Rebel in Paradise

Richard
Drinnon

Rebel in
Paradise

A Biography of
Emma Goldman

The University of Chicago Press
Chicago and London

The University of Chicago Press, Chicago 60637
The University of Chicago Press, Ltd., London

89 88 87 86 85 84 83 82   1 2 3 4 5

Library of Congress Cataloging in Publication Data

Drinnon, Richard.
  Rebel in paradise.

  Bibliography: p. 315.
  Includes index.
  1. Goldman, Emma, 1869–1940. 2. Anarchism and
anarchists—United States—Biography. 3. Anarchism and
anarchists—Jews—Biography. I. Title.
[HX843.G6D74 1982]   335'.83'0924 [B]   82-8531
ISBN 0-226-16364-4 (pbk.)   AACR2

For TWEED DRINNON

PREFACE

"To write," observed the late Albert Camus, "is already to choose." To choose Emma Goldman as a subject is already to say something forcibly, one way or another, about the writer's values. Even a simulated indifference to the thrust of her personality is scarcely conceivable. I may as well record here at the outset, then, that I like her and trust her. No doubt my basic sympathy for the radical style in politics helped shape this empathy and understanding. As she herself often repeated, "Wenn Du es nicht fühlst, wirst Du es nicht erraten"—if you do not feel a thing, you will never guess its meaning. Still, it is somewhat reassuring to recall that when I began research on her life I began skeptically, for her autobiography and the other accounts of her career seemed to make her too extraordinary a woman to be taken seriously. And, along with everyone else, I regarded her anarchism as a particularly bizarre form of political lunacy. Months of research passed before I learned that my skepticism was pseudo-sophistication and my condescension was only conventional ignorance.

Emma Goldman was in truth a remarkable woman of many parts. She was an anarchist lecturer and publicist, an agitator for free speech and a popularizer of the arts, a leading feminist and a pioneer advocate of birth control, a sharp critic of Soviet Communism and an untiring supporter of the Catalonian revolutionists during the Spanish Civil War. She was, above all, an often temperamental, sometimes unreasonable, but always courageous, compassionate, intelligent human being.

To many of her friends the most famous radical of her day and to many of her enemies assuredly the most notorious, she provoked either warm support or furious opposition. Mr. J. Edgar Hoover, for instance, warned in his peculiar prose that she and her friend Alexander Berkman were "beyond doubt two of the most dangerous anarchists in this country and if permitted to return to the community will result in undue harm." Of the large number of Americans who agreed, perhaps a Brooklyn man expressed his feelings most shrilly: "For God sake dont let Berkman and Goldman & the rest of that bunch of defamers of these United States get away with it this time," implored Mr. Theodore De Munel, "but send them bag and baggage out of this country at once." In fundamental disagreement was John Dewey who held that Emma Goldman was "a romantically idealistic person with a highly attractive personality." Another philosopher, Bertrand Russell, found "both her and Berkman very interesting, and, although I have never been an Anarchist, I had much sympathy with them."

Although this book is, first and foremost, a critical biography of the woman, it is also an inquiry into the meaning and significance of such opposition and such support. In her person Emma Goldman confronted Americans with an archetype rebel who challenged their social, intellectual, and political convictions. Their reactions to her, over the years, said something about their changing capacities to accept an open society in which there could be real disagreement. This is a study, that is to say, both of the Rebel and of the Paradise against which she rebelled. To keep the accompanying organizational compromises and risks down to a bare minimum, I have focused all but a small fraction of the attention on her. The interstitial general chapters are short and infrequent. In the end, if my dual purpose is realized, the Times will not have swallowed the Life but instead will have made it less two dimensional and more understandable.

I try to acknowledge some of my many intellectual and research obligations in a section which follows. Here I wish to mention some special debts. Mulford Q. Sibley first awakened my interest in Emma Goldman and anarchism by his open-minded consideration of all shades of theory in the political spectrum. I am indebted to him for this and for the example of his teaching, thinking, doing. Kenneth M. Stampp has also been unfailingly helpful with encouragement and careful criticism. And in our continuing dialogue about things that matter, many of which touch on issues treated in this volume, Warren Olson has helped me more than he can know. I am grateful to all of these friends. Finally, I owe a special debt of gratitude to Anna Maria Drinnon, who has done all of the things expected of a writer's wife and then has cheerfully done more, and to Donna and Jon Drinnon, who have patiently humored their father through all the vicissitudes of a first book.

R. D.

BERKELEY, CALIFORNIA

ACKNOWLEDGMENTS

One of the delights of historical inquiry is the remarkable generosity of friends and colleagues. For their careful and critical reading of all or part of the manuscript, at its various stages, I am grateful to the following: Alice Felt Tyler, Mary Turpie, the late Tremaine McDowell, Ben Willerman, Theodore Caplow, all of the University of Minnesota; Carl Schorske, Gene Brucker, and Henry May, all of the University of California, Berkeley; Alfred Kazin of New York. Henry Nash Smith of the University of California gave me valuable advice and encouragement at a number of points.

My indebtedness to a number of individuals outside the academic world is substantial: Stella Ballantine helped in every way possible this study of the life of her aunt; Ben Capes, the late Rudolf Rocker, Lillian Kisliuk, Ann Lord, John Beffel, and others patiently replied to my letters and kept me from committing some especially egregious blunders.

Librarians have been helpful well beyond the call of professional duty. I owe a special note of thanks to the memory of Agnes Inglis, who worked so many selfless years to develop the Labadie Collection at the University of Michigan. Mme G. Adama Van Scheltema, Professor A. J. C. Rüter, and the staff of the International Institute for Social History in Amsterdam kindly opened the sealed portions of the Goldman-Berkman Archives, for which I offer thanks. My thanks also to Edward Morrison of the New York Public Library, James T. Babb of the Yale University Library, Bess Glenn of the National Archives, Josephine Harper of the Wisconsin Historical Society, and Wade A. Doares of the Columbia University Journalism Library.

I wish to express my appreciation for a Greater University Fellowship at Minnesota in 1953–54, a Fulbright Grant in 1954–55, and a summer 1958 Faculty Fellowship at the University of California, Berkeley.

Alfred A. Knopf kindly gave me permission to quote from *Living*

My Life. Harper and Brothers graciously extended permission to quote from Ignazio Silone's essay in *The God That Failed.* Random House granted permission to use the "Death of Emma Goldman," from Karl Shapiro's *Person Place and Thing.*

CONTENTS

ILLUSTRATIONS

ABBREVIATIONS

Through chapter xxvii footnotes are primarily explanatory. Readers interested in documentation are referred to my "Emma Goldman: A Study in American Radicalism," a 1957 doctoral dissertation in American Studies at the University of Minnesota, copies of which may be obtained through the customary interlibrary loans or from University Microfilms, Ann Arbor, Michigan. Beginning with chapter xxviii I have employed a more detailed annotation, for much of the evidential foundation for this and succeeding chapters is not to be found in my earlier study.

In the footnotes I have used these abbreviations:

- EG: Emma Goldman
- AB: Alexander Berkman
- IISH: International Institute for Social History, Amsterdam
- NYPL, EGP: New York Public Library, Emma Goldman Papers
- LC: Labadie Collection, University of Michigan Library, Ann Arbor
- WMC: Weinberger Memorial Collection, Yale University Library, New Haven
- DJ: U.S. Department of Justice files, National Archives, Washington
- INS: U.S. Immigration and Naturalization Service, Department of Justice files, National Archives
- DS: U.S. Department of State

PART ONE

Young Rebel

And by what destiny or virtue does one, at a certain age, make the important choice, and become "accomplice" or "rebel"? From what source do some people derive their spontaneous intolerance of injustice, even though the injustice affects only others? And that sudden feeling of guilt at sitting down to a well-laden table when others are having to go hungry? And that pride which makes poverty and prison preferable to contempt?

IGNAZIO SILONE in *The God That Failed*

men, the Russians seemed determined that they should live on air—if they stubbornly insisted upon living. Catherine the Great began by drawing a *cordon sanitaire* around them in the recently acquired territory; the area within was then called the Pale of Settlement. The Jews, it was thought, could at least be made to stay where they were, saving the rest of Russia from contamination. But this only kept the problem from spreading. Nicholas I decided to root out the evil by "Russianizing" the outsiders. From this point on, although Russian policy oscillated, certain general constants emerged: Jews were, for the most part, confined to the narrow Pale of Settlement area; they were forced to remain in the villages and towns in which they were registered; they were excluded from public service and agriculture; and they were rarely allowed in any other than the clothing industry. All this meant that they could only subsist in submarginal little ghetto shops in Kovno and other cities—cities which in turn were in the larger ghetto, the Pale of Settlement.

In the nineteenth century Russia was an immense, unbounded, enslaved, illiterate, peasant country, as Nicolas Berdyaev once said, presided over by a strong bureaucracy made up of the otherwise idle nobility and directed by an absolute monarch whose power had religious sanction. Hauntingly unstable, official Russia seemingly had need of the Jews as scapegoats. The Jews offered the Czar and his nobles a means of releasing popular tensions; officials did not hesitate to use the ancient myth of the Christ-killing, Christ-denying Jews to whip up the passions of the masses to divert their attention from the rotting political and social structure. There was thus a contrived projection on the Jews, as particularly obnoxious strangers, of much of the floating aggression and frustration which such a system bred. One consequence was the lush growth of restrictive enactments which hedged in their lives; another consequence was the savage violence which erupted in pogroms, organized massacres of the pitiable pariahs.

3

Under this exceedingly heavy paw of the Russian bear, two young Jews established a home in Kovno in 1868. Failure set the tone for their marriage from the first day. The sad young bride, Taube Bienowitch, a native of Urberig and the daughter of a physician of some eminence and culture, had earlier married a man named Labe Zodokoff. This union produced two daughters, Lena and Helena, before Zodokoff died. Taube's capacity for romantic love died with her first hus-

band. When a few months later another marriage was arranged for
her, she went into it not with love or the hope of love, but as the
only thing to do under the circumstances. Unlike the young widow,
Abraham Goldman, a native of Kovno, had great expectations for his
marriage. Inevitably his passionate desires went virtually unrequited
by his cold bride. Their relationship became more strained when Abraham invested the inheritance of Taube and her two daughters in a
business and promptly lost all their money. At about this point the
Goldmans' first child was born.

Emma Goldman was born in this place and to these parents on the
twenty-seventh of June, 1869. She was thoroughly unwelcome. Taube
seems to have regarded her primarily as additional pain and a continuing burden. Abraham had fervently wished for a son, and he now regarded a daughter as an irritating addition to his other failures. Even
after the subsequent birth of two sons, Herman in 1873 and Morris
in 1875, he could not forgive his daughter her sex.

Shortly after Emma's birth and the failure of his business, Abraham
packed his family off to the small Baltic town of Popelan, where he
became the innkeeper and manager of the government stage. There
he was a butt for the charge that he, both a Jew and a petty official,
was contributing to the drunkenness of the peasants. While the responsibility rested elsewhere, the barn-like inn, in truth, was usually
filled with sodden, quarreling peasants and government employees.
Taube, in poor health and depressed spirits, was kept busy directing
the efforts of servants. Lena and Helena, Emma's half-sisters, worked
long hours in a futile attempt to maintain some order amid the chaos.

As she grew up, Emma escaped to the meadows, when they were
green, accompanying Petrushka, a peasant who had charge of the family's cows and sheep. Frolicking there with the young shepherd, enchanted by the notes of his flute, she experienced a joyous feeling of
freedom from the hateful inn and her scolding parents. Sometimes
at the end of one of these glorious days Petrushka would carry her
homeward on his shoulders, suddenly break into a trot, throw her into
the air, and press her to him. Her delight in this game had erotic overtones—indeed, it may have been from this time that she associated
innocent sexual pleasure with freedom from the guilty restraints of
the world of rules. Her warm relationship with Petrushka, in any event,
led her to an affection for the Russian peasants which was later to assume almost mystical proportions.

Thus affectionately aware of them as human beings, she was horrified one day by the spectacle of a peasant, half-naked, being lashed with a knout. This initial exposure to official brutality shocked her profoundly: for nights afterward her dreams were awesome visions of grimacing gendarmes, bleeding bodies, dripping whips.

Not long after this disturbing experience, her family moved to Königsberg. Taube had become seriously ill after the birth of her second son in 1875 and Abraham suffered an accident which was sufficient to lose him his precarious footing in Popelan. Dogged by misfortune, the Goldmans moved in with Taube's relatively prosperous family, the Bienowitches.

4

Apart from a few wretched months a year or so earlier, Emma had had no schooling. Now with the aid of the city's rabbi, a distant relative, Emma was enrolled in a *Realschule*. The rabbi insisted on monthly reports of the progress of Emma and her brother Herman, but this was a minor humiliation compared with those suffered at the hands of her teachers.

With one exception, they were a grim lot. The religious instructor, a German Jew, took a sadistic pleasure in beating the hands of his recalcitrant or obtuse pupils with a ruler. He beat Emma especially often as the ringleader of those who were so foolish as to rebel against his cruelty. Another teacher, who used his position to prey on his girl pupils, was dismissed after Emma violently resisted his overtures. Had it not been for her teacher of German, she would have learned almost nothing.

A typical follower of Moses Mendelssohn, this teacher wished to bring the European Enlightenment to the dark ghetto. Rejecting instruction based solely on traditional law and ritual, she worshipped instead at the shrine of German literature and music. Genuinely interested in Emma, she did all she could to transmit her enthusiasm to her eager pupil. In her home the two read E. Marlitt, Berthold Auerbach, Frederic Spielhagen, and other nineteenth-century German authors. Emma soon joined her teacher in venerating the German royal house and shedding tears over Napoleon's treatment of good Queen Louise. She entered fully into her teacher's rather pathetic world of vicarious life through the German royal family. Painfully grateful for the older woman's interest and affection, Emma spent every moment she possibly could in her company. On one occasion the teacher took her to the opera *Il Trovatore*. Then Emma's musical imagination, earlier awakened by Petrushka's flute, burst forth and carried her above her mean surroundings to ecstasy. The passionate story made real her own romantic conception of love.

Fired by the goal of studying medicine and being of service to humanity, Emma studied heroically, with the encouragement and help of her beloved teacher, for the entrance examinations to a German *Gymnasium*. Despite eyestrain as a result of overwork, she passed the difficult ordeal—a large accomplishment for a Jewish girl. Only a certificate of good character from her religious teacher stood between her and her dream. The religious teacher, however, dramatically refused her the certificate; unforgiving to the last, he assured her that she did not have the proper respect for authority.

There was now no reason why Emma should not accompany her mother in a move to join Abraham in St. Petersburg, where the latter had charge of a cousin's dry goods store. So in the cold winter of late 1881 the family waded through the deep snow and across a half-frozen brook into Russia. Patrolling soldiers, warmed by a few rubles, magnanimously allowed the wandering Jews entrance into Mother Russia.

CHAPTER II

ST. PETERSBURG

In the 1880's St. Petersburg was a bizarre, meretricious city. In the city proper the palaces were pathetic copies of those in Venice, Amsterdam, and Berlin. Even so, there was at least some pretense toward the grandeur and open vistas of the cities which were plagiarized. In the suffocating Jewish section there was no such pretense. Here narrow quarters housed almost twenty thousand outcasts who nervously tried to exist by running little shops, by working in the clothing trades, or simply by living off each other's misery. In the spring of 1881, when Emma Goldman and her mother arrived, the ghetto was filled to overflowing with Jews who had streamed in to avoid persecution—the refugees had arrived, someone remarked, with death literally nipping at their heels.

Inside the ghetto the savage wave of violence had momentarily silenced those who had argued that the Jewish problem would be solved by the importation of Western art and science. Jewish liberals were plunged into despair by the calloused indifference of their Russian counterparts who were not above seeing in anti-Semitism the beginnings of a popular awakening. Hardly enjoying their moment of triumph, the orthodox nationalists vigorously re-emphasized Jewish consciousness, separateness, culture. Even part of the political left was so dismayed by the actual pogrom propaganda of the Russian populists that they formed their own Socialist labor movement. Only a few of the younger generation, still convinced that nothing less than the radical solution of larger social problems would help the oppressed Jews, continued their activity in movements stemming from Russian nihilism and populism.

Outside the ghetto, events had just reached a climax with the assassination of Alexander II. The roots of this and other assaults on Russian authority went directly back into the 1860's, when some individuals rose in an intellectual revolt against the domestic despotism and social hypocrisy of the Russian system. While nihilism now has come to mean the identification of a crude self-interest with truth and justice, this intellectual revolt then meant precisely the reverse: it was an angry rejection of crude self-interest and authoritarianism. "A nihilist," defined Arkady Petrovich in Turgenev's *Fathers and Sons* (1862), "is a man who does not bow down before any authority, who does not take any principle on faith, whatever reverence that principle may be enshrined in." Such were the quite innocent outlines of Russian nihilism. To be sure, nihilism helped clear the way for the populism of the next decade, when idealistic young Russians attempted to go among the people on a mission of education and socialistic propaganda. But only after these peaceful aims were blocked by widespread arrests and persecution did the populists adopt terrorism as a tactic. Assassinations and attempted assassinations followed, so that when Emma and her mother reached St. Petersburg in 1881, Russia was in a state of virtual civil war.

2

The shop Abraham Goldman was managing closed shortly before the arrival of his family. Taube borrowed three hundred rubles from her brothers to start a small grocery. Lena migrated to the United States; Helena—and eventually Emma—helped out by working.

Emma had six more months of schooling before she went to work full time. These few months were enough to bring her into contact with radical students and open up to her a whole new world of thought. Back in Königsberg she had developed some sympathy for the populist martyrs without having any real awareness of what they were fighting for. When a maternal uncle had been arrested in 1875 for his activities in one of the radical circles in St. Petersburg, an oppressive gloom had settled over the Goldman household—gloom which lifted only after Taube hurried to the capital and made a successful if abject plea to the chief of the imperial police that her brother should not be exiled to Siberia. Emma became increasingly skeptical of her mother's assurances that such officials were kind and humane; she rather came to agree with her teacher, who insisted that they were wild beasts who flogged peasants and tortured imprisoned idealists. Now, however, after her contact with radical students in St. Petersburg, Emma learned what the populists were after and she came to admire those who were willing to risk their lives to achieve their disinterested ends.

During these first months in St. Petersburg she also managed to secure copies of Turgenev's *Fathers and Sons*, Ivan Goncharov's *The Precipice* (1869), and Nikolai Chernyshevsky's *What Is To Be Done?*

(1863). The first two of these novels, notwithstanding Goncharov's admitted caricatures of the nihilists, impressed her. But Chernyshevsky's artistically inferior novel had such a remarkable impact that a large part of her later life was consciously patterned after Vera Pavlovna, the heroine of *What Is To Be Done?*

In the novel Vera Pavlovna is converted to nihilism and therewith reborn into a world of easy comradeship of the sexes, free intellectual inquiry, and co-operative labor. She abhorrently rejects her mother's avaricious and typically Philistine aim of auctioning her off as a valuable sex-object. Instead she lives in free companionship with a poor medical student who had rescued her in the first place from intellectual death and the legal prostitution proposed by her mother. Vera also starts a co-operative sewing shop to insure her complete independence, and she seriously plans to further her development by studying medicine. Obviously more interested in equitable distribution than in maximum output, Vera longs for an ideal world of associations of producers acting freely together, unrestrained by any political bureaucracy. Once she had incorporated these views, Emma Goldman had, in embryo, her later anarchism. But at this time Chernyshevsky's heroine was important, above all, in strengthening Emma's determination to live her own life.[1]

3

Emma's independent views were highly dangerous. The Jewish community looked upon the adolescent girl as little more than a chattel and, more specifically, as the property of her father. Whatever the departure in the actual give and take of the home, the Jewish girl's formal status was essentially the same as it was in ancient times when she was placed in the same category with an ox, an ass, or other private property. When Abraham Goldman exercised a father's right by making arrangements to have her marry at fifteen, Emma boldly objected. Abraham's reception of her refusal was in keeping with tradition: "I had protested," she recalled, "begging to be permitted to continue my studies. In his frenzy he threw my French grammar into the fire, shouting: 'Girls do not have to learn much! All a Jewish daughter needs to know is how to prepare *gefüllte* fish, cut noodles fine, and give the man plenty of children.' I would not listen to his schemes; I wanted to study,

---

[1] When it came time to write her autobiography, the primary source for these early years, Emma Goldman chose the appropriate title, *Living My Life* (New York: Alfred A. Knopf, Inc., 1931).

to know life, to travel. Besides, I never would marry for anything but love, I stoutly maintained."[2] To Abraham romantic love was an aberration; to Emma it was one of the most important forces in life.

Their conflict over this question was merely part of a larger and continuing battle. Undoubtedly Abraham felt himself to be the aggrieved party. He had never recovered from his disappointment that Emma was a girl. Added to this were his repeated economic failures which frustrated all his plans and increased his bitterness and aggression toward the members of his family. In truth the first patriarch Abraham's wanderings through the Fertile Crescent in search of livelihood were hardly more desperate and demanding than Abraham Goldman's search in Czarist Russia: chief of his small clan of wanderers in enemy territory, he easily fell into the habit of regarding his children, and to a certain extent his wife, as members of a patrol subject to the iron discipline of an emergency. He could hardly have been expected to be patient with the rebellious Emma. Had he been able to grasp intellectually the outlines of Russian anti-Semitism, had he been able to visualize some of the forces sweeping over the ghetto, he might have been more patient and he might have accepted his economic reverses with better grace. Unfortunately he never revealed any marked ability to reason out his position, but instead responded with a typically lower-middle-class hostility, thriftiness, distrust for any new ideas, and an envy of the successful which disguised itself as moral indignation.

Whatever the origins of his inner tensions—some of them may have stemmed as well from his sexual incompatibility with Taube, as Emma later suggested—Abraham devoted himself to the task of knocking the rough edges off his unwanted girl child. To make matters worse, Emma never revealed any capacity for meekness and the docile smile which might have turned away parental wrath. Thus the conflict between the two often threatened to become total. She was whipped, forced to stand in the corner for hours, or made to walk back and forth with an overflowing glass of water in her hands—a lash was her reward for each spilled drop. Once the whipping was so vigorous that Emma's screams prompted her younger brother Morris to bite their father in the leg. Another time Abraham, infuriated by her low marks in school for behavior, attacked her with his fists; Helena, fearing serious injury, came to her rescue, but Abraham stopped only when he became exhausted with his exertions and fell to the floor unconscious. Despite all this, Emma had ambivalent feelings toward her father: she liked him

[2] *Living My Life*, p. 12.

for his handsome, dashing qualities; she feared him at the same time for his unreasoning rages.

Taube might have been a source of comfort and a refuge, but she never showed much warmth to any of her children except Morris, the youngest. Though she had her own hysterical quarrels with Abraham, she never permitted herself to support Emma beyond urging her husband to be less severe in his punishment.

Of the two older half-sisters, one was also actively hostile to Emma. Lena blamed her for being the daughter of the man who had lost her and Helena's inheritance in the ill-fated Kovno store. A bright exception to all this was her other sister, Helena. Helena protected Emma when she could and gave her much of the love their mother withheld. Notwithstanding this closeness, Emma and Helena were very different: though Helena joined Emma in thinking Abraham harsh and autocratic, she did not dare open rebellion.

Emma pitied her precious Helena for her timidity. Emma could and did engage in an open running battle with her father. She blocked his efforts to arrange her marriage; she fought for the right to choose her reading matter; and she eventually fought herself completely free of him.

In 1885 Helena made arrangements to follow Lena to the United States. She offered to pay Emma's fare. With Helena going, nothing inside and little outside the family tied Emma to Russia. After the first few months in St. Petersburg she had been forced to leave school and work full time knitting shawls at home. Piecework, however, troubled her eyes and she then went to work in a cousin's glove factory. At the time Helena proposed to emigrate, Emma was working in a corset factory in the Hermitage Arcade in downtown St. Petersburg. Cut off from further education and forced to a routine of uninteresting factory drudgery, she felt that life would be unendurable without her sister.

A final battle remained, for Abraham would not permit Emma to go. He was immovable until Emma played her final card: she threatened to jump in the Neva. Only then did he give her his grudging permission. Late in December, 1885, Emma and Helena left St. Petersburg for Hamburg. There they secured passage on the "Elbe" for America.

CHAPTER III

ROCHESTER: FLOWER CITY
IN THE GARDEN

America, free America, asylum for the oppressed and weary, hungry and ragged of all lands: From the pastures on the sides of the warm Sicilian hills to the factories on the cold banks of the Russian Neva, the dream was nearly always the same, of Columbus country, of Goldene Medinah, of Zion, of golden, glorious, free America. Things were bungled beyond patching up in the old countries, so the vision went for the politically conscious, but in America, now, there a man could be a man, live without scraping, skimping, and always bowing and touching his forelock.

By a happy coincidence, Europe's formal recognition of this dream arrived the same year as Emma and Helena: Bartholdi's "Liberté éclairant le monde" was set down on Bedloe's Island in time for the two sisters to see the silhouette of Europe's great tribute against the New York skyline as the "Elbe" pulled into Castle Garden. American liberty's tallest and most imposing symbol thus appropriately landed at virtually the same time as the little girl who was to become one of freedom's most vocal and energetic champions.

2

Possessed by the dream of America as Paradise, Emma and her sister viewed New York with great emotion. They, too, they thought, would find a place in the generous heart of the new country. Fleeing from parental cruelty and lack of understanding, Czarist autocracy, and Russian pogromy, they expected much from the United States.

Their first experience was disenchanting. Once, when Castle Garden was a fashionable resort, audiences there had thrilled to hear Jenny Lind's clear soprano voice; now the two sisters heard only a medley of the voices of angry officials, distressed men, and hysterical women. Most disquieting were the officials, who behaved pretty much like officials in Alexander's Russia or Bismarck's Germany. Roughly herded off the ship, the sisters were appalled by the antagonism and harshness of the guards and especially by the insensitive treatment of pregnant women and children. Shocked, all they could think of was escape to their sister Lena in Rochester.

Lena was delighted to see them, but in difficult circumstances. Her husband, working long hours as a tinsmith, brought home only twelve dollars a week. While Lena willingly offered her two sisters shelter, she could do little more. Helena shortly found a job retouching negatives for a photographer. Emma went to work for Garson, Meyer and Company; she sewed ulsters ten and a half hours a day for two dollars and fifty cents a week.

Emma had looked forward to working for Leopold Garson, chairman of the United Jewish Charities of Rochester, owner of a model factory, and reputedly a philanthropist. Working for Garson was another major disenchanting experience after her arrival, for again reality veered sharply from her expectations. While the Rochester factory was better lighted and more spacious than the corset factory in St. Petersburg, the pace was also faster and the discipline over the workers was much more complete. Talking and singing, which had made work in St. Petersburg less onerous, were forbidden in Garson's model plant. One could not go to the toilet, Emma always insisted, without permission. Later she also wrote a friend, in the only comment of its kind among her letters, that not only did Garson "exact labor in his factory for nothing, but also insisted on the pleasures the young female wage slaves could give him. He had them or out they went."

Emma's immediate problem, however, was her grossly inadequate income. After paying Lena a dollar and fifty cents for room and board and spending sixty cents for carfare, she had only forty cents a week left for clothes, amusement, books, incidentals. When Lena gave birth to a child, Emma felt she should contribute more for her keep. She resolved to ask Garson for a raise. As she was ushered into his ornate office, a vase full of American Beauty roses fascinated her. Sometime earlier she had admired these flowers in a florist's shop and had learned to her distress that she did not have enough left over from her weekly wages to buy one of them. Garson interrupted her reverie by brusquely demanding what she wanted. She tried to explain her problem to him, adding that she did not make enough to buy even an occasional book or a twenty-five cent theater ticket. Garson told her flatly that her tastes were rather extravagant, that his other "hands" were satisfied, and that if she was not, then she might look for work elsewhere. Work elsewhere seemed preferable.

In her experience with Garson, Emma had brought into focus before her the strains and stresses which existed within the Rochester Jewish community. She saw that the Russian Jew was made welcome by the German Jew primarily because he provided cheap labor for the latter's clothing establishments. She was angered by the hardly hidden contempt of the German Jew for his eastern cousin as a newcomer from a semi-barbarous country which had not prepared him for equal rights.

Many other Russian Jews felt that it was through exploiting them that the German Jews came to control Rochester's important clothing industry. In this case class lines and national origins coincided. Revolt was in the air when Emma came to Rochester, with the Russians moving toward organization in the Knights of Labor and the Germans banding together in the Chamber of Commerce and employers' protection groups. Emma naturally sympathized with her countrymen and became increasingly critical of capitalistic German Jews and of capitalism in general.

She next found work in the factory of a man named Rubenstein. Here the conditions were more tolerable. Rubenstein did not drive his workers with Garson's thoroughness and, moreover, he paid Emma four dollars a week for her labor.

3

While working at her new job, Emma met Jacob Kersner, a young Russian Jew who also professed to love reading and dancing. Anxious to make friends in the unfamiliar city, Emma was pleased by his Russian—her English was still halting—by his apparent indifference to making money, and by his proposal to take her places in an attempt to dispel the loneliness which both of them felt.

After four months of courtship, Emma reluctantly consented to their engagement. Abraham and Taube, who had followed their daughters to America, were pleased by the prospect that their stormy Emma would settle down and establish a home. To help pay expenses, Kersner moved in with the Goldmans as a boarder. A lack of privacy within the house and the closeness of Kersner were constant irritants to Emma. Despite her drive and high ambitions, she finally decided to accept what seemed inevitable. Unlike Chernyshevsky's Vera Pavlovna, she accepted the ceremony which bound her legally to a man. She and Kersner were married according to Jewish rites in February, 1887.

On their wedding night Emma found that her groom was impotent. As she lay beside Kersner, completely bewildered, she recalled every erotic experience she had had up to that night. She remembered her relationship with Petrushka in Popelan, and she recalled the time in Königsberg when Taube had given her a stinging slap at the onset of her menstrual periods: her mother had grimly informed her that such periods were necessary for a girl "as a protection against disgrace." Finally, she recalled an affair in St. Petersburg with a young hotel clerk who had managed to inveigle her into one of his rooms and roughly introduce her to her first serious sex experience. Helena had followed her to the hotel and Emma with terror and guilt had heard her sister out in the hall asking for her. After this, Emma admitted, she "always felt between two fires in the presence of men. Their lure remained strong, but it was always mingled with violent revulsion. I could not bear to have them touch me."[1] Such were her thoughts as Kersner slept.

Marriage to Kersner came to seem a sprung trap. His condition did not change, although, after Emma's urging, he put himself under a doctor's treatment. And all his interest in books and ideas evaporated. Although he had graduated from the Odessa *Gymnasium*, in Rochester he soon adopted the habits of other workers. He developed a passion for cards—an obsession which made it difficult for Emma to keep their household going. At home he was impossibly jealous, probably because of his own lack of virility. While his character seemed to disintegrate, Emma's was undergoing a change which pulled them even further apart.

Her preoccupation with the case of the men allegedly responsible for the Haymarket Bombing gave her developing radicalism more range and depth. By the time of the execution of Parsons, Spies, and their comrades, as we have already observed, she had to be restrained from assaulting a woman who scoffed at all the concern over the Chicago martyrs. With her interest spurred in the cause the dead men represented, she found life with Kersner increasingly meaningless and insupportable.

A short time later she left him. They were divorced by the same man who had performed their wedding ceremony less than a year earlier.

4

Immediately after leaving Kersner, Emma went to New Haven to work in another corset factory. There she met a group of young Russians who worked their trades by day but argued socialism and anarchism by night. Both the interminable arguments and the occasional

[1] *Living My Life*, p. 23.

meetings, at which speakers from New York sometimes appeared, struck Emma as her first meaningful experiences since her arrival in America. But in poor health and perhaps a little homesick, she returned to Rochester a few months later.

Kersner soon sought her out and pleaded earnestly with her to come back to him. He even promised to poison himself, if she did not. Frightened that he might actually commit suicide, Emma consented to a second and equally hopeless marriage. This time, however, she secretly took a course in dressmaking to increase her economic independence. For three months she waged a daily campaign to persuade Kersner to let her go her own way. Finally, after a particularly bitter quarrel, she left him for good and moved in temporarily with Helena.

Of all the members of her family, Helena had been the only one to stand by Emma during this long ordeal. Lena had joined the older Goldmans in opposing her divorce and in urging her to remarry Kersner. Now Abraham and Taube were so angered by this final divorce that they forbade Emma to enter their house. To them it was axiomatic that a woman stayed with a man for life, no matter what the nature of her problems. In a final emotional scene, Abraham denounced her as a "loose character" who had always disgraced the family. Exasperated, Emma turned on her father and charged him with being the cause of her joyless youth and her present predicament. If she had not become a harlot, she cried distractedly, it was not his fault, but because of Helena's love and devotion. On this note their conflict of two decades ended.

To the rest of the Rochester Jewish community, Emma had become a *Meshumed* and a *Radikalke*, or an apostate and, almost as wicked, a shameless, emancipated woman. Feeling against her reached the point of active hostility, as neighbors treated her contemptuously on the street.

While Emma was prepared to fight for her ideals, she could see no point in waging the battle in Rochester. With Helena's help, she left for New York City on the fifteenth of August, 1889. Already a convinced radical, she would seek there her peculiar fortune.

CHAPTER IV

THE MAKING OF A RADICAL

The London *Times* detected psychological possibilities in *Living My Life* when it was published in England in 1932: "Emma Goldman tells a story that competes with romantic fiction and at the same time reveals a personality that might well form the subject of a psychological treatise." Such a study is out of place here, but a brief interlude of speculation is not. Why did Emma rebel against her father's authority? Why was she so impressed by the fight of the Russian radicals against Czarist autocracy? Why was she so profoundly stirred by the execution of the Haymarket martyrs? Why, in fine, did she choose to become a rebel rather than an accomplice?

2

Emma tried her own hand at answering these questions.

Forced to deal systematically with the why's of her life in her autobiography, she informed her friend Evelyn Scott that she could accept neither the theory that she was the prime mover of everything that happened in her life, nor that she was a mere puppet in the hands of circumstance. "Circumstances play havoc with most of us," she believed, "destroy many of our good intentions, paralyze our energies and make us do the very reverse of what we so passionately would like to do. And I also believe that those of us who have enough strength of character and perseverance overcome circumstances." As she saw it, her task in writing would be to distinguish between the influence her background had in molding her and the extent to which her personality influenced her background.

Enthusiastically supporting Emma's choice of approach to character, Miss Scott, the perceptive Tennessee-born novelist, sent off a quick reply: "that back-and-forthness of influences, the times forming the man, the man's personality forcing an expansion of consciousness on the times—that is so exactly the point of view with which I agree."

Yet, Emma was not always able to handle the complex back-and-forthness of influences when she attempted to explain her radicalism. On one occasion she startled members of the Rochester City Club by informing them that Rochester and America had made her an anarchist. She insisted that her early experience with American capitalism, especially its execution of the Chicago anarchists, had made her a radical. The background was all-important here. On another occasion, however, she informed a reporter that "I do my work because I cannot look on and see wrong without a protest. I could no more help crying out than I could if I were drowning. I am an anarchist of the Topsy variety—I was just born so." And in a lecture on Mary Wollstonecraft, she concluded: "Mary was born [a rebel] and not made through this or that individual incident in her surroundings." Here inherited predispositions were all-important.

Contradictions aside, Emma's interpretation of her own radicalism certainly slipped away from her fruitful idea of the interaction of personality and background. In the final analysis, she placed all her stress on innate factors. As she wrote to another friend, "no amount of preachment can change what is inherent in people. It might bring out human traits either for freedom or against it, but it can put nothing into [a] barren soul." Environment only "acts on character as dew and sunshine on plants."

3

Ironically, her account was not unlike that of some of her critics. They, too, relied heavily on the "just born so" argument. Among those who described her as a "madwoman," "a mental as well as moral pervert," or as having an "unbalanced mind," Theodore Roosevelt was merely the most famous. In his first message to Congress, Roosevelt, in direct if nameless reference to Emma, blasted her and her kind as "merely one type of criminal—more dangerous than any other" and went on to insist with his notorious forcefulness that such were "in no sense, in no shape or way, a 'product of social conditions,' save as a highwayman is 'produced' by the fact that an unarmed man happens to have a purse." Unfortunately, Roosevelt did not get as far as Emma in showing just what it was, if not social conditions, that produced such anarchists.

Now is there anything to be said for her radicalism as merely a Topsy-like growth? Certainly it was not the simple product of her glands, nor was it because she had a particular kind of physiognomy, nor was it because she had a certain body type—the pseudoscientific conception here is of the "leanness of the 'fanatical agitator,'" and Emma was a plump 120 pounds and under five feet when she was eighteen. Nevertheless, it would be a mistake to dismiss completely the importance of her biological heritage. An individual with a low energy level—say a thyroid deficiency—could not have withstood the demands of an autocratic father, surmounted unfavorable circumstances, searched for alternative possibilities in books and elsewhere, and later so untiringly served the cause she had adopted.

Certainly she had remarkable energy. As an editor of the Baltimore *Evening Sun* once stated, Emma Goldman probably had "more of sheer vitality, courage and audacity than any woman in America has ever possessed." Probably she did have a sound constitution.

Yet even here one must proceed with caution, for she was frequently bothered by her health. She returned from the New Haven corset factory because of sickness. And later, in 1893, she lost weight and grew too weak to walk across the room. On her return to Helena's in Rochester she was discovered to have tuberculosis. In the middle of plans to send her to a sanatorium for the winter, she felt impelled to return to New York and her agitation there; without informing anyone of her change in plans, she left Rochester before her doctor and sister had a chance to object. Seemingly her iron-willed dedication to her calling helped her to shake off the attack of tuberculosis. She also suffered from menstrual cramps and was so incapacitated at these times that a specialist urged an operation; she was told that without one she would never be free from pain.

Indeed, she very nearly became a hypochondriac. In an entry made in his diary while he was editing her autobiography, Alexander Berkman wrote: "But at some places in her Mss. I have to laugh . . . aloud. She never misses an opportunity, in & out of places, to say how 'terrible' she felt, what [an] awful headache she had, how her soul was in pain. Just now . . . I had to cut out 1½ pages telling of her toe pain. 'My principal suffering was from my feet. The small toe of my left foot folded over the one next to it' etc." A hypothetical hypochondria can, however, account for only a part of her physical distress, which at one time or another included consumption, varicose veins, a tendency to fall, and, unknown to her, perhaps even diabetes.[1]

All this suggests that her native energy and the energy which flowed from her profound commitment to her ideals were so intertwined and so supplemented each other that no strong statement may be made even about her physical endowment. The most one can do is to assume pro-

[1] After Emma Goldman died, a friend wrote: "They found E. to be diabetic. She had never known."

visionally that she inherited a sound constitution with a relatively high level of energy.

More certain is the matter of her native intelligence. Except for conduct, she did well in school, as her feat in passing the *Gymnasium* entrance examinations shows. Moreover, friends and enemies were in general agreement about her intelligence. Federal Judge Mayer, an extremely hostile witness, found it a source of regret during her and Berkman's trial in 1917 that "the extraordinary ability displayed by the two defendants has not been utilized in support of law and order. The magnetic power of one of the defendants [Emma Goldman], if thus utilized, might have been of great service in reforms legitimately advocated. . . ." Another unfriendly observer, United States Attorney Francis Caffey, asserted that "Emma Goldman is a woman of great ability and of personal magnetism, and her persuasive powers are such as to make her an exceedingly dangerous woman. . . ." As a final witness, Inspector Thomas J. Tunney of the New York Police considered her " a very able and intelligent woman and a very fine speaker." Now these officials were probably inclined to exaggerate her intellectual abilities as one way of emphasizing the gravity of their work; but since their response accords with that of many others, we may assume that she was endowed with considerable intellectual powers at birth.

Experimental studies in social psychology have indicated just such a general relationship between intelligence and radicalism. In Emma's case, her intelligence made her more sensitive to the radical intellectual currents moving around her and made her willing to experiment, to break new paths in an attempt to solve old difficulties. Her intelligence also made her less likely to be satisfied with the contradictory hodgepodge of attitudes of the average person. She was prompted to seek a coherent world view. Anarchism, which attempted just such an integration, thus appealed to her.

4

In her attempt to come to grips with the reasons for her own radicalism, Emma Goldman undoubtedly underestimated the significance of her family. Probably a certain amount of unrecognized sexual rivalry between Emma and her mother contributed to the distance between them. Taube's slapping and her generally unenlightened response to Emma's first menstrual period widened the gap. Emma may have associated her mother's actions with the latter's possessiveness of Abraham, but, more certainly, she felt that her mother's authority had been used to give guilty overtones to innocent biological stirrings. Reacting against her mother, Emma was likely as a mature person to identify with the child against the suppressive parent and to be opposed to the conventional morality which tends to make sex a guilty force.

Her relation to Abraham was more decisive. Beyond question she was sexually attracted to her father. Her attitude toward him was fundamentally ambivalent: "My father was handsome, dashing, and full of vitality. I loved him even while I was afraid of him. I wanted him to love me, but I never knew how to reach his heart. His hardness only served to make me more contrary." Abraham's autocratic actions ultimately provoked hate, but for years there was also this attraction of love and a desire to please him.

This ambivalence carried over to her attitude toward other men. After her adolescent affair with the hotel clerk in St. Petersburg, she was torn between an attraction to men and a distaste for close physical contact with them. When she eventually overcame this revulsion, she still refused to give any man a directive role in her life—she had not thrown over Abraham's authority merely to accept that of someone else. Part of her general reaction to men, leadership in general, the family, God, and perhaps even capitalists as authority figures, then, was probably rooted in this early relationship with her father.

Thus the interplay of sexual forces within the Goldman household was important. Alexander Berkman, after forty years of their close relationship, acutely reminded her that "sex has played a very great role in your life and your book would have been lacking if that role had not been mirrored in it." Emma replied that she had always maintained that sex is a dominant force. Indeed, she had attended lectures delivered by Freud in Vienna in 1895 and in her memoirs she did give early sexual experiences a prominent place. Nevertheless, she rightly rejected attempts to reduce all the complex forces acting on her to the rather simple-minded explanation of pure sex. Playwright Laurence Stallings, for instance, once wrote that Emma's life lent itself to the "perfect analysis": a good analyst could show that her subconscious was in complete control of her outward ego and could establish that sexual force was attached to "every move of her long, disputatious, theatrical life." Sexual force, however, is in some way attached to every move of every individual and the analyst would be distorting the evidence if he were to attempt to show that in every instance her "subconscious was in complete control." The evidence tends rather to support Emma's contention in a letter to English novelist Ethel Mannin: "But one thing

I can assure you," she wrote, "the struggle to maintain my own individuality and freedom was always more important to me than the wildest love affairs." While she exaggerated when she said that her struggle for self-autonomy always took precedence, she correctly pointed out that it did at certain crucial points.

Understandably she rejected attempts to put her entire personality in sex and attempted rather to assign sex its proper place in her personality. One may also justifiably reject the attempt to reduce the importance of her family to an abstract interplay of sexual forces. While the latter were not unimportant, it bears repeating, they were merely a part of a complex array of forces which blocked her way to achieving some measure of self-autonomy. Abraham and Taube both attempted to bend her will to theirs, to act as suppressive social agents. Emma rebelled against this attempt in order to have inner freedom and room for development. As an intelligent girl she was increasingly attracted to ideas, to the universe of symbols. In order for her to develop, she had to find some meaning in this symbolic universe of language, art, myth, and religion.[2]

5

It is a curious fact that in her interpretation of her radicalism, Emma Goldman also failed to appreciate both the importance of this symbolic world and the importance of her coming to it as a Jewess. What if she had not been a Jewess, asked the London *Times*, not a member of a group which has always suffered from spiritual claustrophobia? To ask the question, as they say, is almost to answer it. Her life would have been very different.

The truth·is, she was born on the fringe of two cultures, the Jewish and the Russian, that of the ghetto and that of the outside. By 1869 the walls between the two were crumbling. She was made irresistibly aware that the cramped ghetto was not the only world. Living fully in neither world, she was forced to make her way through two antagonistic cultures. This experience in itself encouraged a wider outlook and the habit of digging for the roots of questions—one definition, incidentally, of a radical. Inevitably values appeared somewhat arbitrary, not God-given but man-made, not universal but personal. While such a marginal position was not conducive to serenity and probably contributed to her symptoms of neurasthenia, it also promoted self-consciousness and a

[2] See Ernst Cassirer, *An Essay on Man* (Garden City, N.Y.: Doubleday & Co., Inc., 1953).

feeling of isolation from any pattern of accepted ways. In her case a radical picking and choosing of values was almost inevitable.

And by virtue of her birth Emma Goldman became one of the heirs of a great ethical tradition which persistently stressed the rights of man and social justice. As Ahad Ha'am once wrote, prophetic Judaism emphasized absolute justice and evidenced sharp intolerance of evil in any form.[3] While prophetic Judaism was eclipsed by priestly Judaism, the former continued to provide an element of tension. Thus, while Emma had a generous contempt for rabbis as pathetic symbols of Russian authority, she still was one of the "People of the Book": the prophetic tradition and the folk literature of the Bible, its gorgeous imagery and thunderous accounts of renunciation and bravery, had an inevitable impact on the sensitive and intelligent little ghetto girl. She dreamed of becoming an avenger like Judith: she would cut off the head of evil and run with it through the streets so that all could see and feel relieved. Who could doubt that the prophets whispered a captivating message down through the centuries to Emma? Perhaps the central theme of her life was expressed by the searching and anguished question of Jeremiah: "Wherefore doth the way of the wicked prosper?" And her many responses to this question were delivered with all the passion of Amos' castigation: "Hear this word, ye Kine of Bashan." She, too, would speak judgments "with thee to the end of days."

6

This, of course, is not the first time that it has been suggested that modern radicals owe a great deal to the prophets. While Ernest Renan may have been guilty of oversimplification when he found the forerunners of Saint Simon and other radicals in the prophets, he had his eyes on a valid insight. And this insight is helpful when one essays an understanding of the impact nihilism—most notably, Chernyshevsky's novel—had on Emma. Both she and the Russian radicals were drawing on the same tradition.

Chernyshevsky's nihilism, moreover, had an especial appeal to Emma, for it promised, among other things, individual autonomy, sexual freedom, and an outlet for energies devoted to lessening the gulf between corrupt society and social justice. Emma soaked in the ideas of Chernyshevsky as rain is soaked in by the desert sands. Like his Vera, she desired to launch a co-operative sewing shop. Like Vera, she wanted to

[3] See his classic essay, "Priest and Prophet," *Contemporary Jewish Record*, VIII (April, 1945), 234 ff.

study medicine—in 1895–96 she managed to study nursing and mid-wifery in Vienna and in 1899 she actually made a serious, if short-lived, effort to enter medical school and become a doctor. Like Vera, she insisted on physical and mental privacy, for which a room of her own was always indispensable. More importantly, in her distrust of the state and ruling classes, her condemnation of luxury, and her ideal of a free association of producers, Vera deeply influenced Emma and prepared her for anarchism.

7

Certain broad historical forces also played some part, if not a primary one, in making Emma a radical. Czarist Jewish policy helped shape her life, not only through Abraham's economic failures, but also through its general oppressiveness. The Russian government's vigorous suppression of even mild forms of dissent reinforced her distaste for authority and the state. Such a traumatic experience as witnessing the lashing of the Popelan peasant, for instance, probably helped make her a rebel. Is it unreasonable to assume that the persecution of the Jews and political heretics aroused in Emma some empathy, a sensitivity to the pain of others?

But it was in America that her rebellion came to full flower. The injustice of the Haymarket tragedy shocked her beyond words. In addition, the intolerable chasm between America as Paradise and the actuality of work in Garson's factory simply demanded some kind of action. No longer could she naïvely regard America as the land of economic opportunity. The realization was forced on her that American society tended to be a closed community of Protestant, Anglo-Saxon origin. She and other "New Immigrants" found economic paths littered with obstacles and assimilation difficult. How could she take advantage of freedom and economic opportunity, she reflected, on a miserable wage which did not even leave enough at the end of the week for a book or a theater ticket? At this point she rejected once and for all the goal of the Big Money and became an implacable foe of the economic system which created such a discrepancy between individual worth and social rewards. Her goal became a new society in which there would be a close correspondence between merit, effort, and reward. Anarchism, she became convinced, promised just such a society.

8

There was thus more to Emma Goldman's radicalism than her own rather ingenuous interpretation revealed. True, she seems to have been born with relatively great energy and intelligence potentialities. But this is about as much as one can do with her born rebel argument. Actually, she seems to have become so bewildered by the problem that she sought refuge in an obscure argument that she "was just born so"—one is reminded of H. G. Wells's comparable defeat and his consequent bizarre explanation of his own character on the basis of the texture of his brain.

Any explanation of her radicalism must rest on a conceptual bridge between psychology on one bank and sociology on the other. Thus it was not only important that she was born with relatively great energy and intelligence, but also important that she was born into a religious tradition which placed great emphasis on absolute justice and symbolic satisfactions. This inheritance meshed nicely with her innate potentialities. Next, about midway on the bridge, were the power relationships within the Goldman family. These relations reached out in one direction toward innate sex drives and in the other toward the values and customs of Jewish and Russian societies. Abraham's and Taube's sexual lure and rivalry, respectively, but more inclusively their disposition of authority within the home, were of central importance in causing Emma to adopt radical attitudes. By oppressive and unthinking treatment they sought to seal off all the forces pushing her toward intellectual development and self-government. Moreover, her peripheral position in relation to two cultures helped her to see that rules are often unthinkingly accepted and arbitrary. The gap between ideality and reality in America reinforced her growing rebellion. Specific experiences such as the whipping of the peasant, her marriage to Kersner, and the Haymarket incident, as well as general historical developments such as Czarist persecution of the Jews and the American exploitation of the immigrants—all these helped touch off active rebellion. So much for the push part of a push-pull relationship.

Now for the pulls. Nihilism and anarchism promised to close speedily all gaps between the is and the ought: authoritarian hierarchies were to be overthrown in favor of a society of free equals; individual independence was to be guaranteed; merit and reward were to be brought together; the restrictive family was to give way before more universal ties. The pull of such a systematic solution to all her difficulties must have been virtually irresistible. This attraction, in conjunction with the pushes from behind, made a radical of Emma.

Her radicalism, then, was the product of a unique constellation of forces. But it was more than a "product," for she could have acted differently at crucial points, had she chosen to do so. While her personality has been hammered into parts and analyzed, the whole personality is greater than the sum of its parts.

Greater than the sum of its parts—Emma recognized this in spite of her confusion about the sources of her radicalism. Toward the end of her life she wrote these lines which read almost as if they had been taken from a page of one of Nicolas Berdyaev's books:

Individuality may be described as the consciousness of the individual as to what he is and how he lives. It is inherent in every human being and is a thing of growth. . . . The individual is not merely the result of heredity and environment, of cause and effect. He is that and a great deal more, a great deal else. The living man cannot be defined; he is the fountainhead of all life and all values, he is not a part of this or that; he is a whole, a growing, changing, yet always constant whole.[4]

The confusion was still there, but so was the basic insight. The individual is more than an object, she was arguing; he is also a subject. Applied to her own personality, this insight meant that to some important extent she was a radical by choice.

[4] Emma Goldman, *The Place of the Individual in Society* (Chicago: Free Society Forum, n.d. [Library of Congress, 1940]), p. 3. Berdyaev would have said *personality* rather than *individuality*.

PART TWO

Daughter of the Dream

There is nothing wrong with Miss Goldman's gospel that I can see, except this: She is about eight thousand years ahead of her age. Her vision is the vision of every truly great-souled man or woman who has ever lived. . . . life is death without the dream. The dream is the reality to which we move . . . universal peace and beauty, Emma Goldman, the daughter of the dream.

WILLIAM MARION REEDY, St. Louis *Mirror*, November 5, 1908

CHAPTER V

THE DREAM

The young radical naturally chose not to knuckle under to her family in Rochester. When she arrived in New York City that hot Sunday morning, August 15, 1889, she was on her own and determined to launch her career of world-changing. Gladly leaving behind her unpleasant past and obscure origins, she excitedly stepped from the Weehawken ferry: What would the future hold for her? Would those in power learn of her existence? Would the people listen to her? Or would her large demands on life be quickly snuffed out, sparks landing in the sea of indifferent faces of the bypassers? Despite the heat, the city seemed cold.

She checked her sewing machine, the cornerstone of her plans for a co-operative shop and economic independence, in the baggage room at West Forty-second Street. Starting out on foot, she carried her small bag containing a few articles of clothing and five dollars—all the material accumulation of her twenty years. Three hours later, tired and footsore, she walked into the photography shop of her aunt and uncle on the Bowery. Their invitations to stay rang hollowly and did not hide their dismay at the arrival of an unexpected guest. She hurriedly left. Before the day was out she had found Sachs's Café on Suffolk Street, the meeting place of East Side radicals. There, as the waves of Russian and Yiddish words caressed her ears, she suddenly felt more at ease, as though she had finally come home. A place for her to stay was soon arranged; and Alexander Berkman, a young, studious-looking anarchist to whom she had just been introduced, asked her to go to hear Johann Most speak that evening. A glorious day! Imagine hearing the incomparable Most a few hours after beginning her new life.

2

She had read Most's burning attacks on the Haymarket executions when she was in Rochester—his paper, *Freiheit*, had seemed a cry of sane rebellion in a wilderness of cruelty. Shocked now by her first view of him, she was repelled by his badly twisted and bitter face. All this was forgotten, however, as soon as he started to speak, for he seemed transformed into a figure of primitive power. Never had she heard such invective and wit. Almost hypnotized, she eagerly accepted him as an idol and teacher.

Within weeks of her arrival, she was reading books Most recommended and often going out with the scarred old rebel. He opened up for her the world of music, literature, the theater. One evening in a café, after they had attended Carmen together, Emma told him of her enraptured reactions to her first opera, which she had attended in Königsberg with her teacher-friend. After she finished, Most musingly remarked that he had never heard the stirrings of a child more dramatically told. She had great talent, he added quickly, and would become a great speaker. He would help her, so she could take his place when he was gone.

As their friendship deepened, Emma began to realize the importance of Most's evaluation of her speaking abilities. From his remarks and anecdotes Emma learned of his native oratorical and histrionic talents which had been blighted by an unfortunate childhood and an early jaw infection which was badly cared for. As she listened, she realized that his facial deformity had made it impossible for him to fulfil his desire to become an actor. He could only have played the clown. Apprenticed instead to a bookbinder, he had become a genuinely tragic, Andreyevian figure whose emotions were slapped by everyone: by prospective employers who were afraid he would frighten customers out of their shops; by girls and women who disgustedly repelled his advances; and later by the press which, especially in America, used the whiskered and bushy-headed Most as the model for their bomb-carrying anarchist caricatures. At the point of suicide several times, he brooded over his twisted face, illegitimate birth, cruel home life. Pathologically bitter against those around him, he was well on the way to becoming a confirmed vagrant when he discovered socialism.

Most told his spellbound young protégée of his growing ability to sway audiences of workingmen and of the recognition of his work by governments which honored him with imprisonment. With some pride he described his election to the Berlin Reichstag in 1874 and his flight to England in 1878, following the wave of reaction which swept Germany. He angrily related how he had commenced publication of a radical weekly in England without first obtaining permission from the conservative German Socialist leaders and how he had then been expelled from the party in 1880 for this indiscretion and for his insurrec-

tionary views. Finally, he rather boastfully told Emma of his triumphant arrival in the United States in 1882. When he came, the Socialist
movement was boiling with dissension.

Many of the disputes could be traced back to the previous decade.
In 1872 there were approximately five thousand Socialist members of
the First International in the United States. That same year Marx,
frightened by Bakunin's growing power, dumped the headquarters of
the International in the laps of the startled and isolated German So
cialists in New York. But such evidence of strife in Europe was fully
matched by the immigrant radicals in America. Of the two main camps,
the Lassaleans put all their faith in political action, arguing that the
"iron law of wages" made union activity futile; the Marxists, on the
other hand, insisted that political action should go hand in hand with
economic action in trade unions. This basic disagreement hastened the
moribund First International (International Workingmen's Association) to an early end in 1876.

Despite all this bickering, the times seemed ripe for radical action.
Captains of industry, fanatically engaged in the acquisition of huge
economic empires, presented a challenge which only the dull-witted
could miss. The Molly Maguires in the Pennsylvania coal fields an-
swered this challenge with murder and robbery; they seemed to give
promise of a kind of revolutionary mettle. The great railway strikes of
1877, which began in West Virginia and spread to Maryland, Pennsylvania, New York, and a number of other states, certainly furnished
substantial evidence of labor's restiveness and growing militancy. For
a moment it seemed possible that the Socialists could join forces with
the native radicals, many of whom were Greenbackers, and the trade
unionists in a fight for fundamental changes. Yet few could forego the
delights of internecine strife. The battle between "political" and "economic" Socialists continued in the Workingmen's party and later in
the Socialist Labor party. After supporting Greenbacker James B.
Weaver for president in 1880, the Socialists—there were about fifteen
hundred left—made another amoeba-like split. The left wing affiliated
with the International Working People's Association, the old Baku-
ninist "Black International."

At this point Most made his entry. Quickly assuming leadership of
the scattered forces of the left wing, he almost singlehandedly united
the faction from the Socialist Labor party with the other anarchist
groups. With the help of Albert Parsons and August Spies, he wrote the
Pittsburgh manifesto, a statement of principles which, almost miracu-

lously, was acceptable to all the different groups. Thus by the mid-1880's, just a few years after his arrival, there were some seven thousand American anarchists in eighty organized groups; in Chicago alone there were about two thousand anarchists, and leaders such as Parsons had important ties with the local unions. Most's energetic activities had been in no small measure responsible for this surge of anarchist strength, but even he could do little against the nationwide attack on anarchism which followed the Haymarket Square tragedy of 1886.

Most's account of the ups and downs of anarchism made it clear to Emma that by the time she entered the movement, it was in serious decline. Caught up by her idol's stories of heroes and villains, of sublime acts of self-renunciation and bravery and of despicable acts of self-serving and cowardice, she clenched her teeth in a vow to help him regain lost ground and take new positions.

3

Six months after her arrival in New York, Most, true to his promise to make a speaker of her, sent Emma Goldman on a tour back to Rochester and on to Buffalo and Cleveland. She was to urge the futility of the struggle for an eight-hour workday. As he explained the issue to her, even if the shorter workday were established, it would be no gain, for the masses would be distracted from the real issue of the struggle against capitalism. This argument seemed compelling and Emma presented it in her lectures. But in Cleveland she was questioned closely by a white-haired worker. What were men of his age to do, he asked, since they were not likely to live so long as to see an anarchist society come into being? Why should they work two extra hours a day for the rest of their lives? Immediately the falsity of Most's position flashed across her mind. What was worse, her own position was even more false, for she was simply parroting her teacher's views.

Certain that she would have to think for herself, she told Most of her experience when she returned to New York. In a flash of anger, he informed her that she would think either his way or not at all. "Who is not with me is against me," he shouted. Emma was willing, very willing, to be with him, but not on those terms. She would not enlist in his regiment of the anarchist army.

After this experience she must have sensed the irony in the fact that the man she had sought out as her idol, the man who was the subject for the popular stereotype of the bomb-throwing radical, was only equivocally an anarchist. Actually during his years in the Berlin Reichstag

Most had given no evidence that he despaired of political action. He then held that violence was wrong so long as socialism was accepted by a minority only and unnecessary once the majority had been won over. Only when Bismarck's complete suppression of civil rights lost Most his place in the Reichstag did he change his views. He seems to have been an anarchist primarily because he could not be a Prussian Social-Democrat. His autocratic behavior, in any event, clashed sharply with his new doctrine.

Anarchist in spite of himself, Most made no contributions to anarchist theory. The famous Pittsburgh manifesto (1883), for which he was primarily responsible, was simply a restatement of the ideas of Michael Bakunin, the Russian communist anarchist. In the manifesto Most argued first—and the order was significant—for "destruction of the existing class rule by all means"; second, for co-operative organization of production; and third, for the "free exchange of equivalent products by and between the productive organizations, without commerce and profit-mongering." His political thinking added up to federalism, producer co-operatives, and, above all, guerrilla social and economic warfare.

Most's program, his "fierce call to battle against the enemy," satisfied Emma's rejection of polluted society, but it offered her little or no satisfaction for her pent-up desire for a more humane society. Saddened by Most's arrogant attitude and dissatisfied with his emphasis on hate and destruction, she gradually became attracted to Die Autonomie, a German anarchist weekly published by Joseph Peukert, Most's rival and enemy. She soon came to believe, in spite of Most's warnings against the paper, that its stress on individual freedom and group independence was what anarchism had come to mean to her. Her close association with Most was therewith at an end.

Yet Emma did not give up a certain admiration for Most. In spite of his fulminations on the extermination of "bourgeois vermin" and on the art of Revolutionäre Kriegswissenschaft, he did have something to offer his former protégée. That something was the example of a man who refused to be bowed by imprisonment, ridicule, calumny. Most seemed proof of the indestructibility of the individual human spirit, for each imprisonment only increased his defiance. The image of such burning rebellion flaming forth against the concentrated wrath of governmental power always captured Emma's imagination and wholehearted admiration.[1] In spite of everything, she continued to believe that she was lucky to have known such a fighter.

[1] Perhaps Henry James also appreciated Most's imaginative appeal and used him as a model for the mysterious Hoffendahl in the Princess Casamassima (1886).

4

Fortunately and quite understandably, Peter Kropotkin became Emma Goldman's true teacher and inspiration. A Russian prince who had one of the best minds of the nineteenth century, a geographer of the first rank who had elected to devote his life to anarchist theory and agitation, Kropotkin spoke to what was deepest in her. His articles in *Die Autonomie* and his other writings impressed her as the work of a benevolent, compassionate, unwaveringly principled thinker. Unlike Most, Kropotkin had more to offer than a *mystique* of violence. Unlike Benjamin Tucker and other native American individualist anarchists, Kropotkin had more to offer than their rather arid preoccupation with the widest possible extension of laissez faire.[2] Besides his advocacy of a com-

[2] Once Tucker even went so far as to chide William Graham Sumner for his lack of consistency in laissez faire championship. While agreeing with other anarchists in much of his critique of the state, church, and society, Tucker differed from the communist anarchists in his belief that the abolition of the state would allow free associations—meeting in the hallowed marketplace—to wipe out social evils. Clinging to the institution of private property, Tucker recommended free banking as the pry-pole which would topple monopolies to the ground and restore competition. See his *Instead of a Book* (New York: Benjamin Tucker, 1893). Other American individualist anarchists such as Josiah Warren, Lysander Spooner, Stephen Pearl Andrews, and Joseph Labadie argued much the same position.

Emma Goldman learned of the American libertarian background as she gained proficiency in the use of American-English, but she never worked closely with the individualist anarchists. She knew Tucker, but he did not impress her as a "large nature." As time went on, she drew rather on other figures in the American background, on Emerson, Whitman, and, especially, Thoreau. Contrary to uncritical thinking on this subject, there was in America a native radical tradition which meshed nicely with anarchist theory. This tradition went back to the emphasis on conscience and inner light of Roger Williams and John Woolman; to the colonial distrust of arbitrary governmental power and the negative state ideas which radicals insisted should be embodied in the Constitution in the form of the Bill of Rights; to the communitarianism of the 1830's and 1840's and the "no government" arguments of some of the abolitionists. Thus while the content and form of her dream came primarily and directly from Russian sources, this dream could put down roots in the hospitable soil of a native tradition.

Also contrary to popular misconception, the anarchist tradition elsewhere has had a long and illustrious past. In the East, Chuang Tzu, a follower of Lao Tzu, over two millennia ago lauded "the days when natural instincts prevailed, men moved quietly and gazed steadily." In the West, Zeno (Greek contemporary of Chuang Tzu) argued anarchistic views against Plato's omnicompetent state. Later Ovid looked back with yearning on a time when "everyone of his own will kept faith and did the right." There were more than traces of anarchism in the ideas of other thinkers, from the Hebrew prophets to the leaders of the Reformation. The first systematic statement of the anarchist position was made by William Godwin in his *Enquiry concerning Political Justice* (1793). Other notable figures in the anarchist tradition include Pierre Joseph Proudhon, who wrote *What Is Property?* (1840)—his warning against confusing theoretical anarchy with chaos has been disregarded from his day to ours; Max Stirner, the German individualist who maintained that the individual conscience is all; and Michael Bakunin, the Russian rebel and great antagonist of Marx. Bakunin had insights which gave his writings an almost blinding brilliance, but unfortunately they were also

munism of goods, which seemed much more likely to meet the problems of an industrial age, Kropotkin spoke to her from a Russian tradition —in which Chernyshevsky was one of the significant figures—which she had already made her own. Her whole life seemed to be a preparation for his teachings; she straightway became convinced that Kropotkin was anarchism's "clearest thinker and theoretician."

In truth Kropotkin did advance his theories with unusual clarity, despite the rich complexity and wide range of his thought. A keen student of biology, Kropotkin took as his departure a theory of evolution which stressed co-operation as well as competition. When in both individual and social life the normal processes of evolution are blocked, he argued, then there is after a time an inevitable explosion of energies which can be described as "accelerated evolution" or revolution. Thus in *Paroles d'un révolté* (1885) he contended for the necessity of revolution to break through the inertia of the ignorant and the selfishness of the powerful. Social revolutions acted to clear the way for the progress of social life from the lower to the higher forms of organization. Thus, while Kropotkin personally hated violence, he viewed it as an inevitable concomitant of significant social change. One of the primary roles of anarchists, however, was to help make the conflicts constructive by channeling them into definite issues and focusing them "upon the broad ideas which inspire men by the grandness of the horizon which they bring into view."

His critique of nationalism and capitalism emerged once he began to describe the individuals and institutions which attempted to thwart individual and social development. As he later put it in *Mutual Aid* (1902), the vital growth of society in the ancient Greek and in the medieval cities was brought to a halt by the state which "took possession, in the interest of minorities, of all the judicial, economical, and administrative functions which the village community already had exercised in the interest of all." In opposition to natural social organizations, the state oppressed individual spontaneity and blocked the further evolution of society. It also followed that private property, which was protected by the state, and religious authority, which sanctified state oppression and economic exploitation, denied mutual aid and

---

episodic and marred by a lack of concentrated direction. Kropotkin correctly asserted that Bakunin had influence on those who came later primarily through his "powerful, burning, irresistible revolutionary enthusiasm" which captured the imaginations of men and made anarchism a force to be reckoned with in France, Italy, and Spain. It was with Kropotkin that anarchism came to its fullest and finest theoretical expression.

perpetuated the rule of an elite. The new rulers simply appropriated for themselves the benefits of the combined efforts of present and past generations.

Kropotkin painted the outlines of the free society of the future with bold brush strokes. It will come into being, he contended, once the oppressive institutions of private property, the church, and, above all, the state no longer act as obstacles. Voluntarism will be the root principle of this new order. All agreements will be from the bottom up and free of compulsion. Men will be free to draw from a common pool of goods whatever they need. Moreover, this society will be no mechanistic, utilitarian nightmare, but one in which intellectual, artistic, and moral pursuits will be encouraged. As Kropotkin later summarized his argument,

This society will be composed of a multitude of associations, federated for all the purposes which require federation: trade federations for the production of all sorts—agricultural, industrial, intellectual, artistic; communes for consumption, making provision for dwellings, gas works, supplies of food, sanitary arrangements, etc.; federations of communes among themselves, and federations of communes with trade organizations; and finally, wider groups covering all the country or several countries, composed of men who collaborate for the satisfaction of such economic, intellectual, artistic, and moral needs as are not limited to a given territory.[3]

Such, in brief, was Kropotkin's Edenic dream which Emma Goldman gradually made her own. Henceforth it became, after a few modifications and changes of her own, the consuming passion of her life. She devoted all her amazing energies to make it a reality.

[3] *Memoirs of a Revolutionist* (Boston: Houghton Mifflin Co., 1899), p. 398.

CHAPTER VI

HOMESTEAD: IN THE BEGINNING WAS THE DEED

Shortly after her arrival in New York, Emma Goldman had looked for a job, since even the noblest dreams must be supplemented by bread. Dissatisfied by a few wearisome weeks in another corset factory, she rented a room on the East Side, set up her sewing machine, and commenced contract work on silk waists from a nearby factory. Under this ancient putting-out system she was freed from the strain and galling discipline of work in the shop and was able to equal her former earnings. Moreover, she had more time for her real calling.

As her fame as a speaker spread, she was given increased recognition in radical circles. At the Anarchist Congress of 1890 she was elected to the Anarchist Executive Board, but she soon withdrew after a spirited difference with the rest of the Board over the issue of "German centralization." When Joseph Barondess of the needleworkers called on her to help in the strike of the newly organized cloakmakers, she was able to convince scores of girls that they should support the union. Already her days were an exciting round of meeting followed by meeting, cause followed by cause. And one of the most exciting figures in her new life was Alexander Berkman, the young anarchist she had met that first day in the city.

2

The youngest member of a family of four children, Berkman was born in Vilna, Russia, in November, 1870. Unlike Emma—whose background was otherwise quite similar—Berkman grew up in relatively comfortable surroundings. Joseph Schmidt Berkman, whom he later characterized as his "bourgeois father," was a prosperous wholesaler of "uppers" for leather shoes. Yetta Berkman, his "aristocratic" mother, was from the even more prosperous Natansohn family. Not subject to the restrictions applied to the movements of poorer Jews, the Berkmans moved to St. Petersburg when Alexander was eight or nine.

In the capital conditions helped Berkman become a radical intellectual—one of the Russian type, as Berdyaev observed, "whose sole specialty was revolution." One day as he was reciting his lesson in school, a bomb exploded outside—he and his classmates soon learned that Czar Alexander II had just been assassinated. For Berkman, already possessed of a political awareness, this event called for what amounted to an ideological interpretation. Training for his specialty had in fact commenced at an early age. Much later, in his notes for a projected autobiography, Berkman made some rather peculiar entries for this period when he was just becoming an adolescent: "Visiting university students initiate me into Nihilism. Secret associations and forbidden books."

A small, dark, intense boy, Berkman seems always to have been concerned with forbidden books, forbidden ideas, forbidden ideals. Just as Emma chose Vera Pavlovna as a model of excellence, so Berkman shaped his life after Rachmetov, the most striking of Chernyshevsky's characters. Rachmetov gave up everything—home, sweetheart, children, security—to serve his ideal. Berkman schooled himself to become, as he put it, just such a "titan of resolution." As a boy he prepared himself for the final nobility of dying for a sublime cause: "Why, the very life of a true revolutionist," he declaimed passionately, "has no other purpose, no significance whatever, save to sacrifice it on the altar of the beloved People." Indeed, Berkman felt that he could even surpass Rachmetov in revolutionary zeal and resolution:

In spite of my great admiration for Chernishevsky, who had so strongly influenced the Russian youth of my time, I can not suppress the touch of resentment I feel because the author of "What's To Be Done?" represented his arch-revolutionist Rakmetov as going through a system of unspeakable, self-inflicted torture to prepare himself for future exigencies. It was a sign of weakness. Does a real revolutionist need to prepare himself, to steel his nerves and harden his body? I feel it almost a personal insult, this suggestion of the revolutionist's mere human clay.[1]

Such inflexible commitment made Berkman's early years understandably turbulent. As a *Gymnasium* student he was considered brilliant but too rebellious. Eventually he was expelled for a mordant essay entitled, "There Is No God." Then, angered by the refusal of the Russian authorities to admit his brother Max to a university because he was a Jew, he decided to go abroad. The brothers separated in Hamburg, Max to pursue his plans to study in Germany, Alexander

[1] *Prison Memoirs of an Anarchist* (New York: Mother Earth Publishing Assoc., 1912), p. 9.

to secure steerage passage to the United States. His ship docked in New York during the great snowstorm of the winter of 1888.

3

Both in background and in temperament Alexander Berkman and Emma Goldman had much in common. From their first meeting that August evening they were drawn to each other. She quickly discovered that Berkman too had been dismayed by the Haymarket tragedy and by the gap between the America of his dreams and the reality. In conversations without end they exchanged beliefs and enthusiasms. Berkman declared that Lingg, the Haymarket martyr, was right when he said: "If you attack us with cannon, we will reply with dynamite." Emma quite agreed. One day, in fact, incensed by the press caricatures of Most, she asked Berkman if he did not think one of the "rotten newspaper offices should be blown up—editors, reporters, and all?" Fortunately Berkman did not think the press needed to be taught this kind of lesson, for to his mind it was merely "the hireling of capitalism." They had to strike at the root.

Berkman's intensity and uncompromising dedication seemed sublime to Emma. In the tradition of the Russian revolutionists, they became lovers without being bound together by law. Too, relatively fresh from the horrors of her own married life, she abhorred the thought of conventional marriage.

Together with two other young anarchists, Emma and Berkman formed a little commune and rented a four room flat on Forty-second Street. Everything was shared as befitted real comrades. Emma kept the house and worked on her silk waists; her friend, Helen Minkin, continued to work in a corset factory; Berkman, who had first worked as a packer in a shirt factory, now worked as a cigarmaker; Fedya, the fourth member of their group, continued his free-lance painting. The expense of Fedya's oils and canvases often strained the group's treasury, but no one thought to complain. Sometimes Fedya would sell one of his pictures and then celebrate the occasion by presenting Emma with an armload of flowers or some other gift. This liberality provoked the only serious trouble the comrades had, for the consistent Berkman bitterly resented such extravagance at a time when so many were out of work and the anarchist movement needed money so badly. Fedya chose not to respond in kind to Berkman's attacks, but merely shrugged them off with a laugh and the remark that Berkman was a fanatic with no sense of beauty.

In their memoirs Berkman and Emma both used the name "Fedya" to protect their friend who had become a nationally known commercial artist. Their choice of a pseudonym was probably significant. A Fedya in Tolstoy's The Living Corpse (1911) was aware of the ills of society, but weakly abandoned his convictions to run off with a band of gypsies. Assuredly Berkman looked upon his cousin and best friend as something of a sybarite, as having the same indecisive character as Tolstoy's Fedya. And intellectually Emma agreed with Berkman. Yet she was also attracted by Fedya's thoughtfulness and his love of beauty. Was it possible, she wondered, to love more than one man? When she told Berkman of her feelings, she was startled by the "beauty" of his response. "I believe in your freedom to love," he told her and added that he was aware of his possessive tendencies, which he hated as he hated everything else from his bourgeois background. Not even the normally invincible monster of jealousy could destroy their common ideal.

The comrades lived on a flood-tide of enthusiasm. With no hesitation they earnestly formed a pact "to dedicate ourselves to the Cause in some supreme deed, to die together if necessary, or to continue to live and work for the ideal for which one of us might have to give his life." They decided that perhaps Berkman might serve the cause more effectively by returning to Russia and revolutionary work there. By way of preparation, Emma and Berkman moved to New Haven, where Berkman worked to learn the printing trade. To her joy, Emma now was able to give substance to her old goal of a co-operative dressmaking shop. Though the venture commenced well, it came to an untimely end when one of the members had a lung hemorrhage and had to be taken to a sanitorium. Then, in the winter of 1891, Emma moved to Springfield, Massachusetts, where Fedya had secured work with a photographer. Shortly after her arrival, they opened their own studio in Worcester and invited Berkman to join them.

Unfortunately, an epidemic of camera shyness struck their neighbors. Customers were so rare the three comrades dejectedly prepared to return to New York in defeat. Just at this point, however, they received word of a new series of atrocities in Russia. Spurred on to secure funds to return to their dark native land, the trio gave up their studio, borrowed $150 from their landlord, and opened an ice-cream parlor. Emma's delicious coffee, sandwiches, and other delicacies made the place quite popular. The entrepreneurs were dangerously close to economic success when news reached Worcester of the lockout of the workers at the Homestead, Pennsylvania, plant of Carnegie Steel Company, Ltd.

Closely following all the news of the Homestead struggle, they mistakenly thought the time had come for "the awakening of the American worker, the long-awaited day of his resurrection." One afternoon Emma happened to read in a customer's paper of the eviction of the locked-out workers from their company houses and of the threat of Henry Clay Frick, Carnegie's chairman, to bring in Pinkerton detectives. Therewith the trio decided Homestead, not Russia, was where they were needed. Closing the parlor for good, Emma and Berkman left for New York with the day's receipts.

Back in New York, Berkman drafted an explosive appeal, "Labor Awaken." They were in the process of trying to find someone to translate it into English from German when they were stunned by news of the July 6, 1892, battle between the Pinkertons and the Homestead workers.

For radicals with their views the chain of events leading up to this battle was certainly shocking enough. The Amalgamated Association of Iron and Steel Workers, a thoroughly conservative union of skilled members, had a contract with Carnegie which expired in June, 1892. On the surface the dispute between the workers and the company seemed simple. The wage scale was based on the selling price of steel billets. Management contended that a drop in the price of billets and the introduction of new machinery made a lower scale necessary. Frick proposed a scale which meant an average 18 per cent wage reduction for the men involved. The two sides were still negotiating when Frick abruptly declared that there would be no further conferences. It then became apparent that the real issue of the dispute was the union itself. Intent upon destroying it, Frick wired Robert A. Pinkerton for three hundred guards so that the plant could recommence operations on the sixth of July. The guards were to land at the plant from barges and defend it from behind the three-mile-long board fence—a formidable barricade topped by barbwire and pierced by loopholes—which Frick had constructed. But when the Pinkertons arrived in the early morning hours of July 6, the locked-out workers were ready. In the ensuing battle three Pinkertons and ten workers were killed. That the Pinkertons were ultimately repulsed did not lessen the rage of Berkman, Emma, and other radicals. Private armies of thugs had been used to kill workers.

The moment of decision seemed at hand. "The time for speech was past," Berkman observed. "Throughout the land the toilers echoed the defiance of the men of Homestead. The steel-workers had rallied bravely to the defense; the murderous Pinkertons were driven from the city. But loudly called the blood of Mammon's victims on the banks of the Monongahela. Loudly it calls. It is the People calling. Ah, the People! The grand, mysterious, yet so near and real People. . . . " Such a call was not to be denied. Emma agreed with Berkman that it was the psychological moment for an *Attentat*. Berkman resolved to assassinate Henry Clay Frick, the man responsible for the Homestead battle.

A week of feverish preparation was lost: the time bomb Berkman constructed, following Most's directions in the *Science of Revolutionary Warfare*, failed to go off. Years later Emma looked back on that bizarre week with some incredulity of her own: "Sasha's experiments took place at night when everybody was asleep. While Sasha worked, I kept watch. I lived in dread every moment for Sasha, for our friends in the flat, the children, and the rest of the tenants. What if anything should go wrong—but, then, did not the end justify the means? Our end was the sacred cause of the oppressed and exploited people. . . . What if a few should have to perish?—the many would be made free and could live in beauty and in comfort."[2] Fortunately the lethal device never did go off, whether because of errors in Most's directions, Berkman's blunders, or, as seemed more likely to him, "wet dynamite."

A change in plans was imperative. To her great disappointment, Emma could not accompany Berkman to Pittsburgh, for they had only fifteen dollars left after the abortive experiment with the bomb —barely enough to get Berkman to the steel city and leave him a dollar for his first day. She saw him off on the train and then she was left with the difficult task of raising money for a revolver and a new suit of clothes. The new suit was to help Berkman gain admittance to Frick's office; the revolver was to kill the steelmaster.

It was as though they were characters in a Russian novel. As if to sustain this illusion, Emma next followed the example set by Sonya Marmeladov in Dostoevsky's *Crime and Punishment* (1866). Sonya became a prostitute to support her family. Emma felt that she could do no less for Berkman: he was giving his life; she could at least give her body. So on Saturday evening, July 16, 1892, Emma decked

[2] *Living My Life*, p. 88.

herself out in some cheap finery and joined the procession of girls soliciting on Fourteenth Street. The incident came to an end with a peculiar twist: Despite her firm intentions, she repelled the advance of a number of interested men. Much later, with most of the evening past, she was still tramping the streets, growing more and more disgusted by her lack of will power. She made one last try, but this time she was approached by an elderly man who took her to a saloon, bought her a beer, and sent her on her way with ten dollars and the admonition to stay out of the profession—she was obviously a novice and had no "knack" for it.

After she paid for the high-heeled shoes and fancy lingerie she had only five dollars left. She had to have more. As a last resort she wired Helena that she was ill and needed fifteen dollars. Worried about cheating her beloved Helena, who was also poor and needed the money, she feared that the deception was "criminal." But the great end of liberating the "People" made this a relatively small matter.

4

As with most men of some consequence, Henry Clay Frick was both an expression of his time and something more. He was a classic example of the industrial capitalist who became prominent in the last third of the nineteenth century. Then all the problems of rapid industrialization, urbanization, and the formal end of the frontier seemed to join together to make the captain of industry a figure of colossal proportions. By the watershed of the nineties, the captain of industry and the master of finance emerged in decisive control of the economy and, to an impressive extent, of the society as well. "A banker's Olympus," as Henry Adams was to remark, became "more and more despotic over Esop's frog-empire. One might no longer croak except to vote for King Log, or—failing storks—for Grover Cleveland; and even then could not be sure where King Banker lurked behind."

Take, for instance, the supreme symbol of the times, the trust. The whiskey trust, the oil trust, the sugar trust, and a host of other trusts were gobbling down all the little frogs. In 1892 Carnegie Steel Company, Ltd., was formed with a capitalization of $25,000,000; under Frick's able guidance the Carnegie interests enhanced in value to such an extent that nine years later Carnegie could dispose of his holdings for many times this amount. Morgan and his associates then formed the United States Steel Corporation with an ostensible capitalization of $1,402,847,000. Both a horizontal and a vertical trust, United States Steel was seemingly the kind of amalgamation explicitly forbidden by the Sherman Anti-Trust Act. Yet the Supreme Court much later held that the Sherman Act did not apply to this trust of trusts.

Along with the growth of huge industrial concentrations went the growth of the megalopolis. These great industrial and financial centers, where corruption was at a frenetic pitch, unashamedly concentrated on bigness, wealth, power. Chicago, for instance, extended its "urban imperialism" throughout the Mississippi Valley and reached out to influence cities as far away as San Francisco.

Then there was the frontier, used up, it was thought, like passenger pigeons and buffaloes. After three centuries of escaping from their problems, Americans were suddenly faced with the frightening possibility that all avenues of flight were closed.

As Alfred Kazin has so well remarked, "the image of a closed frontier, of a corporation economy, of a city proletariat oppressed and rebellious, darkened the mind." Darkened the mind is just the right phrase, for Americans finally began to sense the implications of the awesome concentrations of power, such as Carnegie's and Frick's, in an America turned back upon itself. Yet the attempts to make such power responsible resembled somewhat an *opéra bouffe*. For a few heady years the Populists and Bryanites seemed to think that "free-silver" was the key which would unlock the golden door! But even if William Jennings Bryan had won the intensely contested election of 1896, there was not a shadow of a possibility that King Banker and Robber Baron could have been reined in, to change the figure, by a silver bridle. Nor did the Sherman Act offer much hope, especially after it had been devitalized by the Supreme Court decision in the Knight Case, wherein it was held that the Act did not apply to trusts for the control of manufacture, but only to trusts for the control of commerce. On the other hand, the Act was used against Coxey's Army of walking protesters and against Gene Debs and his American Railway Union. The income tax was another favorite weapon of Populists and their friends which was ruled unconstitutional by the Supreme Court.

For a time—before much of the frustration and blocked idealism was channeled into the initially idealistic and finally imperialistic Spanish War—serious class conflict seemed to many to lie just ahead. Even if the power of a few was so great that one-eighth of the families owned seven-eighths of the country's property, the other seven-eighths of the people gave promise of asserting themselves. Nowhere was this better illustrated than in Chicago, the city of the Gold Coast and the Jungle. There two monuments to the Haymarket tragedy symbolized the mood of increased desperation and class hostility. Shortly after the executions of 1887, American radicals placed an imposing statue over the grave of the martyrs in outlying Waldheim Cemetery. An erect, rebellious, compassionate figure of Justice stood looking sadly out on the world which killed the men who were fighting for freedom—for the freedom which she represented. No radical of the time could look on this statute without experiencing the aching hope that August Spies's inscription on the base of the statue was truly prophetic: "The day will come," Spies predicted, "when our silence will be more powerful than the voices you are throttling today." In violent conflict with this view was a monument down in Haymarket Square which the forces of capitalism, law, and the present order had erected. This statue of a helmeted policeman with one of the flowing mustaches of the time and a club conspicuously at his side—not incidentally a male, authoritarian figure—was dedicated by Chicago "to her defenders in the Riot of May 4th 1886." With reassuring firmness the policeman demanded, with upraised hand, that the radicals cease their activity: "In the name of the People of Illinois I command Peace."[3] To the friends of the established order the statue gave a welcome feeling of security, power, confidence.

This was the time of violent conflict and great change of which Frick was so representative a figure. Yet the age was what it was in some measure because he lived in it and made his mark on it.

Frick was born in 1849 in Westmoreland County, Pennsylvania, four generations removed from the maternal ancestor who came from the Palatinate. His grandfather was a pious Mennonite and the original distiller of Old Overholt rye whiskey. Frick worked on his father's

---

[3] The statue, radical legend has it, was knocked from its pedestal by a derailed streetcar November 11, 1927, on the fortieth anniversary of the executions. Its waggish history continued, for it was then placed in Union Park, at the corner of Ogden and Washington, where it now stands. In this location the policeman seems vainly intent upon preventing the facing statue of Mayor Carter H. Harrison from defiantly proclaiming that "Genius is but audacity. . . ." Moreover, the model for the statue was officer Thomas Birmingham, the "handsomest and most perfect specimen of the Chicago Police Department" and one of the "heroes" of the riots of 1886. Birmingham was befuddled by all the attention he received when he was stationed as a showpiece in Haymarket Square during the World's Fair of 1893. Shortly thereafter he became "intemperate," was dismissed from the force, and died a pauper in the Cook County Hospital in 1912.

small farm until 1863, when he was given a job in his uncle's store. There his chief interest was in bookkeeping, and whatever love of artistry he had was revealed by his ornate chirography.

Assuredly Frick was called to business if anyone ever was. Business became his life: to make his mark he could waste no time—idleness was the major sin—through aimless talk, sociability, or inactive contemplation. A typical day in the 1860's, when he was bookeeping for his grandfather, went like this: he rose at seven o'clock; he walked to the distillery; he worked from eight to six; he went to business college in the evening, where he studied accountancy and banking until nine-thirty; he then went home to bed. He had few acquaintances, and he was not much of a reader. His favorite books were the *Sayings of Marcus Aurelius, Memoirs of Cellini, Autobiography of Franklin*, and, in later years, William George Jordan's *Self Control: Its Kinship and Its Majesty*. After his grandfather's death in 1870, he went into the coke business, borrowing money from his mother's estate, his father, and neighboring farmers. Working with the energy of one possessed, he consolidated his holdings. By one evening in 1879, largely through extraordinarily able management of what Henry George called "unearned increment," Frick had "made his million." But it was only the first of many. Permitting himself another look at his accounts, his biographer proudly asserts, he verified his count, lighted a five-cent Havana cigar, and strolled in his measured, stolid way around the corner to his room in the Washabaugh House.

His sleep was probably untroubled, for he apparently never questioned the nature of his calling or inquired into the assumptions he had internalized as a boy. He showed none of the inner uncertainty of Carnegie and never felt it necessary to argue stridently for specious "laws" of accumulation and of competition as had Carnegie in his famous *Gospel of Wealth*. For Frick the competitive order of the universe was given and needed no justification. Nor did he find it necessary as had Carnegie to express some insincere sympathies for the rights of workmen to organize. Frick was always unashamedly and explicitly on the side of the employer and was forthrightly prepared to hire men to replace "hands" who stubbornly questioned his right to manage his property as he saw fit. When he became manager of Homestead and chairman of Carnegie Steel in 1889, the overwhelming power and monstrous discipline of the steel mills found their final and fullest expression in his person. After the battle of the

The Goldman family in St. Petersburg, 1882: Emma, Helena, Morris (in Helena's lap), Taube, Herman, and Abraham. (*Emma Goldman Papers, New York Public Library.*)

The "new immigrant" in 1886, shortly after her arrival.

The redoubtable Johann Most in the 1890's

Alexander Berkman when he was
living in Berlin in the 1920's

Ben L. Reitman in a characteristic pose

Edward Brady in the 1890's

sixth of July 1892, Frick showed himself to be almost as inflexible as one of his steel billets.

5

The July 6 riot caused great concern throughout the United States. Naturally radicals were most condemnatory. A Socialist Labor party mass meeting, for instance, adopted a resolution proposed by Daniel De Leon and Lucien Saniel which asked that "H. C. Frick and Robert and William Pinkerton be executed as murderers." And it was this event of course which so enraged Emma Goldman and Alexander Berkman and put the latter on a train for Pittsburgh.

An ancient rabbinical legend promised that if there were just one instant of righteousness throughout all Jewry, then the Messiah would appear on earth. Berkman may have thought of himself as at least an apostle of the revolutionary Messiah as he sought to make right-eousness prevail in Pittsburgh for "the twinkling of an eyelash." Frick, in turn, was immovably righteous in his conviction—to him beyond question—that his stand in opposition to the union was sanctioned by the structure of the universe itself: of all the verities, the right of man to do what he willed with his property was the most eternal. Thus, two of the most determined and opposed men of the age met in Frick's office in the Pittsburgh Chronicle Telegraph Building at 1:55 P.M., Saturday, July 23, 1892.

Berkman used the alias of Simon Bachman, the head of a non-existent agency of strikebreakers, to gain admittance to Frick's office. Frick was in conference with Vice-Chairman John Leishman when Berkman brushed by the Negro attendant. Let Berkman speak for himself now:

"Fr——," I begin. The look of terror in his face strikes me speechless. It is the dread of the conscious presence of death. "He understands," it flashes through my mind. With a quick motion I draw the revolver. As I raise the weapon, I see Frick clutch with both hands the arm of the chair and at-tempt to rise. I aim at his head. "Perhaps he wears armor," I reflect. With a look of horror he quickly averts his face, as I pull the trigger. There is a flash, and the high-ceilinged room reverberates as with the booming of a cannon. I hear a sharp piercing cry, and see Frick on his knees, his head against the arm of the chair. I feel calm and possessed, intent upon every movement of the man. He is lying head and shoulders under the large armchair, without sound or motion. "Dead?" I wonder. I must make sure.[4]

4 *Prison Memoirs*, pp. 33–34.

Frick was not dead. Berkman, while grappling with Leishman, fired two more shots at Frick before a carpenter, who had been working in the building, knocked him to the floor with his hammer. But then Berkman again heard Frick's voice: "Not dead? . . . I crawl in the direction of the sound, dragging the struggling men with me. I must get the dagger from my pocket—I have it! Repeatedly I strike with it at the legs of the man near the window. I hear Frick cry out in pain—there is much shouting and stamping—my arms are pulled and twisted, and I am lifted bodily from the floor." Then, according to the New York *Times* reporter, although there was some movement to lynch "Bachman" on the spot, he did not shrink or show fear. Frick, still conscious, reportedly asked that Berkman not be harmed—the law could take its course.

Both men, in any case, showed considerable bravery. Frick was soon back at his desk, working as usual after a remarkably short convalescence from his multiple wounds—two from bullets and two from Berkman's knife. Frick kept his head and did not rush up and down the country calling for the extermination of all radicals.[5]

6

After his deed, Berkman had intended to commit suicide. While he had no wish to escape, he did want to live long enough to explain "to the people the motive and purpose of my act." Accordingly he had hidden on his person a capsule containing fulminate of mercury which he planned to use after his trial. However, the afternoon after his attack on Frick he was discovered "chewing" the capsule, and it was forcibly removed from his mouth. Seemingly he could not wait to explain his act.

He had little opportunity to make any explanation during his trial. The date was kept secret until the morning he was to go to court. What was even more grotesque, as he walked into Judge McClung's courtroom, he found the jury already seated! Striving for consistency, he declined legal defense on the grounds that he did not believe in "man-made-law" and that an *Attentat* could not be "measured by the narrow standards of legality." His trial was a naked formality. He was formally charged with six counts: felonious assault on Frick, with intent to kill; the same for his alleged assault on Leishman; feloniously entering the offices of the Carnegie Company on three occasions, three separate

---

[5] Frick's commendable reaction did not of course reach the level of that of Voltairine De Cleyre, a Philadelphia anarchist. Under similar circumstances she refused to prosecute a would-be assassin after he had shot her three times. She even made an appeal in the anarchist press for aid in his defense.

indictments; and unlawfully carrying concealed weapons. Berkman argued, and lawyers generally conceded the validity of his position later, that the lesser charges were all included in the major charge of assault on Frick; moreover, he maintained that he had visited the offices of the Carnegie Company only once. The court overruled his objections. Leishman testified that Berkman attempted to kill him; other witnesses testified that he had been in Frick's office three times; Frick testified; and the trial was virtually over. Berkman still had his speech to read in his own defense, however, and the court assigned an interpreter to him. To his horror Berkman discovered that the interpreter was a blind old man who haltingly translated his German sentences word for word. After a third of the paper was read, the judge stopped the pathetic performance and the trial was over. Berkman was sentenced to twenty-one years in Western Penitentiary and to one year in the Allegheny Workhouse.

Justice was not blind that day. Berkman was not advised in advance of the trial date so he could prepare himself; he was given no opportunity—and this may have been crucially important—to examine the talesmen. Most importantly, the multiplication of the charges against him was simply a way to circumvent the maximum sentence of seven years for such a crime; unfortunately, his failure to take formal exceptions blocked any appeal to higher courts. Next, all the evidence indicates that Leishman lied when he testified that Berkman sought to kill him, for Berkman's every action was directed toward killing Frick. With comparable logic, if there had been a dozen men in Frick's office, rather than two, the authorities would have lodged twelve charges against him, a charge of intent to kill for each one of those present. Next, Berkman maintained that he alone was responsible for his act, but the same witnesses who swore that he entered the Chronicle Telegraph Building three times also testified that they had seen him there in the company of Carl Nold and Henry Bauer, two Pittsburgh anarchists. On the strength of this testimony Nold and Bauer were later successfully prosecuted, although Bauer, a follower of Most, was actually hostile to Berkman, suspected him of being a spy, and therefore was hardly willing to join him in such a desperate venture. Very probably Nold and Bauer, despite the verdict in their case, were not implicated. Finally, the proceedings were rushed through with unseemly haste, as the court sought quick revenge rather than lasting justice. Perhaps the Carnegie Company hurried the proceedings along. Berkman always maintained that Reed and Knox, the Carnegie attorneys, handled the prosecution in court and simply used the district attorney as a figurehead—the latter felt that this was so obvious he was constrained to inform the jury that he was not in the employ of any individual or corporation.

7

Yet Berkman was most assuredly guilty of attempting to assassinate Frick. He committed his deed for propaganda purposes and to destroy Frick. He failed in both ends. Frick lived and became even more immovable, if that were possible, in his opposition to labor. And Berkman only later learned of his and Emma's profound misjudgement of the temper of the Homestead workers. In a moving passage in his *Prison Memoirs* Berkman related his attempt to explain his act to Jack Tinford, a Homestead worker who was in jail awaiting trial for throwing dynamite at the Pinkerton barges. Tinford whispered to Berkman that it was too bad he did not kill Frick. "Some business misunderstanding, eh?" asked Tinford. When Berkman tried to explain, Tinford angrily replied that the Homestead men showed their respect for authority by welcoming the militia; they would have nothing to do with anarchists; it was none of Berkman's business; he had only harmed the steelworkers. Tinford preferred murder that he could understand, murder over a "business misunderstanding." And this of course was the general reaction of American workers everywhere. To be sure, a Pennsylvania militiaman, W. L. Iams, proposed three cheers for the man who shot Frick—for which he was strung up by the thumbs and dishonorably drummed out of the militia (a punishment which involved disfranchisement). But generally the reaction to Berkman's act was startled incredulity or suspicion. Americans found it almost impossible to believe that Berkman did not commit the act for personal gain. Four years later, for instance, the Homestead leader John McLuckie told Emma that he and his fellows believed that Berkman had never intended to kill Frick and had only committed the act to arouse sympathy for the steelmaster. They believed that Berkman had been quietly released from jail shortly after his trial.

Historians have long judged that Berkman's act broke the back of the steelworkers' struggle by alienating public sympathy from the workers and by bringing glory to Frick. This judgment has not stood up under careful scrutiny. Actually the success of the lockout was assured by the arrival of the militia in Homestead. And as Henry David has pointed out, while Berkman's act was universally condemned, a number of journals went on to show carefully that the deed was committed by a person wholly unconnected with the struggle. (Berkman argued that if Frick had died, Carnegie would have hastened to settle with the workers—this was an interesting thesis but by its nature had to remain simply conjecture.)

Meanwhile in New York, Emma and Fedya had decided to blow up the Allegheny County courthouse should Berkman be condemned to death. Fortunately they did not have to act on this decision, although Fedya did resolve to finish what Berkman had commenced. After his arrival in Pittsburgh, however, according to his account of the affair, he hurriedly left when "due to some mysterious reason his presence there became known." He then prudently spent some time in Detroit. As his reputation as a commercial artist became established, he gradually dropped out of the anarchist movement. It was highly unlikely, in any case, that he was capable of a deed such as Berkman's.

The *Attentat* brought about a final rupture between Emma Goldman and Johann Most and led to one of the most shameful chapters in anarchist history. There had been, to repeat, a certain hostility between Most and his two former followers for some time. Emma and Berkman had criticized Most's domineering behavior. There was also an unanarchistic jealousy between Berkman and Most over Emma. Hence, when Emma and Berkman joined the *Autonomie* circle, a group centered around Most's rival and enemy, Joseph Peukert, Most vowed he would have nothing more to do with them. But the worst was yet to come.

At the time of Berkman's *Attentat* Most had only shortly before been released from another year in prison—this time for a speech delivered after the execution of the Chicago martyrs. In a talk delivered immediately after Berkman's act, Most advanced the view that the attempt on Frick's life was probably a newspaper fake and that Berkman was some crank or perhaps even Frick's own man who had acted to create sympathy for him. Emma was understandably horrified by this attack on Berkman. Now Most's timing seemed to go completely haywire. After a decade of urging the supreme value of the *Attentat* and at the height of the condemnation of Berkman's act, Most decided that he had overestimated the importance of terrorism: it was, he felt, impracticable in a country with an immature revolutionary movement. While his argument was quite sound, if belated, its timing suggested that the motives of his turnabout were geared to his fear of returning to prison (he had just completed his ninth year) rather than to sober reflections on revolutionary tactics. In any case, his seeming opportunism and the injustice of his insinuations against Berkman incensed Emma. Not only the whole bourgeois world but Most as well had joined in the cry against Berkman. She challenged Most to prove his accusations and branded him a coward and a traitor. Most made no reply. At his next lecture she again asked him to prove his insinuations. Most merely muttered something about a "hysterical woman," whereupon Emma quickly took a horsewhip from beneath her gray cloak, leaped before the startled Most, and repeatedly lashed him across the face and about the head, finally breaking the whip over her knee and throwing the pieces at him. She had moved so swiftly that the horsewhipping was over before anyone had a chance to interfere.

And on this note of inglorious personal violence closed the episode of Berkman's deed. The twenty-two-year-old Berkman was in prison for twenty-two years—it was thought he would never come out alive. Frick was stronger than ever. Emma had horsewhipped her former teacher-idol and in so doing had further divided the scattered anarchist forces. When the unreconciled Most died in 1906, Emma and Berkman became the central figures in American anarchism. But by then there was little left of the movement.

Although the act proved disastrous in most of its consequences, it had the effect of making final Emma's adamantine opposition to the bourgeois world. Only a lack of funds had kept her from accompanying Berkman to Pittsburgh. She had sent him money for the revolver. Her complicity in the crime was unmistakable—although not publicly proved. She felt as if half of her were in Western Penitentiary in stripes. Hence she had a very strong additional reason for making Berkman's deed meaningful, for carrying on the struggle against the present, and for attempting to bring about "an instant of righteousness."

CHAPTER VII

BEING AN EVIL DISPOSED
AND PERNICIOUS PERSON

A year after Berkman was committed to the penitentiary Emma was in jail awaiting trial herself. The *World*'s Nellie Bly, who had a keen nose for good copy, went down to the Tombs to visit her. Already Emma's reputation was such that Nellie expected to find "a great raw-boned creature, with short hair and bloomers, a red flag in one hand, a burning torch in the other; both feet constantly off the ground and 'murder!' continually upon her lips." But as Nellie put it in her customary hyperbole, she emitted "a gasp of surprise" when she saw the anarchist menace, for the supposed monster was a modest five feet tall, not showing her one hundred and twenty pounds, "with a saucy, turned-up nose and very expressive blue-gray eyes that gazed inquiringly at me through shell-rimmed glasses." She decided that Emma was actually quite attractive, with her light brown hair, "falling loosely over her forehead, full lips, strong white teeth, a mild, pleasant voice, with a fetching accent." Her appearance and able exposition of her views so impressed Nellie—and, of course, she was thinking of the copy Emma made—that she wrote a very favorable article on Emma for the *World*, wherein she outraged her readers by styling the "little anarchist" a "modern Joan of Arc."

2

The intervening year between Berkman's trial and Emma's was marked by no diminution of activity. Her flat was raided by police who searched for evidence linking her to Berkman's act. When they found none, they harassed Emma's landlord until he forced her to move. No one would rent her a room. She moved in briefly with her grandmother, but she could not stay there long. She then managed a few fitful naps each night by riding streetcars until the early morning hours. Finally a landlord on Fourth Street near Third Avenue took her in without asking questions about her past. Not until later did she realize that she had moved into a house of prostitution. But since the girls vied with one another in being kind to her, she decided to stay until her money for rent ran out. Luckily permanent quarters of a sort soon turned up in the Bohemian Republic, a lodging place of Czech revolutionary immigrants.

Almost all the German and Jewish anarchists, following Most's lead, had repudiated Berkman's act. Yet Emma, with the help of a few of the East Side radicals and some native Americans, notably Dyer D. Lum, launched an effort to have Berkman's sentence commuted. Throughout the winter she worked tirelessly to this end. But in the spring she became ill and was advised by physicians to leave New York. In Rochester a lung specialist discovered that she had incipient tuberculosis. Helena and her doctor planned to send Emma to a sanatorium for the winter.

Emma's sense of duty, however, ruled out such an extended period of inactivity. This was 1893, the year of the great Panic and the beginning of four hard years of depression. Throughout the summer conditions became worse: there were some eight thousand business failures and perhaps four million men were unemployed. A cloakmaker's strike in New York was only one of the many labor disturbances which broke out all over the country. To Emma it seemed that capitalism was again showing its inherent contradictions; she felt called upon to return to New York to aid the strikers and to help organize the unemployed. Although still ill, she left Rochester, leaving notes of explanation for Helena and her doctor.

Her health improved marvelously once her life again became full. She organized the first Jewish and Italian groups of girls for the cloakmakers' union, and she threw herself into a round of committee meetings, public talks, food collection. She also helped Joseph Barondess, a radical labor leader, organize mass meetings in Union Square. For a meeting on the twenty-first of August they secured a permit, stating that the object of the occasion was to "promote local, state, and public works for the unemployed."

Three to four thousand bitter, angry people, mostly unemployed, crowded into Union Square that Monday evening. They were especially aroused by the unwillingness of the state legislature to do anything for the homeless and hungry. Emma quickly sensed their mood. As often happened at such times of crisis, she spoke almost in tongues, phophet-like, seemingly possessed by a truly incandescent indignation and sympathy; on these occasions she was so inspired—so filled as with an extra-human energy—that she drew her audience part of the way up to her own heights of feeling and consciousness. The gist of what she said was that the unemployed should distrust the state and labor politicians; she adjured them to stand up and demand what was rightfully theirs—and they could commence by demanding bread, an obvious first step for the starving. Her words were greeted by wild applause and the waving of countless outstretched hands—hands which seemed to her "like the wings of white birds fluttering."

3

Early the next morning she left for Philadelphia to carry on her work for the unemployed there. Several days later, just as she was entering Buffalo Hall to address some three hundred people, she was arrested. One unlucky anarchist, Albert Hanson, rushed into the hall and cried, "Miss Goldman has been arrested. Arouse!" for which he was himself later arrested for inciting to riot. Members of her audience rushed toward her, but the police drew their guns and threatened them back. A German comrade managed to run up to her and hold out his wallet as an offer of economic assistance, but he was promptly arrested for trying to pull Emma away from the police.

After her extradition papers arrived, Detective-Sergeant Charles Jacobs escorted the anarchist agitator back to New York. According to Emma, Jacobs became quite friendly on the train. He informed her that his chief proposed to quash the charges against her and offer her a sum of money in return for her co-operation in keeping the police informed of the activities of New York radicals. His suggestion that she become an informer—a paid one at that—provoked an instantaneous response: she threw the remainder of a glass of ice water in his face. The next morning she was taken before Thomas F. Byrnes, Superintendent of Police. Byrnes, who had been told of course of her rejection of his bribery attempt, turned to her furiously: Such a fool, he thundered, deserved to be put away for years. When he had finished his tirade, she told him that she would tell the whole country how corrupt the Chief of Police of New York could be. Byrnes raised a chair as if to strike her, but changed his mind and had her taken back to her cell.

Violence certainly was not beyond Byrnes. While he did not have quite as lurid a reputation as one of his inspectors, "Clubber" Williams, he was known as "a manhandler of criminals." Young Lincoln Steffens, who was covering Mulberry Street for the New York *Post*, spent his mornings at this time in interested observation of the "broken heads" —the mercilessly clubbed radicals and labor men—who were brought in and out of Byrnes' office. And very probably Byrnes, whose connections with the underworld were so close that he knew the beat of every New York "dip," or pickpocket, wished to establish through Emma closer connections with the radical world. The head of New York's "finest" resigned the following year during the Lexow investigation: it was proved that Byrnes' force collected monthly blackmail from bawdyhouse madams, gamblers, saloon-keepers and, furthermore, received percentages from the takes of pickpockets, gunmen, streetwalkers.

This was the police department which was determined to "get" Emma Goldman.

4

She was indicted on three counts, all for speeches inciting to riot. The formal charges were for unlawful assemblage. Bail was set at two thousand dollars.

After her bail had been raised by a sympathizer, Emma had to decide if she would conduct her own defense. At first she thought she would, since after all she did not believe in law and lawyers. But friends urged her to seek counsel, and Berkman wrote that while he still thought it inconsistent for an anarchist to have a lawyer, he felt that Emma could propagandize in court more effectively if her right to speak were protected. The matter was decided when former Mayor A. Oakey Hall offered his services for nothing.

Hall was a bizarre counsel for Emma. He had been Tweed's mayor in the 1860's, at which time he had helped his boss lick up a phenomenal amount of municipal boodle. By the 1890's Hall was on the outside looking in at the Tammany preserves; he desperately hoped to use her case as the first step of a comeback. Though he may have come, as he professed to Emma, to some liberal ideas and to an antagonism to the police and their corrupt methods, he was hardly "a great jurist" as she so generously called him.

Ostensibly the central issue of the trial was what Emma had said at the Union Square meeting. The star witness for the prosecution was Detective Jacobs. Jacobs admitted he was no stenographer, but he maintained that he had been able to take down a verbatim account of the German portion of her speech. Certainly she had exhorted the people to riot and insurrection: "But with idle talk," Jacobs testified Emma had said, "you will accomplish very little. You must have courage. You want bread but who will give it to you? No one. Nobody will give it to you. If you want it, you must take it. If you do not get it when you ask for it, upon your demands, take it by force." Now this was very probably not a verbatim account of her talk. In the first place, the staccato syntax was unlike her usual style, oral or written, though conceivably such a series of short, pounding sentences may have come at the climax of her talk. But not this series of sentences. Although Emma achieved her share of contradictions, it was highly improbable that she voiced such a manifest contradiction within the space of a few sentences: "You want bread but who will give it to you? No one. . . . If you do not get it when you ask for it, upon your demands, take it by force." It sounded as if she had whirled about and stopped where Jacobs wanted her: "take it by force." Further, it was virtually impossible for Jacobs, not a trained stenographer, to have taken down a word-for-word account while he was standing on a crowded platform in the middle of a noisy square. And Jacobs was probably testifying falsely when under cross-examination he told Hall he was not "gratified" to hear things of an "incendiary nature." If Jacobs and Byrnes planned to force her to become a spy, then Jacobs was gratified to hear her utter a call to riot—or, failing that, to hear a speech which could be reported as a call to riot. Certainly Jacobs and Byrnes, especially after Emma refused to play on their team, had a real stake in making a strong case against her.

But Emma, of course, had an equally strong motive for denying their contentions. She testified that everything Jacobs said was untrue. She noted that she was in the habit of preparing speeches beforehand and then committing them to memory. Reading from the speech which she had memorized for this occasion, she insisted that the lines Jacobs had misquoted were as follows: "No, workmen, you ought to protect what belongs to you—what you yourselves have produced, and, in the first place, you ought to take bread, to procure bread in order to quench your momentary needs. Workmen, you must demand what belongs to you. Go forth into the streets where the rich dwell, before the palaces of your dominators . . . and make them tremble." Unfortunately it was quite possible that these words did not constitute an exact account of what she said. Caught up by the bitterness and tenseness of her audience, she may well have departed from her memorized lines. Furthermore, Emma's veracity, usually beyond reproach, was thrown into question by her testimony under cross-examination. When asked about Berkman's act, she responded that she did not approve of it, though she felt sympathy for him and admired his courage. In responding thus she was merely restating a claim (which she had made a year before) of innocence of complicity in the attempt on Frick's life. Since Emma was very much Berkman's accomplice, however, her denial throws in doubt the rest of her testimony. At this time she believed that the ends justified the means: in order for her to continue to seek her ends, she may have thought that any means were justified to avoid capitalist injustice.

After hearing the evidence the jury, convinced that Jacobs' testimony was accurate, found her guilty. But the jury was admittedly prejudiced before it heard a word of testimony. Most of the talesmen said they would be influenced by the fact that Emma was an anarchist and atheist. And Assistant District Attorney McIntyre in his cross-examination scarcely referred to the meeting, but persisted in questioning her about her political and religious beliefs:

Q.—Do you believe in a Supreme Being, Miss Goldman?
A.—No, sir, I do not.
Q.—Is there any government on earth whose laws you approve?
A.—No, sir, for they are all against the people.
Q.—Why don't you leave this country if you don't like its laws?
A.—Where shall I go? Everywhere on earth the laws are against the poor, and they tell me I cannot go to heaven, nor do I want to go there.

In this way McIntyre played on the prejudices of the jury (quite in the manner established by Meletus two millennia before in the trial of Socrates), introduced extraneous prejudicial testimony to confuse the issue, and in general made it more difficult for the jury to decide her case on its merits. As the New York *Times* pointed out in one of its editorials, her disbelief in God and law was in itself damning: "How far this will go toward convicting her it is easy to determine."

In his remarks to the jury Judge Randolph B. Martine added evidence that Emma was being tried for her opinions. Martine rather regretfully granted her that "you are a woman beyond the average in intelligence." He did not know what her "advantages have been in the way of education," but it was clear that she did not "believe in our laws." Judge Martine felt quite sure "such a person cannot be tolerated in this community by those who believe in law, and I am happy to say that the greater number of our people do believe in law. . . . I look upon you as a dangerous woman in your doctrines." After this frontal assault on her beliefs and doctrines, little doubt remained that Martine was not primarily concerned with her deeds. One wonders if the jurist expected to discover an anarchist who was a believer in the laws in which he took such a proprietary interest—he and the jury shared fully in the popular attitude toward agitators that Finley Peter Dunne burlesqued so well. Agitators " 'must niver agytate' themselves," mocked Mr. Dooley, "and they and the police ought to be 'the Best iv Frinds.' "

Whether Emma advised the Union Square crowd to take bread "by force" was thus not the basic issue in her trial.[1] What she said was of less importance than what she believed to the press, the jury, the judge. The police would have had no difficulty at almost any time in working up a case against an anarchist; in 1893, the year of Governor John Peter Altgeld's pardon of the remaining Haymarket martyrs, they could exploit especially intense feelings against anyone with her views. And since all this was true, her conviction could not be justified: her beliefs were beyond the purview of the court.

5

The epilogue was a year in prison on Blackwell's Island.

There she was almost immediately placed in charge of the sewing shop. The other prisoners kept aloof from her at first, for they had been warned about her disbelief in God and government. But her firm refusal to drive the women in their work made her enormously popular. She realized that "these poor creatures so hungered for kindness that the least sign of it loomed high on their limited horizons. After that they would often come to me with their troubles. . . ."

A short while later, since the prison officials felt that she was not stern enough in handling the women in the shop, she was given another job, prison nurse. Even the prison officials were impressed by her tender care of the sick prisoners. According to one overly sentimental report that appeared in the New York *Herald*, the authorities were surprised to see this "inciter of violence" walk "among those cots, raising the sick with tender touch and looking into poor wan faces with a sympathetic smile." To the prison staff "Emma Goldman was an anomaly, but they liked her as they found her." Actually the officials were mistaken: her actions and beliefs were not anomalous but of one piece.

[1] While what she actually said was not of crucial importance, she very probably did not urge her hearers to rise up in an immediate, futile, suicidal insurrection. Throughout her speaking career she conducted herself with considerable responsibility, often ignoring or warning her audiences against police provocations to violence. Given her ideas on the social revolution, she knew it could not be started by one speaker in New York. More likely, she simply urged her Union Square audience to stiffen their backs, to prepare for the inevitable arrival of the *future* social revolution, to organize and think along anarchistic lines, and, finally, to demonstrate down Fifth Avenue until they were given bread. What she had in mind was probably something such as was tried by Frank Tannenbaum twenty years later, when, during the depression-ridden winter of 1913–14, he led the unemployed on a march to St. Alphonsine's Church, where they demanded food and shelter. Tannenbaum was a frequent visitor at the Ferrer School, where Emma was active; it may be, as the New York *Times* suggested, that Emma had something to do with the idea behind this march.

CHAPTER VIII

AFTER BLACKWELL'S ISLAND

When Emma Goldman was released from Blackwell's Island in August, 1894, she was greeted by an enthusiastic reception committee. A meeting in her honor at the Thalia Theater on the Bowery was jammed, and a hundred or so well-wishers were turned away for lack of space. She had returned a famous or an infamous figure—depending on one's politics and social views.

At this time Justus Schwab's saloon at 51 First Street was where, as Emma put it, "everyone gathered." Everyone radical, that was—to the press it was the "headquarters of international infamies." Still in search of a good story, Nellie Bly visited Schwab's once and was shocked by the fact that women and men entered the saloon through the same door. As she went down three steps, she faced a tall bar, "innocent of glasses" and, worse, with "no free lunch." There were a dozen or so glasses behind the bar, but these were almost hidden by books—some six hundred of them. A strange saloon indeed! As though this were not enough, she next spied a blackboard on which appeared some rather shocking sentiments: "Free speech is to thunder away in the hills of New Jersey where no man hears." And "The bright sun rises in his course and salutes a race of slaves." And "Arrest every petticoat who endangers the welfare of the Republic." True to his contempt for the fearful burghers who had locked Emma up for a year, Schwab gave the "petticoat" a hearty welcome on her return. It was with real pleasure that she took her place in the convivial, argumentative circle which included not only other anarchists, but members of the literati such as Ambrose Bierce, James Huneker, Sadakichi Hartmann, John Swinton.

The friendship of these notable American liberals was especially important for her development. When in prison she had received an inscribed copy of *The Life of Albert Brisbane* from his son along with an appreciative note. This biography had given her some insight into the American radicalism of the 1840's. After her release she was asked to dinner by John Swinton. Swinton, a former editorial-writer for the New York *Times* and later editor of the New York *Sun*, had a radical past as an abolitionist sympathizer, a defender of Walt Whitman, and a friend of political exiles who sought asylum in the United States. Through her conversations with Swinton and others she came to some understanding of the anti-capitalist strain in American life and therewith scored an achievement which had proved to be almost impossible for foreign radicals. She abandoned her superficial idea that America was barren of idealists and resolved to devote herself to propaganda among native Americans. On this decision hinged much of her significance as a figure in American life. Had she been content to propagandize in German and Yiddish among the hermetically inclosed foreign language groups, she would have been of only passing historical interest.

During these years she met Lillian Wald, Lavina Dock, and other settlement workers who were concerned with the problems of the underprivileged East Side. Despite her admiration for these sincere idealists, "capable of fine, generous deeds," she was skeptical of the results of their work. What good did it do to teach the poor to eat with a fork, she wondered, "if they have not the food?" An unintended consequence of the settlement workers' efforts, she felt, was to create "snobbery among the very people they were trying to help." For her part, Lillian Wald, though she was to know Emma well later on, was not concerned with Emma's fundamental criticism of society and her anarchism. Like most American liberals Lillian Wald preferred a piecemeal, pragmatic approach. Her biographer put it well when he wrote that "she did not give the matter much thought at the time. Doctrines as such did not interest her. People did." Nevertheless, despite her differences with Lillian Wald and other liberals, Emma came to know more of them and to respect their motives.

She also came to know some of the leading single taxers and learned to appreciate their Jeffersonian insistence on free speech. While working on an appeal for Berkman she met Ernest Crosby, for instance, and was impressed by his sympathetic understanding for a man with whom he could not agree—Crosby was a Tolstoyan and abhorred violence. In later years she was given a great deal of support by such single taxers in her free speech fights.

Thus gradually but effectively did she break through to the native outside.

2

Among those she met while working for a commutation of Berkman's sentence was Edward Brady, an Austrian who had spent ten years in prison for the distribution of anarchist literature. Brady was the most scholarly person she had known, for he did not limit his interest, as did Most, to social and political subjects. With Brady she read some of the classics of literature—the writings of Goethe, Shakespeare, Rousseau, and Voltaire. After she learned to read French they took up Molière, Racine, and Corneille. While her "sweet companionship" with Brady developed, she deepened her own intellectual interests.

Notwithstanding her preoccupation with Berkman's tragic situation —and Brady was aware that Berkman was on her mind much of the time—their friendship "ripened into love." For the next seven years her personal life was tied to Brady's.

Although their affection for each other was deep, there were recurrent conflicts during this time over Emma's professional agitation for anarchism. Brady felt that such a life was unnatural for a woman. Showing what Emma felt to be a typical German patriarchal attitude, he wanted to have her all to himself, to protect, love, and watch over. She resented being treated as "property." He wanted her to give up speaking, settle down as his wife, and bear him a child—he was convinced that she was attracted to the movement merely because her impulse to motherhood was unsatisfied. But she rejected his demand to choose between her work and her love and this ultimately led to their separation.

3

Her experience in the prison hospital enabled her to work as a practical nurse after her release. Dr. White, the prison physician, employed her in his private office and her friend Dr. Julius Hoffman sent her to his patients. She also worked part time in the Beth-Israel Hospital. But practical nursing even then had little to recommend it: the hours were long, the pay was low, and the practical nurses were treated like servants. She realized that she would have to become a trained nurse if she were to obtain a suitable position. At the urging of Brady, she left New York in August, 1895, to take midwifery and nursing courses at the Allgemeines Krankenhaus in Vienna.

On the way she stopped off for a lecture tour of England and Scotland. She learned to cope with the hecklers in Hyde Park and met such figures of the libertarian movement as the granddaughters of Dante Gabriel Rossetti, Olivia and Helen (who were at that time publishing the *Torch*), her beloved teacher Peter Kropotkin, the already legendary Errico Malatesta, and Louise Michel, "La Vierge Rouge" of Paris Commune fame.

By the first of October she was in Vienna, ready as "Mrs. E. G. Brady" to commence her studies. She prudently did nothing to antagonize the Hapsburg Empire but devoted herself to work. Studying obstetrics, children's diseases, and related subjects, she had a number of interesting lecturers, among whom was a young man named Sigmund Freud. At the end of her year she took two examinations and received two diplomas, one for midwifery and one for nursing.

When she returned to New York in the fall of 1896, she could justly reflect that her year abroad had been fruitful. Her eager mind and energy had carried her a good way toward her long-time goal of a profession in medicine. She had been able to participate in the cultural life of Vienna—she had heard Wagner's *Ring des Nibelungen* performed and had seen the incomparable Eleonora Duse play the lead in Hermann Sudermann's *Heimat*. And, more importantly, she had read Nietzsche, Ibsen, and the others who were producing the "new literature." Through her self-directed reading she had become in large part a self-educated person—though her lack of systematic formal education was to handicap her in some ways for the rest of her life.

As a midwife Emma came in contact with only the poorest of the immigrants on the East Side—those with some resources preferred, like their American sisters, the services of a doctor. Ten dollars was the most she could expect from a delivery and often the payment was much less. She was appalled by the poverty and hopelessness of her patients, for she was brought into a very close relationship with the workers whose plight had at times been rather abstract to her. Most of all she was horrified by the despairing struggle of the wives of the poor against frequent pregnancies. Especially galling was her inability to help these unfortunate souls.

Emma had an especially memorable experience during this period. One Christmas Eve, Dr. Hoffman called her to care for a female morphine addict. A little later she discovered that her patient, Mrs. Spenser, was the madam of a bawdyhouse. To Emma's great surprise she learned that Detective-Sergeant Jacobs, who had helped send her to prison in 1893, was the paramour of Mrs. Spenser and that ex-Assistant District Attorney McIntyre regularly visited Mrs. Spenser's "high class" house where, she heard, the girls preferred "twenty others to that filthy creature." With great satisfaction Emma recollected that it was McIntyre who had earnestly warned the jury that if Emma were acquitted, it "would be to lift aloft the flag of anarchy and let it wave over the ruins of law and order"; McIntyre had also said, carried away by his oratory, that Emma was one of the "aliens who would just as soon as not run a knife into any one or blow up half the town with dynamite bombs." And now, thought Emma, it was this pillar of law and order who was the unwelcome visitor at Mrs. Spenser's house!

4

In 1899 the generosity of two friends, Herman Miller, president of the Cleveland Brewing Company, and Carl Stone, another well-to-do friend, made it possible for Emma to pursue her goal of studying medicine. The two men undertook to provide for her until she should become a doctor. Miller bought her some clothes and gave her five hundred dollars for her passage and her first months abroad.

By this time she was such a public figure that when she sailed aboard the "St. Louis" the Olympian New York *Times* reported her departure as a matter of course. En route to Switzerland she again stopped off in England and spoke in London's Athenaeum Hall and in the East End. In spite of Kropotkin's attempts to dissuade her, she resolved to conduct meetings against the Boer War. Although jingoists threatened to break up her meeting in South Place Institute, she faced down the opposition and made the meeting a success.

In London she met Hippolyte Havel, an emigré Czech revolutionist. With Havel she repeatedly visited Whitechapel and other districts in London's East End, where they observed in fascinated revulsion the almost hopeless wretchedness of the slum-dwellers—people whom they took to be the victims of English capitalism. Their common sympathy for these poor people established a bond between them. Just past a final separation from Brady, Emma shortly felt that love was again making its claims. When she left for Paris, she took Havel with her.

A few weeks later a letter arrived from Carl Stone which reminded her that her allowance was for the study of medicine; Stone insisted that she had to choose between her propaganda and new lover and her studies. Emma recollected that he wrote: " 'I am interested only in E. G. the woman—her ideas have no meaning whatever to me. Please choose.' I wrote back at once: 'E. G. the woman and her ideas are inseparable. She does not exist for the amusement of upstarts, nor will she permit anybody to dictate to her. Keep your money.' " When she learned that Miller also had changed his mind about financing her,

her plans to be a doctor necessarily came to an end. Had she wanted this career deeply enough, she might have deferred her efforts in behalf of anarchism and her affair with Havel. The reaction of her backers was understandable. On the other hand, she assuredly did not believe that she would have to set aside her doctrines and her personal life when she accepted their assistance. Her rejection of the attempt of Stone and Miller to control her life with a subsidy was equally understandable.

While she was still in Paris, Victor Dave, a French anarchist friend, made arrangements for her to attend a secret meeting of the Neo-Malthusian Congress. There she met Paul Robin, Madeleine Verne, and the Drysdales. Thought of her former patients on the East Side made her eager to learn of different kinds of contraceptives and the actual methods of birth limitation.

She had also planned to attend the Anarchist Congress, but at the last minute the French authorities forbade it to convene. She attended a few secret meetings in private homes, but the circumstances prohibited all but a very brief consideration of the most pressing problems.

At the conclusion of these surreptitious meetings she returned to the United States, docking in New York on December 7, 1900.

CHAPTER IX

THE ASSASSINATION OF McKINLEY

On the sixth of September, 1901, President William McKinley was holding a reception in the Temple of Music—which stood, forebodingly it proved, next to the Court of Lilies—at the Pan-American Exposition in Buffalo. Leon Czolgosz, a young American of Polish descent, had come to Buffalo perhaps because of the low Exposition train rates. On this afternoon Czolgosz entered the line of people waiting to shake hands with the President. As he reached the head of the line he raised his right hand, which was apparently bandaged, and fired two shots through his handkerchief at McKinley, hitting him once in the chest and once in the stomach. Clubbed to the floor by soldiers and secret service men, he seemed to expect immediate death. "I expected after I shot him," he said later, "that I would be catched at it." Asked to explain his act, he replied: "I done my duty." Eight days later McKinley died.

2

Earlier that year Emma had lectured in Cleveland before the Franklin Liberal Club. In her talk she denounced the rule of government and cited anarchism as the only path leading toward freedom; but she also took occasion to attack the popular misconception that anarchism meant bomb-throwing and general violence. She for one, she declared, did not believe in violence; she added that anarchism in any case had no necessary connection with violence. During the intermission a young man asked her to suggest something for him to read. Later Emma remembered him, for he had "a most sensitive face."

Several weeks later, as she was preparing to leave the home of Abe Isaak, editor of the Chicago anarchist paper, *Free Society*, a caller was announced and, on leaving the house, she discovered that he was the young man of the sensitive face. He introduced himself as Nieman and on the elevated train he told Emma that he had been a member of a socialist local in Cleveland but found its members dull; he now wanted to know some anarchists. At the station Emma found friends waiting and she asked Havel to introduce Nieman to some of their comrades.

After her departure several Chicago anarchists became suspicious of Nieman, since he knew next to nothing about anarchism, kept asking about secret societies, and repeatedly referred to acts of violence. Then a letter from Cleveland anarchists arrived which warned them against the young man and informed them that Nieman was an assumed name. On the first of September, five days before McKinley was shot, Isaak's *Free Society* carried a warning notice against another agent *provocateur* —Nieman, or, as it turned out, Czolgosz, was thus branded a spy. Emma, by this time in Rochester, was angered by such an unsubstantiated charge and protested vehemently to Isaak. After the assassination she always feared that the injustice of the spy charge in *Free Society* might have spurred Czolgosz on to an act to prove his loyalty.

On September 6 she was in St. Louis. A friend warned her that the papers would connect her with the act. She scoffed at the notion, but the next day she was shocked by these headlines: "ASSASSIN OF PRESIDENT McKINLEY AN ANARCHIST. CONFESSES TO HAVING BEEN INCITED BY EMMA GOLDMAN. WOMAN ANARCHIST WANTED." When she read that nine of her friends in Chicago were being held until she was found, she determined to return there immediately.

Upon her arrival friends prevailed upon her to go into hiding at least until she could collect the $5000 reward the Chicago *Tribune* was offering for an exclusive interview. This money could then be used for her defense. She was tucked away in the home of J. Norris, a properous friend who lived in a fashionable neighborhood. On September 10, however, before the interview had taken place, police stormed into her room demanding to see the anarchist menace. Emma easily slipped into the role of an inarticulate Swedish serving girl and the police were ready to leave when at the last minute they found a pen with her name on it. Emma Goldman, *alias* Lena Larson, gave herself up.

3

After Emma's hearing, Mayor Carter Harrison commented: "I believe she is exactly what she says she is—a rank anarchist. She is a woman of decidedly great ability, and even if she were connected with a deed of that sort, I think she is too smart to get caught at it." Notwithstanding Harrison's doubt of her implication, the officials in Chicago determined to connect her with Czolgosz's crime one way or another. The police subjected her to the "third degree," but even grilling her for several days brought them no success.

In New York the Buffalo police worked feverishly on Czolgosz to have him implicate Emma. But after hours in the "sweat box," Czolgosz still stubbornly refused to involve her. In his first statement he insisted: "I said to the officer I done my duty in shooting the President. I was working under my own instructions." As for Emma: "One woman I saw at the Cleveland Club was Emma Goldman. She said she did not believe in voting and did not believe in government. Said all government was tyranny. She said she believed in Anarchy. I am an Anarchist. Anarchy as I understand it means self government. That time in Cleveland was the only time I saw Emma Goldman."

In a statement signed at 10:20 P.M. that night (September 6) he was more explicit in his answers to leading questions:

Q.—Have you ever taken any obligation or sworn any oath to kill anybody; you have, haven't you; look up and speak; haven't you done that?
A.—No sir.
Q.—Who was the last one you heard talk [against rulers]?
A.—Emma Goldman.
Q.—You heard her say it would be a good thing if all these rulers were wiped off the face of the earth?
A.—She didn't say that.
Q.—What did she say? What did she say about the president?
A.—She says—she didn't mention no presidents at all; she mentioned the government.
Q.—What did she say about it?
A.—She said she didn't believe in it.
Q.—And that all those who supported the government ought to be destroyed; did she believe in that?
A.—She didn't say they ought to be destroyed.
Q.—You wanted to help her in her work, and thought this was the best way to do it; was that your idea; or if you have any other idea, tell us what it was?
A.—She didn't tell me to do it.

In a statement made at 6:00 P.M., September 7, Czolgosz admitted that he had also seen Emma in Chicago, but he insisted that she had not talked to him, for "the women were all talking together." Except for some minor discrepancies, Czolgosz's statement was substantially the same as Emma's.

Czolgosz's words were misquoted at the time and have often been misquoted since. Observe that after the most vigorous grilling by officials wildly casting about for any tie to Emma, however flimsy, Czolgosz resolutely maintained that he had acted alone, under instructions from no one.

Not to be denied their game, the police followed every possible trail. Earlier that year Emma had spent a holiday in Buffalo at the invitation of her friend Dr. Kaplan. The police hauled Hattie Lang, Emma's landlady in Buffalo, down to the station to make a sworn statement. She told them that Emma Goldman had arrived on a Saturday afternoon toward the middle of July. Emma had gone out with Drs. Kaplan and Saylin to visit the Exposition; returning early, she "had seen the illumination"—not a flash of daemonic inspiration but undoubtedly the Tower of Light, a post-Edison marvel of 35,000 light bulbs shining down from a tower 400 feet high. And to the mortification of the questioners, Hattie Lang turned up nothing any more sinister.

In Rochester the Goldman family was submitted to police questioning and popular persecution. Emma's teen-age niece, Stella Cominsky, was mercilessly interrogated for two days, but she stoutly maintained that her *Tante* Emma was innocent. Her other nephews and nieces had innumerable jeers to bear at school about their aunt who was a "murderess." But her father suffered most. Abraham Goldman lost many of his customers in his little furniture store, was ostracized by his neighbors, and was even excommunicated from his synagogue.

Despite the lack of evidence anywhere implicating Emma, the Buffalo authorities did not give up. Superintendent of Police William S. Bull had a theory, which he never abandoned, that Czolgosz "was an anarchist and that he had been guided by others in all he did." Present at the questioning of Czolgosz, Chief Bull maintained that it was plain to anyone that the assassin was in love with Emma Goldman. Bull dispatched Detective Mathew J. O'Loughlin to Cleveland to look into Czolgosz's background. On his return O'Loughlin reported that "Czolgosz... became a follower of Emma Goldman and either travelled with her or followed her. He went to Detroit where he remained for a certain time and then to Chicago, and possibly to other places." But Czolgosz had admitted on September 7 that he saw Emma in Chicago. Thus O'Loughlin's report provided nothing really new, except the misleading information that Czolgosz may have traveled to Chicago with Emma and that he became her "follower." George E. Corner, the Cleveland Police Chief who kept a close eye on radicals in his city, came much closer to the truth when he admitted that he had been unable to connect Czolgosz with the anarchists.

Though the effort to break down Czolgosz's story continued, he never changed it. On the way to Auburn Penitentiary after his trial, he was reported to have reaffirmed: "I knew Emma Goldman and some others in Chicago. I heard Emma Goldman speak in Cleveland. None of these people ever told me to kill anybody. Nobody told me that. I done it all myself." In Auburn attempts to implicate Emma continued. Revealing a contempt for the truth himself, Superintendent Collins questioned Czolgosz: "You know Emma Goldman says you are an idiot, and no good, and that you begged a quarter of her?" "I don't care what she says," wearily replied the prisoner. "She didn't tell me to do this."

Although there was "No Evidence Against Emma Goldman," as the New York *Times* reported (September 13), Erie County District Attorney Thomas Penney unsuccessfully proposed to extradite Emma. He affirmed that there was "sufficient evidence to warrant him in bringing Miss Goldman to Buffalo for trial for conspiracy to assassinate the President." Since he really had no evidence, however, he could not go before the grand jury then in session and obtain an indictment. So he proceeded on the extraordinary assumption that such an indictment was unnecessary before applying for extradition. Penney apparently thought that if he could just have Emma in Buffalo, a case could be created—and perhaps a political future for himself as well. On Penney must be placed the responsibility for keeping secret the parts of Czolgosz's confession which cleared Emma.

Why was Penney unsuccessful in his attempt to extradite her? No evidence may explain his failure. On the other hand, Emma thought that the insistence of the Illinois officials on direct evidence of complicity was prompted by Chicago Police Chief O'Neill. A journalist friend on the Chicago *Tribune* informed her that O'Neill was feuding with several of his captains whom he wanted to put in prison for perjury and bribery; he objected to their attempt to extricate themselves from their difficulties by claiming glory in the arrest of Emma. After questioning her and being convinced of her innocence, O'Neill then worked to have the charges against her dropped. In any event, the attempt to extradite her failed and after fifteen days in jail, during which time a policeman hit her in the mouth and knocked out one of her teeth, she was released.

4

The wild hysteria which swept the country in September, 1901, made her release surprising. Not only her relatives had been persecuted. Johann Most might well have been electrocuted if he had remained in Buffalo where he worked from 1897 to 1899. As it was, Most was arrested for reprinting "Der Mord" ("Murder"), a half-century-old article by the German republican Karl Heinzen. Although only one copy of the *Freiheit* in question had been sold, and that to a policeman on the day McKinley was assassinated, Most was tried and sentenced to another year on Blackwell's Island. The night of the shooting a young orator excited a good deal of attention on 125th Street in New York when he made a speech denouncing the anarchists and proposing that they be treated to the "South Carolina Method": he asked his hearers to follow him to Paterson, an anarchist stronghold, help him "begin the slaughter" and join him in burning Paterson to the ground. The New York *Times* candidly admitted: "A number of policeman were near at the time, but they made no effort to stop the man in his petition for volunteers." An alleged anarchist was mobbed in New York and an anarchist who played violin in a saloon was arrested in New Mexico. The mayor of Marietta, Ohio, was nearly killed for approving the assassination. In Chicago William Randolph Hearst, whose papers had violently attacked McKinley before his assassination, sat with a gun always on his desk. And so it went.

Understandably Americans were upset and stirred to unreflective wrath by the assassination of their head of state. The dazed Czolgosz had committed an atrocity which was a shock to all those who cared about their political system. Moreover, "an act upon the King," as Thomas Erskine truly said, "is considered to be parricide against the state, and the jury and the witnesses and even the judges are the children."[1] People who looked to the king, or the president in this case, as the symbol of the father state, naturally were wrathful when this symbol was knocked to the ground. But the orgy of national feeling and its attendant persecution of innocent individuals went well beyond this predictable response.

What was behind this late-summer's madness? Of considerable importance was the fact that Czolgosz said he was an anarchist; by this time the press had made anarchists into extra-human diabolic figures

[1] Quoted by Robert J. Donovan, *The Assassins* (New York: Harper & Bros., 1955), p. 105.

without a touch of humanity about them. If they were not human, they could be treated as infuriating objects. Yet perhaps more importantly—here the public reactions to the assassinations of Garfield and McKinley might be fruitfully contrasted—the head of the United States was struck down during a time of rising nationalism and just as the country was hitting its industrial and imperialistic stride.[2] As Louis E. McComas from Maryland lamented to his fellow senators, "this tragedy came just when our Republic had advanced to the front rank of international powers and when we began to realize our illimitable greatness."[3] Anything or anybody standing in the way of this march to illimitable greatness had to be ground down, abolished, destroyed completely. This was literally what happened to the befuddled Czolgosz: after 1,700 volts of electricity coursed through his body, the top of his head was hurriedly sawed off to see if he was really insane and then a carboy of commercial sulphuric acid was poured on his body as it was lowered into the grave.

All the more remarkable, therefore, was Emma's attitude toward the assassin. Friends warned her that her expressions of sympathy were

[2] The assassination of Garfield makes a more meaningful comparison in a number of ways than that of Lincoln. McKinley and Garfield were more on the same level of popularity and more equal in ability and accomplishments. Charles Guiteau, the assassin of Garfield, was given a notably fair trial in which he was even allowed to harangue the court. Popular feeling, while certainly not favorable, never reached the heights of animosity it scaled against Czolgosz and anyone even erroneously assumed to be associated with him. It is true that a guard shot at Guiteau through the door of his cell and that a drunk shot at him one day when the assassin was returning from court. But scores of people took his side, and he received many sympathetic letters and wires. One wire, for instance, was signed "A Host of Admirers"; it encouraged him to believe that "all Boston sympathizes with you. You ought to be President." (Quoted by Donovan, Assassins, pp. 54–55.) Almost no one sympathized with Czolgosz; no one proposed him for president.

[3] Other expressions of this pounding religion of nationalism, as it may be described, are not difficult to find. Toward the end of the century the doctrine that America was to become a super power gained wide and joyful acceptance. Item: Henry Watterson predicted the United States was "destined to exercise a controlling influence upon the actions of mankind and to affect the future of the world as the world was never affected, even by the Roman Empire—itself." Item: Senator Albert Beveridge modestly claimed that God "has marked the American people as His chosen nation to finally lead us in the regeneration of the world." Item: Josiah Strong thought it "manifest" that the "destinies" of men were in the hands of "the Anglo Saxon" and added that "the United States is to become the home of this race, the principal seat of His power, the great center of His influence." Item: Rather paradoxically, Alfred Thayer Mahan felt that the all-powerful Americans were weaker than their destiny, for "whether they will or no, Americans must now begin to look outward." Item: Henry Cabot Lodge also took a sanguine view when he spoke of obeying "our blood" and occupying new markets; with the most energetic fatalism he cried that "fate has written our policy for us; the trade of the world must and shall be ours. . . ." Add five, fifty, or five hundred of these statements together and one still has the religion of nationalism, the doctrine of America's illimitable greatness.

extremely dangerous. Clarence Darrow sent a lawyer from his office to caution her of her peril of being held an accessory to the crime if she persisted in her stand. But she quite consistently regarded Czolgosz as "the poor unfortunate, denied and forsaken by everyone." No amount of popular hysteria could sway her from this view.

In a life filled with high drama Emma often showed exceptional courage. But her refusal to join the pack in its cry against Czolgosz approached the sublime: in jail in Chicago, in imminent danger herself of a long prison term or worse, she managed a breath-taking disregard for self in her willingness to extend sympathy to the pathetic slayer. Even reporters, who held a professional disbelief in the possibility of any idealism, were genuinely puzzled by her expressed willingness to nurse McKinley, even though she sympathized with Czolgosz. In vain did she try to explain her solicitude for both of the protagonists in this tragedy. However, there was one person who could understand her civilized compassion. From prison Berkman wrote his approval:

You were splendid, dear; and I was especially moved by your remark that you would faithfully nurse the wounded man, if he required your services, but that the poor boy, condemned and deserted by all, needed and deserved your sympathy and aid more than the president. More strikingly than your letters, that remark discovered to me the great change wrought in us by the ripening years. Yes, in us . . . for my heart echoed your beautiful sentiment. How impossible such a thought would have been to us in the days of a decade ago! We should have considered it treason to the spirit of revolution.

As he added, "at 30 one is not so reckless, nor so fanatical and one-sided as at 20." Assuredly, Emma in her attitude toward McKinley and Czolgosz showed greater wisdom and compassion than a decade earlier when she proposed to Berkman that a newspaper office should be blown up.

After her release, Emma returned to New York, though she was admonished by friends that it was folly to do so. They felt certain that she would be sent to Buffalo and prosecuted. But it was unthinkable to her that Czolgosz should be left to his doom without someone making an effort to help him. Back in New York no landlord would rent her a room; she finally had to move into the room of a young prostitute. This girl, with the depth of sympathy sometimes revealed by members of her profession for those in need or trouble, gave her room up to Emma and moved in with a friend.

When she undertook to organize meetings for Czolgosz, her old friend Brady had to tell her flatly that she could find no hall in New York for such a meeting and that she was the only person willing to speak for the man. She replied that while no one was expected to eulogize his act, there had to be some radicals capable of sympathy for the doomed man. She was wrong. Absolutely nothing could be done for Czolgosz. Helpless, Emma had to stand by and watch him hurried to the death chamber.

With reason she was contemptuous of the assassin's trial. He was tried on the twenty-third and twenty-fourth of September, just a few days after McKinley's death. The court appointed Loran L. Lewis and Robert C. Titus, former justices of the New York Supreme Court, as defense counsel. These "two superannuated and apparently self-satisfied ex-judges," as Dr. Allan McLane Hamilton called them, made the barest pretense of defending their unwelcome client. No attempt was made to secure a minimally prejudiced jury. In his report of the trial Dr. Carlos F. MacDonald, a noted New York alienist, observed that "it was difficult to avoid the impression that each of the jurors in this case held a mental reservation to convict the prisoner. Had Czolgosz been on trial for the murder of a common citizen, instead of the President, it is safe to say that not one of the jury as completed would have been accepted by the defense; and instead of getting a jury in approximately one hour and a half, that feature of the trial alone would probably have occupied several days." During the trial Lewis and Titus found it impossible not to help the prosecution. Lewis delivered a maudlin apology for having to appear as counsel for the assassin of the "beloved" President, "one of the noblest men God ever made . . . [whose] death was the saddest blow to me that has occured in many years." So spoke Czolgosz's "defense." After approximately five and a half hours of actually trying Czolgosz, the jury retired for thirty-four minutes—"for appearance's sake"—and returned with the absolutely predictable verdict. All in all, as the New York Times put it without intentional irony, "the time was wonderfully short for our system of punishing criminals."

Despite the fact that the Times felt it was all done in a "dignified way" and rhapsodized on "A Model Trial," there was no doubt it was a "travesty of justice," as Dr. Hamilton held. It probably was also a monstrous miscarriage of justice, for the sifted evidence strongly indicates that Czolgosz was insane. Dr. Hamilton, who attended his trial, thought he was "clearly demented." After the trial two noted alienists,

Walter Channing and L. Vernon Briggs, made a painstaking inquiry into the life of Czolgosz and concluded (unlike the "defense" and prosecution doctors who had made no attempt to study his past history) that Czolgosz was insane. They thought the slayer was probably a victim of dementia praecox and concluded that he suffered from two delusions: that he was an anarchist and that it was his duty to assassinate the President.

In view of such evidence, Emma certainly exaggerated Czolgosz's strength of character and intellectual curiosity. Contrary to what she thought, he was probably not a misguided young man who was on the way to becoming an anarchist but rather a man in need of psychiatric care who sought in anarchism aid in carrying out and explaining his act. As an overreaction to the popular vindictiveness and because of her own memories of the act she and Berkman planned together, she tended in fact to eulogize the demented assassin. At the Anarchist Congress of 1907 she did not reprove Baginsky, her fellow American delegate, when he advanced the ridiculous claim that Czolgosz's act "was a blow in the class struggle." On the other hand, both she and Berkman thought that Czolgosz's act should not have been committed. And certainly the deserted, denied, and abused aspects of Czolgosz were what most touched her heart. Thirty-six years later in war-torn Barcelona she still remembered the anniversary of the execution of that "poor forsaken boy, Leon Czolgosz."

CHAPTER X

MEANS AND THE DREAM

In the late 1920's Theodore Dreiser was writing his *Gallery of Women* (1929) and, since he wanted to include Emma because of her "unescapably dramatic and colorful" past, he asked about some pivotal incidents. In one of her letters to Dreiser, Emma had this to say about her connection with violence: "I have never in my life induced anybody to acts of violence. The only time I was consciously connected with such an act was Berkman's. And it was at his insistence that I did not take my stand with him. When you read my memoirs you will understand why, and what it cost me in regret and misery not to have shared his fate with him. But as to urging anyone to acts, that is too absurd." This was an accurate summary of her relationship to acts of violence.

The evidence was conclusive that she did not urge Czolgosz to murder McKinley. It was less conclusive on her Union Square address of 1893, but, in spite of the verdict, she probably did not then exhort her hearers to riot and insurrection. After the McKinley tragedy some attempt was made to involve her in the bombing of the Los Angeles *Times* building in October, 1910, the explosion in an apartment building on Lexington Avenue in New York in July, 1914, and the Preparedness Day explosion in San Francisco in July, 1916. But she was not in any way responsible for these incidents. That left, as she wrote Dreiser, only the 1892 attempt on Frick's life. This one incident raised in sharp outline the complicated problem of the relationship of her means to her end, the dream.

2

A good criminal lawyer might have made a number of points in exculpation of Berkman's act and Emma's connection with it.

In the first place, their motives for their action were less self-serving than the motives which propelled Carnegie and Frick. Unlike these two, they were not avidly seeking great personal power and wealth. Insofar as motives were ever pure and free of selfishness, their motives were idealistic and selfless.

Next, Carnegie and Frick did represent irresponsible power which sooner or later had to be made responsible. In Frick, fittingly located in smoky Pittsburgh, they saw a symbol of the post-frontier, urban, industrial America. To them Frick was monopoly-capitalism incarnate, with his callous, principled disregard of the reasonable wishes and expectations of his workers. To them he represented concentrated capitalistic power which was responsible to no public agency or group of outside individuals. When Frick managed to have National Guard soldiers march into Homestead, they were strengthened in their anarchistic conviction that Frick and his fellow capitalists controlled state agencies also. At the risk of almost certain death they determined to do something to help free the apotheosized People from this irresponsible power.

Moreover, this was a period when many disputes were settled by violent means. It was, as Charles Beard wrote, "a baronial epoch when physical force was a normal part of high business procedure." Somehow the same people who were horrified by the Molly Maguires and such sporadic acts of violence as Berkman's were undisturbed by the frequent outrages committed by Pinkerton armies of strikebreakers. Frick struck the first blow in 1892.

Further, a defensible philosophical argument might be advanced that individual violence is at least as justifiable as the organized national violence called wars. Everyone is to a large extent shut up in his own consciousness—everyone, whether he likes it or not, is in what Ralph Barton Perry years ago called "The Ego-Centric Predicament." The implications of this predicament are debatable—indeed debate on this subject between idealists and realists has been a basic philosophical preoccupation. It is safe to say, however, that this dilemma makes it difficult if not impossible to prove demonstrably false the argument of the anarchists that the individual—the I—is the basic reality; the state is merely an abstraction. From this point of view it is defensible to argue that it is more justifiable for individuals to use violence for their own ends than it is for them to participate in the large-scale violence of abstractions such as the state, which is composed of collectivities of individuality-denying persons. Looked at from this philosophical position, Berkman's act was more defensible ethically than Theodore Roosevelt's so-called charge up San Juan hill (at the top of which, he exultantly reported, he killed a Spaniard with his own hand, "like a Jackrabbit").

There is also a certain validity in the contention of Emma and Berkman that "force begets force"—more precisely stated as violence begets violence. Only a mind closed to a frank discussion of the problem of violence would refuse to recognize an element of truth in this claim of Berkman: "The bomb is the echo of your cannon, trained upon our starving brother; it is the cry of the wounded striker. . . . the bomb is the ghost of your past crimes." Are warships built for "educational purposes"; is the army a "Sunday school"; is the gallows a "symbol of brotherhood"? Berkman asked. One necessarily must answer no and therewith recognize that the large-scale violence exercised by the state sets a pattern for and dwarfs acts of individual violence. The symbol of violence nowadays is not the anarchist's puny bomb, but the state's magnificent hydrogen horror.

The issue may be sharpened by a further examination of the customary ambivalent attitude of the overwhelming majority of the people toward violence. This attitude admits of simple statement: state violence, of course defensive, is sacrosanct; individual violence is murder. Now the Russian terrorists, and at this point Emma and Berkman were two of them, did not believe that violence in any form is sacrosanct, but on the contrary concluded that it is, in the words of Albert Camus, "necessary and inexcusable." This conclusion cuts far deeper than the usual approach to the dilemma. "Mediocre minds," wrote Camus, "confronted with this terrible problem, can take refuge by ignoring one of the terms of the dilemma. They are content, in the name of formal principles, to find all direct violence inexcusable and then to sanction that diffuse form of violence which takes place on the scale of world history."[1]

Still it is more than a matter of "mediocre minds." Those interested in a preservation of the present find personally compelling reasons for believing as they do. With pungency John Dewey wrote that these people, "who decry the use of any violence are themselves willing to resort to violence. . . . Their fundamental objection is to change in the economic institution that now exists, and for its maintenance they resort to the use of force that is placed in their hands by this very institution. They do not need to advocate the use of force; their only need is to employ it." Thus most of those who condemned Berkman's act committed or approved of violence themselves. An extreme illustration in point was the sanguinary offer made by Senator Joseph R. Hawley after McKinley's death: "I have an utter abhorrence of anarchy

[1] *The Rebel* (London: Hamish Hamilton, 1954), p. 140.

A drawing by V. Gribayedoff of the "high priestess of anarchy" and her friends in Justus Schwab's "anarchy den" and saloon at 51 First Street in New York. (*Culver Service.*)

MOTHER EARTH

VOL. X.　　　**MAY, 1915**　　　**No. 3**

**BILLY
SUNDAY
TANGO**

A cover of the "distinguished gadfly." Robert Minor scourged the strenuous life in a revivalist setting.

A cover from the competition. The irreverent gaiety of the *Masses* is evident in John Sloan's light approach to a dark subject.

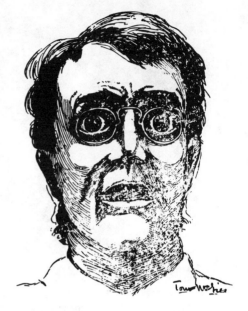

The Symbol, from the front page of the New York *World*, August 17, 1897. The caption read, "Anarchist Emma Goldman, who prefers Hell to Heaven."

The Woman

and would give a thousand dollars to get a good shot at an anarchist."[2]

Yet this is not the place to rest content with the *tu quoque* arguments of a defense lawyer. Idealists, who profess to stand for more, have to be judged more strictly than others who express contentment with the world's ways. After all this has been said in exculpation—to gain perspective and understanding it had to be said—the point still remains that Berkman's act was inexcusable. The deed was an instance of misguided idealism which bordered on insensate folly.

Emma and Berkman foolishly tried to apply Russian revolutionary tactics directly to American problems. Whatever the arguments for such an act in Russia, the attempted assassination was out of place in a country where they both had considerable opportunity to spread their ideas through persuasion. Two misapprehensions led to their act: First, they thought conditions in America were as oppressive as those in Russia. This was an instance of their general inability—common to anarchists— to distinguish between more and less coercive states. Second, and tied to this first mistake, was their almost complete lack of understanding of how Americans would receive their act. Still more Russian than American, they played out their tragedy in a revolutionary idiom which was absolutely foreign to the American ear. Berkman's fellow prisoner Jack Tinford and other Homestead workers stopped short at the idea of "some business misunderstanding." The misapplication by Berkman and Emma of suspect tactics to a different set of conditions meant that almost no one could even imagine what motivated them.

It was, moreover, always defective reasoning to suppose that desirable social change could be brought about by such acts of violence. If all the major agencies of violence were in the hands of the capitalist class, as Emma and Berkman held, all the more reason was there for seeking peaceful means of effecting radical change. The position that only violence could clear the way for social change became (in the West) ever more disastrous as the twentieth century approached. Technological change and concentrations of power made such barricade tactics as obsolete as the Pony Express.

But the really grievous error of Emma and Berkman was not this sort of miscalculation of practical exigencies. It was rather their assumption that the end justifies the means. Such thinking led Emma to lie to and

2 The *Nation* feared that if Hawley's hand were no steadier than his mind, an anarchist could pick up an easy thousand dollars. Voltairine de Cleyre, incidentally, offered herself as a target to Hawley, provided he would first give her a few minutes to explain anarchism to him. Hawley, whether because he feared conversion or missing, did not accept her offer.

cheat her beloved Helena; led Emma and Berkman to tinker with a time bomb in a crowded tenement, endangering the lives of innocent people; and led them to think that through taking a human life the day of freedom and human brotherhood would be brought closer. The fullness of life was to be achieved by destroying life.

That Emma was involved only once in such an act of violence indicates that she soon outgrew her idea about the end justifying the means. Years later she was sharply critical of her earlier position. Arthur Leonard Ross, her lawyer, advised her to omit from her autobiography the incident of soliciting on the street in order to make enough to buy Berkman a revolver. He correctly pointed out that this established her complicity "pro confesso" and warned: "A bourgeois president of a bourgeois country could no more see in the story the humane promptings of a girlish heart than I can see Vesuvius from my office window." Emma refused to omit the incident for a number of reasons:

The principal being that my connection with Berkman's act and our relationship is the leitmotif of my 40 years of life [since]. As a matter of fact, it is the pivot around which my story is written. You are mistaken if you think that it was only "the humane promptings of a girlish heart" which impelled my desperate act. . . . It was my religiously devout belief that the end justifies all means. The end, then, was my ideal of human brotherhood. If I have undergone any change it is not in my ideal. It is more in the realization that a great end does not justify *all* means.

She also came to be ashamed of her horsewhipping of Most, as her attempts at a reconciliation before his death in 1906 showed. Much later she wrote Max Nettlau, the anarchist historian: "I admit that nothing Most, or anyone else might have done, since 1892, would induce me to horsewhip them. Indeed, I have often regretted to have attacked the man who was my teacher and whom I idolized for many years."

In fine, she was to reverse herself almost completely on violence as a means. In 1928 she wrote Berkman that she wished she could adopt the position of Tolstoy or Gandhi: "I really do. I feel violence in whatever form never has and probably never will bring constructive results." But she could not become a Tolstoyan because she could not escape her old conviction that changes will always be violent.

3

Her assumption of the inevitability of violence rested on Kropotkin's evolutionary theory. Kropotkin held, it will be remembered, that violence attends great social changes as surely as showers come in April. Emma never seems to have realized that in adopting this view she indulged in a form of historicism which she repudiated in other areas. On violence, she held, in effect, that whatever has been in the past must be in the future. Incongruously with the rest of her theory, she rejected the possibility that *methods* of achieving social change might also be radically changed. She also became entangled in the thicket of cultural and social determinism. Generally she believed that individuals could act on their own responsibility—that they could, for instance, be less slavish. But when it came to acts of violence she argued that the individuals concerned were caught tight in a net of forces which finally made them lash out violently. While she never really adequately resolved this confusion in her thinking, she did find a way to account for such acts as Czolgosz's: his was a supersensitive nature which cracked under heavy pressure. Other stronger individuals, presumably, could stand up under this pressure and still exercise their individual wills.

Much of the popular indignation against Emma was the result of this theory of the inevitability of violence and this sympathy for overly sensitive individuals. A popular outcry was raised not because she committed violent acts herself, but because she refused to join in the condemnation of individual violence. Although after 1892 "never again had I anything directly to do with an act of violence," she pointed out, "I have always taken my stand on the side of those who did. I have fought shy, all my life, from joining the cry of 'Crucify!' Even if I did not agree with the act[s] I understood the impelling motives of them." To the authorities and to the public generally such an attitude seemed conclusive proof that she abetted acts of violence. Her earnest efforts to understand these acts and to extend sympathy to the unfortunates who committed them seemed to most Americans wilful irresponsibility at best. Yet such understanding and sympathy were always in order and rare: many leaped at the chance of joining the hounds, but few thought of comforting the hares.

4

Paradoxically, in 1892, at the moment of their extreme negation and attempted destruction, Emma and Berkman created for themselves a value of enduring worth. Their willingness to sacrifice their lives to the end of human brotherhood proved beyond question the imperative nature of their ideal and its supreme importance in their lives. Not without reason their 1892 *Attentat* became the "leitmotif" for the lives of both.

Undoubtedly violence seemed to them both "inevitable and inexcusable." Berkman would have planned the assassination so he could have escaped undiscovered and unpunished had he thought otherwise. But he went to Pittsburgh with the intention of deferring suicide after his act only long enough to make an explanation. Emma also looked on the act as inexcusable and felt guilty all her life that she had not shared Berkman's fate. If such violence was inevitable, as both of them thought, the least they could do was to exchange their lives for the life they took. In this sense they refused to exalt their ideas above human life and in this sense they affirmed the supreme value of human life. Others would come after them, also professing the ideal of brotherhood, but content to exalt their ideas above human life: these men would assassinate in dark streets or in concentration camps.[3]

Attempting assassination for their idea, yet not valuing it above human life, Emma and Berkman lived on the plane of their idea. Still, they made a fundamental mistake: even a willingness to pay with their lives did not make assassination justifiable. Means have to correspond with the end—especially when the end is the great dream of human brotherhood.

[3] Or contrast their act with that of the pilot who pushes a button that blots out many lives: his great desire is to return to his field unharmed. (Like most soldiers, his sustaining faith is that it is always the other fellow who dies.) Abstractions—defense of homeland, nation, way of life—are placed above the value of human life.

PART III

Agitator of Anarchy

I enclose for the information of the Spanish Government two pictures, with personal description of Emma Goldman, the agitator of Anarchy.

Secretary of State Elihu Root in a letter to William H. Buckler, American Legation in Madrid, December 4, 1907

CHAPTER XI

NATIONAL BUGABOO

All this while Emma Goldman had not been getting a good press, as they say. She was the victim of American journalism's unremitting quest for sensationalism and of its almost instinctive hatred of dissent. Up from the front pages floated a kind of super-witch named Emma Goldman and away went the composure and appetite of breakfasting burghers. No one could accuse reporters of letting themselves be handicapped by the truth. Two illustrations are a great plenty: In 1892 the New York *World* tremulously informed its readers of the discovery of an "Anarchy Den" at 340 Fifth Avenue. It was puzzling though, for nothing about the rooms gave evidence that Emma Goldman and Alexander Berkman, "anarchists of the worst type," lived there, "except their uncleanliness." A little leg-work or, better, a little candor would have solved the reporters' puzzle: Emma had not curled up in this particular den—she never lived on Fifth Avenue and she was almost compulsively clean and neat. And in 1897 the Detroit *Journal* boomed the shocking news: "One Dynamite Bomb and One Death, She Says, Are Worth Ten Years Talking and Preaching"—or so went the banner.

This was unrestrained enough, but after McKinley's assassination, the sky was no limit. Certainly it was almost impossible to detect any similarity between the vilified representation and the woman. "From the newspapers you would judge her to be an ignorant, vulgar, shrieking harridan, with a bomb in one hand and a bottle of vitriol in the other," William Marion Reedy once wrote. "What is she then? Anything but what the papers say." Just two examples again from reports which were so plentiful they seemed entries in a sort of public diary:

New York *World*, September 14, 1901: Emma Goldman "is a wrinkled, ugly Russian woman." She "would kill all rulers"; it was she "who inspired McKinley's assassination." Working in secret, she plots with "slayers who are singled out from her body of anarchists." And to make sure its readers got the point, the newspaper repeated the charge: "She has been in more than one plot to kill."

New York *Journal*, September 16, 1901: Not only was she bloody-minded and bloody-handed, but now it was established that she did it all for the Czar! "A well known Russian in Washington" reported that he had seen a secret document which established beyond question that Emma Goldman was a paid agent of the Czar.

Pulitzer and Hearst were supremely unconcerned that she was no murderess and no more an agent of the Czar than Theodore Roosevelt was a Spanish spy. Yet it might be objected that Pulitzer and Hearst were merely representatives of the "yellow press." John Dewey, for one, insisted that Emma Goldman's "reputation as a dangerous woman was built up entirely by a conjunction of yellow journalism and ill-advised police raids. She is a romantically idealistic person with a highly attractive personality."

Still, the record of the New York Times, "one of the ornaments of American civilization," was not appreciably different from that of the New York Journal. To the Times Emma Goldman was at one time or another a "mischievous foreigner,'" a paranoiac, a degenerate, a creature, "apart from the mass of humanity," a leader of "the Army of the Unwashed," and the chief of a tribe of "frousy-haired specimens."

But historians of the Times have asserted that by 1901 the paper had mended its ways. Its coverage of the assassination of McKinley was said to be a marvel of modern journalism: "The stories were factual, without lace-trimming; the editorial comment was sober." Actually the Times was just warming up to its intemperate, fanciful attacks. On September 7, for instance, it cited Czolgosz's confession: "He says he was induced by his attention to Emma Goldman's lectures and writings to decide that the present form of government in this country was all wrong and he thought the best way to end it was by the killing of the President." This gross distortion was accompanied by a malignant piece which was entitled "The Assassin's Preceptor" and which was literally loaded with factual errors such as providing the wrong name for Kersner and misdating Emma Goldman's arrival in the United States by six years. Then, after the screaming headlines announcing that Czolgosz was her pupil, on September 13 there were a few murmuring lines in the second column of the second page which reported that the authorities had "No Evidence Against Emma Goldman." On September 25 ten lines appeared toward the bottom of the sixth column of the second page conceding that Emma had been freed because there was no evidence to hold her. False charges of implication were worthy of monumental columns on the first page; admissions that these charges had no evidential basis were buried on an inner page.

Thus the creation of Emma Goldman as a mythical monster was the work of all the major newspapers. The general view of this female anti-Christ must have been not unlike the caricature which stretched across three front-page columns of the *World* of August 17, 1897. An inhuman creature, "Red Emma" glared madly out at one, in keeping with the representation of her as a vampire, ready to kill again, lick up the blood, and batten on the corpse. She seemed the quintessence of all the black, unconscious, hellish forces in life. No longer was she presented as a crank or an eccentric or a starry-eyed idealist or even a local menace. To an increasingly nationalistic age she had become a national enemy.

2

Mere mention of the name Emma Goldman became enough to frighten little children. In 1901 Margaret Leech, who has since written at greater length about McKinley, was living in the Palatine Hotel in Newburgh, New York. Then seven years old, Miss Leech gave poetic expression to her fearful revulsion:

> I am oh so sorry
> That our President is dead,
> And everybody's sorry
> so my father said;
> And the horrid man who killed him
> Is a-sitting in his cell
> And I'm glad that Emma Goldman
> Doesn't board at this hotel.[1]

S. N. Behrman, the playwright, has recalled that when he was a boy, "parents cited her to us constantly, using her name somewhat as English parents used Napoleon's in the first decades of the nineteenth century, to frighten and to admonish." If this were so, what could be more natural than that parents should decide to deport her to some remote rock where she could live out her last days like Napoleon? This was pretty much what happened.

In an article in the *North American Review* Senator Burrows of Michigan regretted that Emma Goldman had not been deported "long before she had an opportunity to convince the McKinley assassin that

---

[1] Miss Leech's poem appeared in the New York *Times* (November 1, 1959) review of her *In the Days of McKinley* (New York: Harper & Bros., 1959). Now old enough to have a more balanced view, Miss Leech characterizes Emma Goldman in her book as that "rabble-rousing anarchist leader"—it is as if Miss Leech had set out to demonstrate personally the longevity of tribal hatreds.

the murder of a President is a divine duty." Assistant Attorney-General James Beck told the New York State Bar Association that "the late President might never have been assassinated had the Goldman women [sic] been deported ten years ago, as she could have been . . . for it was Emma Goldman, according to Czolgosz, who fired him to do the fatal deed." In these heady days of the New Imperialism, lawmakers were increasingly in favor of an American Devil's Island for such undesirables. Senator Hoar of Massachusetts proposed to his colleagues that they send all the anarchists to an "island Paradise." Senator Vest of Missouri offered a resolution to the Judiciary Committee asking it to determine the expediency and necessity of amending the Constitution in order to establish a penal colony for anarchists "on some suitable island." But there were those, of course, who were in favor of more rough and ready methods. Some made proposals that all anarchists "be strung up" and Senator Hawley made his daring offer of a thousand dollars for just one "good shot at an anarchist."

On the executive level the concern was equally great and fittingly bi-partisan. Former President Grover Cleveland declared: "We can hardly fail to see . . . behind the bloody deed of the assassin, horrible figures and faces from which it will not do to turn away. If we are to escape further attack upon our peace and security we must boldly and resolutely grapple with the monster of anarchy." In his first message to Congress President Theodore Roosevelt decreed that Czolgosz "was a professed Anarchist, inflamed by the teachings of professed Anarchists, and probably also by the reckless utterances of those who, on the stump and in the public press, appeal to the dark and evil spirits of malice and greed, envy and sullen hatred. . . ." As for the anarchists, "we need not have one particle more concern than for any ordinary murderer."

Robert A. Pinkerton, the master detective of his day, agreed that there was a need for a penal colony on some island and a need to discard "any squeamish scruples" in attacking "the evil in a rough-handed, common-sense way." One way to detect the evil more readily was to have an enlarged and properly trained national secret police. Reminding his readers of James McParland's success in bringing the Molly Maguires to justice, Pinkerton claimed that such "a man on the inside could have landed information years ago that would have put Goldman, and the other preachers of anarchy who inspired Czolgosz, within the hands of the law."

When the legislators finally moved against Emma and other anarch-ists in "An Act To Regulate the Immigration of Aliens into the United

States" (32 *Statutes* 1213) of 1903, they lamely based their definition of anarchism on New York's "Anarchy Act" (*Penal Law*, Article XIV) of 1902. Under the New York law, "criminal anarchy" was defined as the doctrine which advocates that organized government be overthrown by force or violence or the assassination of public officials or by any unlawful means. (To advocate "criminal anarchy" became a felony, punishable by up to ten years in prison, or by a maximum fine of five thousand dollars, or by both.) This definition of anarchism was taken over virtually intact in the national immigration law, and it became the basis for all subsequent legislative efforts to exclude or deport those with objectionable opinions. Belief and association were the two fateful concepts which were the dubious heritage of this statute.

Something of the quality or at least the state of mind of the congressmen who passed the act was reflected by Section 34, which provided "that no intoxicating liquors of any character shall be sold within the limits of the Capitol building of the United States." Probably the relevance of this provision to the regulation of immigration was not as obscure as it at first glance appeared. But observe the over-all Alice-in-Wonderland aspects of this measure:

—Czolgosz was convicted by a New York court under existing laws. He was electrocuted and carbolic acid was poured over his body. More than this no law, anti-anarchist or otherwise, could have done. Yet the frenzy was so great that something more was desired.

—Czolgosz, one must repeat, probably was not an anarchist. He more likely suffered from mental delusion (as did, for instance, John Schrank, who shot and wounded Theodore Roosevelt in 1912).

—Even if Czolgosz had been an anarchist, he could not have been deported before his act, for he was born in the United States. Contrary to the hopes of Beck, Pinkerton, and others, the federal law did not undertake to deport citizens.

—Perhaps it is worth repeating that Emma Goldman did not "inspire" Czolgosz to kill McKinley. The only time Czolgosz heard her talk she insisted that anarchism had no necessary connection with violence.

—In any case, even if the law had been in effect in 1886, it would not have kept Emma out, for she was not then an anarchist. Nor would it have applied to her in 1894, as she was then, for the time being at least, a citizen through her marriage to the naturalized Jacob Kersner.

In a word, Congress passed a law, in part designed to prevent a recurrence of such assassinations as McKinley's, which did not apply to either of the alleged principals![2]

This act marked the first major move of the government against Emma Goldman and her cause. To be sure, it was not a camouflaged bill of attainder nor was she alone responsible for its passage. But she was believed to have been responsible for McKinley's death. This misapprehension—which was true for those who held it—was clearly behind the passage of the law.

3

Attacking with overwhelming force, the press and the government constituted adversaries which no one could be expected to oppose singlehandedly. At this point Emma Goldman could have left the field in good grace and with no reflection on her courage. Yet she undoubtedly would have continued to battle these enemies joyfully had she not felt betrayed from within her own ranks. Her inability to rouse fellow radicals to some protest over Czolgosz's farce of a trial plunged her into a slough of despair. If her erstwhile radicals friends were to run for shelter at the first real test, she reflected, how valuable was the radical movement? She felt an imperative need to stand aside for a time and take stock of both herself and her cause.

Indicative of her mood during these black days was her decision to seek night duty. Nursing poor Jews and Italians at night gave her a way to make a living while she was immersed in almost complete solitude. After several moves—for again she found it difficult to rent a few rooms, even under an assumed name this time—she secured shelter in the heart of the ghetto. To her flat on the fifth floor of a crowded tenement on Market Street she would return exhausted after a long night and sleep through much of the time when the world was up and doing. Her circle of friends became smaller, and she avoided the meetings which had yesterday been the center of her life.

But this mood could not continue. No matter what her motives, had she not herself withdrawn into a well of silence when the forces of suppression became especially violent? And, she asked herself, were her

[2] The New York Anarchy Act also had a curious history. In January of 1907 Emma and Berkman were arrested under its provisions, but their hearings were repeatedly postponed and the charges against them were finally dropped. The act did enable the New York City Police to harass landlords of the halls where Emma wanted to talk about the drama, birth control, or anarchism, but this was about the extent of its effectiveness. The first real application of the law came seventeen years after its passage when Benjamin Gitlow was indicted for publishing and circulating the famous "Left-Wing Manifesto." Gitlow, however, was not in fact an anarchist, but a Communist!

motives as pure as she had made herself believe? She had not been able to stand alone and laugh at repudiation. As though coming back to life, she emerged from her darkness and threw her energies into the fight of the anthracite coal miners in 1902. An exceedingly strenuous and difficult tour put her back in fighting trim.

When the bill to exclude and deport alien anarchists was passed in 1903, she had the rather bitter pleasure of observing liberals finally become aware of the perils of the reaction. While they might have prevented the passage of the act at the psychological moment, she argued, still the belated resurgence of their support for libertarian causes was welcome. One consequence of this changed atmosphere was that Emma herself ceased to be considered a pariah by the leading forums. The Manhattan Liberal Club, the Brooklyn Philosophical Society, and the Sunrise Club again invited her to speak. Renewing old friendships, she was again in touch with native radicals and liberals.

4

This broadened base of her support was important, for she soon had her chance to contest the new law. Seven months after its enactment John Turner, a well-known English trade union leader and anarchist, came to the United States. Emma and her friends arranged his lecture tour. He was delivering the first of his talks, ten days after his arrival, when immigration officials took him from the stage of the Murray Hill Lyceum in New York. As *Outlook* reported the incident, "when the anarchist speaker was put under arrest, his audience was inclined to rescue him by force, and a riot was threatened, but Emma Goldman, the Anarchist leader, sprang to the platform and succeeded in controlling her followers." She also succeeded in staying the rush to deport Turner.

While she had no faith that the Supreme Court would hold the law unconstitutional, she did believe that a fight could be made which would be excellent propaganda. Working under the assumed name of E. G. Smith for the benefit of faint-hearted liberals who were still frightened by her real name and under her own identity for those who were not afraid of her ideas, she managed to organize a permanent Free Speech League. The League included Peter E. Burroughs, Benjamin R. Tucker, H. Gaylord Wilshire, Dr. E. B. Foote, Jr., Theodore Schroeder, Charles B. Spahr, and a number of other eminent liberals. Hugh O. Pentecost, whom Emma and her friends retained as counsel, immediately instituted habeas corpus proceedings in Turner's behalf. The deportation order was sustained, and the case was then appealed to the Supreme Court. Turner, who had a leave of absence from his union, bravely agreed to stay for the fight, even if it meant months of inactivity on Ellis Island. To cover part of the expenses of the appeal Emma collected and turned over to the League some sixteen hundred dollars. Clarence Darrow and Edgar Lee Masters were asked to represent Turner before the Supreme Court.

Darrow and Masters argued two main points in his defense. First, they denied that he was an anarchist as defined by the 1903 law. They held that he was not an *advocate* of anarchism, but a philosophical anarchist who "regarded the absence of government as a political ideal." Second, they contended that the law was definitely unconstitutional, for it was antithetical to the First Amendment. It constituted an abridgement of the right of free speech and press.

Chief Justice Fuller's opinion for the Court (Turner v. Williams, 194 U.S. 279 [1904]) stressed that Congress has *unlimited* power to exclude aliens and deport those who have entered in violation of the laws. Even "merely political philosophers" could be excluded if "Congress was of the opinion that the tendency of the general exploitation of such views is so dangerous to the public weal that aliens who hold and advocate them would be undesirable additions to our population, whether permanently or temporarily, whether many or few." As for the Bill of Rights, it has no application to aliens seeking admission: "those who are excluded cannot assert the rights in general obtaining in a land to which they do not belong as citizens or otherwise." The rights of the alien individual, Fuller seemed to be saying, are as nothing when compared with reasons of state: as long as governments endure, "they cannot be denied the power of self-preservation."

With this decision America formally abandoned its claim to being an asylum for the politically oppressed of foreign lands. In one of his letters to Emma, Peter Kropotkin bitterly remarked that the actions of bourgeois society in the Turner case showed that it "throws its hypocritical liberties over-board, tears them to pieces—as soon as people use these liberties for fighting that cursed society." This expressed Emma's view exactly. Although she felt that the Turner campaign had some propaganda value, she still was angered by the predictable disposition of the case. Granting that the government had won this first round, she braced herself for a long fight.

CHAPTER XII

MOTHER EARTH

During the summer of 1905, a year after the Turner case, Emma Goldman and her niece Stella Cominsky camped out on an island in Pelham Bay, near New York. While they were there, they received word that Paul Orleneff and Mme Alla Nazimova, the talented Russian actor and his leading lady, were stranded without means in New York. Emma invited Orleneff and his company to join them under the stars. A close friendship soon sprang up between the actor and his hostess. Convinced that Orleneff was an artist of genius, Emma helped him get established, became his interpreter, and, at his urging, his manager. That winter she accompanied him on tour, traveling under the name "Miss E. G. Smith." She must have played her part with poise, for a startled Chicago reporter who later learned of the deception remarked that, because of her "noted refinement" at society gatherings, "one might have thought her the daughter of a noble Russian family in reduced circumstances."

The grateful Orleneff wished to repay her for her substantial contribution to his successes. Remembering that Emma had once told him of her desire to publish a magazine, Orleneff offered to give a special performance to start the venture. A torrential downpour on opening night and Orleneff's difficulties with creditors cut the proceeds down to a fraction of what was expected. Nevertheless, with only two hundred and fifty dollars as capital, Emma went ahead with her plans.

The name of the new publication was to be "The Open Road," borrowed from the title of "Song of the Open Road" by Walt Whitman, the patron poet of American radicals. "Allons!" invitingly chanted Whitman, "whoever you are come travel with me!" In the same spirit the magazine was to invite participation by young idealists in art and letters, "those who breathe freely only in limitless space." Unfortunately the open road passed through limited space: an editor of a magazine by that title in Colorado threatened to sue Emma for infringement of copyright.

Abandoning her first choice, she sought for another name which would adequately express her purpose. Out buggy-riding one day—although it was February, there was a hint of spring in the air—she saw traces of green on the dark fields which called to her mind the image of life germinating in the womb of Mother Earth. That was it! That was precisely the name for her magazine. So in the red month of March, 1906, appeared the first sixty-four-page issue of *Mother Earth*.

2

Well might Emma remark that the title "rang in my ears like an old forgotten strain." *Mother Earth* was a singularly apt name for her monthly. At one stroke it indicated the background of her thinking and her economic and social purposes. The forgotten strain led directly to Chernyshevsky and Kropotkin, on the one hand, and to Jefferson, on the other. Indirectly it led back to Locke and beyond to the writer of Psalm 115, who held that the earth belongs "to the children of men." In *Mother Earth* Emma's overriding economic concern was precisely to remake the earth, in Jefferson's words, "a commonstock for man to labour and live on." The happily chosen title also invoked ancient mother-goddesses of fertility to act as silent witnesses to the original purity and innocence of the procreative urge and to the need for freedom in sexual relations. The title suggested her purpose of combating the obscene approach to sex of the Anthony Comstocks—curious men whose lives were devoted to public interference with private relations.

Emma and her friends made every effort to have the first issue a success. Max Baginsky contributed "Without Government," a theoretical examination on a popular level of the fundamentals of anarchism. Harry Kelly reported on "The British Elections and the Labor Parties." "Internationalist" wrote on "National Atavism," in which he assailed the national idea, with particular reference to the Jewish question and Zionism. There followed a short account of the arrest of Charles Moyer, Bill Haywood, and G. A. Pettibone for the murder of former Governor Steunenberg of Idaho and an appeal for action to prevent another legal murder such as that of 1887. Emma herself contributed a rather perceptive article on "The Tragedy of Woman's Emancipation." These articles were complemented by an opening blast against "Comstockery" by John Coryell, an imaginative sketch by Edwin Bjorkman, a translation by Alice Stone Blackwell of a poem by Maxim Gorky, and a review of the *Letters of Henrik Ibsen*.

Thus Emma had reason for pride in her fledgling, for it was, on the whole, a creditable work. The pattern established here was followed in subsequent issues until a special issue in October, 1906, systematically reconsidered the case of Leon Czolgosz. The resulting shock caused some to withdraw their support. *Mother Earth* remained afloat, however, and continued its independent course.

3

In the meantime Alexander Berkman was finally released from prison. For fourteen long years Emma had waited with hopeless impatience for this day. When it came, she was filled with apprehension: Could they take up even a part of that life together which had ended in July, 1892?

As Berkman walked toward her along the station platform, she was paralyzed by terror and pity. Ingenious and sustained attempts by prison officials to break his will and his health, months and years of solitary confinement, the agony of watching other prisoners crack or break under the galling confinement and calculated injustices—all had left their mark on the proud young man who had gone defiantly, even joyously, to Pittsburgh that day an eternity ago. A milky prison pallor and thick glasses covered his face; an over-sized hat did not quite cover the shame of his freshly shaved head; an ill-fitting suit merely emphasized his uncertain gait. Emma could only press the roses she had brought into his hand and kiss him. Although waves of unsaid words threatened to sweep them both off the platform, Berkman too could not talk. "I hold the flowers to my face," Berkman later remarked, "and mechanically bite the petals."

Despairingly Emma tried to break through the wall which separated them, for Berkman was unquestionably her great love. But she quickly realized that her desire to take up where they had left off was idle. The long days and the longer nights in an unchanging prison world had erected in Berkman barriers which she would never scale completely.

And to Berkman she seemed almost as strange as the first horseless carriage he saw whir by. Not only had many of his friends scattered or died, but even Emma was no longer his "little Sailor." His disappointment was deep:

. . . my companion of the days that thrilled with the approach of the Social Revolution, has become a woman of the world. Her mind has matured, but her wider interests antagonize my old revolutionary traditions that inspired every day and colored our every act with the direct perception of the momentarily expected great upheaval. I feel an instinctive disapproval of many things, though particular instances are intangible and elude my analysis. I sense a foreign element in the circle she has gathered about her, and feel myself a stranger among them. Her friends and admirers crowd her home, and turn it into a sort of salon. They talk art and literature; discuss science and philosophize over the disharmony of life. But the groans of the dungeon find no gripping echo there. The Girl is the most revolutionary of them all; but even she has been infected by the air of intellectual aloofness, false tolerance and everlasting pessimism. I resent the situation, the more I become conscious of the chasm between the Girl and myself. It seems unbridgeable; we cannot recover the intimate note of our former comradeship.[1]

Perhaps Berkman might have overcome his feeling of alienation had he been given a chance. Instead he was tenderly escorted into a situation which made it impossible for him to find his own way back to freedom: the flat was Emma's flat, the friends her friends, the work her work. Unaware of how galling his position was, she smothered him with maternal protectiveness. Always the Great Mother, Emma made a motherly mistake. As she later admitted, she made the usual error of assuming that she knew best what was good for her boy. Berkman found it intolerable. "Through it all," he remarked, "I feel the commiserating tolerance toward a sick child."

Everything she did for him seemed to increase the distance between them. In misery she watched him fight to regain his footing only to be overwhelmed by the changed attitude of comrades, his memories of prison horrors, and his feeling of uselessness. At the point of suicide several times, he became seriously ill; she could only numbly take him into her home and nurse him back to health. The matter seemed insoluble until Emma was arrested one night, charged with violating New York's Criminal Anarchy Law. Aroused by the brutality of the police, Berkman saw at last that he had work to do.

When his spirits again began to descend into a well of depression, Emma offered him the editorship of *Mother Earth*. Perhaps, she reasoned, this work would help him find himself and also free her for a fund-raising tour for the chronically needy publication. Her desire was realized, for Berkman's real recovery commenced at this point.

4

As editor from 1908 to 1915, Berkman contributed substantially to the measure of success enjoyed by the magazine. Already a writer of some power, he went on to develop a simple, lucid style which was relatively free of revolutionary clichés. Consequently Emma's monthly was

[1] *Prison Memoirs*, p. 493.

spared much of the turgid rhetoric and pseudo-scientific jargon which cursed other radical publications.

Over the years *Mother Earth* played a significant role in American radicalism. It acted as a rallying center for isolated individuals, as an outlet for their ideas and feelings, and as a source of support for them in their difficulties. Its influence was felt beyond the immediate circle of its readers, who numbered from 3,500 to perhaps almost 10,000 at one point. C. E. Scott Wood, the distinguished poet and lawyer, justly dubbed *Mother Earth* a "gadfly" which stung the "mammoth" by soliciting aid for the victims of Lawrence, Paterson, Calumet, Ludlow, for Arturo Giovannitti and Joe Ettor, Matthew Schmidt and David Caplan, Becky Edelson and Margaret Sanger. Very likely the magazine influenced liberals to think more radically on a number of civil rights issues. And, not least, it sounded a radical note in the animated discussion of the day on the relationship of the sexes.

Mother Earth also had some importance as a medium of the arts. Frequently there were in its pages translations or reprints from translations of the writings of Tolstoy, Dostoevsky, Gorky; borrowings from Thoreau, Whitman, Emerson; stories by Floyd Dell, Ben Hecht, Sadakichi Hartmann, Maxwell Bodenheim; and poems by Scott Wood, Lola Ridge, Arturo Giovannitti, Bayard Boyesen, Joaquin Miller. There were a number of critical studies and reviews of current works. Finally, on occasion the covers were designed by artists. An obvious cover (December, 1907), for instance, was done for Emma by the French artist Grandjuan: a portly, supremely satisfied figure in a top hat—labeled, in case there were any so dull as to misunderstand, "Capital"—was placed before a chained Mother Earth and given a revolver and a paper marked "Law" to keep back the horny-handed workers. On a quite different level were the drawings of Robert Minor, Berkman's friend who had a genius for trenchant radical cartoons. Perhaps the best of his covers for *Mother Earth*—Minor also drew for the *Masses*—was that of May, 1915, which showed a very limber, very big-mouthed Billy Sunday doing a tango with a very distressed-looking Jesus, whom Sunday had taken down from the cross for this dubious purpose.

Yet, in spite of all this, *Mother Earth* fell short of fulfilling the avant-garde role Emma had planned for it. Little or nothing was done to encourage experiments in style. All the various literary enthusiasms—the imagism, symbolism, futurism which tumbled through the pages of Margaret Anderson's *Little Review*—bypassed Emma's magazine.

Even more importantly, not one young writer or poet of importance was first published in *Mother Earth*.

Perhaps more than anything else, *Mother Earth* lacked a sense of humor. Although there were occasional bright patches of satire contributed by Scott Wood and bits of biting sarcasm from the pens of the publisher or editor, the reader was weighed down by the deep Russian seriousness of its pages. No one seemed to have any ability to laugh at himself or his opponents—the causes were too sacred and the issues too momentous for that. Emma and Berkman could never rise to the satire, gaiety, and impertinence (or sink to the frequent prankishness and irresponsibility) of the *Masses* editors. The July, 1913, *Masses* cover by John Sloan, for instance, captioned "The Return from Toil" and showing six laughing prostitutes strolling jauntily down the street, would have been out of place on *Mother Earth*. Involving broken lives and pointing to deeper social evils, prostitution deserved a more solemn, serious treatment—or so Emma and Berkman might have argued. Thus, *Mother Earth* had no great appeal to the laughing rebels who clustered around the old *Masses*. Even George Bellows, Max Eastman has recalled, who "threatened sometimes to leave us for Emma Goldman's paper . . . could never quite carry out his threat." Despite the generous admixture of anarchism in his thought and art, Bellows must have been repelled by the anarchist publication's lack of humor. Such humor may well have been a precondition for any real fusion of social and artistic rebellion.

Well aware of her magazine's shortcomings, Emma tried a number of times to account for them. She argued that a number of radical writers had been alienated by the issue which was devoted to a consideration of Czolgosz and his act. But long after that issue was forgotten, the situation did not change. Then she suggested that the magazine's weaknesses were "partly because of the scarcity of brave spirits, partly because those who are brave cannot always write," but mainly because "those who are brave and can write are compelled to write for money." Her argument had a measure of validity, for supporting *Mother Earth* brought no financial returns and many professional hazards. But the fact remained that other radical literary magazines had no money and still received active support from writers and artists. Although the *Masses* was on record as favoring the revolution, artists were not frightened away.

A large part of the explanation for *Mother Earth's* relative lack of literary and artistic importance was to be found in its editor and publisher. Berkman's interests were almost completely devoted to political and economic struggles—strikes, demonstrations, the problem of political prisoners. The magazine naturally reflected his interests. Although Emma had other intentions, she, too, was preoccupied with political and social questions. Inevitably the main courses in *Mother Earth* were politics, economics, and social studies, with literature, poetry, and drawings thrown in for dessert. A successful little magazine of the arts required someone who was a professional writer, poet, critic, or at the very least, someone such as Margaret Anderson, who read poetry with the feeling that it was her religion.

Thus, contrary to what Emma Goldman had hoped, her magazine did little to encourage "the young strivings in the various art forms in America." Yet one must add that *Mother Earth* could hardly have been all things to all radicals—it was something to be a distinguished gadfly.

CHAPTER XIII

AMSTERDAM ANARCHIST CONGRESS

In the spring of 1907 a number of anarchist groups asked Emma to be their delegate at an anarchist congress to be held in Amsterdam that summer. Leaving *Mother Earth* under the able direction of Alexander Berkman, she and Max Baginsky, the other American delegate, sailed for Holland in August. The irony of monarchical Holland permitting an open anarchist conclave was not lost on Emma, for she remembered very well that the Chicago police in the democratic United States had stopped such a meeting in 1893 and that the Paris police had frustrated anarchist plans to hold a congress in republican France in 1900. Her respect for the doughty Dutch increased. In the few free days before the other delegates arrived, she and Baginsky went sight-seeing in old Amsterdam, wandering along the winding canals, poking among the goods in the open markets, or dodging the scrub-water of the unbelievably industrious housewives.

2

By the eve of the Congress, Emma Goldman held political views much more mature and coherent than those of the intense enthusiast who had joined the anarchists in New York almost two decades earlier. As late as 1897, when the editor of the *Labor Leader* asked her for a statement of her position, her nonchalant response had been less than adequate: "I am really too much of an anarchist," she had airily replied, "to work out a program for the members of that society, in fact I do not bother about all the trifling details, all I want is freedom, perfect, unrestricted liberty for myself and others. . . ." But she could not remain unaware that a wave of the hand would not banish the "trifling details" and that a belief in perfect freedom did not constitute a political philosophy. By 1907 she had gained sufficient footing in anarchist theory and her adopted language to make vigorous statements of her views in lectures and essays.

For the most part, she merely restated Kropotkin's arguments in her sweeping criticisms of capitalism, Christianity, and nationalism. In an age of potential abundance for everyone, she argued, private property is a cruel anachronism which condemns the great majority of men to be wage slaves, condemns them to sell themselves and submit to the judgment of a master. But even more importantly, private property makes man into a mere part of a machine, "with less will and decision than his master of steel and iron. Man is being robbed not merely of the products of his labor, but of the power of free initiative, of originality, and the interest in, or desire for, the things he is making."

Christianity, she held, is a superstition which constitutes one of the strongest supports of capitalism. Based on man's fearful ignorance, the church drains off moral energies which might have been directed toward a rebellious effort to improve man's condition in this world. Following Stirner and Nietzsche, she believed that "Christianity is most admirably adapted to the training of slaves."

But she reserved her heaviest charges for the state, which she regarded as the master cause of modern man's difficulties. Quite simply, the state is "organized exploitation, organized force and crime." Attracting the blindest passions of mankind, the state is the focal point for the twin evils of patriotism and militarism. Dealing with the same phenomenon William Graham Sumner called ethnocentrism, she held that patriotism "assumes that our globe is divided into little spots, each one surrounded by an iron gate. Those who have had the fortune of being born on some particular spot, consider themselves better, nobler, grander, more intelligent than the living beings inhabiting any other spot. It is, therefore, the duty of everyone living on that chosen spot to fight, kill, and die in the attempt to impose his superiority upon all the others." When these dark passions are caught up by the state, there goes abroad in the land the military spirit which "is the most merciless, heartless and brutal in existence." Precisely as had Tolstoy, she described the soldier as a "professional man-killer," who kills not for the love of it, like a savage, or in passion, like a homicidal maniac, but as an obedient tool of his military superiors. Thus the state, not anarchism, is the real destroyer of personality and the promoter of disorder. The alleged violence of anarchism is condemned by people "who would yet be delighted over the possibility of the American nation soon being able to hurl dynamite bombs upon defenseless enemies from flying machines"—a prescient observation, written as it was a number of years before the First World War.[1]

[1] This particular quotation made up part of her article, "What I Believe," which appeared in the New York World, July 19, 1908, almost a year after her return from Amsterdam. There is every reason to believe, however, that she held this or a similar view

Private property, the church, and the state, then, were in Emma's eyes the primary evils. One can visualize her ideal for the future simply by imagining a society without these institutions. Power that the monopolization of wealth gives the few over the many, she contended, would disappear with the introduction of complete communism. Each would take from the common storehouse whatever he needed; most men would be happy to contribute according to their abilities; even if there were a few who manifested mental illness by their laziness, a free society could afford to let them dream under the shade of a tree. In all cases, the evils of compulsion would greatly outweigh its possible economic advantages. And in a free society the worker would no longer be a cog on a huge productive gear. In words which call to mind Marx's passage on the unfragmented individual (the fisherman-hunter-shepherd-critic), she wrote that a "perfect personality, then, is only possible in a state of society where man is free to choose the mode of work, the conditions of work, and the freedom to work. One to whom the making of a table, the building of a house, or the tilling of the soil, is what the painting is to the artist and the discovery to the scientist—the result of inspiration, of intense longing, and deep interest in work as a creative force."

Similarly, once the "nightmare of Gods" is dismissed as unbecoming to adult individuals, then the church will no longer be able to exploit the fears of men and enjoin obedience and submission. The free individuals of an anarchist society will be atheists, for atheism "is the concept of an actual real world with its liberating, expanding and beautifying possibilities as against the unreal world, which, with its spirits, oracles and mean contentment, has kept humanity in helpless degradation."

Finally, by definition the anarchist future will be stateless. Then there will be the free opportunity and spontaneity which are necessary for men to grow and realize their potentialities. There will be associations of free individuals which in turn will federate with larger associations. The end result will be, in her words, "a social order based on the free grouping of individuals for the purpose of producing real social wealth; an order that will guarantee to every human being free access to the earth and full enjoyment of the necessities of life, according to individual desires, tastes, and inclinations."

---

a year earlier. Actually, the fundamentals of her political outlook had been formed by 1907 and were to remain unchanged, except for a few details, until after 1920 and her experience in Russia.

But will not an effort to bring about this ideal society lead to revolution? "Indeed it will," she emphatically replied. "No real social change has ever come about without a revolution.... Revolution is but thought carried into action." Although after the Congress of 1907 she was to direct her attention more closely to the general strike and to other syndicalist tactics, she remained convinced that they were merely preparatory and that the social revolution itself was indispensable for the introduction of anarchism. A cataclysmic outburst of evolutionary energies which were suppressed too long or, better, a blinding collision of the past and the future, the revolution was capable of changing overnight the personalities of whole populations. Old ideas would instantaneously collapse; anarchism would then build on their ruins.

3

Such were the ideas which Emma took with her into the Anarchist Congress when it convened. Although her arguments were phrased in her own words, they were not in conflict at any essential point with those of Kropotkin. Nevertheless, at the very beginning of the Congress Emma found herself opposing her old teacher's ideas on the subject of organization.

The opening address of the Congress was delivered by Amédée Dunois, a Swiss delegate. Dunois maintained that anarchism was federalistic rather than individualistic. He attacked the individualism of Henrik Ibsen, asserting that the egocentric views advanced by Dr. Stockmann in *An Enemy of the People* were opposed to anarchism.

Now Emma, convinced that Dr. Stockmann was profoundly right about the primary importance of the morally courageous individual, felt compelled to contest Dunois's position. With the help of Baginsky, she argued that while it was true that anarchism stood for federalism and organization, it was equally true that anarchism stood for individualism.

Let no one think, she continued, that she was opposed to all organization as such. She was merely against some forms of organization: against the state, which is an "arbitrary" institution cunningly imposed on the masses; against the present organization of industry, which is "ceaseless piracy"; against the army, which is "only a cruel instrument of blind force"; against the public school, which is "a veritable barrack," where the human mind is drilled and manipulated into submission. On the other hand:

Organization, as we understand it . . . is a different thing. It is based primarily on freedom. It is the natural and voluntary grouping of energies for the achievement of results beneficial to humanity; results which should endow life with meaning, worth, and beauty.

It is the harmony of organic growth which produces variety of color and form, the complete whole we admire in the flower. Analogously will the organized activity of free human beings, endowed with the spirit of solidarity, result in the perfection of social harmony, which we call Anarchism. In fact, Anarchism alone makes non-authoritarian organization of common interest possible, since it abolishes the existing antagonism between individuals and classes.

A stateless society, therefore, is not enough. The individual first has to be regenerated—reborn in a secular sense. No organization which is a harmonic, organic growth will "result from the combination of mere nonentities. It must be composed of self-conscious, intelligent individualities." Then public opinion will not be tyrannical, for society will be composed of libertarians with a respect for the right of others to be different.

Although the Congress accepted Emma's argument in behalf of individual as well as collective action, Errico Malatesta, the remarkable and venerable Italian anarchist, soberly observed that if Dr. Stockmann were in a factory, he would descend from his lofty pedestal. Emma and Baginsky replied that anarchism does not mean Kropotkin or Ibsen. It means both: "While Kropotkin has explained the social conditions which lead to a collective revolution, Ibsen has portrayed, in a masterly manner, the psychological effects which culminate in the revolt of a human soul—the revolt of individuality." There is an imperative need, she concluded, to "unite the external, the physical, and the internal, psychological motives of rebellion against the existing institutions."

Without doubt Emma saw the root of the problem and saw it clearly. It was the old enigma of the individual and society. "Under any circumstances," Kropotkin had written, "sociability is the greatest advantage in the struggle for life."[2] No, replied Ibsen's Dr. Stockmann, "the strongest man in the world is he who stands most alone."[3] Con-

[2] *Mutual Aid* (Harmondsworth-Middlesex, England: Penguin Books, Ltd., 1939), pp. 60–61.

[3] *An Enemy of the People* in *The Works of Henrik Ibsen*, ed. William Archer (New York: John Wiley & Sons, Inc., 1912), V, 216. Out of fairness to Kropotkin one must add that he detected in Ibsen "a certain vision of an individualism to come" which will be superior to both "misanthropic bourgeois individualisms" and "Christian Communism" (quoted in George Woodcock and Ivan Avakumovic, *The Anarchist Prince* [London: T. U. Boardman & Co., Ltd., 1950], pp. 280–81).

trary to all the rules of either/or logic, she believed both men were right. She was as keenly aware as Ibsen of the tragedy of the modern individual and mass organization; she was as apprehensive as Kropotkin of the power-obsessed, socially irresponsible individual. Caught between these two positions, she tried to fuse them into a higher synthesis of individualistic communism.

What emerged was a peculiar kind of elitism which envisioned individuals so strong-willed they could reject the fatal lures of authoritarian power. This anarchist elite would urge others to rebel, to exert their own strength, and to refuse direction by other individuals, including other anarchists. Put in another way, she tried to find a place in her thought for heroes. These Titans, unlike Nietzsche's or Carlyle's, would be distinguished by their efforts for social justice and their own renunciation of power: they would urge all men to be heroes. Hence Emma could, for her own purposes, quote Emerson on the crudeness and docility of the masses and on the need to break them up and draw individuals out of them.

This effort at the Anarchist Congress constituted her nearest approach to an original contribution to anarchist theory. Obviously it was less than a complete success. The immensely formidable nature of the problem had baffled better minds than hers. In her thinking she continued to fly a never-ending flight from an elite pole to what may be described as a populist pole. Happily the result was not hopeless confusion but an outlook charged with a fruitful tension.

4

As the little volume *Congrès Anarchiste tenu à Amsterdam, Août 1907* (1908) makes plain, the anarchist gathering was marked by an absence of the tumultuous incoherence predicted by the unfriendly press. It also reveals, however, that a rather ironic problem confronted the delegates during the first sessions. Emma Goldman supported the proposal of F. Domela Niewenhuis, the pioneer Dutch labor leader and prominent Protestant theologian, that the anarchists attend, as a group, a meeting of the Anti-Militarist Congress (L'Association Internationale Antimilitariste Congrès), which was to convene immediately after the close of their own sessions. To this purpose Emma read a proposal she and Dr. R. Friedberg, a German delegate, had formulated. Then in the minutes occurs this passage: "F. Domela Niewenhuis demande le vote de la proposition Friedberg-Goldman." After voting (par tête), "la proposition Malatesta obtient 38 voix; la proposi-

tion Friedberg 33. La proposition Malatesta est donc adoptée." Later
in the week the issue of voting bothered some of the delegates. Georges
Thonar pointed out the apparent inconsistency of counting heads and
admitted that he took part even though he was an adversary of all voting. Malatesta could see nothing inconsistent about voting. Pierre
Monatte introduced a fine distinction and insisted that voting was not
inconsistent if no one used parliamentary machinery. He thought it
unfortunate that some could not understand the difference between
the anti-parliamentary spirit and the raising of hands to manifest an
opinion. Christian Cornelissen held that voting was blamable only if
it obligated the minority. But R. de Marmande cogently replied that
voting was in any case indispensable: Without a vote after discussions,
how was one to know the opinions of others? Later Emma wanted a
vote on another proposition, but this time Malatesta drew back from
the issue and insisted that a declaration of principles was sufficient.

In practice, then, Emma acted very much like an individualistic
democrat. Her actions were footnotes to the observation made by
Bernard Shaw over a decade earlier: "Anarchism means simply the utmost attainable thoroughness of democracy." To be sure, there were real
differences between conventional democratic theory, with its emphasis on majoritarianism tempered by checks and balances—and anarchism, with its emphasis on individualism tempered by social responsibility. But a forest of confusion may be bypassed by realizing that
Emma was simply an extreme federalist-democrat. She was differ-
entiated from more orthodox democrats in that she placed ultimate
reliance on her own conscience; her liberal contemporaries (George
Creel and Louis F. Post, for example) put their ultimate reliance on
the majoritarian state (as their repudiation or rejection of the con-
scientious objector during World War I conclusively showed).

5

Emma Goldman was honored by being named chairman of the afternoon session of the last day of the Congress (August 31, 1907). At
the end of the day she asked Malatesta to say a few words in closing.
Malatesta pronounced the Congress a success, in spite of the poverty
of the movement and the difficulties caused by different languages and
the diversity of national origins. It was with a feeling of achievement
that the anarchist comrades sang "L'Internationale" and adjourned.
Emma herself returned home satisfied by the experience, for, aside
from having met some of the foremost anarchists of the world and

renewing her acquaintance with others, she had been able to express her political outlook in its most fully developed form.

Now, like all political perspectives, Emma's had its weaknesses. She mistakenly followed Marx in the assumption that under capitalism the poor would get poorer and more numerous. Her crude atheism was little more than a restatement of the ideas of Chernyshevsky and Bakunin, both of whom had been uncritically influenced by the positivism and popular science books of their day. In her criticism of the state she too simply assumed that it was always on the side of injustice, that it was never in fact responsive to popular pressures, and, most egregiously, that it was the same wherever it was found. She tended to be vague about the means to achieve her ideal society. Despite her concern with the means/ends problem and her personal distaste for violence, she still believed that real social change could come only through a revolution which would inevitably be violent.

On the other hand, she cogently argued against a system of property relationships wherein the eradication of poverty was not in direct ratio to technological progress. Her criticism of the psychological consequences of modern industrial capitalism put her in the great tradition of John Ruskin, William Morris, Kropotkin, and Thoreau, all of whom lashed out against a system which dehumanized man and made him a mere appendage of the machine. While she overstated her case against the church, she did score when she pointed out that it was often only an arm of the state, when she insisted that its morality was shaped by dominant economic groups, and when she maintained that the uniqueness of the individual was lessened by his unquestioning obedience to a transcendental deity. One can at least see the force of her underlying fear that the pattern set up by submission to a heavenly father translates easily into submission to physical fathers, to benign capitalists as father-figures, and to the fatherland. In her criticism of society, Emma fought her way clear of some of the naïve features of Kropotkin's overwhelming faith in the "people." She was thus able to face up to the problem of the tyranny of public opinion and the danger that society was closing in on the individual.

Although she was myopic when it came to distinguishing between concrete states, she did see that the national state, no matter what its name, time, or location, presents the problem of power in its most menacing form. She saw that the state by its nature is jealously preoccupied with security and offhand about or contemptuous of individual freedom; that it is of necessity based ultimately on coercion;

that it has inherent bureaucratic tendencies. In a sentence, she saw that it is the strong tendency of the modern state to fashion all life in its own image. Line and staff organization then takes over and the free individual who is also a citizen is replaced by the civil servant who is also, within ever narrowing limits, an individual. Dissent becomes disloyalty.

In some crucial respects, then, Emma Goldman's anarchism did not compare unfavorably with the competing political theories of the time. Jack London's *Iron Heel* (1907) was one of the few indications that any other radicals or liberals dimly sensed the perilous potentialities of the state and the possibility that centralized economic and political power in the same hands might well result in the rule of a managerial elite. Unfortunately London himself was intrigued and not appalled by the "Iron Heel." To be sure, there were still a few Jeffersonians around who regarded the state as potentially malevolent—who remembered that the people should be eternally alert "to know ambition under all its shapes and prompt to exert their natural powers to defeat it." Some of them, such as Henry George, tended to believe social magic would conjure the state into an affable tax-collector-constable. But for the most part, Populists, the later Progressives, independent liberals, and Socialists—all rushed to embrace the more or less omnicompetent and presumably benevolent state.

In an exaggerated but also symptomatic way, Edward Bellamy's *Looking Backward* (1888) revealed the peculiar blindness which afflicted these worshipers at the shrine of the state: Bellamy welcomed the total state as long as it was socialistic and distinguished by the absence of competition! Bellamy's anticipation of conscripted industrial armies seems scarcely to have bothered his American contemporaries, for *Looking Backward* exerted an extraordinary influence on the thinking of the time, not only through the short-lived Nationalist clubs, but also through the social gospel movement, populism, socialism. The experiences of the years since 1888 make the attraction his book had well-nigh incomprehensible to the modern reader. George Orwell's horrified apprehension of 1984 makes much more sense than Bellamy's delighted anticipation of the year 2000. And therewith the unusual foresight of Emma's views is documented, for she was one of the few who enlisted early in the fight against the all-embracing state.

Hence, her criticisms went to the root of some of the most urgent problems in the modern world. She saw that power could be made more manageable by breaking it down into smaller units and placing on the people most immediately concerned the responsibility for making decisions. Then, she observed, organizations will be functional, organic growths, "the complete whole we admire in the flower." She saw that a distinction needed to be made between relatively inflexible abstract organizations such as the state and the more primary, flexible organizations such as communities. Many years later Karl Mannheim, the German sociologist, was to restate this view in modern terms: "the task of this philosophy [anarchism] is still to teach mankind again and again that the patterns of organization are manifold, and the organic ones should not be and need not be overridden by rigid organization. The natural forces of self-adjustment in small groups produce more wisdom than any abstract thinking and so the scope for them within the plan is even more important than we can guess."[4]

From the standpoint of the general Western liberal tradition, the anarchism for which Emma stood is perhaps superior ethically to any other political theory. No other theory makes so primary an appeal to the individual responsibility and intelligent self-expression of man. For all of its practical weaknesses, the developed political outlook she brought back from Amsterdam had a fundamentally sound core. Thanks to it, Emma Goldman had the early and relatively rare insight that responsible individual freedom is the touchstone of supreme importance in the modern world.

---

[4] Quoted by Herbert Read, *Anarchy and Order* (London: Faber & Faber, Ltd., 1954), p. 14 n. Mannheim and other sociologists, of course, have long had the monumental work of Ferdinand Tönnies to draw on. In *Gemeinschaft und Gesellschaft* (1887), Tönnies brilliantly discussed—and deplored—the modern drift from the small, face-to-face association to the large, impersonal organization which achieves its consummation in the integral state. Relationships of a brotherly or father-child character are increasingly replaced by relationships of a ruler-subject character—by the extension of the penal code and police power. The uncontested rule of these state-*Gesellschaft* relationships means that culture itself is doomed, "if none of its scattered seeds remain alive and again bring forth the essence and idea of *Gemeinschaft*." In a sense, Emma's lifework was directed to keeping such scattered seeds alive and thereby to "fostering a new culture amidst the decaying one."

CHAPTER XIV

THE KERSNER CASE

After the Congress, Emma next spent a few pleasant days in Paris, where she met Stella Cominsky and laughed with her over what the American Consul, who was Stella's employer, might do if he knew that he had taken into his establishment the devoted niece of Emma Goldman. At this time Kropotkin lived only a few doors from Emma's hotel on the Boulevard Saint-Michel and he as usual inspired her by his "large and beautiful" nature. The leading syndicalists of the Confédération du Travail impressed her with their intense activity, especially in editing an excellent labor paper and in conducting night classes to teach the workers all the intricate details of the industrial complex. Sébastien Faure's anarchist school was even more impressive, for there Emma saw children actually educated to be free. Just before she left Paris, she met her old acquaintance Jo Davidson, the sculptor, and with the odds and ends of her own ménage she happily helped him furnish his new studio.

Her stay in London was much less pleasant. Upon her arrival she read press dispatches from America which announced that the Immigration Service would refuse readmission to the notorious Emma Goldman. She was not especially worried, for she believed her marriage to Jacob Kersner had made her citizenship secure. But letters from several friendly attorneys were alarming: apparently Washington was seriously determined to keep her out of the United States.[1] After a lecture in Holborn Town Hall in London, she observed that she was being followed by a number of detectives who were presumably from Scotland Yard. Every attempt to elude her unwelcome escort proved futile. Early the next morning, however, Rudolf Rocker, the German leader of the local Jewish anarchists, managed to smuggle her into the home of a relatively unknown comrade who lived in the suburbs. After three

---

[1] Immigration officials had for some years felt a peculiar responsibility for Emma Goldman. In 1901 Commissioner of Immigration Powderly expressed himself in favor of a law which would put the "strong hand of justice" on her. Powderly of course had his own hand in mind, but even the Anarchist Exclusion Act of 1903 gave the Immigration Service no opportunity to deport her.

days of hiding, she went to Liverpool and embarked for Montreal. From Canada she quietly returned to New York in a Pullman.

Chagrined immigration officials reacted immediately. Commissioner Sargent announced from Washington that steps would be taken at once to put her under arrest with the view of deporting her. Before this threat was carried out, Emma rashly crossed into Canada to deliver several lectures. The level of official interest in her was high, for John E. Jones, the American consul at Winnipeg, informed the State Department that Emma unexpectedly left that city on the afternoon of April 6, 1908, "in an effort to evade the Immigration authorities." She was intercepted at the border and taken before a Board of Special Inquiry. The victory in this particular skirmish, however, was all Emma's: she showed her questioners that she had been in the United States some twenty years, while the 1903 law applied only to aliens who had been here for three years or less. She further produced a copy of her ex-husband's citizenship papers to show that she was a citizen by marriage. Exceedingly disappointed, her inquisitors reluctantly allowed her to cross over to Noyes, Minnesota. Yet the New York *Herald* (April 9, 1908) rather ominously relayed a quasi-official announcement that the Department of Commerce and Labor wanted to deport Emma Goldman and that "steps are being taken now to determine her citizenship."

Despite such threatening rumbles from Washington, Emma went ahead with plans for an extended tour of Australia. Invited the year before, she now decided to accept the invitation and at the same time lecture in various cities on her way out to the West Coast. Fortunately, difficulty with the San Francisco police over her right to lecture delayed her long enough for a wire from her sister Helena to reach her before she sailed. The telegram informed her that Jacob Kersner's citizenship had been revoked. Emma immediately canceled her passage, realizing that if she left the country, she might never get back in.

"Steps" had indeed been taken to determine her citizenship. What were they?

2

Twice defeated within a few months, the Immigration Service bureaucracy had angrily laid plans for an extended campaign against Emma Goldman. Since, strictly speaking, her present status did not enable the officials to exclude or deport her under the 1903 law, they had to follow another course. As it happened, a denaturalization law, passed in 1906, offered the alternative sought. This act (34 *Statutes*

601) permitted the cancellation of certificates of citizenship on the ground of fraud or illegal procurement. If Emma was through some mischance a naturalized citizen, then hopefully fraud or illegal procurement could be proved. Perhaps Kersner, her former husband, had secured his papers illegally. The chance warranted intensive investigation, even though his papers had been conferred almost a quarter of a century earlier and he had since disappeared.

Federal authorities directed Special United States Attorney P. S. Chambers of Pittsburgh and Naturalization Examiner Abraham Zamosh to conduct the inquiry. Their report, which they submitted to Attorney-General Bonaparte in March, 1908, provided the basis for further action.

One bit of incidental information turned up by Chambers and Zamosh led to cabinet discussions and one of the first of our modern loyalty investigations. They discovered that Stella Cominsky, Emma's niece, was a stenographer in the American consulate in Paris. With all the customary gravity, they insisted upon the importance of their evidence: "It seems very certain from our information that this position was secured for the purpose of gaining inside information for the assistance of anarchists. This girl herself is an avowed anarchist[,] being an ardent admirer of Emma Goldman, and is her pupil. This position as a stenographer was secured through the influence of Emma Goldman[!], who took her personally to Paris last year." On March 24, five days after the submission of the report, Bonaparte relayed this information to Secretary of State Elihu Root, asking for all the information he might have on the accuracy of the matter "to which I called your attention at the cabinet meeting." Root immediately warned Consul-General Frank Mason in Paris and requested him to investigate the charges. In reply Mason cabled on March 30, 1908, that "story Goldman had an influence quite absurd." He later added that Stella Cominsky had been hired as a record clerk through the suggestion of the Directress of the American Women's Club; the latter was an "American Protestant of the most orthodox type, and about the last person in Paris to knowingly harbor or give any countenance or aid to an anarchist." Although Miss Cominsky handled no correspondence or dispatches and Mason doubted her subversive intentions, he showed that a seed of suspicion had been planted in his mind: "Still, she is a woman, whose parents are of European origin and belong to the race which has furnished many anarchists." But the Consul-General ultimately refused to believe that she was a "young woman of other than honorable character and antecedents," though he did gallantly accept her resignation when she decided to return to America with her friends Hutchins and Neith Hapgood.[2]

Thus Chambers and Zamosh were not the most reliable of reporters: Stella Cominsky was not a stenographer but a record clerk in the consulate. Of course Emma had nothing to do with her being hired, for her niece got the job through being introduced to the Directress of the Women's Club by Arthur Bullard, another compatriot. Nor had Miss Cominsky accompanied Emma to Paris—she had been there a month when Emma arrived from Amsterdam. Nor, finally, did her position enable her to gain "inside information," had Emma wanted it.

In addition to this unanticipated spy story, Chambers and Zamosh found what they went after. They reported that Emma had indeed married Kersner in the spring of 1887 and that she had secured a divorce from him in late 1888 or early 1889. But Kersner's father, they wrote, was "cooperative": he acknowledged that his son became a citizen a short time after he came to this country. His son was pressured into becoming a citizen, the elder Kersner reportedly said, so he could vote for Cleveland.

The day after this report was submitted, Attorney-General Bonaparte ordered Chambers and Zamosh to make the investigation "into the citizenship of Emma Goldman desired by the Department of Commerce and Labor and this Department." Translated, this meant that they were to prepare the case which would deprive Kersner of his citizenship—and therewith Emma of hers.[3]

3

As he proceeded with his preparation of the government's case, Chambers became concerned over a fundamental question. Does not the denaturalization of the husband, he asked Attorney-General Bonaparte, *ipso facto* mean the denaturalization of the wife? "In this particular case the wife's interests are the only ones in which the government is particularly interested, and the question just raised, therefore, becomes the all important one here." If Kersner were deprived of his citizenship, and if it were later found that Emma Goldman, "not having been made a party to the suit[,] is not affected thereby, the

---

[2] As Mrs. Stella Cominsky Ballantine writes, "how differently it would be handled by a member of the State Dept. today!"

[3] To understand all this, the reader must recall that a federal act of 1885 (*Revised Statutes*, Section 1994) automatically conferred citizenship on a woman who married a citizen and who was herself eligible for citizenship. This law was in effect until 1922.

whole object to be obtained by the suit would be lost." Chambers urgently requested advice.

Bonaparte asked Assistant Attorney-General William K. Harr to write a memorandum on the question. In his findings Harr argued that it is a fundamental principle of law that "no one be deprived of property rights without notice and opportunity to be heard being first accorded him." But the present case was "anomalous," he went on, for if Kersner's citizenship were cancelled, then the question of Emma Goldman's status would be raised effectively only if she went abroad. Harr was certain then that a number of Supreme Court decisions would make any action of the immigration authorities final, "unless an abuse of authority appears. The fact that their decision is wrong does not constitute ground for the interference of the courts." All in all, Harr said in effect, the "anomaly" of the case was such that Emma's fundamental rights could safely be disregarded. Moreover, it was good strategy: "If Emma Goldman is made party to this suit, and her husband's certificate is cancelled, she will be put on her guard and will not be apt to go abroad again. Hence I think it advisable, as a matter of policy, not to join her in this case."

Thus reassured, Bonaparte asked Oscar B. Straus, Secretary of the Department of Commerce and Labor, for his opinion. Straus replied negatively to the question of whether "to make Emma Goldman a party to the said proceedings." After a consideration of the subject, Straus wrote, "I doubt seriously the wisdom of taking that course. *It would too obviously indicate that the ultimate design of the proceedings is not to vindicate the naturalization law, but to reach an individual, and deprive her of an asylum she now enjoys as the wife of an American citizen.*"[4] Now convinced that appearance if not justice was on his side, Bonaparte informed Chambers that he did not think it "necessary or advisable" to make Emma Goldman a party.

4

The trial was hardly more than a formality, since no one appeared to contest the government's action. Chambers had served notice on Kersner through publication in the Rochester newspapers. United States Marshal Compton of the Western District of New York had reported failure "to locate the Defendant in my District." Thus, at least publicly, the government professed ignorance of Kersner's where-

---

[4] Emphases added. One of the lesser ironies was that Straus was himself an immigrant and the first Jew to be elevated to cabinet rank.

abouts. Emma Goldman, the real defendant, was given no notice of the proceedings.

The documents in the case were simple enough. In his citizenship application of October 18, 1884, Kersner claimed that he was born in Belgrade, Serbia, in April, 1863. He swore that he had immigrated to the United States in 1879. Simon Goldstein and Samuel Cohen, both of Rochester, attested that Kersner had been in the United States five years.

In its presentation, the government made two contentions: first, that Kersner was not twenty-one in 1884, but only sixteen; and second, that the defendant had not been in the United States for five years, but only three. As his first witness, Chambers called Abraham Kersner, Jacob's father. Asked about the date of birth of Jacob Kersner, Abraham Kersner replied that his son was born in 1865 or 1866, "I suppose." He also testified that his son came to the United States in 1882. Simon Goldstein, one of Jacob Kersner's two deponents in 1884, was next called to the stand. Questioned about the month of his original affidavit, he obligingly remarked that "it must have been close to election." He testified that he was Kersner's employer at the time and had known him before his marriage to Emma Goldman. So there could be no mistaking the gravity of the case, Chambers wanted to make clear that it was the one and only Emma Goldman who was Kersner's wife: "By Emma Goldman I mean the woman who is recognized as one of the Anarchist leaders of this country." Goldstein confirmed that it was indeed that Emma Goldman. Judge John R. Hazel broke in and questioned Goldstein about Emma Goldman, though she of course had absolutely nothing to do with the "fraud and perjury" of Jacob Kersner's citizenship application.

Judge Hazel found Jacob Kersner not entitled to his citizenship on the grounds that he was born in 1865 and that he came to the United States in 1882. Chambers triumphantly informed the Attorney-General of the verdict, unnecessarily reminding him that "this is the suit which was entered for the purpose of depriving Emma Goldman of her rights of citizenship, she being the wife [sic] of Kersner."

5

When she heard of the decision, Emma thought it likely that the government had paid for perjured testimony in the case: "Some people in Rochester had to be cajoled, intimidated, threatened, frightened, and possibly bribed." She knew the testimony was false, she later wrote, for

Kersner "had been more than five years in the States before he became a citizen and he was more than of age at that time." Thus, "private inquiries" convinced her that the federal authorities had not acted in good faith. And years later, Lena Cominsky, Emma's sister, informed a reporter of the Rochester *Post Express* (October 28, 1919) that Emma had married Kersner in her home in November, 1886, at which time Kersner was a young man of "about 26 or 27," who had been in the United States since "about 1879."

These contentions differed sharply with those offered to the District Court. And Judge Hazel, after hearing the testimony, substantially accepted the government's brief. Yet his decision was questionable. First, Chambers' mishandling of the spy charge against Stella Cominsky strongly suggested that a man capable of such sensational misrepresentation might not have hesitated at coercion or bribery. Second, Kersner's father testified that he "supposed" that his son was born in 1865 or 1866. But Abraham Kersner, like so many members of his generation and faith, was used to reckoning time by the Hebrew calendar. Very probably he had only the vaguest notion of his son's birth date according to the Gregorian calendar; his testimony, coerced or not, was of little value in ascertaining the year of his son's birth. Third, the absence of any mention of the ship which brought Jacob Kersner to this country was suspicious. While lists of steerage passengers were far from exact in those days, still the absence of any reference to the name of the ship and the date of its supposed arrival in 1882 was passingly strange. Fourth, why was Samuel Cohen, the other deponent in 1884, not called upon to testify with Simon Goldstein? He too was subpoenaed by Chambers. And fifth, why was Goldstein so ready to admit perjury for answering falsely in 1884? Although the courts do not examine such decrees collaterally, except on appeal, the absence of the ostensible defendant might well have moved Judge Hazel to inquire further into the background of the self-confessed perjurer's testimony.

On the other hand, Goldstein may well have lied in 1884. The date of Kersner's application, October 18, was suspiciously close to the November elections and 1884 was, after all, a presidential election year. In many instances politicians have herded aliens through the steps of naturalization, with little attention to the formalities, in order to have them at the polls in time for election. Jacob Kersner never evidenced any integrity which would have led him to resist such pressure. Moreover, Emma herself once wrote that Kersner came to America in 1881. Since there was no absolute proof to the contrary then, Judge Hazel's findings probably were roughly accurate. But this was not the point. It was rather that the findings were not established beyond a *reasonable doubt* and here the whole proceedings were most seriously at fault.

There was no counsel present to object to the introduction of such extraneous material as the relationship of the ostensible defendant to Emma Goldman, to challenge Judge Hazel's interest in this completely irrelevant aspect of the case, and to cross-examine the witnesses. Had the government made a serious effort to find and produce Kersner, the latter's counsel might have made a *trial* of what were instead virtually star-chamber proceedings.

But where was the absent defendant? As far as the Rochester community was concerned, he had disappeared in 1890 "as if the earth had swallowed him." Emma was convinced that "no one, not even his parents, knew his whereabouts. He vanished completely." Then in 1909 Marshal Compton reported that he was unable to find Kersner. He could not have looked too hard. According to a later statement of John S. Markell, the former Superintendent of Onondaga Penitentiary in Syracuse, New York, "Jacob Kersner was serving a sentence there when I went there Jan[uar]y 1st 1895, and served under me until Sept[ember] 18th 1895. . . ." Kersner had been convicted in Syracuse of grand larceny and subsequently served a year and a half in Onondaga. Another account in the New York *World* of October 11, 1898, three years after Kersner's release from his first prison term, reported that "Jacob Kerstner [sic], Socialist, husband of Emma Goldman, was sent to Auburn prison for 3 years on a charge of grand larceny." The *World* reported that after this term he would probably be arrested for issuing a fraudulent bail bond to secure his brother's release from the penitentiary. Thus, Kersner's activities had been rather well publicized. While Emma and members of the Rochester community could not be expected to know about his subsequent career, Chambers and Marshal Compton had the court records, prison files, and even newspaper files to help them trace Kersner.

In point of fact, the issue came down to one of two alternatives— *Either:* The government really did not know of Kersner's whereabouts. In this case, depriving him of his citizenship was bizarre to say the least. For all the government knew, it was depriving a dead man of his non-existent citizenship. Or: The government did know of his whereabouts. If so, its actions become even more reprehensible. It was depriving a man, who had already lost his right to vote, of his citizenship without giving him a chance to contest the action. Kersner's record and the threat of future criminal proceedings against him, mentioned above, would have been enough to insure his compliance with almost any plan or proposal the government might mention. Actually, the government may have known where Kersner was. As we shall see, Kersner went to Chicago and lived there under an alias, as Jacob "Lewis." After Chambers and Zamosh finished their first report in March, 1908, Bonaparte directed Zamosh to proceed to Chicago "and make an investigation into the status of Emma Goldman." Why was he sent there unless he and Chambers had discovered that Kersner had gone to Chicago? While this question must remain unanswered, it is worth noting that Mr. J. Edgar Hoover had little difficulty locating Kersner in 1919, when the issue came up again.

In any case, the real intent of the government was to denaturalize Emma Goldman. (Any doubt that the denaturalization act was used as a political weapon should be dispelled by these proceedings.) She was not served with any papers or notified by means of publication. Cabinet officers quite consciously and maliciously decided to deprive her of her citizenship without making her a party defendant in the case. A sad commentary on the whole procedure was that Kersner received more constitutional protection when he was being tried for a felony than he did when he was being deprived of his citizenship; Emma, the real defendant, also would have had procedural rights and constitutional guarantees if she had been tried for burglary or forgery, but in being denaturalized, so much more serious in many ways, she had no protection whatsoever.

The denaturalization of Jacob Kersner was a decisive if unclean victory for officialdom. Hereafter the government could simply wait until Emma ventured out of the country again and it could then refuse to readmit her. Or, failing this, other legislation might be enacted which would make her deportation possible—which was precisely what happened.

CHAPTER XV

LIBERTY WITHOUT STRINGS

A lull in the government's war with Emma followed the Kersner case, as officials watchfully waited for her to venture abroad, while she frustrated their plans by refusing to be so indiscreet. Instead her next few years were filled with struggles of a different kind: with extraordinary energy she fought to gather the scattered forces of anarchism, to keep *Mother Earth* afloat, and to deliver her lectures on anarchism, literature, the role of women in society, and, later, birth control. Of all these struggles, perhaps that of trying to make free speech a practical reality in American communities from Boston to Los Angeles was of the most enduring significance. "Liberty without Strings," to use her own phrase, was the high drama she played over and over again during this period.

Since 1897 she had been touring the country, now appealing for funds for this imprisoned radical and next appearing for that worthy cause. When the police tried to prevent her speaking, a free-speech fight almost invariably ensued. The plot of the drama had an almost classic simplicity: She would arrive in town to deliver her lectures. The police would either censor or attempt to censor her remarks. Thereupon an imposing number of radicals, liberals, and sometimes even conservatives (who happened to believe in a strict interpretation of the First Amendment) would object to the police intervention and assumption of responsibility for what the people should hear. On occasion these protesters would join together to fight police suppression and, if necessary, aid her in court. For instance, Hutchins Hapgood related in his memoirs how he once arranged a meeting for Emma in Indianapolis. Assured of an audience of several hundred, he went to Mayor Charles Brookwalter, a former trade-unionist, to learn whether he had any objections to the meeting. The Mayor informed him that if Emma did not charge admission, she had every right to lecture. The Chief of Police, however, positively interdicted her speaking and the night of the meeting "it was interesting to see the cars of the rich and fashionable audience depart." Despite their desire to hear her, they were denied this pleasure by their servants, the police. Hapgood observed that the suppression was followed by protests from "high minded citizens" who believed in free speech.

2

Another overview of how this pattern unfolded may be obtained by glancing quickly through the files of the Chicago *Inter-Ocean* for March and April of 1908: March 5, Emma Goldman in city; March 7, tells story to public; March 8, clashes with police on meeting; March 9, anarchists gather with Emma Goldman at Waldheim Cemetery; March 16, police drag "Red Queen" from hall; March 20, Rabbi Hirsch defends anarchy in sermon; March 24, William Dudley Foulke writes letter to editor, "The Right to Free Speech"; March 31, prominent citizens aid Emma Goldman—join free-speech movement—Emma Goldman in court with police, on right to talk; April 5, Emma Goldman writes two-page article on activities of police and "conspiracy" to suppress free speech.

Emma had arrived in Chicago shortly after an alleged attempt on the life of Chief of Police Shippy by an obscure young man named Lazarus Averbuch. The police were excitedly determined not to let her speak. Friends advised her to leave town. She predictably refused but found that the police had so terrorized landlords they would not rent their halls.

At this point Dr. Ben L. Reitman, an eccentric Chicago physician of uncertain reputation as the "King of the Hobos," offered to let her speak in the vacant store he was using for gatherings of transients and unemployed men. The police had told him, he informed Emma, that if she were able to find a place, they had no objection to her speaking. Emma accepted the challenge. As Reitman and his hobos were cleaning and preparing the store for the meeting, however, they were visited by fire and building inspectors who forbade them to seat more than nine persons in their makeshift hall.

Emma replied with a ruse. Through friends she arranged a social and concert at Workingmen's Hall and made certain that her name did not appear on the announcements. She proposed to elude the police, appear by surprise, and deliver her prohibited words. Reitman was the only outsider who knew about her plans. Characteristically, he secretly informed a reporter that she would speak at the meeting. Forewarned, the police rushed the platform when she got up to speak. One officer, a Captain Mahoney, literally dragged Emma toward an exit. Fearing that there would be bloodshed, she warned her followers against the police provocation and asked them to leave quietly. Undoubtedly her coolness and quick thinking prevented a serious disturbance.[1]

It was this arbitrary act of the police which so angered independent individuals and moved even some newspapers to protest against police interference with her right to speak freely. Rabbi Hirsch, a prominent Jewish leader, castigated the official stupidity of trying to stamp out ideas by violent methods. William Dudley Foulke, a well-known Republican, wrote a biting letter to the press, insisting on the right to freedom from such official malice and interference. Others also added to the cries of protest. A consequence was the formation of a chapter of the Free Speech League, organized to prevent such occurrences in the future. When Emma returned to Chicago (in 1910), the police, mindful of these protests and the publicity they had given her, actually assured her that she would be allowed to speak unmolested.

Such situations were summed up justly by the Detroit *Sunday Tribune* (April 5, 1908) when it declared that the police were creating in anarchism a "bogie-man for the public to fear" and held as self-evident that whatever the possible danger from an incendiary orator, danger was sure to result from "a battalion of policemen in full tilt."

3

It was during this Chicago fracas that Ben L. Reitman entered Emma's life. Margaret Anderson, of *Little Review* fame, always very unkindly maintained that "the fantastic Dr. Ben Reitman ... wasn't so bad if you could hastily drop all your ideas as to how human beings should look and act." Actually, Reitman's photographs showed him to be not that staggering, but rather handsome in an unsubdued way. As Emma described him, he was tall, with a finely shaped head which was covered by a mass of black curls—his curls, unfortunately, like his fingernails, were successful fugitives from soap and water. Despite this, Emma was stirred by Reitman, attracted to him by a passion which made relatively unimportant her well-founded suspicion that he had informed the police of her meeting. Inner barriers were swept aside as the "Red Queen" and the "Hobo King" became lovers and co-workers.

In the best fashion of royalty, Reitman in effect gave up his throne

[1] Chicago *Inter-Ocean*, March 17, 1908. Her responsible role in such critical situations was sufficient commentary on the argument that she was a helpless victim of her emotions or, as the police maintained, that she was an irresponsible exhorter to mad acts of violence. On other occasions (for example, in 1903 when she persuaded an audience not to attempt a rescue of John Turner) she was credited by the hostile press with having prevented serious violence.

for his love. Meeting in solemn assembly a short while later, his former subjects rather conventionally declared that whereas Reitman had conducted himself in a manner "unbecoming any member of the hobo party" and was "now hitting the road with Emma Goldman, the Anarchist Queen," they renounced all allegiance and informed the public that he was no longer their leader. For all their bottom-rail posturings, Reitman's hobos retained in such full measure the standards of genteel propriety that they were unwilling to see their leader consort with the notorious Emma Goldman.

Reitman's background was no less bizarre than his present associations. When he explored the farthest reaches of his memory, he could not think of a time when he had not known social outcasts, drunkards, pimps, prostitutes, beggars, and crooks. Born in St. Paul, Minnesota, in 1879, he was just a few years old when his peddler father deserted his mother. When he was eight he began to run errands for prostitutes in the slum and vice area near the Polk Street Depot in Chicago. At eleven he ran away from what passed for home, wandering for the next few years in aimless journeys which eventually took him around the world. Still harboring a deep resentment over the epithet "Sheeny Ben" which had been hurled at him by his Chicago playmates, at seventeen he jumped at the chance to be formally converted to Baptist Christianity in a Bowery mission. In 1899 he took a job as janitor in the Chicago Polyclinic. There followed the big opportunity of his life: Some doctors took an interest in him which helped him make the startling jump from a fourth-grade education to medical school; then, as he put it, he "somehow passed medical school and the state board examinations."

As a companion and manager Reitman often embarrassed Emma. His essential frivolity and the quality of his thinking could not fail to upset her. Take, for instance, this rather characteristic passage in "Following the Monkey," his unpublished autobiography: Charged by Mrs. F. J. McBain-Evans with leading her son to take to the road and his subsequent death, Reitman wrote, "my publicity debauch attracted the attention of foreign papers. I was of sufficient interest that had I not met Emma Goldman and had there not been a World War[,] I might have become King of Serbia [Reitman had planned to take 3000 hobos overseas to besiege Belgrade, Serbia]." On tour philogynist Reitman was always on lookout for overnight romances. At one meeting he "met the grandaughter of Brigham Young [he did not say which one] and almost had a romance with her." In Everett, Washington, he had an affair with "a tall, Theosophical looking young woman." More serious were his equivocal honesty and his twilight-world connections. On their first tour together in 1908 Reitman secretly took money from the admissions and literature sales receipts to pay off his debts and support his mother. Later in Spokane he was given six purses containing seventy dollars by "Delicate Dan," a friend who had dipped into the pockets of Emma's audience. Scrupulously honest in money matters, Emma was furious when Reitman told her about the purses the next day. Although she made certain that such a thing never happened again, she was never really able to make Reitman see the absurd aspects of his silently accepting the filched purses of those who came to hear her talk about a more just society.

When they returned to New York together, members of Emma's circle of friends were severely critical of Reitman. His irresponsible antics were offensive, and his practice of holding Sunday school classes in Emma's office seemed ridiculous. Though Emma defended his right to freedom of expression, however much she disagreed with him, other anarchists scoffed at the sight of "Jesus in the sanctum of an atheist." (Years later Reitman scaled the heights of absurdity by asking a group awaiting Emma's atheistic lecture on "The Failure of Christianity" to join him in a prayer to God "to help the poor working people"!) Berkman expressed a common reaction by refusing to believe that Emma could love such an interloper. When the infatuation showed no sign of abating, he still thought that Reitman did not belong in the anarchist movement, that he was no rebel, and that he lacked social feeling. While he admitted that Reitman was of considerable help financially, he believed that "morally he was harmful."

To such criticisms Emma replied, "Hobo will learn." She appreciated the soundness of many of her friends' criticisms, but she still loved Reitman. As she later wrote, she knew him "inside out" in two weeks: she "loathed his sensational ways, bombast, braggadocio" and "his promiscuity which lacked the least sense of selection; still, there was something large, primitive and unpremeditated about Ben which had terrific charm."

In truth, Reitman was hardly more than an overgrown child whom Emma had taken under her wing. He called her his "Blue Eyed Mommy," and she often talked to him as if he were an infant. Moreover, his role as a child of the abyss, a social outcast despised and rejected by respectability, aroused her sympathies. She reminded Berkman and others that they always talked about helping the outcast and criminal, "but when confronted by such a creature you turn from him in disgust

... and drive him back to the depths." Emma's good friend Hutchins Hapgood penetrated to the heart of the matter when he wrote to her that he was touched by the unfailing way "you always spontaneously sympathized with the under-dog. Perhaps the most striking illustration of that was your attitude toward Ben. He was, symbolically at any rate, the under-dog, and I imagine that it was more than your passion for him which explained your love."

Although Reitman was in many ways a trial, he did help Emma in her free-speech fights and in her work in general. Before he became her manager, she had to rely on local individuals to find halls, publicize her meetings, and arrange for her lodging. Such uncertain arrangements were a thing of the past after Reitman became her "advance man." His exhibitionism and Barnum-like flair for the dramatic advertised her lectures as serious appeals to the faithful never could. An index to his usefulness was the sharp increase in the number of people Emma spoke to in 1909, the year after he became her manager.

4

In the January, 1909, issue of *Mother Earth* Emma exulted that it was fun "to put oneself up against a world of stupidity, mental laziness, and moral cowardice." Fun maybe, but she was more prophetic than she realized when she added: "The world hates to be conscious of itself." The American part of the world hated it so much that she was stopped from speaking in eleven different places in the single month of May. Nineteen hundred and nine was assuredly a year of free-speech fights.

It started with a bang. In January she arrived in San Francisco and made the first of a series of appearances which was to include eight lectures and two debates. On her way to her second lecture she and Reitman were arrested and charged with "conspiracy and riot, making unlawful threats to use force and violence, and disturbing the public peace." For these grave offenses bail was set at $16,000 each. Several days later the charges were set aside, and the indictment was merely for "unlawful assemblage, denouncing, as unnecessary, all organized government, and preaching Anarchist doctrines." In court, however, the prosecution could do no more than introduce the testimony of a detective that Emma had made this flaming statement: "The judiciary and police take your money, that's all they do for you." Nothing else could he remember of her speech which lasted two hours; the audience admittedly had been orderly. District Attorney Ward thereupon made some wandering and irrelevant references to the Industrial Workers of the World and to red shirts and red neckties. After this grotesque performance, the judge had no choice but to direct the jury to acquit Emma and Reitman. A "Monster Reception" on January 31, when two thousand people streamed into the largest hall in the city, further vindicated free speech. The police were only passively present.

A little later, at the opposite end of the country, Police Chief Henry Cowles of New Haven reversed the usual procedure by first allowing Emma to enter the hall and then keeping everybody else out. He seems to have felt that technically he was not interfering with her right to speak. But he was interfering with her right to speak to those who wished to hear her and he was interfering with their right to listen.

After highly adverse comments on his action appeared in the press, Chief Cowles wrote Attorney-General George Wickersham a rather plaintive letter. Was there, he asked Wickersham, no federal law, passed after the "death of our late lamented President McKinley," which supported suppression of Emma Goldman's talks? The reasons he gave for refusing to allow her an audience, even in the absence of any knowledge of the existence of such a law, revealed a widespread police attitude: He refused, "as she is an undesirable person, and one whom the good and respectable people of this City do not care to have speak on any subject." Moreover, in his omniscience, Cowles had decided that she was guilty of McKinley's assassination: "I firmly believe that she was the cause of the murder of President McKinley." The Attorney-General was forced to tell the frustrated Cowles that there was no federal law which sanctioned his position.

One Sunday in May, Emma prepared to deliver "Henrik Ibsen as the Pioneer of Modern Drama," the third of a series of lectures in Lexington Hall. Just as she referred to "Henrik Ibsen," the Sergeant of the Anarchist Squad jumped to the platform and shouted: "You aren't sticking to your subject. If you do it again, we'll stop the meeting." In vain did Emma offer assurances that she was "sticking" to her subject, for the scholarly representative of New York's Finest made a sharp distinction between the drama and Ibsen. Since she could not very well lecture on Ibsen without occasionally mentioning his name, the Sergeant was goaded into action by what seemed her open defiance and the audience's obvious amusement. Suddenly the command rang out to clear the hall, people had chairs pulled from under them, and their protests were silenced by clubs. The police roughly saved the audience from hearing more about Ibsen.

According to a New York *Times* report the next day (May 24), "an indignant audience" was turned away from Emma's drama lecture. Actually, indignant was too mild an adjective: the audience was enraged and, unlike most of Emma's other audiences which had been mishandled, its rage carried an impact. Among the native Americans who had hoped to hear about Ibsen, there was, for example, Mrs. Milton Rathbun, the widow of a prominent New York merchant. She spoke out bitterly. Other prominent citizens made their sense of outrage known. Such protests were channeled by Alden Freeman, a member of the Mayflower Club and the Socialist son of Joel Francis Freeman, the longtime treasurer of the Standard Oil Company.

As it happened, Alden Freeman was also a member, along with General Bingham, the Commissioner of Police, in the Order of the Cincinnati. In a letter to the press Freeman recalled that, accompanied by a "high official of the New York Life Insurance Company" and by a member of the New York Bar, a man of "great wealth and highest social position," he had heard Emma Goldman lecture on the drama the year before: "I thought Miss Goldman's treatment of the subject was admirable. It was intellectual, illuminative and brilliant, and, in regard to the Russian plays and Ibsen, superior to lectures on that branch of the subject which I had recently heard by a Columbia Professor." The second time he heard her he was accompanied by the law partner of a Republican senator and by the wife of a former Democratic senator; it was on this occasion that the meeting was broken up by the police: "Most people present were Americans, in whose blood the love of freedom of speech and assembly had been bred. It was probably their first experience with such arbitrariness. . . ." He confessed that he had been "unable to take food since the outrage."

Thoroughly aroused, Freeman arranged to have Emma speak in English's Hall in his home town of East Orange, New Jersey. This time the local police stopped the meeting and set in motion an incident which Freeman later rather floridly compared with the Boston Tea Party: "a score of Orange Chaps, disguised as policemen, plain clothes men and county detectives, defended the headquarters of the English in East Orange and forced the Americans to retreat to a stable. This was the famous *Orange Barn Party.*"

The Barn Party was held in the stables of Freeman's estate in the most exclusive section of exclusive East Orange. Returning good for evil, Freeman invited the police in. Almost a thousand spectators remained outside, unable to join the crowd in the barn. The attendant confusion prompted one socialite to propose that the police guests should disperse the audience outside, so Emma could get on with her speech. Rejecting this proposal, Emma emphatically declared that the police "would make more confusion in one minute than they could stop in five years." Over the cheers and laughter she added, according to one reporter: " 'We are well protected here' looking at the Chief. 'It's cause we know you,' put in the Chief. 'Not at all,' said Miss Goldman, amid laughter, 'for if you knew me you'd know I can take care of myself. I am here to protect you against yourselves.' A great burst of laughter came from the crowd and more cheers." Finally she delivered her talk, which she concluded by thanking her friendly enemies, the police and press: " 'If truth depended on Emma Goldman it would not be worth while, but it depends on justice and human liberty. I am grateful, deeply grateful, to the police and the papers for acting so they make the people think a thousand times more than I could make them.' There was this time a genuine cheer."

Such protests against police censorship finally found explicit expression in a mass meeting of some two thousand people in Cooper Union. The event was sponsored by the Free Speech Committee, of which Louis F. Post, C. E. Scott Wood, Eugene V. Debs, Clarence Darrow, William English and Anna Strunsky Walling, B. O. Flower, William Marion Reedy, J. G. Phelps and Rose Pastor Stokes, and others were members. Every liberal and radical view was represented at the meeting: John S. Crosby, once Henry George's aide, raised the single-tax banner and assailed the unthinking public opinion which allowed police suppression of civil liberties. Gilbert E. Roe spoke for the liberals. Former Congressman Robert ("Anti-Pass") Baker delivered himself of a rousing Populist assault on big privilege. Voltairine de Cleyre represented the anarchists in an intelligent address in which she insisted that "freedom of speech means nothing, if it does not mean the freedom for that to be said which we do not like." Of the many letters of protest and promises of support, one from Eugene V. Debs hit just the right note. Debs maintained for the Socialists that Emma Goldman had a right to be heard: "If she has no right . . . neither have we; and if we suffer her to be silenced, we ought to be silenced."

Even a number of papers, all of which had approvingly reported police suppression of Emma's meetings among the immigrant radicals, were angered by the Lexington Hall episode. In a lead editorial the New York *Evening Sun*, for instance, angrily instructed the police about free speech in the United States: Here the people lived under a Constitution and not under "the imaginary summary jurisdiction of ignorant, illiterate and ridiculous policemen."

The upshot was that when Emma again essayed to talk on Ibsen, two hundred and fifty people were left undisturbed to hear her "awful piece." Mayor McClellan dismissed General Bingham and appointed a new Commissioner of Police. And, more important, a number of citizens had been brought together in the Free Speech League to protect precious civil rights.

So the struggles came and went. In the autumn of 1909 she was able to speak in Providence but was unable to make a collection. In Boston she finally secured a hall, despite police efforts to frighten all the landlords into refusing her. In Malden she could find only a half-finished hall. In Lynn a hall rented from a trade union official was suddenly no longer available and she was forced to find another. In Worcester the Police Chief refused to let her speak "under any conditions," but the day was saved by an Emersonian figure, Episcopal Rector Eliot White, who invited Emma to speak in his home. In Barre, Vermont, she finally was able to speak in the hall of some Italian Socialists, but in Burlington all the hall owners responded to the Mayor's plea to refuse to rent her space.

Thus Emma Goldman stirred up quite a breeze when she came to town, and it seemed as if she was always just over the horizon. Overwhelmed by it all, the Springfield (Massachusetts) *Republican* petulantly inquired: "Is it necessary for America to be perpetually in hysterics over Emma Goldman and Alexander Berkman?" For the time being the answer seemed to be yes: Americans persisted in becoming hysterical when Emma Goldman and Alexander Berkman questioned their cherished beliefs; for their part, the two critics had no intention of gagging themselves.

5

On the contrary, Emma had one of her most successful years in 1910. On one tour alone, she visited thirty-seven cities in twenty-five states, lecturing one hundred and twenty times to large audiences. She and Reitman sold ten thousand pieces of literature and gave away five thousand. They took in over four thousand dollars from the twenty-five thousand paid admissions, over one thousand dollars in literature sales, and three hundred in *Mother Earth* subscriptions and renewals. More importantly, she fought five free-speech fights to a successful conclusion.

It was also on this tour that hardly more than Emma Goldman's presence in Madison set off a chain of events which shook the University of Wisconsin. Scheduled to speak in the evening of January 26, 1910, she arrived earlier in the day and was pleased by the lively interest shown by students and faculty alike. She gladly accepted the invitation of a group of students to speak that afternoon in the hall of the University Young Men's Christian Association. That evening she was pleasantly surprised by the large number of students and sprinkling of faculty members who attended her lecture. The next morning she accepted the invitation of Professor E. A. Ross, the well-known sociologist, to tour the campus. She then left Madison, convinced that her stay had been exceptionally peaceful. She could hardly have been more mistaken.

Even before her arrival in Madison, Professor Ross had become involved when one of his graduate students came to him with the information that someone was tearing down the signs announcing Emma's talks. Ross later interrupted his lecture (ironically, on the development of government from the coercive to the beneficent state!) to deliver this digression to his class in elementary sociology: "I am told that some lady in Madison has been tearing down the posters announcing Miss Goldman's lecture. Now I take no stock in philosophical anarchism, but I do believe in the principle of free speech. For this reason and *no other* I wish to state to you that Miss Goldman speaks this evening at eight o'clock in the Knights of Pythias Hall." The next morning, as we have seen, he took Emma over the campus, "pointing out its beauties."

One consequence was an immediate and ear-splitting explosion in the newspapers of the state. The Madison *Democrat* and the Wisconsin *State Journal* demanded Ross's academic scalp. The Milwaukee *Free Press* agreed that the attempt to "coddle" Emma required a "stinging rebuke." The Beloit *Daily Free Press* also unconsciously burlesqued its name by attacking academic freedom and by printing a spurious version of Czolgosz's confession which directly linked Emma to McKinley's assassination. A few papers described the incident as a "tempest in a teapot," but the attitude of the great majority was summed up by the Madison *Democrat* in angry words: "And so why should there not be consternation in civilized society when a blatant, professed anarchist like Emma Goldman has her coming duly announced by a university professor to two of his classes, when several professors and many students give her welcome and when not a word of condemnation of any part of the vicious proceeding is offered to an indignant public." Evidently for a professor in a state university to give Emma a warm wel-come was like a priest announcing a visit of the devil and then hospita-bly taking the Black Prince on a tour of his parish.

President Charles R. Van Hise, an academic leader of the Progres-sives, hastily reprimanded Ross for the "embarrassment" he had caused the university: "It seems to me you should have appreciated that the announcement by you would be taken, by some people at least, to imply that you sympathize with her doctrines and considering Miss Goldman's past history, that popular passion would be aroused. . . . I trust that in the future you will be extremely careful in handling such matters as are likely to result in misunderstanding as to the position and teaching of the university concerning subjects in reference to which public senti-ment is sensitive." In a pathetic reply, Ross capitulated completely: "I agree entirely with you that for the reasons you state my announce-ment of Miss Goldman's lecture was an impropriety. You can rest as-sured that sort of mistake I shall not commit again." Despite this ab-ject apology and his complete submissiveness, Ross was almost dis-charged by the regents. After extensive investigations, however, he was let off with a sharp reproof for his lack of judgment.

A distinguished scholar was thus publicly disciplined and made to abase himself for what amounted to no more than a friendly gesture toward Emma Goldman and free speech. A great university shuddered timorously at the public outcry raised by her presence. One way or an-other Emma had made the University of Wisconsin spell out what it meant by academic freedom; the results were miserable, both as set forth by the administration and as accepted by Professor Ross. For-tunately there was a brighter side, for, as sometimes happens on the campus, students came to the defense of freedom when no one else would. The Class of 1910 commenced a five-year struggle with the con-servative regents which ended in a considerable victory for the former. In 1915 the "Goldman incident" was officially closed by a plaque which was riveted on the façade of one of the halls. The sentiments expressed thereon added up to a rebuke for those who had shown cowardice in the face of public outcry: "Whatever may be the limitations which trammel inquiry elsewhere," read the memorial, "we believe that the great State University of Wisconsin should ever encourage that con-tinual and fearless sifting and winnowing by which alone the truth can be found." No words could have expressed more effectively what Emma Goldman stood for—she might have been their author. That she was indirectly responsible for the series of events which produced this landmark of academic freedom made her visit in Madison meaningful indeed.

6

While on this same tour in 1910, Emma Goldman learned from *Mother Earth* subscribers that they had not received their January copies. She immediately wired Berkman to find out what had happened.

Berkman was told by an inspector in the New York Post Office that the issue had been held as a result of a complaint by Anthony Comstock. When Berkman finally secured an audience with the formidable vice-hunter, Comstock denied having made the complaint but admitted that the magazine had in fact been held up. At Comstock's request Berkman accompanied him to see the District Attorney. After carefully reading the allegedly objectionable parts—Comstock seemed most upset by a rather academic article by Emma on prostitution—the prosecutor informed them that he could find nothing illegal in any of the articles. Comstock therewith, according to Berkman, promised to have the magazine released. The next day, however, Comstock issued a public denial that *Mother Earth* had been kept from the mails. In response to a telephone call from the New York *Times*, he angrily claimed that the charge was "a scheme of Emma Goldman's [sic] to attract attention to the publication. I have not made any complaint against it, nor is the magazine being held up at the Post Office." When he read this, Berkman telephoned his adversary: "But Mr. Comstock, you know that is a lie. . . ." There was a click—Comstock had hung up.

Angered by Comstock's interference with her magazine and by his duplicity, Emma Goldman and a delegation of friends went to heckle the old man when he delivered an address at the Labor Temple in November, 1910. One newspaper report showed Comstock having quite a time of it. He was asked: "Isn't prudery the chief cause of immorality?" He disingenuously replied that "such a question is too absurd to answer." A young girl wondered "What are obscene books?" The obscenity expert squirmed: "It would be impossible. It would be shameful for me or any one else to describe them publicly." Well, would he put the Bible into the hands of a child? Comstock refused to "listen to such remarks on the word of God." Would he take school children to the Metropolitan Art Gallery? Stumped, he faltered and confessed he did not know. Emma asked him how he could read obscene literature for forty years and still have a pure mind. Comstock believed an agent of God could, "if he keeps his will under subjection and obeys always the laws of God and morality." He went on to add that he thought it was honest for him to use a fictitious name to trap wrongdoers. "Purity is truth!" Emma thundered back. Red-faced and distressed, Comstock was obviously pleased when a woman urged that he be allowed to finish his talk. On her part, Emma left the meeting completely at a loss about "how anyone so limited and unintelligent could wield power over a supposedly democratic nation."

Anthony Comstock and Emma Goldman were, in all truth, polar opposites. An American grand inquisitor for over four decades—agent plenipotentiary of the United States Post Office and the New York state-supported Society for the Prevention of Vice—Comstock lurked everywhere, exposing, as he put it in one of his curious books, *Traps for the Young* (1883). Apparently born ancient, despite his close ties to the Young Men's Christian Association, the old man placed rough hands not only on pornography but also on art and literature—he once referred to Bernard Shaw as "this Irish smut-dealer." In a word, Comstock believed above all else in suppression; Emma Goldman believed in expression.

The fundamental contrast between their points of view came out when Emma Goldman and a group of liberals and radicals met in the studios of George Bellows to form a society to oppose Comstockery. In his memoirs, George Hellman, the Fifth Avenue art-dealer, recalled this interchange between Bellows and Emma:

"If a policeman interferes with a man walking naked on Fifth Avenue, would that be censorship?"

"Are you going to try to reduce this to the absurd?" replied Miss Goldman, somewhat nettled. "But my answer is it would be censorship. Let the man go naked if he wants to."

"Hurrah!" said Bellows, "I sometimes feel like doing that in hot weather."

Over in Summit, New Jersey, Anthony Comstock must have twitched nervously in his sleep.

7

Town fathers did more than twitch when Emma Goldman staged a performance of her "Liberty without Strings" in their particular locality. This was especially true of San Diego in 1912, for the city was gripped by a vigilante terror whipped up against the Industrial Workers of the World. In their dramatic way the wobblies were protesting a new ordinance which forbade outdoor oratory. But as fast as the footloose wanderers streamed into San Diego, literally trying to break into jail, local authorities and citizens clubbed them off the streets or sub-jected them to even harsher treatment. The result was one of the most bitter and violent of the wobblies' many free-speech fights.

As she had done on previous occasions—these melees were waged along lines she had established earlier—Emma immediately joined forces with the radical unionists. She raised funds for them at her meet-ings and helped organize a feeding station for the clubbing victims at the I.W.W. headquarters in Los Angeles. Undaunted by the obvious danger, she went ahead with plans for her talk in San Diego on May 14. Ibsen's *An Enemy of the People* was the appropriate subject of her lecture.

A large crowd of ill-wishers awaited Emma and her manager at the depot in San Diego. By luck they managed to slip through the station unobserved, though the crowd spied them outside and gave chase. Later in the afternoon the vigilantes milled round the U. S. Grant Hotel, where Emma and Reitman had taken rooms. Shortly after the worried manager had secretly transfered them to a suite of rooms on the top floor, they received word that the Mayor and Chief of Police awaited them in the lobby. Downstairs the officials asked Emma to step into one of the rooms where she could talk with the Mayor. Reitman was told to wait. Judging the Mayor's solicitous concern over her safety sheer hypocrisy, Emma contemptuously rejected his proposal that she leave. But on her return to the lobby she could not find Reitman. After a few wretched hours, she concluded that she was in a hopeless predica-ment. Reitman had disappeared. The friends who had charge of the arrangements for her lecture were being watched and obviously could not help her. An unusually courageous offer of the recital hall of the local Conservatory of Music came from its head, George Edwards, an "anarchist in art" and a believer in free speech; but she could never get to the recital hall, let alone publicize her meeting there. Thus baffled, in the early morning hours she boarded a train for Los Angeles, with the vigilantes again in attendance, rushing up and down the platform and screaming at the crew which kept them from boarding the train.

Later in the day Reitman turned up in Los Angeles, a pitiable sight indeed. While Emma had conferred with the guileful Mayor, armed men had forced her unfortunate companion to accompany them some twenty miles out of San Diego. There the vigilantes tarred and, in lieu of feathers, sagebrushed Emma's manager. "We could tear your guts out," he recalled them saving, "but we promised the Chief of Police not to kill you." They stopped just short of this ultimate step: he was brutally beaten; one "gentle businessman" even tried to ram a cane into his rectum; another twisted his testicles; others used a lighted cigar to burn the letters I.W.W. on his buttocks. This painful ceremony concluded on a patriotic note when he was forced to kiss the flag and sing "The Star-Spangled Banner." When he finished, he was allowed to drag himself away in his underclothes and vest.

To Reitman San Diego became an obsession: with bravado he insisted upon returning. While their defeat there rankled Emma, she regarded it as just one more place where free speech was denied. It was her habit to return to such places as a matter of course until free speech was again established. Her strongest motive in assenting to Reitman's urgent requests that they return immediately, however, was her hope that he would be able to free himself of the hold the city had on him. The second act began, then, in May, 1913, almost exactly one year after the first.

This time four detectives and Francis Bierman, the San Diego *Union* reporter whom Reitman and Emma believed to be behind much of the vigilante terror, met them and took them directly to the police station. As if in response to a conjurer's wand, the vigilantes appeared, whooping and honking outside the jail. Fatherly Chief Wilson promised his charges protection out of town if they would go quietly. Emma stoutly rejected his offer until it became apparent that Reitman had disintegrated completely. She then felt forced to accept. By this time the crowd had become huge and ugly. With a melodramatic flourish Chief Wilson ordered the demonstrators to stand back: "The prisoners are under the protection of the law. I demand respect for the law. Get back!" Clicking cameras and whining sirens sounded Emma's second retreat. The San Diego *Union* (May 21, 1913) chortled: "CITY PURGES ITSELF OF ANARCHISTS. DRIVES OUT GOLDMAN AND HER PAL." But in small print there was also Emma's promise "I'm coming back."

Meanwhile, after the harsh treatment of Emma and Reitman in 1912, a small group of people had banded together to form the Open Forum, with a Baptist minister, A. Lyle de Jarnette, as chairman and George Edwards of the Conservatory of Music as one of the leading members. The membership soon grew to several hundred. Finally, through Edwards, a meeting was arranged for Emma in 1915. Edwards and other Open Forum members called on the Mayor and Chief of Police to learn "if this time the police department was to be on the side of 'law and order' or merely messenger boys for the vigilantes." The officials assured them that they would not interfere with Emma. Unencumbered by the timorous Reitman and supported instead by the steadfast Berkman, she again invaded San Diego and at long last delivered her lecture on *An Enemy of the People*. True to her promise, she had come back. "The triumph was big for the Open Forum and for Miss Goldman," Edwards jubilantly observed. "Others have suffered financially and socially, but out of the fire has come the intellectual salvation not only of the martyrs, but of all the inhabitants of the city—a kind of real vicarious atonement in which not even 'belief' is necessary for participation in the fruits thereof."

8

Before the First World War residents of cities from southern California to Massachusetts received the immeasurable benefits of this kind of intellectual salvation. More simply put, Emma's free-speech fights were ultimately successful in a remarkable number of places. Within these communities numerous individuals found that the patterns of their lives had changed. Former Baptist Minister A. Lyle de Jarnette and musician George Edwards in San Diego, California; Episcopal Rector Eliot White in Worcester, Massachusetts; socialite Socialist Alden Freeman in East Orange, New Jersey; young Ben Capes, who, accompanied by four other boys armed with rocks and beanshooters, came to contest her right to speak in St. Louis and stayed to support her from then on—they and others found that after a performance of Emma's drama they had made far-reaching and almost irrevocable commitments to unfettered freedom of expression. Henceforth their townsmen would look upon them differently and, for that matter, they would look upon themselves with different eyes. Four examples will have to stand here for many.

1. Out in Anaconda country Lewis J. Duncan, a Unitarian minister, bravely acted as chairman for one of Emma's meetings in Butte and then went so far as to invite her to speak from his pulpit. What was involved in such intrepid support of the "battle for freedom of speech over Emma Goldman," as he put it, came out in his letter to a friend, June 20, 1908. After "a merry war with the G.A.R." partial success was achieved:

Miss Goldman was heard, but under a boycott of the press and public and corporation influence which keeps the many—all but the bravest souls— away from her meetings and which compels her to small and obscure halls. My fight has alienated many of my church people too and cost me some subscriptions. How far this loss will be made up by accessions from the working men remains to be seen. I am not sanguine about it. The men are afraid of losing their jobs and even those who fear not are so impoverished by the five months shut down and the irregular employment since [the] mines reopened they have little to give to support a preacher except their good will.

That Duncan won some of their good will was likely, for not long after this he was elected Mayor of Butte. Ultimately, however, he was pushed out of public life by group pressures aroused in part by his support of Emma. Though forced to do housework for friends to keep alive, he did not regret his support, for he declared unrepentantly that he "could not have done differently."

2: One evening in the spring of 1908, after Emma had finished a lecture on "Patriotism" in San Francisco's Walton Pavilion, a soldier slipped through the crowd and shook her hand. Thus began the affair Buwalda. Private William Buwalda, with fifteen years of good conduct military service behind him, had come to the meeting merely to practice his shorthand. Convinced she was a crank, he had taken notes until what she was saying and the way she said it captured his imagination and interest. Still under the sway of her influence at the close of her remarks, he impulsively had gone forward to meet her. On his return to the Presidio he was followed by detectives and placed under arrest. Asked by officers during his court-martial what Emma had done to make him commit so grave a crime, he replied simply that she had made him think. The startled officers sentenced him to five years at hard labor. General Funston, his commanding officer, declared he was "lucky not to get fifteen years" for his had been a "great military offense, infinitely worse than desertion."

The aftermath was no less interesting. Emma immediately organized a committe for Buwalda's defense. Ten months later he was pardoned by President Roosevelt. The former soldier thereupon entered the anarchist ranks and was arrested with her during a subsequent free-speech struggle in San Francisco. Scolded by the police for the company he was keeping, Buwalda replied that he would associate with whom he pleased. A more complete change of an individual's life and outlook is difficult to imagine.

3. Agnes Inglis dated her intellectual birth from the first time she heard Emma speak. Before this she felt her life had been a "fantasy existence": private schooling, comfortable means, and "the futile stop-gap social work endeavors associated with them"—she thought of her time spent as a social worker in Hull-House in Chicago and in the Franklin Settlement House in Detroit as so much "do-goodism." Now,

instead of this kind of work, she threw herself into efforts to gain a hearing for radicals in Ann Arbor and bitterly criticized her cherished University of Michigan for its refusal to allow Emma to give a series of lectures on its campus. Moreover, as a member of a wealthy family— her brother was a millionaire industrialist—she had some savings from which she gave generously when Emma needed support. Her cancelled checks were mute testimonies to the extent of her devotion and self-sacrifice. They show also, incidentally, how Emma was able to meet part of the expenses of her various struggles.

Despite her devotion to Emma, however, Agnes Inglis had mixed feelings about the effect her heroine had on her:

She is the biggest person that ever came into my life. But she did not free me. I gained freedom from the things that then bound me, only to become tied in the movement—it became more of a religion and it was more exciting than the church by far. One felt that one must give every cent one could. Emma has a compelling nature. . . . One thing, tho, seems to me to be true. These great personalities sweep on and never really know the little this and thats of it all as the smaller personalities they come in contact with meet it and think about it and go on with their lives.

Here spoke the perennial protestant who was certain to be restive under ties, even voluntary ones, to any movement. But Emma did have a way of assuming that since she was giving every waking hour to the cause, others should be prepared to give as unsparingly. Taking this sort of generosity for granted can have a disagreeable effect; it was just this which Miss Inglis resented—in large part, justifiably resented. Moreover, her remarks pointed up the really novel problem of leadership in anarchist circles—circles composed of individuals committed to no external direction. While Emma was able to avoid most of the problems of a sectarian political movement—the leader worship, formulation of a rigidly defined creed, punishment or expulsion of deviationists—she was unable to avoid now and then a strong suggestion of similarity with the sect leader who exacts complete support from his followers.[2] In fine, Agnes Inglis' perceptive response revealed that support of Emma Goldman in her free-speech fights and other aims did not lead to unmixed blessings.

[2] In part this was because a large number of anarchists escaped from the freedom which Emma urged upon them and instead leaned on their creed and on her. On this point, John Sloan entered a real insight in his diary, November 5, 1911: Emma Goldman "has splendid strength and courage, a really great woman she is. I can't criticize her—her admirers, however, like many Socialists and other followers are horribly appreciative of the points in their creed—as they are trotted forth they smile the 'ah! isn't that a crushing truth?' smile at the platitudes of the propaganda. Just like the Socialists, I say."

4. In 1911 the Chief Probation Officer in St. Louis was Roger Baldwin, a young man whose purity of political and social views was scarcely questionable—while at Harvard he had refused to hear Jack London speak on the grounds that the novelist's socialism was both foolish and dangerous. Hence, when a friend suggested that he accompany her to one of Emma's St. Louis meetings, he refused abruptly: "I won't go near that crazy woman." He yielded, however, after his friend made several uncomplimentary observations on the narrowness of Harvard men. Let Baldwin give his own unexpected response:

Emma spoke in a crowded hall in the slums. It was a working class audience, the kind she was at her best with. I was electrified the moment she opened her mouth. She was a great speaker—passionate, intellectual, and witty. I'd never heard such a direct attack on the foundations of society. I became a revolutionist, though I continued to work at practical reforms.

A short while later Baldwin declared himself to be a "philosophical anarchist," a follower of Thoreau, Kropotkin, and Emma Goldman. He expressed this profound change of outlook by helping Emma gain a hearing in St. Louis before the exclusive Women's Wednesday Club, by arranging other meetings, and by giving her further aid and encouragement, especially after he became active in civil rights work. He went on, of course, to organize the National Civil Liberties Bureau which did such needed work during the Red Scare of 1919–20 and which later became the American Civil Liberties Union. During this time and later, Baldwin made numerous acknowledgments of his great intellectual and moral debt to Emma Goldman. He wrote in one of his letters to her, for instance, "you always remain one of the chief inspirations of my life, for you aroused me to a sense of what freedom really means."

A heightened awareness of the meaning of freedom—this Emma Goldman undoubtedly gave to Agnes Inglis, Duncan, Buwalda, Baldwin, and many others, and this gave her free-speech fights a significance that should not be underestimated. If she had done nothing else than set Baldwin off on his career, her role as the woman behind the man behind the organization of the American Civil Liberties Union would have made her fights for free speech an outstanding success.

9

Of course, she did more. Not only did she influence other Socialists, single taxers, wobblies, social gospelers, and liberals, but she also, in the process, helped to build a bridge from immigrant radicalism to the native radical and liberal traditions. One of the most effective speakers of her time and perhaps the most accomplished woman speaker in American history, she understandably secured an audience outside anarchist circles.[3] Since her ideas were in part merely logical extensions of the Reformation doctrine of the priesthood of all believers and of the classical liberal tradition of individual freedom and distrust of the state, liberals and radicals of other schools could be enlisted to support her views, even if they could not be persuaded to accept them. Remember that in 1903 it was she who was primarily responsible for the organization of the Free Speech League, which had many notable liberals and radicals as charter members. The League supported Emma in a number of her free-speech fights, and she in turn was able to organize its outlying chapters. In some respects the Free Speech League was the real intellectual godfather of the American Civil Liberties Union.

With such native support, Emma Goldman did more than any other person of her time to check police arbitrariness in general and police mistreatment of immigrant radicals in particular. Her dramatic battles against the groping intolerance of the General Binghams and Chief Wilsons aroused individuals and even some newspapers to resist police autocracy and violence. By 1910, for instance, it was no longer as easy for the police to arrest immigrant radicals on "general principles," the capricious grounds they at one time confidently gave the New York *World* (January 28, 1903) as justification for their actions. Moreover, while immigrant rebels gained directly from her struggles, everyone gained indirectly, for police irresponsibility ultimately menaced the freedom of natives as well as immigrants.

Of equal importance, by her example she gave cautious and sensitive men courage to speak their minds. Her uncompromising stand on free speech stiffened the backs of liberals—liberals whose half-loaf psychology made them susceptible to compromise even in the dangerous area of censorship and suppression. Floyd Dell stated this point effectively in 1912: "She has a legitimate social function—that of holding

[3] A large part of her effectiveness came from her charisma—a concept borrowed from Max Weber and applied here to her magnetic power to sway her audiences, to give them a sense of her having extraordinary gifts of body and spirit, of compassionate feeling and penetrating insight. While this power was admittedly nebulous, hostile and friendly critics time and time again attested to its presence when they referred to her "great and dominating power" of holding her audience in a "vice like grip" or to her gift of putting "electric power" behind her words.

before our eyes the ideal of freedom. She is licensed to taunt us with our moral cowardice, to plant in our souls the nettles of remorse at having acquiesced so tamely in the brutal artifice of present day society." Both as someone to defend and as an inspiration, Emma Goldman was invaluable to the liberals.

"For the cause of free speech in the United States," concluded Roger Baldwin (in 1931), "Emma Goldman fought battles unmatched by the labors of any organization." Perhaps. At the very least Emma Goldman's uncounted performances of "Liberty without Strings" were of significance to all those for whom ends were still debatable.

PART FOUR

New Woman

In 1916 Emma Goldman was sent to prison for advocating that
"women need not always keep their mouths shut
and their wombs open."

MARGARET ANDERSON, *The Little Review Anthology*

CHAPTER XVI

DEVIL'S GATEWAY

During these young years of the twentieth century, minds all over America were humming like the telegraph wires Thoreau had found so poetically suggestive two generations before. Gaiety, revolt, and regeneration filled the air. Public holiday was the mood and Washington Square was the midway. The time was the spiritual descendant of the heady, rebellious 1840's, which Emerson had described so well; now as then, "the key of the period appeared to be that the mind had become aware of itself." True, the hum of aware minds often came closer to cacophony than symphony, but the big thing was the fresh thinking and feeling. It was as though many Americans looked out of their bedroom windows on the first bright morning of spring. How fine it was just to be awake and alive!

Even the political backdrop was new—or purported to be new. Theodore Roosevelt, the explosively assertive former President, whose verbal heroism diverted attention from his essential opportunism, charged the hustings with a "New Nationalism." The inattentive blinked when they heard that "malefactors of great wealth" still stalked the land, for they had believed them all slain years before by the Great Trustbuster. Blinded by Roosevelt's verbal gymnastics and perhaps as well by his dental display, social workers, reformers, liberals, and some radicals deserted La Follette and embarked upon the wildest goose chase of them all, the Bull Moose campaign of 1912. The Progressive Convention even boasted the novelty of eighteen women delegates, whose presence was an eloquent testimonial to the growing political importance of restive American women. Jane Addams of Hull-House, the most admired woman of her day, delivered a keynote address. A pacifist, Miss Addams had joined forces with the militaristic Roosevelt to promote "social reform." Later she might well have joined William Allen White in his admission, "Roosevelt bit me and I went mad."

Democrats were also furiously active. "If a machine gun does not cost too much, I will be glad to contribute that to the [Mexican] revolution," pledged Frank P. Walsh in 1911, after Emma had asked him for a contribution. "In the circumstances, I believe, of course, in the power of brute force as well as education. Sometimes education works too slowly." Walsh, a well-known liberal and Kansas City attorney—he was to head Wilson's Commission on Industrial Relations and become his liberal whip in New York—revealed in this letter the painfully simple faith of his time in progress: machine guns and education both led to the same elevated goal, the former perhaps more rapidly than the latter. While Walsh's chief at this time had no intention of sending machine guns to Mexican revolutionaries, he too, of course, had the same devout faith in progress. Even when Wilson wrote in 1911 that "the forces of greed and the forces of justice and humanity are about to grapple for a bout in which men will spend all the life that is in them," he had little real fear that progress was in peril. The forces of greed were about to meet their master in Woodrow Wilson's New Freedom.

Poor Taft, with nothing newer than a fairly vigorous antitrust policy, was left behind by voters eager to move into an era of newness, of New Freedom or even New Nationalism. Nineteen twelve was also the year that Eugene V. Debs, the Socialist candidate who might actually have brought about something new under the sun, received 900,000 ante-Nineteenth Amendment votes.

But the "new" politicians were, for the most part, merely the background chorus. This was the time of the New Poetry, of Harriet Monroe's magazine in Chicago and of Margaret Anderson's *Little Review*, which later migrated to New York. The New Drama was getting under way with the productions of the Washington Square Players and the writings of Eugene O'Neill. The New Painting, officially marked by the Armory Show of 1913, hinted to the shocked public that American art had reached some sort of strange, new dimension. The New Architecture was in full swing—Frank Lloyd Wright already had behind him two hundred projects and realized structures which were startlingly original protests against the preceding "rubbish heap of styles." New developments in philosophy were appropriately marked in 1912 by the publication of a co-operative book entitled *The New Realism*. The New History was given monumental support by the publication in 1913 of Charles Beard's *An Economic Interpretation of the Constitution of the United States*. In a word, a consciousness developed that a decisive turning point had been reached in aesthetic and intellectual pursuits.

The quintessence of all the new movements was that of the New

Woman. In its extreme form feminist agitation threatened to make masculine authority yield equal rights to women in all areas, moral, aesthetic, and economic. Young Margaret Sanger, for instance, even claimed the right in her short-lived magazine, *Woman Rebel*, for women to be not only unmarried mothers, but *lazy* unmarried mothers! She advised her sisters to look the whole world in the face with a "go-to-hell look in the eyes."

In New York—where the humming was loudest—there were three archesymbols of the New Woman. Isadora Duncan, sheathed in her loose-flowing gowns and in a kind of vitrifying creativity, dancing always with her near-magical spontaneity and vitality, gained the profound admiration of young rebels whose parents had frowned upon any kind of dancing. Another center of interest was Mabel Dodge, hostess of the famous salon at 23 Fifth Avenue, directly across from the Brevoort Hotel. Nothing was too new for Mrs. Dodge. Designedly enigmatic, dressed in white and wearing perhaps an emerald chiffon wrap, she stood in her doorway and cryptically greeted lovers, friends, acquaintances, and strangers who came to her "evenings" to discuss Freud and the post-Freudians, Bergsonism, futurism, anarchism, syndicalism, socialism. With justice she later recalled that "the new spirit was abroad and swept us all together"; everywhere "barriers were down and people reached each other who had never been in touch before." Some in fact reached each other when it might have been just as well had they not, as an anecdote in Carl Van Vechten's *Peter Whiffle* (1922) suggested: An ultra respectable elderly lady made unfavorable comparisons between Mabel Dodge's modern pictures and the old masters in Henry Clay Frick's collection. She and her substantial husband became apoplectic when Van Vechten irreverently remarked that he had not seen the Frick collection but by way of amends offered to introduce them to the man who had shot Frick. Fortunately most who came to the salon were less violently stimulated by each other. One of the most famous evenings was given over to an informal debate on direct action between its supporters—Emma, Berkman, Big Bill Haywood—and its critics—William English Walling, Walter Lippmann, and other Socialists.

The other archetype New Woman was, of course, Emma Goldman. The office of *Mother Earth*, at 210 East Thirteenth Street, was more the "home of lost dogs," as Hutchins Hapgood characterized it, than it was a salon; still it was one of the centers of feminist agitation and lively thinking. Mabel Dodge, whose establishment eclipsed, in some respects, this humming office, nervously went with Hapgood to visit Emma. Apparently she was rather surprised not to find the anarchists drinking nitroglycerin punch: "I knew she stood for killing people if necessary," she ingenuously wrote, "But what a warm, jolly atmosphere, with a homely supper on the table, and Emma herself like a homely, motherly sort of person giving everyone generous platefuls of beefsteak . . . and fried potatoes! She looked to me, from the very first, rather like a severe but warm-hearted schoolteacher and I am sure that that was essentially what she was. . . ."

In pleasant contrast to the deep, pervasive seriousness of the pages of *Mother Earth* were the occasional frolics of its staff. A carefree note was struck several times a year in "Mother Earth Balls"—relaxations which suggested the possible outlines of leisure after the revolution. In 1912 a reporter for the *Evening Post* (February 24) obviously enjoyed his assignment to a "Ball." He described the refreshments on counters laden with "a steaming Russian samovar, cakes, pies, sandwiches, fruit"; Emma's appearance as she hurried "about in her long, checkered, kitchen apron, somewhat plump, and beaming at the many friends who crowd around her counter"; the lively dancing; and the singing of "Oh, I love my boss" and other wobbly songs. Emma's most famous party was a "Red Revel" in March, 1915, which celebrated *Mother Earth's* tenth year of publication. A cordial invitation was extended to all those of "red revolutionary blood" who could for a moment forget the war and the "blunders and crimes" against internationalism committed by European radicals. Eight hundred persons, representing "every profession from the dramatist, painter, composer, poet, actor, to the scavenger," accepted the invitation. Carlo Tresca, the Italian-American anarchist, was one of the revelers: he remembered that Emma appeared dressed as a nun and that she vainly tried to execute a waltz called the "Anarchist's Slide." For a woman so lightheartedly to flaunt the proprieties created almost unimaginable consternation among the traditional minded.

2

Not that the public needed newspaper accounts of red revels to become convinced that Emma Goldman was a criminal hoyden and a trollop. For years it had been exposed to shocking accounts such as that of her sitting in an East Side "barroom" at a table with men, her chair tilted back, reading a book. In a day when women were still slyly puffing cigarettes in closets or bathrooms, Emma smoked in public—so obvious a breach of public decency that she was often ejected from restaurants.[1] She further outraged conventional sensibilities by publicly mentioning such unmentionables as the murderous steel-reinforced corsets which were still squeezing the life out of women. On one occasion, for instance, a woman fainted during the course of Emma's talk to the Manhattan Liberal Club on the "Tragedy of Woman's Emancipation." To her startled hearers she remarked that this woman was a case in point: "She is an example of woman's emancipation. If she had her clothes looser she would not have fainted."

Such uninhibited behavior in itself condemned her beyond all hope of social salvation. When the public further heard her attack the traditional family structure and advocate "free love," its horror was simply deepened. Emma Goldman was a demoniac modern Eve, allied with the serpent, to all those for whom the flesh was evil—to all those, and their numbers should not be underestimated, who oscillated strangely and tragically between regarding woman as an angel or a demon, as a force of light or a force of darkness, as a mother or a mistress, as God's doorway to salvation or the Devil's gateway to sin. To these people "that woman" came to be looked upon as a sort of well of impurity. On the other hand, to many of those for whom the flesh had no terrors, she was looked upon as a well of purity in a swamp of lecherous hypocrisy.

Now just what did she mean by "free love"? Obviously she did not mean the wrangling lack of love which characterized the relationship of Abraham and Taube Goldman; she did not mean anything similar to her own suffocating marriage to the impotent Kersner. On the contrary, to Emma free love meant the mutual, essentially private attraction of two responsible human beings to each other. It meant the tender and passionate feeling she had for Berkman, Brady, Reitman, Max Baginsky, Hippolyte Havel. This feeling rested on an inner sincerity which was not so much antithetical to conventional morality as it was beyond any mere outward conformity. Paradoxically, given their number, her affairs of the heart were in the main built on lasting foundations of tenderness and mutual esteem. With the one exception of her relationship with Most, who never wavered in his rejec-

[1] The times change. In 1904 a woman was arrested for smoking on Fifth Avenue; in 1929 the railroads ceased prohibiting women from smoking in dining cars. In 1934 the New York *Sun* reporter who accompanied Emma on a train ride from Toronto to Rochester remarked that she was the only woman in the Pullman who was not smoking— Emma had given up the habit early, for she correctly anticipated that she might be sent to prison, which almost inevitably meant annoying deprivation.

tion of her apologies and attempts at reconciliation, her love affairs did not end in a flurry of degrading reproaches and recriminations. Quite the contrary. Brady remained her very good friend until his death. Havel and Baginsky remained her close friends after their more intimate association with her had ended. Even Reitman, from whom Emma eventually separated in 1917 over his equivocal stand on the war, continued to regard his ten years with her as the most "glorious" years of his life.[2] While Emma had to give up her desire to assume her old relationship with Berkman upon his release from prison, the two still continued their extremely close working partnership. Their friendship continued for almost half a century, through revolution, war and peace, health and sickness, agreement and disagreement.

In her relationships with the men she loved there was more than a little maternal feeling. Since her powers to bear and nurse a deeply desired child were never allowed outlet—why and how they were not will be discussed later—some of her maternal longing seemingly focused on the men of her choice. This was one reason why many other friends besides Reitman were impressed by her motherly qualities. To mention only a few, Kate Richards O'Hare, a keen observer, felt that Emma was primarily "the tender, cosmic mother"; Leonard Abbott thought her "motherly and compassionate"; Art Young found her to be "more maternal in appearance and manner than destructive"; and Roger Baldwin was struck by "the warm tenderness of a mother which lay just under that defiant, unyielding public exterior."

Beyond serious doubt her sex life was, as Waldo Frank once observed, the "response of a motherly heart rather than of a lusting body." Emma herself emphatically rejected the notion that love and physical sex are synonymous. Later, in a letter to the writer Frank Harris, she set forth her position forcefully:

Well, Frank dear, when I read your first volume [of My Life and Loves], I realized at once how utterly impossible it is to be perfectly frank about sex experiences and to do so in an artistic and convincing manner. Believe me, it is not because I have any puritannic feeling or that I care in the least for the condemnation of people. My reasons for the impressions regarding the facts of sex are that I do not consider the mere physical fact sufficient to convey the tremendous effect it has upon human emotions and sensations.

---

[2] At the time of Emma's death, decades later, Reitman was quoted as saying that "they have taken away my savior and I know not where they have laid her . . . she gave me a soul." While this expression of his grief was in keeping with his ingrained exhibitionism, it was nevertheless genuine.

. . . I feel that the effect of sexual relation is psychological and cannot be described in mere physical terms.

In point of fact, she approached love quite idealistically.

Nevertheless, her refusal to make a sharp division between her public and private selves, her complete frankness, and her deep contempt for those stuck fast in the cake of custom aroused guilty horror in the hearts of many—many who had a public self which spoke for the record and a private self which whispered to a mistress or lover; many who felt that anything out of the ordinary had better be kept clandestine; and many who clung to tradition even in the selection of their vices. On the underside of the righteous denunciations of her were sly snickers of the dirty-story kind. There were absurdities, too. Take, for instance, the scandalized protests of divorcees who objected to staying in the same Reno hotel with the "Free Lover." Or the Cincinnati brewer who rapped on her hotel room door late one night and demanded to be admitted; when Emma jumped from her bed, shouting that she would wake the whole house, he begged to be allowed to make a quiet retreat: "Please, please! Don't make any scene. I'm a married man, with grown children. I thought you believed in free love." Thus did the brewer and others mistranslate her appeals for the creative richness of a love free from legal coercion, economic motivation, and social compulsion into exhortations for a sort of "Wild Love."

3

For years Emma Goldman had returned the conservative fire directed her way by delivering lectures which were corrosive criticisms of the institution of marriage. Then she put some of these lectures (along with others) in essay form and published them in 1911 under the title of *Anarchism and Other Essays*. These essays showed that she was drawing on the same tradition of hostility to conventional marriage as had the utopian Socialists, the Anabaptists and earlier heretical Christian sects, and, to a certain extent, Plato and other Greek thinkers—all of whom, in one way or another, had rejected the exclusiveness of an institution which was anchored to private property. The essence of Emma Goldman's criticism was that marriage caused man (and woman herself) to look upon woman as an object, a thing.

Under present circumstances, Emma held, woman obviously is "being reared as a sex commodity." Since her body is capital to be exploited and manipulated, she comes to look on success as the size of her husband's income. The girl is taught to ask only this question: "Can the man make a living? . . . her dreams are not of moonlight and kisses, of laughter and tears; she dreams of shopping tours and bargain counters." The woman who enters a marriage of convenience and the prostitute are on the same level: both subordinate sexual relationships to gain.[3]

A potentially free being, Emma argued, woman becomes a lifelong dependent when she marries. Even her supposed citadel is *his* home, wherein she moves, "year after year, until her aspect of life and human affairs becomes as flat, narrow, and drab as her surroundings." Such dependency rules out the development of a free personality.

As an economic convenience, marriage is also productive of jealousy. This degrading phenomenon she sharply distinguished from anguish over a lost love. She argued that while the latter is virtually inevitable, jealousy is not; and she cited anthropological evidence from the writings of Lewis Henry Morgan and Elie Reclus to show that it is not inborn. It results rather, she felt, from possessiveness and bigotry. The male's conceit is hurt to realize that there are "other cocks in the barnyard"; the female's jealousy results from economic fears for herself and a petty envy of others who gain grace in the eyes of her supporter. In the final analysis, she concluded, the foundation of jealousy is marriage, for it rests on the ownership of woman—the possession of woman as a commodity or object.

She did not rule out the probability that some marriages are based on love and that in some instances love continues in married life, but she maintained "that it does so regardless of marriage and not because of it." And after all, she asked, how can love, "the defier of all laws," be coerced; "how can such an all-compelling force be synonymous with that poor little State and Church-begotten weed, marriage?" The question was rhetorical: *legitimate love,* she believed, is the final absurdity.

4

Emma Goldman repeatedly asserted that the tragedy of the woman's emancipation impulse was symbolized by the devout faith of women in equal suffrage. Nothing indicated any more clearly that the movement had become enmeshed in externals. Universal suffrage, she upset her feminine audiences by saying, was the modern fetish: "Life, happi-

---

[3] She really put the prostitute on a higher level, for she went on to quote approvingly Havelock Ellis' contention that "the wife who married for money, compared with the prostitute, is the true scab. She is paid less, gives much more in return in labor and care, and is absolutely bound to her master. The prostitute never signs away the right over her own person. . . ."

ness, joy, freedom, independence,—all that, and more, is to spring
from suffrage." By way of answer to her sisters who expected miracles
from the vote she merely asked them to look at the record of the then
four states with equal suffrage. Were politics "purer" therein? As a
matter of fact, she asserted, the antiequalitarianism, antagonism to
labor (present from the time of Susan B. Anthony), and Puritanism
of the woman suffragettes tended to make politics even more of a
moral swamp than it had been.

All the narrowness of vision and inner emptiness were rooted, she
thought, in modern woman's overreaction to her traditional sexual role.
In some Whitmanesque lines she observed that "the great movement
of true emancipation has not met with a great race of women who could
look liberty in the face. Their narrow, Puritanical vision banished
man, as a disturber and doubtful character, out of their emotional life.
Man was not to be tolerated at any price, except perhaps as the father
of a child, since a child could not very well come to life without a
father."

Thus did Emma Goldman take issue with Charlotte Perkins Gilman,
Ida Tarbell, Jane Addams, and other leaders of the woman's struggle.
She felt that their emphasis was misplaced—that they tended to advance the mistaken idea "that all that was needed was independence
from external tyrannies; the internal tyrants, far more harmful to life
and growth—ethical and social conventions—were left to take care of
themselves; and they have taken care of themselves." While she agreed
with them in rejecting for woman the role of a mere sex commodity,
she differed with them on the appropriate response of the New Woman
to the problem of sex. Many of the feminist leaders joined Mrs. Gilman—whose important *Women and Economics* (1899) Emma had
obviously read—in bewailing the "over-sexed" woman, in advocating
the inherent value of chastity, and in holding that "excessive indulgence
in sex-waste has imperiled the life of the race." On the contrary, Emma
maintained, the "tragedy of the self-supporting or economically free
woman does not lie in too many, but in too few experiences." In fine,
she attacked not only the New Woman's fixation on the suffrage
panacea, but also her epicene tendencies—her tendency to become a
"compulsory vestal."

5

Such views on marriage, the right to vote, and sex produced a reaction
among women which may be described as fascinated revulsion. They
were repelled by her suggestion that women might safely escape the

sacred shelter of marriage; they were angered by her questioning of the adequacy of the vote; and they were shocked by her frank advocacy of a full sexual life for woman. Yet their dissatisfaction with the lot of women raised the possibility in their minds that she was right—or at least partly right. A reviewer in the "socialist number" of the old *Life* detected this uncertainty, for he advocated that *Anarchism and Other Essays* "ought to be read by all so-called respectable women, and adopted as a text-book by women's clubs throughout the country." While he had no idea they would all agree with Emma Goldman, he felt her essays would give them another point of view of importance, for "she stands for some of the noblest traits in human nature." New Women, many of whom were affiliated with the General Federation of Women's Clubs (which soon had over a million members), did read her book and fearfully attend her lectures, titillated by their own daring. They emerged shaken and frequently convinced that their fears had been justified: Emma had made them think.

CHAPTER XVII

POPULARIZER OF THE ARTS

As much a dramatic personality as Sarah Bernhardt or Eleonora Duse, Emma Goldman would probably have been drawn to the stage had the drama not been in a state of ferment and innovation.[1] As it was, there was an obvious connection between the struggle of women for equal rights and the New Drama associated with the ground-breaking works of Henrik Ibsen. Back in the 1890's, while in Vienna, Emma had read his plays almost as if they constituted a new revelation: here was art and social rebellion fused into one symmetrical whole; here was support for the woman who rejected the role of plaything and dependent; and, not least, here was a vigorous argument for the individual against the mass. Swept along by her enthusiasm, she became thoroughly familiar with the plays of Ibsen, Strindberg, Sudermann, Hauptmann, Brieux, Shaw, Galsworthy, Yeats, Chekhov, Gorky, Andreyev.

After her return to New York she joined a group of artists and actors in the organization of the Progressive Stage Society, one of the early forerunners of the little theater movement. The society gave weekly performances of foreign plays, but the relative lack of interest of New York audiences made the venture short-lived. Then in 1905 and 1906 she managed the Orleneff troupe, at which time she became acquainted with various theater personalities, among them Ethel and John Barrymore, Arthur Hornblow, Minnie Maddern and Harrison Grey Fiske. Later she knew and worked with Maurice Browne, who founded the Chicago Little Theater in 1912, and with a number of the members of the Provincetown Players.

As early as 1897 she had commenced lecturing on the New Drama, in this first instance on one of Shaw's plays to a group of miners far beneath the surface of the earth. Their understanding of her talk en-

[1] The inherent drama of Emma's life—her connection with Berkman's attempt on the life of Frick, her many free-speech fights, her general struggle against the forces of suppression and tyranny—made her seem almost a figure of the theatrical world. In any case, the dramatic aspects of her career were obvious. The late Mme Nazimova, for instance, once told the playwright S. N. Behrman that "she would like to do a play about Emma Goldman and play the part of Emma."

couraged her to prepare, down through the years, more and more lectures on the drama. She was convinced that through her discussions of modern plays she was able to spread her radical ideas. Under anarchist attack for lecturing on highbrow drama to middle-class intellectuals, she angrily retorted that "creative effort which portrays life boldly, earnestly and unafraid, may become more dangerous to the present fabric of society than the loudest harangue of the soap-box speaker."

Whatever their effect on the fabric of society, her lectures helped prepare an audience for the new icon smashers. "It is largely through Emma Goldman's lectures," Rebecca West declared, "that the works of George Bernard Shaw became popularly known in the United States." Miss West's tribute may have been too generous, for others, particularly the producer Arnold Dayly, probably did more to make Shaw known in this country. It remains true, however, that Emma Goldman was one of the first to appreciate Shaw and that she had been lecturing on his plays for six years when Dayly first staged *Candida* in 1903 and set off the Shaw vogue.

The lively pen of Margaret Anderson has provided us with some idea of how Emma's drama lectures sounded to a sympathetic and intelligent listener. Miss Anderson, who had become an anarchist after hearing Emma speak only once, attended a series of the latter's lectures in Chicago's Fine Arts Building in 1914. She was in some measure disappointed, for she concluded that a few of the lectures had the serious shortcoming of not being interesting. Emma had divided her plays into nine nationality groups, which meant that some evenings she discussed three or four plays:

As a result of such an arrangement, all she could do in an hour's time was to tell the story of each play and point out its social value. And she did it well; instead of being indiscriminate and uncritical, as some of her critics have it, she proved how creatively critical she is: she understands what the authors were trying to do and she doesn't distort and misinterpret in an effort to say something clever on her own account. . . . But it is not enough from Emma Goldman. Unless she can link up a drama talk with her special function—with her own reactions—the essence of her personality is lacking and the thing misses fire.

Obviously it was one thing for Emma to outline the plot of a play to a group of miners so they could understand it; it was quite another thing for her to analyze critically the structure of a play and tie it to the history of the drama in a way that would impress the sophisticated members of her audience.

2

In the early teens a young stenographer named Paul Munter attended Emma's discussions of the drama in New York's Berkeley Theater. At the conclusion of the six-week series he presented her with a neat typescript of her lectures—the gift was both a mark of affection and proof that he could keep up with her rapid delivery. Berkman went to work on the typescript, doing most of the editorial revision— while Emma was a fluent speaker and writer, her handwriting was almost illegible and her spelling indescribable. A short while later Emma's second book, *The Social Significance of the Modern Drama* (1914) was published in Boston by Richard G. Badger.

In her Foreword Emma made clear that she did not mean to support the exponents of art for propaganda's sake, for she criticized those who were caught up by radical jargon such as "bloated plutocrats," "economic determinism," "class consciousness," and the like: "since art speaks a language of its own, a language embracing the entire gamut of human emotions, it often sounds meaningless to those whose hearing has been dulled by the din of stereotyped phrases."

Emma tumbled from this high ground into a morass of aesthetic theory, however, when she went on to argue that art is "preëminently the reflex, the mirror of life. The artist being a part of life cannot detach himself from the events and occurrences that pass panorama-like before his eyes, impressing themselves upon his emotional and intellectual vision." For her, then, art was mimesis. But why was she ready to settle for the reflection rather than the real thing? Certainly Venus in the flesh was more beautiful than her distorted and cold reflection in some mountain pool. Emma sensed her difficulty at this point, for she granted that "perhaps those who learn the great truths of the social travail in the school of life, do not need the message of the drama." The drama was merely the Extension Division of the Great School of Life.

Underlying her mimetic theory of art was a quite naïve assumption, common to the radical critics of the time, concerning "life" or "reality": reality in a capitalist society was a kickable lump of ugliness and horror. Had enough artists stumbled across this lump and depicted it realistically, then the social revolution would have been at hand. It was that simple. And after the revolution, when classes were abolished, there would be no real need for art, for life would then be in itself an all-satisfying mountain of beauty and happiness.

In truth, though she was reluctant to admit it, she evidenced more than a trace of hostility to art as an independent enterprise. There was more than a hint of fear that art acted to divert potential forces of social rebellion into "mere" aesthetic activity. Art had to get properly into harness and be true to life. "The world will be beautiful enough when it becomes good enough. Is there anything so ugly as unjust distinctions, as the privileges of the few contrasted with the degradation of the many? When we want to beautify we must begin at the right end." So declared Henry James's revolutionary Princess Casamassima, not Emma. But the latter's theory moved in this direction.

Since these ideas led away from the rest of her thinking, her adoption of them was curious. In its formal statement her theory moved toward a mechanical realism and a totalitarian objectivism in which the artist became merely the scribe of an imperious reality. The rest of her thinking implied an organic art and a creative subjectivism in which the spontaneous artist triumphed over the constricting forces of a too narrow reality—the logical literary expression here was lyrical poetry. In a sentence, most of her ideas implied the insight that art not only reflects but also *illuminates*.

One reason for the discrepancy was that she was still under the spell of Chernyshevsky, who deprecated traditional art as "futile diversion." Too, she was influenced by the crudely instrumental theories of art held by other radicals of her day. But perhaps more important still was the unresolved tension in her thought coming from her simultaneous commitment to the mass of mankind and to a peculiar kind of elitism. Her aesthetic sentiments rested on a faith in the regenerative power of the masses. Elsewhere she lamented that the "intellectuals of America have not yet discovered their relation to the workers. . . . They seem to think that they and not the workers represent the creators of culture. But that is a disastrous mistake. Only when the intellectual forces of Europe had made common cause with the struggling masses, when they came close to the depths of society, did they give to the world a real culture." On the other hand she joined Ibsen in supporting the individual against the mass. Thus did this root tension crop up again.

3

No other critic ever abandoned more of his formal aesthetic theory in the practice of his craft than did Emma. In the pages of her *Social Significance of the Modern Drama* there was no insistence that the playwrights heed inflated *pronunciamentos* against deviating from revolutionary realism. On the contrary, like Whitman she contained multitudes and had no fear of contradicting herself. Romantics, realists, and naturalists were all grist for her mill. She wrote as sympathetically and understandingly of Edmond Rostand's romantic poetic *Chanticleer*, as of Strindberg's naturalistic prose *Countess Julia*; as enthusiastically of Hauptmann's realistic *Weavers*, as of his symbolic *Sunken Bell*. Indeed, she explicitly refused to rank her artists: "life is sufficiently complex to give each his place in the great scheme of things." In practice, then, she recognized the author's right to his idiosyncratic choice of subject and style of expression. More consistently with the rest of her anarchism, she did not presume to tell the individual what he should say, or how he should say it—actually, her criticism boiled down to a socially oriented impressionism.

Notwithstanding the great improvement of her practice over her theory, her method had deep flaws from the standpoint of serious dramatic criticism. In her book, precisely as Miss Anderson observed of her lectures, she tried to do too much. Within a little over three hundred pages she essayed to discuss the modern drama of Norway and Sweden, Germany, France, England, Ireland, and Russia, considering, in all, thirty-two plays by nineteen playwrights. Dizzied by such a kaleidoscopic whirl past the great names of the modern theater, the alert reader sensed that the book lacked inner unity—that the removal of its covers would have sent the chapters flying in all directions, as if they were marbles spilled from a boy's pocket.

The book did reveal Emma's ability to get inside a play and dig out the author's explicit meaning. Her summaries and description of themes were enlivened by her intense feeling about social problems; her close attention to the play itself and her exegesis of the text gave her essays a curiously modern air—though, of course, she did not have the literary training which would have enabled her to ferret out subtle and implicit meanings. But in the end her method amounted to little more than homily-hunting.

By way of illustration, let us consider her discussion of four of Ibsen's problem plays. The theme of *The Pillars of Society* she took to be the disintegrating effect of the "Social Lie," "Duty," and "Provincialism." After a quick and accurate summary of the plot, she arraigned Consul Bernick as an oppressive, patriarchal husband and a posturing Christian who jeopardized human life by sending out his unseaworthy ship, the "Indian Girl." She thought Ibsen's message clear: the "Indian Girl" was the symbol of a society which was also beyond patching up; Truth and Freedom were the real pillars of a new society. She held

An Enemy of the People to be Ibsen's enunciation of his own faith in the man who stood alone and his distaste for the "compact majority, the damned compact liberal majority." In her discussion of *A Doll's House* and *Ghosts* she explained and heartily seconded Ibsen's attack on "the lie of the marriage institution." The essence of his attack, she felt, was to be found in the actions of two of his most memorable characters: in Nora Helmer, who refused to be treated as a doll by her loving, honorable but obtusely patronizing husband; and in Mrs. Alving, who tragically accepted, because of her sacred marriage vows, continued life with her depraved husband. Finishing her essay with a flourish on Ibsen's "bugle call, heralding a new dawn and the birth of a new race," she obviously felt that she had extracted some messages for her day.

Unfortunately, Ibsen's meaning in all his works was "as clear as daylight" to Emma. This was simply another limitation of her approach, for Ibsen, of course, placed some rather formidable obstacles in the path of those who would understand his work. What, for instance, was Ibsen doing in *The Wild Duck*? Was he mocking his own ideals, as James Huneker thought? Asking himself if telling the truth was really worth the effort, as Georg Brandes thought? Concluding with despair that if life could not reconcile itself with truth, then death was preferable, as William Archer thought? Or heading off his disciples from forgetting that men not strong enough to bear the truth needed illusions, as Bernard Shaw thought? Significantly, Emma did not choose to discuss *The Wild Duck* in her book. It did not have as inspiring a message as *A Doll's House* or *Ghosts* and tended to throw in doubt Ibsen's exact position on the "Social Lie." Indeed, Ibsen's position on this question was less daylight clear than Emma thought. In *An Enemy of the People* Dr. Stockmann was happily married and in *The Wild Duck* even the impending marriage of the old roué Werle to Mrs. Sörby promised to be happy. In her haste to make her points forcibly, Emma tended to bypass ambiguities and complexities, the qualifying statement and the tentative inference.

4

After the New Drama Emma Goldman's major literary interest was in the poetry of Walt Whitman. To her the "great old Walt" was easily "the most universal, cosmopolitan, and human of the American writers." In her lectures on Whitman, which she continued to revise and deliver over a period of decades, she tried to give her audiences proof that Whitman merited this praise. In her study she had the advantage of a warm friendship with Horace Traubel, whose reminiscences and biography of Whitman helped her understanding. Her lectures also revealed extensive reading of other studies of Whitman and a fairly close reading of *Leaves of Grass* (1855) itself.

One of the keys to Whitman's poetry, Emma held, was the fact that the Good Gray Poet "never saw the inside of a college or university . . . [this] was fortunate because it helped him to retain originality and independence of thought. He was a prolific reader, however, and in his 'loafing' he learned more of people, conditions and nature than most men who received the so called highest education." Hence, Whitman was able to retain the "inexhaustible force of spontaneity" which made him an "irrepressible outlaw" compared with academic poets. Another key, she later decided with remarkable insight, was Whitman's "bisexuality": the more she read and studied, "the clearer it is to me that it was his sex differentiation which enriched his nature, hence enriched his knowledge of and his understanding for human complexities. Walt Whitman's idea of universal comradeship was conditioned in his magnetic response to his own sex. So was his extraordinary sensitiveness to the nature of woman conditioned in the fact that he had considerable femininity in him. All combined . . . to make up his greatness as a poet and rebel and needs no apology or defense."[2]

Starting thus with the man—for she accepted Whitman's view that whoever touched the *Leaves* touched the man—she went on to examine his poetry. In it, she found, the individual was brought "exultantly close to the universe": "Just as man appears to the great old Walt, so does he appear in anarchism, all equally related to life, all interwoven with society, yet each unto himself a personality." His rebellion and iconoclasm made Whitman one "with the liberating factors of life." But Emma honored him above all for his lines on the "sweet still sane nakedness in nature." The genteel tradition, so paralyzing to life, almost suppressed Whitman's great poetry: "Because *Leaves of Grass* sings the beauty and wholesomeness of sex, of the human body freed from the rags and tatters of hypocrisy, the professors, Uncles and Aunts demanded to know if the author is not really a dangerous, immoral character." It was Whitman's great achievement to liberate the

2 Gay Allen, a modern student of Whitman, offers persuasive evidence which substantiates, in the main, Emma's earlier insights into the life and work of her idol. See Allen's *Solitary Singer* (New York: Macmillan Co., 1955), pp. 187, 211, 218, 421–25, esp. 424.

senses from a Puritanism which "outrages all that makes for health and beauty and naturalness." Emma was convinced that no song ever written could compare with his "Children of Adam": "A Woman Waits for Me" and "One Hour of Madness and Joy" gained Whitman a "niche among the immortals."

Unlike some of her drama lectures, these studies of Whitman were interesting and penetrating. But again in her haste to use Whitman for some of her favorite beliefs, she glossed over or omitted considering serious problems presented by his poetry. She used him propagandistically in the sense that she took from his poetry only those parts which were useful to her. Once while working on one of her lectures, she wrote a friend that Whitman's optimism was "sickening": " 'All is well, everything for the best, the tyrant as well as the rebel, the slave as well as the master, all is well in the universe[.]' The only question is why then make an effort for anything if all is well and ordained by some force? I wonder why Whitman himself tried anything, or was so enraged when he came face to face with some wrong?" Such complaints indicated that she was at least partially aware of Whitman's excesses, of his frequent histrionics, and of the flatulencies of much of his work as the "official poet" of democracy. Surely she must have been aware, though she did not say so, of the strain of crude nationalism in his poetry. But her private doubts and questions never found expression in her lectures. Like Whitman's political poetry, her lectures were marred by the suppression of doubt and tension.

5

Thus, for all of her intense concern and frequent insights, Emma Goldman betrayed a certain lack of understanding in her lectures on the drama and poetry. This was less true of her remarks on music and sculpture. Like most Russian Jews, she had an almost inborn taste for music—a taste which expressed itself early in her enchantment over the plaintive notes of Petrushka's flute and later in her absorption in the music of Wagner and Beethoven, her favorite composers. She was also able to accept sculpture more nearly on its own terms, as she made clear in her appreciation of the work of Rodin, Meunier, Jacob Epstein, an early visitor to her flat in New York, and Jo Davidson, a friend whose work she frequently admired though she as frequently disapproved of his choice of subjects.[3] But, for the most part, Emma was guilty of

[3] Davidson, incidentally, was to design the impressive plaque for the headstone on Emma's grave in Waldheim Cemetery on the outskirts of Chicago.

imposing nonartistic demands on artists. "She was good," John Sloan noted in his diary after hearing her lecture on "Art and Revolution," "but here and there demanded too much social consciousness from the artist. For instance, she said that if the great painter (therefore revolutionist) should paint a wealthy lady he would show the parasite covered with diamonds—this is too far, takes it out of art—which is simply truth felt by the painter."[4] Parasites should be covered with diamonds and capitalists should be bloated! Indeed she went too far.

Yet, after all this has been said, the important thing was that she was able to do so much in this area in addition to all of her other activities. Avoiding the narrow economism which severely limited the outlook of so many other radicals, she made an impressive effort to state the anarchist position in all relevant fields. Only with superhuman effort, however, could she fight for free speech in San Diego and elsewhere and at the same time play a leading role in advancing aesthetic awareness. Even the energetic Margaret Anderson had time to do little else than edit her *Little Review* and solicit funds for the next issue. To become a first-rate critic—the vigor of her mind and her feeling for the drama made this quite conceivable—Emma would have had to devote the major part of her energies to this end. But this would have meant that she might well have had to become less of something else—less a champion of free speech, less a mother of the hungry and cold, less a public rebel.

While she was not "an able critic of the drama," as the New York *Times* once too generously asserted, she was a writer of presentable surveys and the first to pursue systematically the theme of the social significance of the modern drama—a theme since developed by Ramsden Balmforth and Eric Bentley, among others. She was an above-average guide to works of literary merit—she was one of the first to recognize the importance of Shaw and O'Neill—although she had occasional lapses of taste, as when she characterized the posing Bret Harte as "America's most human writer." As editor and publisher of

---

[4] For this and the quotation in an earlier chapter from Sloan's diary I am indebted to Mr. Joseph J. Kwiat. The artist Robert Henri, Sloan's friend and mentor, was an anarchist and regarded himself as a follower of Emma Goldman. He once painted her portrait—it has since mysteriously disappeared—which she disliked, ironically enough, because it was not a close likeness. It is only fair to add that later in her life Emma resolved some of the contradictions in her thinking about art. She came to see that art does more than mirror life: in 1935 the Montreal *Gazette* (February 28) quoted her as saying: "Art in part is a rebellion against the realities of its unfulfilled desire." Belatedly she came up with this insight that art and social criticism have a common origin and are both concerned with new visions.

Mother Earth she brought before her readers some good poetry, reprints of good literature, and critical discussions of several authors. She helped create an audience for the rebel writers and artists of her day (and, to turn the coin over, she also played a definite role in introducing literary people to radical ideas).

Through her lectures she infected her listeners with some of her genuine enthusiasm for such writers as Ibsen and Whitman. One accomplished woman has recently remarked, for instance, that "Emma made me what I am. Can you imagine the effect she had on an East Side girl of seventeen who knew nothing of the world of culture? She introduced me to Strindberg, Shaw, and Ibsen. I used to travel clear across town to hear her lecture Sunday nights on literature, birth control, and women." A former Rhodes scholar working on his doctorate in American literature at Yale wrote to Emma that he hated to think what he would have been like if he had started his studies before he received a "breath of humanism in knowing you." A young scientist also obviously felt that he owed her a great debt, for he wrote that "you made literature, poetry, history live for me. No longer could I merely be interested in self-culture, or in getting rich." As a final illustration, the writer Henry Miller has observed that his meeting Emma in San Diego was "the most important encounter of my life. She opened up the whole world of European culture for me and gave a new impetus to my life, as well as direction."

These tributes and others like them show that Emma was a gifted teacher and an extraordinary popularizer of the arts. They help substantiate the following contention of Van Wyck Brooks, the critic and historian of the writer in America: "No one did more to spread the new ideas of literary Europe that influenced so many young people in the West as elsewhere,—at least the ideas of the dramatists on the continent and in England—than the Russian-American Emma Goldman. . . ."[5]

[5] *The Confident Years* (New York: E. P. Dutton & Co., 1952), p. 375.

CHAPTER XVIII

BIRTH CONTROL PIONEER

When Nora Helmer slammed shut behind her the door of her doll's house, as Emma Goldman justly observed, Ibsen's heroine opened the great rebellion of women against male domination. To be sure, industrialization and urbanization made the fight of women easier, as many of the functions of the traditional family were taken over by the state, the school, the factory. But women helped to make themselves free and by the lyric years before the First World War they had come a considerable way. Not so long before, men had argued that women should not be admitted to higher education, since in a botany course, for instance, the lecturer would be obliged to point out that plants have sex organs and therewith the feminine students would be made unfit to associate with their respectable sisters. By 1913 Dr. A. A. Brill, a pioneer American follower of Freud, was able to lecture on "Masturbation" to the ladies of the Child Study Association. The old sex piety was giving ground. Despite the valiant efforts of Comstock and his successors, nudes became common in art; an increasingly frank discussion of the relationship of the sexes found its way into fiction; the traditional role of women was openly attacked in problem plays; and even the feminist ideas advanced by such extremists as Emma Goldman and Isadora Duncan gained ground. While the great majority of American women continued to darn socks and prepare suppers, they did so, so to speak, with one eye on the door through which Nora had escaped.

To thoroughgoing social conservatives such as Theodore Roosevelt, the conduct of modern women was scandalous. They so lightly regarded the sacred shelter of marriage that, in increasing numbers, they sought their freedom—in 1914, for example, the number of divorces finally reached 100,000. Worse yet, they had allowed the birth rate to fall, especially in families on the higher social and economic levels. Muttering darkly of the "race suicide" of which they were guilty, T. R.

led the forces which vainly rushed to block the escape of women from the kitchen and, it must be said, the bedroom.[1]

2

To Emma Goldman and many of her sisters voluntary parenthood was a crucial step in the emancipation of women. "Woman no longer wants to be a party to the production of a race of sickly, feeble, decrepit, wretched human beings," she declared in lecture after lecture. "Instead she desires fewer and better children, begotten and reared in love and through free choice, not by compulsion as marriage imposes." In a lecture on one of Brieux's plays (she subtitled her lecture, "Why the Poor Should Not Have Children") she endorsed "the demand that woman must be given means to prevent conception of undesired and unloved children; that she must become free and strong to choose the father of her child and to decide the number of children she is to bring into the world, and under what conditions."

Emma Goldman's belief in the right of women to regard conception as a choice dated from the beginning of her career. When a medical examination in the early 1890's revealed that she had an inverted womb, which would continue to give her pain and prevent her from having a child, she refused to undergo an operation on the ground that she did not want to add a child of her own to the thousands of poor children around her. Instead she would give her love to all children and to an ideal which promised them the freedom in which they might develop. From the outset, then, she practiced a personal form of birth control. Later in the decade her interest in the subject increased. Working as a midwife and nurse on the East Side, she reluctantly turned down the heart-rending pleas of involuntary mothers to perform abortions, for she feared the consequences of poorly executed operations and she knew of no contraceptive methods. Then in 1900, as we have already observed, through the good offices of her friend Victor Dave, she attended an international Neo-Malthusian conference in Paris. There she sympathetically listened to the arguments for family limitation and observed demonstrations of preventive methods. At the conclusion of the conference she was supplied with printed instructions and contraceptives for her future work.

After her return she took up the question in her lectures and essays. She worked closely with Moses Harman, setting up joint-subscription offers for *Mother Earth* and Harman's *American Journal of Eugenics*

---

[1] T. R. warned that if marriages did not produce an average of four children, the numbers of the "race" would drop. This was the "race suicide" he found so frightening.

and in 1910 publishing an appreciation of Harman which hailed him as the pioneer of the free motherhood movement in America. Still, since she considered family limitation only one aspect of her work, she did not care to risk prison by discussing contraceptive methods in her lectures. She limited herself to supplying information only when privately requested for it. Then in 1914 Margaret Sanger was indicted for her publication of *Woman Rebel:* her arrest was followed by that of her husband, who had, in Mrs. Sanger's absence, sold her pamphlet on *Family Limitation* to a Comstock agent. Emma decided that the time had come when "I must either stop lecturing on the subject or do it practical justice. I felt that I must share with them the consequences of the birth-control issue."

3

On March 28, 1915, Emma lectured to some six hundred people who were assembled for one of the fortnightly dinners of the Sunrise Club. To her audience of physicians, lawyers, artists, businessmen, Comstock detectives, and liberals of both sexes, she recounted the background of the movement for "Family Limitation" and then frankly discussed the use of various contraceptives. Arrest seemed so certain for this first public discussion of contraceptive methods that she took a book with her to read in jail.

Unexpectedly, no arrest followed until August, when she and Reitman were on tour in Portland, Oregon. Charged there with circulating "literature of an illegal character," they were found guilty by the municipal court and fined one hundred dollars each. Scott Wood, the poet-lawyer friend who lived in Portland, helped with an appeal to the circuit court. Circuit Judge William Gatens set aside their conviction because of insufficient evidence and took occasion to remark "that the trouble with our people today is that there is too much prudery. . . . We are all shocked by many things publicly stated that we know privately to ourselves, but we haven't got the nerve to get up and admit it. . . ." Pleasantly surprised, Emma went ahead with her work, encouraging local radicals to take up birth control agitation.

On her way East she lectured in the major cities on "Birth Control" or "The Right of the Child Not To Be Born." She found her audiences attentive, especially when composed of men. "Women," she wrote a friend, "are impossible. They snicker and giggle and pretend to be shocked and make the men present so conscious they too act silly. It's just been hell to speak on Birth Control with many women present."

In April, 1915, Margaret Sanger had complained to Emma and the leaders of *Mother Earth* that she had expected more support from her radical friends; she earnestly appealed for funds to carry on her fight. In a note Emma reassured her that "MOTHER EARTH and those connected with her never have and never will hesitate to stand by our brave friend, Margaret H. Sanger." Good as her word, Emma collected forty dollars for Mrs. Sanger in Chicago, twenty in St. Louis, and additional amounts in other cities.

4

Emma was finally arrested in New York on February 11, 1916, for a lecture "on a medical question" at the New Star Casino. A protest meeting followed on the heels of her arrest. According to one reporter, the meeting in Carnegie Hall was attended by four police stenographers, untold numbers of police plain-clothes men, and several thousand of Emma Goldman's admirers. Her arrest had brought the increasing public support for birth control to a sharp focus: Leonard Abbott, an old friend of Emma's and an associate editor of *Current Literature*, presided at the meeting. Drs. William J. Robinson and A. L. Goldwater spoke against her arrest and for birth control. Bolton Hall, single taxer and attorney, and Theodore Schroeder, the well-known Free Speech League lawyer, discussed the legal aspects of birth control. John Reed and Anna Strunsky Walling also protested Emma's arrest. A letter from Margaret Sanger, endorsing the purposes of the meeting, was read.

After several hearings, the trial was set for the twentieth of April. The night before Emma went to court, Anna Sloan and a number of her other friends gave her a dinner at the Brevoort Hotel. Again many leading representatives from the professional and artistic world were present: Goldwater and other physicians, Henri, Bellows, Sloan, Minor, Boardman Robinson, and other artists, John Cowper Powys, the English writer, and Alexander Harvey, editor of *Current Literature*—all participated. Rose Pastor Stokes, wife of J. G. Phelps Stokes, millionaire industrialist and railroad-owner, handed out sheets of contraceptive information. Asked by a New York *Times* reporter why she thus defied the law, she replied that she "simply wanted to do what Emma Goldman did." The failure of the police to arrest Mrs. Stokes prompted Max Eastman to write in the *Masses* of the rule of the police that "whoever goes free, Emma Goldman should be punished."

The trial the next day was more a spectacle than a contest of the law. One reporter observed that hundreds went to it, "as to a play, with Emma Goldman in the leading role." The scores of artists, intellectuals, and radicals who observed Emma tilt with the forces of suppression were not disappointed. She delivered an impassioned plea for birth control, which included statistics on the high birth rate among the poverty-stricken and references to her experiences as a nurse with tragic East Side cases. She closed with a quotation from John Galsworthy's *Justice* (then playing on Broadway): "Your honor, back of every crime is life, palpitating life."

His honor, of course, found her guilty and gave her the choice of paying a one-hundred-dollar fine or spending fifteen days in the workhouse. Amid cheers and applause from the spectators, she chose the latter. For the first time in over a decade, she returned to jail for a much needed rest. Upon her release from the Queens County Jail, she was greeted by another large meeting at Carnegie Hall, this time announced as a "Birth Control Meeting To Welcome Emma Goldman from Prison."

During that summer Emma was busy with the Tom Mooney case, but she continued to discuss methods from the platform. In October she was arrested again in New York for handing out birth control information, but for once she was acquitted, partly because she was innocent of this particular charge and partly because she was defended ably by her counsel, Harry Weinberger, an energetic single taxer.

Earlier she had warned her followers that birth control was only a "small phase" of their total program. Now, in the early part of 1917, she turned her attention to other issues, justly feeling that she had done more than her part in the campaign. She had spread birth control ideas from one end of the country to the other, she had helped organize groups to carry on the propaganda, and she had gained the cause public attention through her arrests. She now felt content to leave the leadership to those who looked upon birth control as a panacea for every social problem.

5

Foremost among those who asserted the overriding importance of birth control was Margaret Sanger. Mrs. Sanger was also a registered nurse who had been shocked by her work among involuntary mothers in the same immigrant slum area where Emma had worked a decade and more earlier. A left wing Socialist, she was close to the anarchists working out of the *Mother Earth* offices. Indeed, Hutchins Hapgood recalled that in 1913 "I met Margaret Sanger . . . in Provincetown; a very pretty woman and at that time friend of Emma Goldman and other anarchists from whom she got her first ideas of birth control." Mrs. Sanger went abroad in 1913 to learn more about family limitation, asking the old French anarchist Victor Dave, among others, for help. On her return she published *Woman Rebel*, a venture in personal journalism along the same lines as *Mother Earth*. Emma's influence on Mrs. Sanger was indisputable. As one student of the movement has observed, "Margaret Sanger borrowed much from Emma Goldman and the anarchists in the terminology and theory of reform which characterized 'The Woman Rebel.'" As a matter of fact, in the first issue of *Woman Rebel* there was an extract from Emma's essay on "Love and Marriage" which urged the right of women not to have children, if they so decided, since they were not machines.

Arrested for the April, 1914, issue of her magazine, Mrs. Sanger fled to Europe to escape trial. In her absence her pamphlet *Family Limitation* (1914)—secretly printed by Bill Shatoff, an anarchist—was distributed publicly. After her return to the United States, she was supported by Emma and other radicals. By the time the government dropped its case against her, Mrs. Sanger had made of her birth control agitation a full-time occupation. Finally despairing of meaningful support from the "wives of the wage slaves," as she called them, she turned "to the women of wealth and intelligence" for help. With considerable ability she guided the movement into respectably conservative channels by emphasizing the need for legislation which would give doctors, and doctors only, the right to impart contraceptive information. Her name has since become almost synonymous with the struggle for birth control.

In setting forth her own accounts of these early years, Mrs. Sanger has ignored or minimized the role Emma played. In *My Fight for Birth Control*, published in 1931, Mrs. Sanger did not refer to Emma's activities—though this involved some awkwardness, as, for example, when she mentioned the arrest of Bolton Hall, Ida Rauh, and Jesse Ashley but failed to mention that they were arrested for distributing Emma's pamphlet, "Why and How the Poor Should Not Have Many Children," or that Emma was arrested for the same incident! In 1938 she referred in her *Autobiography* to the avid public interest in birth control in 1916 and to the attendant problem of preventing emotional "scatter-brains" from confusing the issue. In a chapter suggestively entitled, "Hear Me for My Cause," she wrote that "Emma Goldman and her campaign manager, Ben Reitman, belatedly advocated birth control, not to further it but strategically to utilize in their own program of anarchism the publicity value it had achieved."

To Margaret Sanger birth control was the very *Pivot of Civilization* (1923), as she entitled one of her books. Like the progressives of her day, she was preoccupied with a contrivance, a sort of contraceptive counterpart of a compounded Australian-ballot-direct-election-of-senators-initiative-and-referendum. Naturally she resented Emma Goldman's refusal to consider birth control a panacea; naturally she wished to de-emphasize the radical sources of the movement, once she began to make her primary appeal for support to the "women of wealth and intelligence." Almost equally understandable, given her single-minded commitment to "My Cause," was her disinclination to consider seriously the contributions of other leaders such as Emma Goldman, Mary Ware Dennett, a distinguished liberal, Dr. William J. Robinson, a pioneer medical exponent, or such earlier figures as Moses Harman. Nevertheless, however understandable, Mrs. Sanger's misstatements did a needless disservice to her own contributions to the campaign for planned parenthood.

6

On a number of counts, then, Emma Goldman was one of the significant women in the years before the First World War. She helped rout the worst of the lingering Victorian prudery and sanctimoniousness. She helped enlarge the range of choice open to women through her vigorous attacks on their objectification. She also effectively criticized those women who made a fetish of some one issue, such as suffrage or birth control. Her own views were provocative and her practice was much less wild than was commonly thought—first and foremost she was a motherly figure, not a libertine. In short, "the revolution in morals" of these years owed a good deal to her efforts.

Recognition of her significance for the feminist cause was not long deferred, though many soon tended to forget it. In 1922 the *Nation*, for instance, wanted to add her name to a list of the twelve greatest living women: "Emma Goldman is a great woman and an American despite the fact that we disagree with her about almost everything and that the house committee has stricken her from the rolls of this rather exclusive country club called the United States. As a publicist she makes Ida Tarbell seem inconsiderable." A decade later her name was on a list of the world's greatest women, compiled this time by John Haynes Holmes, beside those of Jane Addams, Annie Besant, Margaret Sanger, Mme

Curie, Helen Keller, and others. Two English writers also considered her one of the most remarkable women of the epoch. Margaret Goldsmith chose her as one of the *Seven Women against the World* (1935) and novelist Ethel Mannin dedicated her *Women and the Revolution* (1939) to Emma "because your whole life has been dedicated to the revolutionary cause, and because you are the greatest living woman revolutionary."

Such high praise, however, was hardly matched by the views of a majority of her contemporaries. It was especially far from the opinions of her adversaries in the government. To them she was simply the most dangerous Red at large.

PART FIVE

Red

If what I do displeases you, leave the place; war allows no free talking.

JULIUS CAESAR

Freedom of speech is always a liberty, but never a license.

J. EDGAR HOOVER

CHAPTER XIX

"MUNI! MUNI!": THE MOONEY
CASE, 1916

For almost a decade after Kersner's denaturalization in 1908 the stalemate in the struggle between the government and Emma Goldman was not effectively broken. Her stubborn refusal to go abroad reduced her enemies to methodically keeping her dossier up to date. On two occasions, however, the disappointment of interested officials lightened momentarily: Perhaps, they hoped, a case could be made that she was implicated in or at least had advocated acts of violence.

It seemed clearly incriminating that she refused to turn against the McNamara brothers who had confessed dynamiting the Los Angeles *Times* in 1910. Yet her refusal to join in the condemnation of the dynamiters was based on her conviction that this tragic affair was merely another manifestation of the principle that employer violence inevitably begets labor violence. Nothing at all could be done to tie her directly to the McNamaras, who were militant but essentially conservative Roman Catholic trade-unionists—they had no more radical affiliations than their membership in the American Federation of Labor. Her only indirect connection with the affair was through her friendship for Matthew Schmidt and David Caplan, both of whom were indicted with the McNamaras. After Schmidt came out of hiding in 1914, Emma invited him to her flat one afternoon to visit with Lincoln Steffens, Hutchins Hapgood, Berkman, and others. A certain Donald Vose, whom Emma had taken into her home on the strength of her friendship for his mother, came in while they were talking and was introduced to Schmidt. A few days later Schmidt was arrested. Emma then learned that Vose had been hired by detective William J. Burns to spy on her in an attempt to locate Schmidt. Sickened by the fact that she had housed such an informer, she wrote a denunciation of "Donald Vose: The Accursed," which appeared in *Mother Earth*, January, 1916. It was this article which Attorney-General Mitchell Palmer later used to contend that Emma was implicated in the Los Angeles bombing.

Palmer had slightly more grounds for claiming that the July, 1914, issue of *Mother Earth* showed that Emma had advocated violence. This issue of her magazine was dedicated "to our martyred dead," Arthur Caron, Charles Berg, and Carl Hanson. The three had lost their lives in a Fourth of July explosion in a crowded tenement house on Lexington Avenue in New York. Either a bomb had been placed in the apartment belonging to Louise Berger, one of the *Mother Earth* group, or the three men staying there were destroyed by the premature explosion of a bomb of their own which they intended to use in their fight against the Rockefellers.[1] Which of these two possibilities it was will probably never be known.

Emma was on tour in the West when she received the July issue of her magazine. She was dismayed, for it was "filled with prattle about force and dynamite." One article in particular excited her ire. Charles Robert Plunkett, a writer she had never heard of, stated wildly that "as for me, I am for violence. Not only defensive violence, but offensive violence." Plunkett found dynamite the answer to about everything: "They have guns, they have cannon, they have soldiers, they have discipline, they have armies—and we have dynamite. To oppression, to tyranny, to jails, clubs, guns, and navies, there is but one reply: dynamite!" Almost wishing that Plunkett had been consumed by his own inflammatory words, Emma wanted to throw the entire issue into the fire. The magazine was already in the hands of its subscribers, however, and her bitterness was not decreased by the reflection that Berkman, who was in charge of the magazine during her absences, was directly responsible for the inclusion of such explosive material. As the publisher of *Mother Earth*, she was formally responsible. Besides, no matter what the pressures, it was unthinkable that she would ever try to shift any of the responsibility to her old friend.

Nevertheless, in the end these attempts by federal officeholders to tie her directly to outbreaks of violence failed for lack of real evidence. Then, as if their frustration had finally mated with irony, surprised federal officials found themselves on the same side with Emma and Berkman in opposing California's drive to execute Tom Mooney.

2

On July 22, 1916, a bomb went off during a Preparedness Day parade in San Francisco. Eight persons were killed and forty wounded. De-

[1] The explosion occurred shortly after the Ludlow massacre in Colorado, Upton Sinclair's "mourning parade"—in which Caron participated—before Rockefeller's offices on 26 Broadway, and the free-speech fight at Tarrytown, where Rockefeller had his home.

MONSTER ANTI - MILITARY
MASS MEETING

SUNDAY NIGHT, MAY 3
At East Turner Hall, 2132 Arapahoe St.

ADMISSION FREE

To Protest Against the Outrages committed upon the Working Class of Colorado by the Thugs and State Hirelings; Against the Importation of Federal Troops, and Against this country's War with Mexico.

WORKINGMEN REMEMBER

Whenever a country has gone to War the Workingmen and Women have always been the losers, and whenever Federal Soldiers have Invaded a Strike Region, Workers Have been KILLED and the Strike has been LOST.

DON'T BE FOOLED

Come All Who Are Against Exploitation and Murder

SPEAKERS

EMMA GOLDMAN   S. MEYERS and Others

DR. BEN R. REITMAN, Chairman
Anti-Militarist League of Denver

NOTE—Emma Goldman will deliver a Series of Lectures on the Revolutionary Significance of the Modern Drama, from May 4 to 9, at 8:00 p.m., in Building Trades Club Hall, 1749 Arapahoe Street.

Farewell
to America !

Emma
Goldman

SPEAKS FOR THE
LAST TIME BEFORE
HER RETURN TO EXILE

Thursday, April 26
1934, at 8:00 p.m.

•

WEBSTER HALL
119 East 11th Street
New York City

•

"The Decay of
German Culture"

Chairman: ROGER N. BALDWIN
Auspices: Libertarian Workers Committee

ADMISSION 35 CENTS
TICKETS AT BOX OFFICE

As the shadows of the conflict in Europe glided toward America, Emma braced herself to speak against war "so long as my voice will last." At this Denver meeting in 1916, she condemned preparedness, Pershing's chase into Mexico after Villa, and the use of federal troops in Colorado's bloody labor disputes. (*Labadie Collection, University of Michigan Library.*)

Two decades later she was still speaking out against war. The terms under which she was permitted a brief visit to the United States, however, forced her to voice her opposition under the guise of discussing the literary plight of Hitler's Germany. (*Labadie Collection, University of Michigan Library.*)

A prison "mug shot" and identification card of Leon Czolgosz, dated one month before his execution for the assassination of President McKinley.

Alexander Berkman, Emma Goldman, and their police escort at the time of their return from federal prison, September, 1919. Uncle Sam, pointing from the poster in the background, was obviously not through with them. (*Culver Service.*)

Emma, with her dapper attorney, Harry Weinberger, in December, 1919, on her way to Ellis Island to be banished from the Promised Land. (*Toronto Star.*)

"The Sailing of the Buford," from the *Liberator*, February, 1920.

tective Martin Swanson, retained by capitalists interested in the city's utilities, helped pin the crime on Thomas J. Mooney, a "troublesome factor," as he was called, in Bay Area labor disputes, and on Warren Billings, a minor labor organizer. District Attorney Charles Fickert, who had refused to prosecute graft charges against the President of United Railways, was more than willing to prosecute Mooney, the enemy of United Railways. Mooney and Billings were arrested, without warrants, on July 26. (Two days earlier a fund of $400,000 had been raised by members of a "Law and Order Committee" to rid the community of "anarchistic elements.") "Private" detective Swanson took charge of the investigation, directing the work of public law enforcement agencies. Swanson also let it be known that he was going to "get" Alexander Berkman—according to one witness, he vowed to hang Berkman along with Mooney.

As it happened, both Berkman and Emma Goldman were in San Francisco at the time. Berkman had come out West to publish and edit the Blast, a radical labor weekly. Emma was in San Francisco for a series of lectures. One of them, on "Preparedness," was originally scheduled for July 20, but, when she learned of another antipreparedness lecture on the same evening, she deferred her talk until the twenty-second. Exceedingly fortunate was this change, for if she had given her lecture before the parade, she almost unquestionably would have been held responsible for the tragedy.

As it was, both she and Berkman were in danger. Six days after the explosion the police forebodingly informed the San Francisco Examiner (July 28) that correspondence found in the home of Edward C. Nolan, who was arrested with Mooney and Billings, showed he was "identified" with Emma Goldman's activities. This misinformation was a faint indication of the profound duplicity of the police and of the fantastic lengths to which they would go in their efforts to connect Emma with the bombing—it later developed that Emma's correspondence with Nolan was merely to the effect that she was coming to San Francisco to deliver some lectures on art! District Attorney Fickert also let it be known that he saw "Berkman's hand in the bombing" and that he was considering a move "to take into custody every Red of any prominence in San Francisco." A frame-up was indeed under way.

To make matters worse, liberals and trade-unionists, still stinging from the confession of the McNamaras, were prepared to leave Mooney and Billings to the care of Swanson, Fickert, and the "Law and Order Committee." Just as they had assumed without question in 1910 that the McNamaras were innocent, now almost the entire left assumed that Mooney and Billings were guilty. Even Fremont Older, a normally staunch civil libertarian, abandoned his ideals and expressed the general sentiment toward Mooney: "Let the son of a bitch hang," he exclaimed.[2] Berkman and Emma were virtually the only radicals prepared to speak for the accused men. Had they believed Mooney and Billings guilty, they still would have tried to make sure the two men had adequate defense. As it was, Berkman, who knew both men well, was convinced of their innocence. He and Emma immediately began efforts to help them.

As a start, Berkman fought in the columns of his *Blast* against the hysteria which threatened to annihilate the accused men and possibly others as well. He prevailed upon his friend Bob Minor to come to San Francisco and devote his considerable artistic talents to the cause. Official recognition of the impact of the magazine soon came in the form of a raid on its offices. The raiders had a search warrant, but they gave no receipt for the mass of documents, subscription lists, and other materials which they seized; they filed no return on the warrant until compelled to do so during Mooney's trial.

Berkman, Emma, Minor, and M. Eleanor Fitzgerald, Berkman's companion, organized the first Mooney-Billings Defense Committee. After some weeks of frustrating effort, working constantly against the supine acquiescence of liberals, the committee fanned a spark of interest in the case among western radicals and trade-unionists.

In the meantime, Berkman asked Emma to find a prominent, able attorney who would defend Mooney. She reluctantly interrupted her vacation in Provincetown, where she had gone for a month's rest, to make a personal appeal to her friend Frank P. Walsh, who was then in charge of Wilson's New York campaign headquarters. Walsh was sympathetic and interested, but his overriding concern at the moment was to work for the man who had kept America out of the war. Declining with regret, Walsh assured Emma that it was the first duty of all liberal-minded and peace-loving persons to re-elect Woodrow Wilson.[3]

Where Emma had failed, Berkman succeeded. Intent upon securing a competent lawyer, Berkman traveled across the country, interest-

---

[2] Older soon regained his balance and worked selflessly to have Mooney freed. He wrote Emma in 1931 that for fifteen years he had been "doing amends" for his initial blindness in the Mooney case.

[3] Walsh too, by the way, later gave generously of his time and talents to help the imprisoned Mooney. But by then two things had happened: (1) Wilson had become the peace-loving war-President; (2) Mooney had almost lost his life and had lost his freedom.

ing unions in the case on his way. In New York he sought out W. Bourke Cockran, the highly paid and well-known Tammany lawyer and Democratic party orator. Cockran was so impressed by Berkman's eloquent description of the conspiracy against Mooney that he offered to take the case without pay. While in the East, Berkman also managed to rouse the interest and support of radicals and Jewish labor unions.

Thus Berkman, with Emma's help, set in motion a nationwide campaign in Mooney's behalf. Years later, when the latter's defense had been taken over by the Communists, Berkman's extraordinary achievement was consciously ignored in the presentation of the history of the struggle. Mooney apologetically wrote Berkman that a contemporary Communist-written account of his case did not "do justice to you and your comrade—the reason is—their [the Communists'] hatred of both of you. . . ." Notwithstanding this familiar effort to rewrite the past, Berkman clearly played a role second to no one. Primarily because of his tireless agitation, Mooney had competent legal defense, some funds, and a measure of radical, labor, and liberal support—support "in those early days," as Mooney appreciatively wrote, "when the going was tough."

3

Alas, all this was not enough. On February 7, 1917, Mooney was convicted and sentenced to hang. That the verdict flew in the face of perjured testimony and transparent official persecution made little difference. After all, the $400,000 fund raised by the "Law and Order Committee" did some testifying in its own right. Mooney was to die.

And Fickert was now free to proceed against other "Reds." In his "Brief of the People of the State of California," written for the United States Commission on Mediation, he flatly asserted that Emma Goldman's connection with the explosion was indisputable: since "Emma Goldman, the anarchistic leader in the United States," was visiting San Francisco, "it cannot possibly be doubted but that Mooney and his associates, added to their general motive of being desirous of stopping the Preparedness Day Parade, had the further motive of being desirous of showing to their leader and champion the boldness and fearlessness of her followers here in San Francisco." Moreover, the close friendship of Emma and Berkman was a "matter of common notoriety"; and "we have shown the intimate relations of Thomas J. Mooney and Alexander Berkman in matters pertaining to anarchy." Perhaps Fickert realized, however, that such evidence would hardly have convinced a lynch mob, for he did not pursue this tack. Instead, he merely used Emma Goldman's name in his prosecution of the case against Israel Weinberg, another defendant. Weinberg was asked these questions before the grand jury:

Q.—Do you know Emma Goldman?

A.—Yes, sir, I have seen her.

Q.—You have received letters from her?

A.—I didn't receive any letters from Emma Goldman.

Q.—You didn't see a letter written to Mr. Nolan by Emma Goldman stating she would be in the city at this time?

A.—No.

As the United States Commission on Law Observance and Enforcement later observed, "the unfairness of this line of questioning lies in the fact that public opinion had been aroused at this time against radicalism, and especially against the doctrines of Emma Goldman and Alexander Berkman."

Fickert was much more serious about trying Berkman. At the time of Mooney's trial, he commenced a series of "leaks" to the press: (1) San Francisco *Chronicle*, January 1, 1917: "The office of the 'Blast,' said Fickert, is the place where the bomb-plot was hatched." (2) *Chronicle*, January 7: Assistant District Attorney Cunha said he would attempt to prove that Berkman and Fitzgerald plotted in 1914 to blow up the home of John D. Rockefeller in Tarrytown. (3) *Chronicle*, January 8: Fickert charged that Berkman bribed a member of the Industrial Relations Committee to color its report. (4) *Chronicle*, January 10: Fickert charged that Berkman was the real power behind the defense. The District Attorney circulated such charges while Mooney's jury was being drawn. The following July, after Mooney had been convicted, Fickert secured a grand jury indictment of Berkman for murder. Fortunately for the latter, he was in New York's Tombs, awaiting an appeal of his and Emma's conviction for conspiring against registration.

Given the atmosphere in San Francisco, Emma immediately sensed that Berkman's extradition would mean almost certain death. She and M. Eleanor Fitzgerald quickly organized a publicity committee to oppose Fickert's plan. Emma and her co-workers secured the support of the United Hebrew Trades, the Amalgamated Clothing Workers, the Furriers, the Bookbinders, and other unions. Their efforts were responsible for the numerous petitions against the extradition which streamed into the Department of Justice. Next the committee laid plans to send a large delegation of labor leaders to Albany to protest to Governor Whitman against Berkman's removal to California.

When the delegation waited on Governor Whitman in October, he assured it that he would study the case thoroughly before taking any action. While the extent of Berkman's popular support was important, the decisive influence on the Governor probably came from Washington. Berkman later wrote that Wilson intervened personally by sending Colonel House to Albany. Whether or not Berkman was correct, House very likely did communicate in one way or another with Whitman—that the administration interest in the entire Mooney affair was high was revealed by a confidential memorandum House sent Wilson a few weeks earlier. The upshot, in any event, was that Whitman refused to act until he had an opportunity to see the minutes of the grand jury which indicted Berkman.

Fickert was nonplused by this unexpected development. To cover his retreat he announced that he would leave "the Berkman matter alone" for the present. He was understandably reluctant to send Whitman the grand jury minutes, for they showed that the San Francisco prosecutor had nothing more to go on than his immeasurable vindictiveness. Had he been of a mind to continue in spite of this, he would have been stopped by the request of the United States Attorney in New York that Berkman be kept in the East until certain federal proceedings against him were decided by the courts.

4

By this time, to the consternation of Fickert and other California authorities, the Mooney case had become an international scandal. As the Mediation Commission, which was itself created largely in response to international protests, reported to Wilson (in January, 1918), "it is now well known that the attention of the situation in the East was first aroused through meetings of protest against Mooney's conviction in Russia. From Russia and the Western States protest spread to the entire country. . . ." How this came about was the most fascinating part of the story.

Through an odd coincidence, Lincoln Steffens was talking to Ambassador David Francis in the American Embassy in Petrograd one day, when they were startled to hear a chanting mob outside. Going to the front door, Francis stood there mystified by roar after roar of "Muni! Muni!" A newspaperman present finally guessed that the Russians were protesting the conviction of Mooney in California, half a world away. The crowd, according to Steffens, accepted Francis' assurance that he would report the matter to his government.

Such demonstrations, which occurred a number of times in Petrograd and Kronstadt in 1917 and early 1918, were answers to messages sent to Russia by Berkman and Emma Goldman. They gave returning refugees the task of arousing Russian workers to demonstrate against the California frame-up. Despite the wartime censorship, they also managed to cable instructions directly to Russian comrades. Thus, when Fickert proposed to extradite Berkman, Emma and the committee cabled that "Uncle is sick of the same disease as Tom. Tell friends." The cable slipped by the censors, and the demonstrators subsequently chanted Berkman's name as well as Mooney's.

President Wilson learned of the protests, of course, through Ambassador Francis. To make sure he felt their full weight, Berkman suggested to Emma that she send Ed Morgan, a wobbly friend, to Washington to increase interest in the case. Emma complied, though she was skeptical that one man could do much. She was quite wrong. Morgan accomplished wonders, peppering Wilson's favorite papers with news items about the demonstrations and then arousing the sympathies of influential officials through detailed accounts of the actions of Fickert, Swanson, and Company. This publicity campaign was just well started when Wilson proposed a thorough investigation of the whole affair; he appointed the United States Mediation Commission to make the inquiry.

The Mediation Commission's findings prompted Wilson to ask Governor William D. Stephens of California (January 22, 1918) that Mooney's execution be postponed until he could be tried on one of his other indictments. "I urge this very respectfully indeed," wired Wilson, "but very earnestly, because the case has assumed international importance. . . ."

At about this point the Kronstadt sailors staged another mass demonstration before the American Embassy in Petrograd. Through their interpreter, Louise Berger, a close friend of Berkman and Emma, the sailors announced their determination to hold Francis as a hostage until Mooney, Berkman, and the other accused men were freed. Francis, in the presence of the demonstrators, cabled Washington and reportedly promised to work for the release of the labor men.

A short while later (March 27), Wilson telegraphed Governor Stephens that he hoped Mooney's sentence would be commuted, for it would have a "heartfelt effect upon certain international affairs." Stephens still refused to act. Then (June 4), Wilson made a final appeal for the commutation of Mooney's sentence: " I would not venture again to call your attention to this case," Wilson begged Stephens to believe, "did I not know the international significance which is attached to it."

Only after a second federal investigation turned up further grave irregularities in Fickert's conduct did Stephens belatedly comply with Wilson's requests. In his statement (November 28), Stephens angrily held that Berkman was responsible for all the international agitation for Mooney: ". . . the propaganda in his behalf following the plan outlined by Berkman has been so effective as to become world-wide." Reluctantly or rather protestingly, as though he were being cheated of his due pound of flesh, Stephens signed the commutation of Mooney's sentence. Official cowardice, cruelty, and stupidity were to keep Mooney behind bars for another twenty-one years, but those who thirsted for his death were denied their ultimate pleasure.

Yet Governor Stephens was right about one thing: it was Berkman, with Emma's help, who was largely responsible for the international demonstrations which saved Mooney's life. A quarter of a century earlier Berkman and Emma Goldman—through misguided idealism—had very nearly taken Frick's life. Now—through well-directed idealism—they helped save Mooney's life. After all the debits and credits were entered, the books showed a decided balance in their favor.

CHAPTER XX

1917

The story has often been told how one day the American people elected as President the man who had "kept us out of war" and how a few months later this man pledged himself to use "Force, Force to the utmost, Force without stint or limit." Wilson's war message to Congress on April 2, 1917, mocked Emma's friend Frank P. Walsh and all the other liberals, pacifists, and radicals who had labored mightily to keep the "militarist" Charles Evans Hughes out of the White House. Although Wilson led the Americans into the roaring conflict on the high plane of a Crusade for Democracy, the hideous carnage had all the symptoms of disastrous militarism. Wallowing about day after day in the deep mud of the interminable trenches or making their way hopelessly through the barbed wire entanglements, men killed each other with rifles, machine guns, artillery, poison gas. For many of those who did not become part of the acres of stinking, bloated corpses, there were the ambulance units, the base hospitals, and then perhaps the poppy fields. Even the survivors did not escape unscathed: the moral exaltation of the early stages of the war was followed by disillusionment and immeasurable spiritual damage.

It was a bitter truth that many of the most conspicuous crusaders for this unutterable futility were Progressives. Earlier, in his important book on *The Promise of American Life* (1909), Herbert Croly had frankly accepted war as a "justifiable engine" of national policy. He was heartily in favor of a state distressingly similar to that which Mussolini later established. To Croly it was axiomatic that the individual's primary responsibility was to the state, not to himself: "individuals should enjoy as much freedom from restraint, as much opportunity, and as much responsibility as is necessary for the performance of their work." Who was to decide the necessary amount of freedom for the individual? The state. Acting in response to such reasoning, the Progressive party platform of 1916 contained a plank calling for universal military training. On the eve of the war, Croly, now a member of the influential

New Republic group, frankly proposed that "the American nation needs the tonic of a serious moral adventure."[1]

Few were more aware than Wilson of the seriousness of the moral adventure on which Americans embarked in that tense spring of 1917. The long night before he delivered his message to Congress, Wilson sat up with the remains of his New Freedom. To Frank Cobb of the New York World he prophetically observed: "Once lead this people into war and they'll forget there ever was such a thing as tolerance. To fight you must be brutal and ruthless, and the spirit of ruthless brutality will enter into the very fibre of our national life, infecting Congress, the courts, the policeman on the beat, the man in the street." Wilson should have added to this list the Chief Executive and his departments, agencies, bureaus, for as he put it in his Flag Day Address of June 14, 1917, "woe to the man or group of men that seeks to stand in our way in this day of high resolution."[2] Woe indeed.

The pity of it was that the entry of the United States into the conflict effectively silenced the humming intellectual and artistic activity of the time. Wilson—the earlier Wilson—was himself an authority on the pity of it, for he had said that American entrance in the war would be a world calamity. Only a few were able to retain such a conviction after the war virus became epidemic. One was Randolph Bourne, once a Progressive and always a searcher for the American promise. Bourne repudiated the hopelessly muddled progressive past with his despairing cry: "War is the health of the state." Wilson, the supreme leader of a People's War, saw in the state an organ of freedom; Bourne lifted the veils from the face of this great friend of the Progressives and saw nothing of the sort: "The State is intimately connected with war, for it is the organization of the collective community when it acts in a political manner, and to act in a political manner towards a rival group has meant, throughout all history—war."

[1] By the 1920's Croly had penitently reversed his field by taking the "redemption of the individual" as his point of departure. By then it was a little late—though perhaps not too late.

[2] Before long, Attorney-General Gregory called for God to have mercy on the opponents of the war, "for they need expect none from an outraged people and an avenging Government." But the rush to embrace a police state was bipartisan. In the summer of 1917, Theodore Roosevelt demanded "one allegiance, one flag, one language" and urged "vigorous police action against orators preaching veiled treason on street corners and elsewhere." On August 15, 1917, Elihu Root warned the Union League Club in New York that "there are men walking about the streets of this city who ought to be taken out at sunrise tomorrow and shot for treason." See Horace C. Peterson and Gilbert Fite, Opponents of War (Madison: University of Wisconsin Press, 1957), passim.

2

Emma Goldman also continued to look upon American entry in the war as a great calamity. Early in 1917 she gave up her work for birth control to devote most of her time to antiwar agitation. In March she informed "Promoters of the War Mania" that "I for one will speak against war so long as my voice will last, now and during war." This assurance had hardly more than reached *Mother Earth* subscribers before the United States formally declared war on Germany.

To Emma and her friends, Wilson's advocacy of conscription was the ultimate affront to the individual conscience. Here was an almost unbelievable regimentation of individuals by the state. She simply could not understand how liberals could in one breath denounce Prussian militarism and in the next propose conscription. Along with Berkman, Fitzgerald, and Leonard Abbott, she organized a No-Conscription League in early May. As a woman not subject to the draft and further as an anarchist who believed that everyone should follow the dictates of his own conscience, she did not feel that she could advise individuals to refuse service. Yet she was determined to stand by those who did so refuse. The No-Conscription League was formed primarily to protect such objectors.

As a first step against conscription, the league scheduled a protest meeting to be held at the Harlem River Casino on May 18. Some eight thousand people, watched over by a hundred policemen, went to hear Leonard Abbott, Harry Weinberger, Louis Fraina, Berkman, and Emma denounce forced military service. Some members of the armed forces present made a number of attempts to interrupt the talks. One was so objectionable that the audience threatened to remove him, but Emma insisted that he be given an opportunity to speak his mind. Confused by this turn of events, the soldier muttered something about "German money" and retreated with his comrades. Although Emma reassured her audience that there was no kaiser money behind the meeting, the next day the New York *Times* skeptically reported "many Germans in the audience" and remarked on the two police stenographers who recorded every word uttered at this "wild anti-conscription meeting."

Undoubtedly the No-Conscription League became the nerve center of the resistance to the draft. During the four weeks after the Harlem River Casino meeting, the league was engaged in a whirl of activities. Chapters were organized in other cities. Youths streamed in and out of Emma's office seeking advice. In a remarkably short time the league circulated 100,000 anticonscription manifestoes.

At the next major meeting, which took place in Hunt's Point Palace on June 4, Emma's quick thinking and courage probably prevented a mass tragedy. Soldiers and sailors showered the platform with light bulbs. A riot threatened when a serviceman proposed to rush the platform. Running to the speaker's stand, Emma warned the audience that the soldiers and sailors had been sent there to cause trouble and that the police were in league with them. She succeeded in quieting her hearers and had them file out without mishap. The seriousness of the situation was undeniable: there were almost 5,000 persons inside the hall, at least 15,000 outside on Southern Boulevard and 163d Street, and battalions of police and police reserves stationed nearby. Emma's actions on this occasion gave point to Leonard Abbott's remark that the way she and Berkman "faced the war fury of 1917 was the most stirring manifestation of sheer physical courage that I have ever seen."

At a final meeting, in Forward Hall on June 14, there was a capacity crowd and lively interest in resistance to conscription. At the close of the meeting, however, all youths who could not produce registration cards were arrested. Once Emma and Berkman realized that the authorities used their meetings to trap young men who had not registered, they decided to concentrate on written propaganda. But time had almost run out for any show of resistance to the war and conscription.

3

Hands of stern repression were preparing to crush all dissent. After the first of the large anticonscription meetings, United States Attorney H. Snowden Marshall of New York recommended to the Attorney-General that draft opponents be treated summarily: "I believe that an exhibition of force at the outset will have a salutary effect upon all those who contemplate resistance. . . ." Of exactly the same opinion, federal Marshal Thomas McCarthy informed the New York Times on June 12 that "I will arrest this Goldman woman if she organizes more meetings." In truth, McCarthy's boisterous enthusiasm almost upset the government's case against Emma and Berkman, for his superiors desired shorthand accounts of several meetings before she was arrested. Authorities in Washington sharply reprimanded McCarthy and bade him to be patient. The buoyant Marshal did not have long to wait, however, for on June 15 he received orders to arrest the anarchists.

He bounded up the stairway leading to the *Mother Earth* and *Blast* offices—Berkman had moved his magazine from San Francisco to New York—and breathlessly informed Emma that she and Berkman were under arrest. In response to her request to see his warrant, McCarthy brusquely replied that none was needed. While the good Marshal may well have had a warrant for their arrest, it is very unlikely that he had any warrant for the unreasonable search and seizure of their personal property which followed. He and the seven deputies in his raiding party turned the offices almost literally upside down, throwing correspondence, books, pamphlets, and other personal possessions in a huge pile on the floor. Emma lost manuscripts, her lectures, subscription lists, correspondence files. All told, the raiders made off with a "wagon load" of materials, the New York *Times* (June 16) noted with satisfaction; especially pleasing was "a splendidly kept card index" of "Reds" which would simplify the work of the secret service. No mention was made of the Fourth Amendment in this list of seized items.

Emma barely had time to change her dress and pick up a book—she decided that James Joyce's *Portrait of the Artist as a Young Man* would be appropriate prison fare—before the impetuous Marshal rushed her and Berkman through the crowded streets to the Federal Building. Mildly reproached by Emma for breaking speed regulations and endangering lives, McCarthy merely replied impatiently: "I represent the United States Government." Not by chance they arrived at the Federal Building after the closing hour; they were, as Emma anticipated, ordered to the Tombs for the night.

The next morning she and Berkman were brought before United States Commissioner Samuel W. Hitchcock. They were charged—under statutes enacted during the Civil War and a provision of the Draft Act of May 18, 1917—with having formed a "conspiracy to induce persons not to register." Assistant United States Attorney Harold A. Content demanded high bail and the Commissioner obliged by fixing the bonds of Emma and Berkman at $25,000 each. Harry Weinberger, their lawyer, futilely protested that this amount was unreasonable.

Weinberger and Fitzgerald organized a drive to raise the entire $50,000. Friends in New York contributed substantial sums. Agnes Inglis telegraphed from Detroit that she would send five thousand dollars as soon as she could; she ran into difficulty, however, for, when she tried to cash some liberty bonds, her banker insisted on knowing whether the money was to be used in the "interest of the country for constructive service." Emma's sister Helena, whose son was soon to enlist in the army, sent a sizable contribution. But for the most part the money came in small amounts from persons scattered throughout the country.

By June 21, the day Emma and Berkman were indicted by a federal grand jury and arraigned before Judge Julius Mayer, $25,000 in cash had been raised. Weinberger again vainly pleaded for a reduction of bail. He referred to the refusal of the National Surety Company to post bond on $120,000 in securities and to the refusal of Assistant United States Attorney Content to accept Brooklyn real estate as security. Declaring that he did not care to be informed of the activities of surety companies, Judge Mayer continued the bonds at their original figures. Since Berkman refused to be bailed out first, the cash was posted for Emma. Not until June 25, two days before their trial was scheduled to commence, was Berkman's bond raised.

Now by almost any standards the government required excessive bail. While the Eighth Amendment probably did not technically protect Emma Goldman, since Kersner's denaturalization presumably made her an alien, the required bail was no less excessive. Government officials clearly intended to set the bonds so high that neither defendant could go free on bail. Their virtual inability to raise the exorbitant sum and the probability that a much smaller amount would have guaranteed their appearance aroused no feeling of fair play among the authorities.

Thus did the war between Emma and the government get entangled in the larger war to save the world for democracy. Emma herself had no illusion about the outcome of her trial. On June 26 she wrote Agnes Inglis that she and Berkman were "as good as convicted now." In this frame of mind she went into court the following day, which happened to be her forty-eighth birthday.

CHAPTER XXI

THE UNITED STATES V. GOLDMAN-BERKMAN

The proceedings began on an incongruous note. Emma argued that since she and Berkman had been imprisoned to within a few days of their trial and that since Berkman had also suffered a painful leg injury, a postponement was imperative. Judge Mayer denied her motion. Therewith she informed him that the defendants refused to take any further part in the trial. Surprised, Mayer retaliated by announcing that the court would appoint a defense counsel. Realizing that participation of some sort was inevitable, Emma and Berkman determined to defend themselves. Harry Weinberger continued to advise them on the legal aspects of their defense.

When the spectators filed back into the courtroom after the noon recess, they were greeted by the curious spectacle of the two leading anarchists in the country engaged in legal tilts with Attorney Content and Judge Mayer. According to Margaret Anderson, "they were charming in court. E. G. was the earnest preacher rather than the fiery fighter and extremely effective. Berkman was uncontrollably temperamental. He even provoked the judge into displays of temper and fought him man to man in a way the latter seemed to like far better than E. G.'s controlled reasonableness."

It took three days to seat a jury. The two defendants submitted each venireman to an extended inquiry designed to reveal some of the broader social issues involved in the trial. "Do you believe in free speech?" Berkman asked prospective jurymen. "Do you believe in the right to criticize laws?" "Do you believe that the majority is necessarily right?" Emma followed by asking them if her views on birth control, marriage, and sex enlightenment of the young would prejudice them against her. The jury which was finally impaneled included a perfumer as foreman, a jeweler, a florist, a vice-president of a business firm, a real estate dealer, two salesmen, two contractors, a secretary, and two unlisted. It was obviously predominantly representative of business and white collar interests; the names of the jurors indicated they were predominantly from Anglo-Saxon stock. No artist or longshoreman, no intellectual or trade-unionist, was on the jury. Aside from the waves of nationalism which were sweeping the country, the background of the jurors indicated an ingrained hostility to the causes which Berkman and Emma represented. The most the defendants could hope for was an independent individual who had the courage to stand out against his fellows—one such as the editors of the *Masses* had later, when a member of their jury informed his colleagues that he would hold for the editors "till hell freezes over."

Assistant United States Attorney Content commenced the case for the prosecution on July 2. The major part of his presentation was absurdly irrelevant to the crime for which Emma and Berkman were indicted. He tried to show (1) that they had misused funds contributed to the No-Conscription League, (2) that by implication they had accepted German money in support of their activities, (3) that they had advocated violence at the Harlem River Casino meeting on May 18, and finally (4) that they had conspired to prevent registration.

Content found it impossible to prove that Emma and Berkman were pseudo-idealists who had made agitation a lucrative business. At the close of the trial the combined bank deposits of Emma and Berkman amounted to $746.96, hardly a handsome fortune for thirty years of effort. Content got no further with this charge than a rather petty criticism of Berkman's method of accounting for contributions and some rather cheap reflections on the honesty of his two opponents.

He was no more successful with his next line of attack. On June 29 the New York *Times* had reported that Content intended to question Emma about a mysterious bank deposit of $3,067 which she had made three days before the trial began; in view of the reports of German money behind the agitation, Content let it be known that he was particularly interested in this matter. Now he inquired about the source of the money. Octogenarian James Hallbeck was called to the stand by the defense. He related that he had walked into the *Mother Earth* office one day and handed Emma a check for 3,000.[1] A California vineyard-owner and an anarchist since the Haymarket executions, Hallbeck was born in Sweden, not Germany. His testimony effectively quashed Content's attempt to taint Emma and Berkman with German money.

[1] There is no discrepancy between the discussion of this deposit and the preceding paragraph where the bank balance of the two defendants at the end of the trial is set forth. This $3,000 contribution and others of a smaller amount were expended for their defense.

Much of the government's case was devoted to establishing the proposition that Emma and Berkman advocated violence. Content's key witness was William H. Randolph, a police stenographer. The latter continued to maintain that Emma had declared at the Harlem River Casino meeting that "we believe in violence and we will use violence." Other prosecution witnesses corroborated Randolph's testimony. One of Content's expert witnesses, however, a stenographer named Charles Pickler, informed the court that Randolph's testimony was "perfectly absurd": it was unbelievable that Randolph, who could take only a little over a hundred words of shorthand per minute under the best of conditions, could stand on a table twenty feet from the speakers' stand and take down Emma's rapid delivery. Exasperated by this unexpected testimony, Content requested that the jury be instructed that Pickler was a defense and not a government witness. (Earlier he had excused Randolph for missing the name of Senator La Follette in Emma's speech on the ground that "La Follette is not an American name"!) Paul Munter, who had taken Emma's drama lectures in shorthand, testified that she lectured on the average of one hundred and eighty words a minute. John Reed, Lincoln Steffens, Anna Sloan, Leonard Abbott, Bolton Hall, and a number of other witnesses who had known Emma for years testified that they had never heard her advocate violence. Moreover, there were other reasons for doubting the credibility of Randolph's testimony: (1) in court he was unable to keep up with her when she read some passages from her speech; (2) under cross-examination he claimed that he was "not at all" prejudiced against the defendants; and (3) he testified that Emma made a statement which would have been completely out of character. Nevertheless, Content did not lose this round, for he countered by reading from the Lexington explosion issue (July, 1914) of *Mother Earth*. A few choice passages on dynamite from the fulminations of such writers as Charles Plunkett were enough to convince the jury that, irrespective of whether she had urged violence in a particular speech, she did in fact advocate violence.

After all this, there was surprisingly little effort to try Emma and Berkman on the charge for which they had been indicted. Randolph testified that Emma had said, "we are going to support the men who will refuse to register and who will refuse to fight." The defense maintained that Emma had said nothing about registration, but had offered the support of the league to those who refused to be conscripted. Emma and Berkman attempted to distinguish sharply between conscription and registration, support and advice, but their efforts revealed hardly more than an underlying equivocation. Undoubtedly they both did everything within their power to oppose compulsory military service, though they may have tried to stay within the law by opposing conscription rather than registration as such. Berkman made a point, however, when he cogently ridiculed the legalistic notion that they who had publicly opposed militarism for thirty years could be said to have "conspired" against the draft.

The outcome of the trial, whatever the arguments, was never in serious doubt. As though the jurors were not already suffering from acute nationalism, Content and his associates missed no chance to play on their inflamed emotions. Much emphasis was placed on the issue of the defendants' belief in violence, though even Content must have been aware that—as Judge Mayer later said—the testimony "about violence was not germane to the case." On at least two occasions everyone, with the exception of the defendants, was compelled to rise when strains from "The Star-Spangled Banner" floated up into the courtroom from a liberty bond band playing in the street outside. Those who did not stand were forcibly ejected from the courtroom. As a final addition to all the extraneous prejudicial matter, Content implied in his address to the jury that Emma had said in 1901 that McKinley ought to be shot.

Passages of Emma Goldman's final summary fully equaled Gene Debs's famous speech a year later in the Cleveland federal court. Taking up the matter of violence, she reaffirmed her belief that "an act of political violence at the bottom is the culminating result of organized violence at the top." The jurors might just as well believe that Jesus advocated prostitution when he defended Mary Magdalene, she declared, as to believe that she advocated violence when she defended the political criminal. Anticipating Debs's moving "while there is a soul in prison, I am not free," Emma cast her lot with the victims of society: "I refuse to cast the stone at the 'political criminal.'. . . I take his place with him, because he has been driven to revolt, because his life-breath has been choked up." Her definition of patriotism gave this much-abused word a genuinely lyrical stature:

Who is the real patriot, or rather what is the kind of patriotism that we represent? The kind of patriotism we represent is the kind of patriotism which loves America with open eyes. Our relation to America is the same as the relation of a man who loves a woman, who is enchanted by her beauty and yet who cannot be blind to her defects. And so I wish to state here, in my own behalf and in behalf of hundreds of thousands whom you decry and state to be antipatriotic, that we love America, we love her riches, we love her mountains and her forests and above all we love the people who have produced her wealth and riches, who have created all her beauty, we love the dreamers and the philosophers and the thinkers who are giving America liberty. But that must not make us blind to the social faults of America.

No oratorical flourishes these—they came from the heart.

Unmoved, Judge Mayer sternly insisted that the trial was not one of political principles. No issue of free speech was involved, he said, for "no American worthy of the name believes in anything else than free speech; but free speech means, not license, not counseling disobedience of the law. Free speech means that frank, free, full, and orderly expression which every man or woman in the land, citizen or alien, may engage in, in lawful and orderly fashion. . . ." Mayer here came dangerously close to what Lenin called "democratic centralism": Mayer ruled that before the registration act became law, everyone might speak vehemently against it, but once a law, "then it became the duty of every person living under this Government to obey that law. Individual opinion might still be fully expressed, and proper agitation for the repeal of such a law continue, but the law itself thenceforth must be obeyed." But, Emma and Berkman must have wanted to ask, what if the law prohibited agitation, even "proper" agitation against it?

The jury took just thirty-nine minutes to return a verdict of guilty. Over Emma's protestations that their sentences should be deferred, Mayer imposed the maximum penalty of two years in prison and a fine of $10,000 each. He expressed his regret "that the extraordinary ability displayed by the two defendants has not been utilized in support of law and order. The magnetic power of one of the defendants [Emma Goldman], if thus utilized, might have been of great service in reforms legitimately advocated. . . ." Looking down on the defendants from the heights of his official certainty, he recommended that they both be deported at the expiration of their sentences: "we have no place in this country," he ruled, "for those who express the view that the law may be disobeyed in accordance with the choice of an individual."

2

By one o'clock the next morning, July 10, 1917, Berkman was on his way to the Federal Penitentiary at Atlanta and Emma on hers to the Missouri State Prison in Jefferson City. On the train Emma found time to write a friend that she went to prison "with an exalted sense of having remained absolutely true to my ideal." Indeed even her enemies had to grant that she was unusually consistent in her opposition to war—the usual pattern was to oppose war only in times of peace. But the trace of martyrdom in her letter was premature. She had scarcely commenced the difficult process of adjustment to prison routine before she learned that Justice Louis Brandeis had signed a writ of error, allowing them an appeal to the Supreme Court. Three weeks after she was hurried away to Jefferson City she was back in the Tombs, again awaiting bail.

This time the government came close to outright intimidation in its efforts to keep its two hated adversaries behind bars. It had already impounded $20,000 of the original $50,000 bail as payment of their fines; it had demanded that 1 per cent of the total bail bond be deducted as clerk's fees; and Attorney Content had let it be known that he was interested in learning the names of those who had furnished their bonds. Now, in spite of the fact that government officials had already seized their bank deposits and hence had a rather full knowledge of the lack of resources of the pair, bail was again set at $25,000 each. Content refused to consider the government's own liberty bonds for bail; he also refused property valued, according to Weinberger, at $250,000. Moreover, Weinberger wired the United States Solicitor-General that the owner of real estate offers for bail had been threatened. The government may also have exerted undue influence on surety companies. Just as Louis F. Post, Assistant Secretary of Labor under Wilson, reported that a surety company in New York "intimated that it had been significantly warned of official criticism if it wrote bail bonds for alien 'reds,' " so now one surety company gave Weinberger "alleged patriotic reasons" for its refusal to post bond for Emma and Berkman. Finally, when Weinberger handed Content $25,000 cash as Emma's bond, the prosecutor's response was almost laughable: "I will not sign any paper," he heatedly declared, "the purpose of which is to set this woman free and I will not be a party of her release from custody."

Weinberger had little difficulty in obtaining Emma her freedom, despite Content's stand.[2] In other areas as well the overeager prosecution suffered setbacks. Judge A. N. Hand ruled that the government could

---

2 Berkman was not bailed out for some time, for Emma and other of his friends feared that he might be kidnapped and taken to California to stand trial for his alleged part in the Mooney case.

not appropriate $20,000 of the money of innocent persons (who had helped Emma and Berkman meet their original bonds) as payment of their fines. In September, Judge Spiegelberg of New York's First District Municipal Court ruled that Marshal McCarthy had no right to execute a judgment on Emma's bank deposit of $329.13; the New York Produce Exchange Bank, which had already delivered the money to the Marshal, was compelled to reimburse her. Ironically the government eventually was even forced to accept its own liberty bonds for bail. The scales swung the other way, however, when the United States Supreme Court ruled, with Justices Holmes and Brandeis dissenting, that the government might deduct 1 per cent from their bail bonds for clerk's fees. In the majority opinion Justice McReynolds ruled that Emma Goldman and Alexander Berkman had been deprived of no constitutional rights, since they had "voluntarily asked to deposit money with the clerk and later requested that he be required to pay it out." McReynolds' dictum was largely rhetoric, and not very persuasive rhetoric, for posting the excessive bail required was hardly a completely voluntary act on the part of the two defendants. But whatever the defendants may have thought of Justice McReynolds' reasoning, it was clear that the general pattern of the government's actions revealed a systematic effort to deny them bail, to punish those who helped them meet the excessive amounts demanded, and to discourage any others from helping in cases in which radicals were involved.

At the same time the government was fighting to keep Emma and Berkman behind bars, it was moving to keep their publications out of the mails.[3] In April, 1917, the New York Post Office Inspector had requested an opinion from the United States Attorney on whether the *Mother Earth* of that month was mailable. The prosecutor then had ruled that this issue was "not such as to make it advisable to institute criminal proceedings." All doubt disappeared with the June registration issue of the magazine—it had a cover representing a tomb, draped in black, and inscribed, "In Memoriam—American Democracy." The Post Office Solicitor ruled that both it and the *Blast* were unmailable. Thereafter, anything that Emma or Berkman wrote was likely to be banned from the mails. In July officials allowed an issue of *Mother*

[3] As early as 1908 Postmaster-General George von L. Meyer instructed a number of his postmasters in the Middle West to furnish the Department of Justice with the names and addresses of *Mother Earth* subscribers. Presumably these names were used by the government in its denaturalization actions. Anarchists were aware of this role of the Post Office Department, as a letter from C. L. James of Eau Claire, Wisconsin, indicated. James wrote Berkman that his copy of *Mother Earth* was being held up: the Post Office Department was "becoming a detective and blackmailing agency."

Earth to pass, for some reason, but the August issue was held up. The Solicitor instructed the Chicago Postmaster to "destroy all issues" and for emphasis he added that he should "completely destroy" them. Thus did Emma's "child," her venture in personal journalism, die during its twelfth year. Emma, her niece Stella Cominsky, and M. Eleanor Fitzgerald started a *Mother Earth Bulletin* in October, 1917, but in May, 1918, it too was declared unmailable. Perhaps representative of the attitude, if not of the level of literacy, of members of the Post Office Department was the letter of a New York official to his chief: "it is apparent that the spreading of anti-war and peace propaganda is being agitated in every from [sic] known to the Socialists and the March, 1918, issue of this bulletin should be denied the use of the mails."

Obviously some representatives of the government would be satisfied with no less than Emma Goldman's complete silence. Foremost among these was the ebullient Marshal McCarthy, who took it upon himself to keep her from speaking during her months of freedom while her appeal was pending. Just before she was scheduled to appear in the Kessler Theater on September 11, McCarthy informed her that he would lock the doors of the hall unless she promised not to speak. Weinberger immediately protested this precensorship to Attorney-General Thomas W. Gregory, who in turn inquired of William C. Fitts, one of his assistants and McCarthys more immediate superior, whether he had given the Marshal any orders to stop annoying Emma. Fitts replied that he had not: "I think the Marshal is over-stepping bounds, but if I order him to let Goldman speak and she plays the mischief, he will then say, 'see, you ordered me to let her alone, now look what has come of it.' My plan is to let Emma and the Marshal fight it out." Fitts seemed bent on caricaturing the bureaucratic mind. Attorney-General Gregory rejected his preposterous view of the Department of Justice's responsibilities and instructed the Marshal to discontinue his unconstitutional actions.

Free from such interference, Emma worked feverishly against Mooney's conviction and commenced a passionate defense of the Bolsheviki and the October Revolution against what she then considered calumny and slander. Her days of precious freedom were too few to waste.

3

For this breathing spell in her contest with the government, Emma owed a great deal to Harry Weinberger, her aggressive, energetic attorney. Born on the lower East Side, Weinberger had made his way through New York University Law School by working nights as a ste-nographer. A pacifist and follower of Henry George, Weinberger made a specialty of cases involving individual freedom or freedom of the press. He first met Emma in 1917, when he successfully defended her against the second set of charges for distributing birth control information. During this same year he gave indispensable aid to Emma and Berk-man in their struggle with the authorities—indeed, so numerous were the legal actions, Weinberger must have devoted most of his time to their cases. His devotion involved considerable sacrifice, for he received hardly more than his expenses.

Other legal help, to be sure, was offered. In July Clarence Darrow offered to take over the case, if he were needed. Darrow proposed to go over the abstract carefully, make suggestions, and render help on the brief, though he preferred not to have his name on it, since "I have had so many of this sort." While Weinberger welcomed Darrow's offer, he did most of the work on the brief himself.

In his argument before the Supreme Court on December 13 and 14, Weinberger pointed out that the trial had failed to bring out any evi-dence of guilt under the indictment, especially since the alleged "con-spiracy" was overt and there was no proof that these overt acts caused anyone to disobey the law. But he concentrated the major part of his attack on the unconstitutionality of the Draft Act. He contended that it violated the Thirteenth Amendment, which forbids slavery or involun-tary servitude; that it violated the First Amendment, which states that there shall be no law prohibiting free speech; that it also violated the pro-hibition against establishing a religion (by providing exemption only for certain religious objectors to war); and that it violated the Fifth Amend-ment and the due process clause. But, whatever the merit of these con-tentions, Weinberger was demanding too much when he asked the Supreme Court to put its will against the national war effort. As Scott Wood wrote a few days before Weinberger argued his case, his only hope was to construct an argument which would enable the Justices to free Emma and Berkman without calling the draft unconstitutional: "That they will never do," Wood predicted, since "they are human beings with no radical education or sympathies."

Of course Wood was quite right. In an omnibus decision delivered on January 7, 1918, Chief Justice White declared the Draft Act constitu-tional (Selective Draft Law Cases, 245 U.S. 366). Congress' power to conscript rested in the constitutional power to declare war and to raise and support armies. The autonomy of the individual conscience counted very little in the face of this power: "a governmental power which has no sanction to it and which can only be exercised provided the citizen consents . . . is in no substantial sense a power." The Court held that the very idea of a government included a reciprocal relationship in which every citizen had the obligation and could be compelled to render military service. In the time-worn polemical style of his predecessors—"all history shows"—Chief Justice White ruled that the idea that the Draft Act established a religion was of an "unsoundness too apparent to require us to do more." He found no greater validity in Weinberger's contention that the draft violated the Thirteenth Amendment:

Finally, as we are unable to conceive upon what theory the exaction by the government from the citizen of the performance of his supreme and noble duty of contributing to the defense of the rights and honor of the nation, as the result of a war declared by the great representative body of the people, can be said to be the imposition of involuntary servitude . . . we are constrained to the conclusion that the contention to that effect is refuted by the mere statement.

White was self-confessedly unable even to conceive of a theory in which conscription was not a noble and supreme duty (a good many untheoretical and involuntary servicemen could have helped White at this point); then the Chief Justice fell back on the rhetorical device of ridicule. The decision suited the times, however, for they called for the affirmation of faith, not for persuasive argument.

Among others before the Court in which conspiracy was involved, their case was held for further consideration. On January 14, Chief Justice White again spoke for a unanimous Court in holding that "a conspiracy to commit an offense when followed by overt acts is punishable as a crime, whether the illegal end is accomplished or not" (Goldman v. United States, 245 U.S. 474). The Court concluded, "after a review of the whole record we think the proposition that there was no evidence whatever of guilt to go to the jury is absolutely devoid of merit."

Emma was on tour when the decision was made public, speaking for "the new-born hope" of Russia. On her return to New York she organized a Political Prisoners' Amnesty League before she was compelled to board a train for her return trip to the Missouri State Prison.

CHAPTER XXII

HEAVY GATES: THE PRISONER

Upon her return to Jefferson City, Emma later observed with pleasure, "my fellow-prisoners greeted me as a long-lost sister." "Long-lost mother" would have been more accurate, for she was in indisputable truth a Great Mother to the unfortunates with whom she found herself during her several periods in prison. The empathy and solicitude which she revealed for her fellow outcasts brought out, in a striking way, the genuineness and extraordinary depth of her compassion. This was reassuring to those who followed her career. Prison was the acid test, for there, as she was fond of quoting Oscar Wilde,

> Pale Anguish keeps the heavy gate,
> And the warder is Despair.

Had she merely professed her dream of a free society, she could not have surmounted this despair and she would not have been able to use her ideals so magnificently.[1]

That she managed to give the other inmates in the Jefferson City penitentiary so much of her time and energy was surprising for a number of reasons. The length of her sentence and the probability of deportation at the end of it must have weighed heavily on her mind. Moreover, the prison routine was particularly harsh. Women prisoners were put to work sewing jackets, overalls, suspenders. In one of her letters written shortly after her return, Emma described a typical day: she rose at 5:30 and cleaned her cell; she then went to breakfast; from 6:30 to 11:30 she worked in the shop; after an hour off for lunch she worked until 4:30; then she had supper and read until 9:00. At this point she was

---

[1] To make a noninvidious invidious comparison in the style of Veblen, Samuel Gompers always insisted that he came to the United States with a burning desire to help the helpless. In the 1870's he was actively engaged in his pioneering union work. But the depth of his feeling for those in need was called into question by his reaction to the only arrest of his life. In the spring of 1879 he was jailed for talking to a picket. In his own words, "that was one of the most uncomfortable days I ever spent, sitting there in the dirt and filth and vermin surrounded by men of unclean bodies and minds who used vile language. Fortunately for the effect on me, there was only one day of it." (Samuel Gompers, *Seventy Years of Life and Labor* [New York: E. P. Dutton & Co., 1925], I, 122–23.)

making about half of the fifty-four jackets which constituted her "task." After a hard week at such a pace she complained to Weinberger of sharp pains in the back of her neck and spine and of the strain on her eyes— she was very nearsighted, which forced her to sit with her neck and back bent in order to see her stitches.

As if all this were not enough, Emma was almost forty-nine years old when she returned to prison. She was, as President W. H. Painter of the Missouri State Prison Board bluntly put it, "having a change in life." All problems of her menopause—the glandular change usually involving depression, excitation, high blood pressure, and sometimes increased sexuality—had to be met under exceedingly difficult circumstances. The wonder was that she was able to give any of herself to the other inmates.

Yet over a year later when Kate Richards O'Hare, Gene Debs's close friend and colleague, entered the prison for violating the Espionage Act, she found that Emma was mothering all the unfortunates. Kate O'Hare contrasted her very favorably indeed with the religious social workers who descended upon the prison:

But no religious organization will ever be able to get to the hearts of these women until it shows an intelligent interest in righting the terrible wrongs that prevail here and bettering the body, brain, and soul-destroying conditions. To these women Emma Goldman is ten thousand times more than all the priests, preachers and religious organizations in the state. They have no conception of her teachings and do not know whether anarchy is a breakfast food or a corn cure; but Emma DID things for them. She fought for them when she felt they were being wronged; she fed them when they were hungry, and cared for them when they were ill and cheered them when they were sad.[2]

Since to her socialist mind Emma's anarchism was the "impractical phantasties [sic] of psychopathic minds," Mrs. O'Hare was not merely another partisan delivering the proper tribute. As Emma said, had she and Kate O'Hare "met on the outside, we should have probably argued furiously and have remained strangers for the rest of our lives."

In prison, however, the two women were drawn together. Mrs. O'Hare seemingly was startled into admiring Emma for her role in the lives of the prisoners. Her letters from prison were filled with evaluations of the impact of Emma's character:

[2] *Letters from Kate Richards O'Hare to Her Family: From April 20, 1919 to May 27, 1920* (St. Louis, 1920). The parallels between the prison role of Emma Goldman and that of Gene Debs must be apparent to the reader. The Atlanta inmates called Debs "Little Jesus."

The Emma Goldman that I know is not the Propagandist. It is Emma Goldman, the tender, cosmic mother, the wise, understanding woman, the faithful sister, the loyal comrade. . . . Emma don't believe in Jesus, yet she is one who makes it possible for me to grasp the spirit of Jesus. . . .

Both women shared their gifts of food and "goodies" with their sisters:

Instead of hurling anarchist texts at me Emma raps on the wall of the cell and says, "Get busy Kate, it's time to feed the monkeys, pass the food down the line." I think it would be a godsend if a lot of theoretical hair-splitters . . . went to prison. . . .

After Emma was released:

Of course we miss Emma very much. . . . We differed as far as possible in our philosophies of life and reaction to prison conditions, but she was a brainy, intellectual woman and a wonderful study in psychology. I too feel that anarchism is but the visible expression of the soul scars of social wounds and should be dealt with by the psychologist and not the police-man and judge and jailer. But Emma is above all things maternal. The mother instinct is her dominant trait and she mothered and babied not only Ella [Antolini, another "political"] and me, but every creature in the prison and the more forsaken the more tender she was in her ministrations. But left to ourselves Ella and I are like two kids whose mother has gone away on a visit. . . . It will be some time before I become accustomed to looking out for myself, so completely did Emma spoil me.

Kate O'Hare believed that she had penetrated to the psychological foundation of Emma's magnetic appeal:

Thwarted in physical motherhood she poured out her whole soul in vicari-ous motherhood of all the sad and sorrowful, the wronged and oppressed, the bitter and rebellious children of men. Warden Gilvin was right when he said the women here worshipped her with an idolatrous worship. They did. And largely it was because the women here are mostly the weak and inefficient, the arrested and infantile who have never achieved adulthood and still sorely need the sheltering mother love.

While the maternal wellsprings of Emma's feeling for prisoners were undeniable, as Mrs. O'Hare perceived, Emma's ideas also played an im-portant part. Much of her compassion was due to her belief that "crimi-nals are victims of our mad social arrangements"; in her twenty months at Jefferson City, she "did not find one I could call depraved, cruel or hard."

Whatever the reasons, Emma obviously had a most unusual influ-ence on her sister-inmates. And at precisely this point she achieved a notable triumph: in following her ideals in prison, she cheated the government of its full satisfaction: it could punish her body, but it could not reach her. Like Thoreau in somewhat similar circumstances, she continued to express herself.

2

Just as "Red Emma" was the leading woman anarchist in America, so "Red Kate" was the most prominent woman Socialist in the country. Born on a Kansas ranch, Mrs. O'Hare was of the indigenous, Mary Ellen Lease ("raise less corn and more hell") variety of radical. By running on the Socialist ticket in Kansas in 1910 she had achieved the distinction of being the first woman candidate for the United States Senate; in 1916 she had been an unsuccessful candidate for the Socialist vice-presidential nomination. Mrs. O'Hare tended to believe that a classless heaven here on earth could be achieved through political machinery; Emma believed that such means would lead to a hierarchical hades. Socialists and anarchists alike had expected a great clash—a sort of Amazonian ideological struggle—to reverberate past the Missouri state lines when the two were shut up in prison together. Their followers experienced a feeling of letdown when no clash occurred.

Actually their views on some issues were not as far apart as they both believed. Differences remained, however, and nowhere were they more interesting than in the area of crime and punishment.

Emma would have solved the prison problem with a breathtaking move: the gates should simply have been opened. "Of course, as far as I am concerned," she wrote from her prison cell, "all the prisoners should be let go—it would be better for society and more benificial [sic] to those who watch over them. More than ever I am convinced that next to the outrage of locking people away where they are degraded to the condition of inanimate matter is the outrage of condamning [!] people to be their jailors and keepers. The best of them gradually grow hard and inhuman or they do not keep their jobs very long." At worst, prisons were places where men were "tortured 'to be made good.'" At best, a process of dehumanization took place in which the individual was degraded to a mere automaton. In both cases they were "universities of crime" which turned out upon society graduates who soon made use of their degrees. Then the cycle was simply repeated. Though Emma felt that something could be done to free prisoners from the brutality of prison officials, provide them with remunerative work while in prison, and increase their self-direction, she was convinced that the primary need "is a renovation of the social consciousness." Most of her faith, then, was in a changed social vision: "Nothing short of a complete reconstruction of society will deliver mankind from the cancer of crime."

Kate O'Hare agreed that possibly "in the last analysis" the solution of the problem of crime and punishment "must be found in the great broad sweep of social justice that shall eventually replace those crimes of society which now play so large a part in the creation of the individual criminal."[3] Her greatest concern, however, was with what was to happen in the meantime: "But criminal laws, criminal courts, and penal institutions are very important parts of our social machinery and we must patch up what we have so that it will operate with as little friction and waste of human life as possible, while we are building the machinery of the new order." After President Wilson commuted her sentence in 1920 she wrote a biting attack on conditions in the Jefferson City prison. For this the Missouri Welfare League later declared that the whole country owed her a debt of gratitude, for "her fearless disclosures of abuses and cruelties in the women's department of the prison were of great value and helped end an intolerable situation there." Fighting for immediate reforms, Mrs. O'Hare went on to become Assistant State Director of Penology in California and was credited with helping make San Quentin a model penal institution.

Unquestionably Kate O'Hare's emphasis on the immediate, meanwhile problems enabled her to accomplish concrete reforms. Had she had the chance, Emma Goldman probably would not have worked as effectively in this area, though she did announce in 1919 that her primary interest had become prison reform and though she was able to give Mrs. O'Hare some very practical advice in the 1920's—Mrs. O'Hare responded generously that the campaign for prison reform was "your work as well as mine." Yet the fact remains that both women, each with her own perspective and emphasis, fulfilled important functions. Mrs. O'Hare had the primary role of institutional development; Emma's primary mission was to arouse social consciousness and direct attention to underlying issues. Like some modern criminologists— Ralph Banay, for example—Emma saw that the prison is simply an anachronism which perpetuates and multiplies crime. She saw that such a malignant tumor requires a major operation, not placebos— that, to put her insight more directly, prisons should be torn down, not patched up.

[3] O'Hare, *In Prison* (New York: Alfred A. Knopf, 1923), p. 164.

A concern with more fundamental issues did not rule out a compassionate concern with the here and now. After all, it was Kate O'Hare herself who declared that "the girls love me too, but never as they loved Emma Goldman. To them I am the dispenser of chewing gum and peppermint drops, a perambulating spelling book, dictionary and compendium of all known wisdom, I am lawyer, priest and physician . . . but I do not and never can fill Emma's place in their hearts."

CHAPTER XXIII

EMMA GOLDMAN AND 59,999 OTHER REDS

Meanwhile the government's campaign against Emma Goldman clanked along. Just a few days after her return to Jefferson City, all the major newspapers blurted this account from their front pages: "Letters which indicate that Alexander Berkman and Emma Goldman were working with the German spy and propagandist of the Indian revolution Har Dayal before they were sent to jail for violating the 'Draft Law,' were published by Attorney-General Gregory in reply to the protests of radical elements against the imprisonment of the Anarchist leaders." Emma Goldman a German spy?

The Department of Justice thought that a case of sorts could be made out that she was. At a moment when the Wilson administration was embarrassed by the international protests over the imprisonment of Mooney, Berkman, and Emma, one high official conceived the fetching idea that if the two anarchists could be associated with the hated Germans, then the radical agitation for them would cease. This man, John Lord O'Brian, Special Assistant to the Attorney-General, thought he remembered that in all the papers plundered from the office of *Mother Earth* there was one letter which might be useful. He immediately wrote Assistant United States Attorney John C. Knox in New York:

. . . it has occurred to me that it might be of very great value just now, because of the agitation in Russia as well as here, arousing sympathy for Emma Goldman among the Bolsheviki element. If the letter has as I think it had a distinctly German *taint* and would *in any way* tend to connect her up *even indirectly* with the German activities you can readily see that it might have just now extraordinary value. [Emphases added.]

Knox responded by sending to Washington photostatic copies of two letters, "from Har Dayal, a Hindu, asking that Berkman send persons from the United States to engage in an Indian revolutionary movement."

Four days after the receipt of these letters, Attorney-General Gregory charged that Emma and Berkman were "apparently working in con-

junction with German spies in foreign countries." At Gregory's request, George Creel's Committee on Public Information passed on
this charge and copies of the Har Dayal letters to the newspapers—
Creel, Emma's old admirer, seemed to go out of his way to document
personally his earlier charge that as far as she was concerned the un-
reliability of the press was "absolute."

"Berkman in Ring of German Spies," dutifully shouted the New
York *Times'* headline on February 25, 1918. But the reader who was
not blinded by nationalism or the newspaper's proud boasts of objectivity saw with surprise that the Hindu's letters in no way proved
that Berkman and Emma were in a ring of German spies. They
showed rather that an Indian named Har Dayal had written Berkman
a request that he send "comrades to Holland, to help a movement
to bring about a revolution in India" and that he requested either Berkman or Emma to give him letters of introduction to prominent anarchists in Europe. Nowhere was there any indication that Berkman
or Emma had complied with Dayal's request, or even that Dayal was
a German spy.

On the contrary, Dayal was apparently an Indian nationalist who
worked openly with the German government to free his country from
English rule. As Emma caustically observed, the mere fact that Berkman had received two such letters from Dayal was no more remarkable
than if the former had received a letter from Bernard Shaw. Emma
recalled that she and Berkman had met Dayal, a "great idealist" and
Tolstoyan, when he was an instructor at the University of California
at Berkeley. If he had ever approached her with such a request, she
had refused, for she did not think "outsiders can free a country." In
any case, it was utterly absurd to contend that she and Berkman were
working with spies for the German government. She asked Weinberger to inform the Attorney-General and the press that she was in
favor of a revolution in Germany to topple that government from
power.

Rich irony lay in the fact that this spy story was concocted by John
Lord O'Brian, prosecutor of the most important wartime espionage
cases. In 1919 O'Brian denounced the popular hysteria which led to
all the false stories of enemy activity in the United States: the accounts
of phantom ships carrying ammunition to Germany, enemy sub-
marines landing on American coasts, mysterious airplanes floating over
Kansas. O'Brian informed his colleagues of the New York Bar Association that "these instances are cited not to make light of the danger

of hostile activities, nor to imply that incessant vigilance was not necessary in watching German activities, but to show how impossible it was to check that kind of war hysteria and war excitement which found expression in impatience with the civil courts and the oft-recurring false statement that our government showed undue leniency toward enemies within our gates." The phantom ships and mysterious airplanes were, however, not a whit less foolish or vicious in their consequences than the spy story O'Brian himself fabricated. Some of the wood which fed the flames of war hysteria was hauled from Washington.[1]

Certainly O'Brian's spy story showed that the government would use almost any means against Emma Goldman—its campaign extended not only to taking away her freedom, but also her good name among radicals.

2

After the Armistice was signed, the spy charge withered on the vine, for it was no longer worth the effort to depict Emma and Berkman as German agents. The attack instead shifted back to her radicalism, as the government began full-scale investigations of dissenting organizations and opinions.

The profound illogicality of the time was revealed by the general lack of awareness that any real shift was involved in turning from German espionage to radical activities. A vulgar pragmatism led to the conclusion that anyone—a radical or an Indian nationalist or an Irish nationalist—who was less than enthusiastic about the war, was necessarily for the Central Powers. Now with the enemy without vanquished, what could be more natural than an assault on the "enemy" obstructionists within?

The Overman Subcommittee of the Senate Judiciary Committee made this transition with ease. Headed by Senator Lee Slater Overman of North Carolina, the subcommittee had already managed to include college professors and newspaper publishers under its authorization to investigate "Brewing and Liquor Interests and German Propaganda." Now that the Germans were defeated, the question arose whether the subcommittee could not abandon brewers and Germans altogether and simply investigate radicals. One witness provided the senators with a seductive theoretical justification. Senator William

[1] O'Brian has since lectured and written on this theme without giving any adequate account of his own or other officials' instigation of part of this "popular" hysteria. See his "The Government and Civil Liberties: World War I and After" in The John Randolph Tucker Lectures (Lexington: University of Virginia Press, 1952).

The exiles out for a stroll with friends in Nice or Saint-Tropez

Emma speaking to English comrades and others. *(Emma Goldman Papers, New York Public Library.)*

The prodigal daughter apparently being questioned by an immigration official or a reporter about her imminent return to the United States. Fenner Brockway observed that she had "a stocky figure like a peasant woman, a face of fierce strength like a female pugilist. . . ." (*Underwood and Underwood.*)

H. King of Utah asked the witness, "would the radical movement now have anything to do with the German propaganda, or the investigation of the activities of the brewers?" In reply, Archibald Stevenson, a New York lawyer and one of the Bureau of Investigation's experts on dangerous opinions, asserted that anarchism was "imported into America" from Germany and that the "Bolsheviki movement is a branch of the revolutionary socialism of Germany." After all, Marx was a German; Lenin was a follower of Marx; therefore Lenin could be looked upon as "a tool of the Germans"!

The senators did not have to be convinced; they only wanted an excuse to believe. The consequence was a strange volume on *Bolshevik Propaganda* (1919), filled with testimony on Russian "free love" bureaus, the "criminal" Red Army, the psychological impact of the "Red Flag" on native radicals. Emma Goldman was appropriately given a prominent place at the beginning of the inquiry, for in the eyes of Senator Overman and his colleagues she was indubitably the Red of Reds. Inspector Thomas J. Tunney of the New York Police testified that he had helped secure the conviction of Emma and Berkman for obstructing the draft and that he found the Hindu letter which had been used against them. This colloquy on Emma Goldman, illustrative of the tone of the inquiry, followed:

Inspector Tunney.—She is a woman about 46 years of age; a very able and intelligent woman and very fine speaker.

Senator Overman.—I know something about her of course. . . .

Senator Nelson.—She speaks good English?

Tunney.—She speaks English very fluently. In fact, I have heard newspaper men say that she is a master of the English language. She and Berkman defended themselves on their trial and they put in a very able defence.

Overman [foreshadowing this early his deep interest in everyone connected with "free love"].—Is she a handsome woman?

Tunney.—No; she is not. I would not call her a very homely looking woman either. She was rather good looking when she was young. She is a very stout woman.

All this was very interesting, but since Emma Goldman was "in a safe place," as Senator Nelson euphemistically put it, the subcommittee dropped for the moment any further investigation of her case.

The Overman investigation was only a small dark cloud scudding across an already troubled sky: a full-scale national storm against heresy was about to burst forth. As Emma herself had clearly foreseen in 1917:

Militarism and reaction are now more rampant in Europe than ever before. Conscription and censorship have destroyed every vestige of liberty. Everywhere the governments have used the situation to tighten the militaristic noose around the necks of the people. . . . The same is bound to take place in America should the dogs of war be let loose here. Already the reactionary riff-raff, propagandists of jingoism and preparedness, all the beneficiaries of exploitation represented in the Merchants and Manufacturers' Association, the Chambers of Commerce, the munition cliques, etc., etc., have come to the fore with all sorts of plans and schemes to chain and gag labor, to make it more helpless and dumb than ever before.

Her prophecy was in large part fulfilled during the Red Scare of 1919.

The immediate background was a complex of disturbing events: the Russian Revolution of November, 1917; the Seattle general strike of early 1919, which probably influenced the decision of the Overman subcommittee definitely to investigate radicalism; the "Bomb Plots" of the spring of 1919, when a person or persons to this day unknown mailed bombs to Attorney-General A. Mitchell Palmer and other prominent persons; the Boston police strike, the steel strike, and the coal strike, all in the autumn of 1919—these events helped touch off the Red Scare.

The key figure was the new Attorney-General, A. Mitchell Palmer. A standing reminder of the decadence of American liberalism, Palmer was the prototype of the Wilsonian Progressive. In 1912 he had been Wilson's floor manager; in 1913 he turned down Wilson's offer of the post of Secretary of War because he was "a man of peace." But he continued his good work in the vineyard of progressivism with such success that he was regarded by many as the father of women's suffrage and the child labor law. Yet the war seems to have undone Palmer, like his master. He developed an impressive hate for Germans and the radicals who seemingly aided and abetted the enemy during time of war. After his appointment to the Cabinet, he was frightened by the explosion in front of his home during the June, 1919, "Bomb Plots"; moreover, as the hopeful heir apparent of the New Freedom (in all its desuetude), he had ambitions to be in the White House. A crusade to make America safe from radicalism must have seemed to Palmer the answer to his most pressing problems: at one and the same time it struck at his radical enemies and promised to further his political ambitions.

Yet, after this has been said, Palmer may have been, in the beginning at least, as much a gull as a devil. Assistant Secretary of Labor Louis

F. Post, who was in a position to know, believed Palmer to have been a victim of "detectives who knew exactly what they wanted." Robert K. Murray, the historian of the Red Scare, also has found some evidence that William J. Flynn, head of the Bureau of Investigation, and J. Edgar Hoover, head of the bureau's newly created General Intelligence (antiradical) Division, both purposely played on Palmer's fears and ambitions to enhance the power of the Bureau of Investigation.

Other organizations and interests brought pressure on Palmer to crack down on the radicals. Labor-spy interests were understandably concerned. Patriotic organizations—the National Security League, the American Defense Society, the National Civic Federation, the American Legion—all came out against "False Idealism," "Parlor Bolshevism," and "The Enemy within Our Gates." The American Legion was in favor of deporting all individuals, aliens or *citizens*, who had the effrontery to defame American life. General Leonard Wood, Theodore Roosevelt's old comrade-in-arms, endorsed a minister's call for the deportation of Bolsheviks "in ships of stone with sails of lead, with the wrath of God for a breeze and with hell for their first port." The Attorney-General did not move fast enough to suit these organizations and individuals.

Certain members of Congress also felt that the executive branch should do less talking about "evil thinking" and more acting. In the House, Albert Johnson of Washington, Chairman of the powerful Committee on Immigration and Naturalization, accepted the view that the Department of Labor was sympathetic to lawless agitators, and he actually initiated an unsuccessful attempt to impeach Post. At about this time Weinberger wrote Emma of a consultation he had in the Department of Labor with Post, John W. Abercrombie, also an Assistant Secretary of Labor, and Anthony Caminetti, the Commissioner-General of Immigration who worked closely with J. Edgar Hoover.[2] Weinberger reported that "the Department there is absolutely panic-stricken over the hammering they have been getting from the House of Representatives and the Senate." During the heated discussion, with "Hoover of the Department of Justice . . . floating around in and out," Post angrily declared that in the present situation even Tolstoy would have to be deported, that it was not up to him, and that the only relief was in the courts and legislatures. Weinberger wondered out

[2] Caminetti, the first Italian-American to be elected to Congress, attempted (as Commissioner of Immigration) to prove that he was fully "100 per cent American."

loud if it was not the same way that Pilate had washed his hands of Christ. Post made no recorded reply.

In the Senate, Miles Poindexter of Washington centered his fire on the Department of Justice. He was especially interested in the disposition of the case of Emma Goldman: "Mr. President . . . a short time ago Emma Goldman, an anarchist, was released from the Missouri penitentiary. She had been ordered to appear before the United States Immigration officials to answer the charge of being an undesirable alien, subject to deportation, and has had her case indefinitely postponed." Poindexter wanted to know why she and other radicals had not been deported. His question was put formally in a resolution, passed October 17, 1919, which asked the Attorney-General to inform the Senate if he had taken action, "and if not, why not, and if so, to what extent, for the arrest and punishment of the various persons . . . who, it is alleged, have preached anarchy and sedition; who it is alleged have advised the defiance of law and authority. . . ." The resolution boiled down to a censure of the Attorney-General, though Senator Poindexter maintained that it did not "reflect" on the Department of Justice.

3

Attorney-General Palmer responded with a lengthy, curious report, entitled *Investigation Activities of the Department of Justice* (1919). A red thread of complaint ran through its texture: unfortunately he could not apply the general statutes on treason and rebellion to radical agitators; he could invoke the Espionage Act of June 15, 1917 against seditious utterances, but he had himself ruled that it applied only to those utterances which weakened the war effort; he was limited to using, therefore, the Immigration Act of October 16, 1918 which provided for the exclusion and deportation, "any time after entry," of those aliens who were anarchists or disbelievers in organized government. The most urgent need of the moment was thus legislation which would make "preaching anarchy and sedition" a crime under general criminal statutes.[3] Until the enactment of such legislation, Palmer pledged continued action with every means at hand against the "60,000 radicals."

Partly because of the Senate's special interest in Emma Goldman and perhaps partly because Palmer himself considered her the most

[3] While Palmer did not get the peacetime sedition act he asked for, there were some seventy sedition bills under consideration in Congress during the winter of 1919–20. Perhaps this was the most effective comment on the war which had been waged to make the world safe for democracy.

dangerous of all the 60,000 Reds, over a hundred pages—more than half of his report—were devoted to "Exhibit No. 6: Emma Goldman." J. Edgar Hoover and his General Intelligence Division had laboriously assembled a detailed dossier on Emma—one that drew heavily on the Chambers-Zamosh investigation made at the time of Jacob Kersner's denaturalization. Hoover and his men had added excerpts from the July, 1914, *Mother Earth* (the Lexington explosion issue) to show that she advocated violence, papers allegedly linking her to the Los Angeles *Times* bombing, the records of her trial in 1893 for inciting to riot, and so on.

But the most grievously misleading part of "Exhibit No. 6" consisted in a novel treatment of all the old, disproved allegations that Emma was responsible for the assassination of McKinley. What a grand jury would not even indict her for in 1901 was evidently in Hoover's mind appropriate for overwrought senators in 1919. By a judicious use of selection and unmarked ellipses the report made Czolgosz's confession seem damning. Palmer introduced this version of the assassin's statements:

Q.—You believe it is right to kill if necessary, don't you?
A.—Yes, sir. [1]
Q.—Did you talk it over with any one or say it was something you had read that suggested it to you, or something else? [2]
A.—Yes, sir.
Q.—Something you had read was it?
A.—Yes, sir.
Q.—Who was the last one you heard talk?
A.—Emma Goldman. [3]
Q.—What did she say or what did she say to you about the President?
A.—She says—she didn't mention no Presidents at all, she mentioned the Government.
Q.—What did she say about it?
A.—She said she didn't believe in it. [4]
Q.—You got the idea it would be a good thing if we didn't have this form of government?
A.—Yes, sir.

The impression all this conveyed was almost totally false.[4] Following the bracketed numbers inserted above, one observes just how misleading the scholarly efforts of Hoover's General Intelligence Division could be: (1) The reader was not warned of a substantial ellipsis after

[4] The reader may compare this version with that introduced above, p. 70.

this response. Czolgosz affirmed that he had planned the assassination only a few days beforehand, in which case Emma could not have been responsible for it. (2) The following question and answer were, for obvious reasons, left out of the Department of Justice version: Q: "Have you ever taken any obligation or sworn any oath to kill anybody; you have, haven't you; look up and speak; haven't you done that?" A: "No, sir." (3) At this point the Department of Justice made another unmarked ellipsis which was of fundamental importance in understanding Czolgosz's confession: The omitted question and answer were as follows: Q: "You heard her say it would be a good thing if all these rulers were wiped off the face of the earth?" A: "She didn't say that." (4) After this answer there were two further omissions of basic importance: Q: "And that all those who supported the government ought to be destroyed; did she believe in that?" A: "She didn't say they ought to be destroyed." Q: "You wanted to help her in her work, and thought this the best way to do it; was that your idea; or if you have any other idea, tell us what it was?" A: "She didn't tell me to do it."

Such a misuse of evidence makes it easier to understand how the Department of Justice could go on to misuse its power during the Palmer-Hoover raids on radicals and supposed radicals. The Department of Justice's actions in Emma's case were consistent with its invasion of private homes, meeting halls, union headquarters; with its unreasonable seizures of private possessions; with its arrests without warrants and its detention of people *incommunicado;* with its third degree tortures and the use of *agents provocateurs.* Above all, its actions were consistent with crying up a Great Conspiracy of Emma and 59,999 other Reds. Yet, after a thorough investigation of the official evidence of such a conspiracy, Louis F. Post found to his amazement that "the whole 'red' crusade stood revealed as a stupendous and cruel fake." A tragicomic fake perhaps, but it set the stage for the dramatic close of the case of the United States *v.* Goldman-Berkman.

CHAPTER XXIV

BACK PAST THE STATUE OF LIBERTY

Months before Palmer reported on the Great Conspiracy, J. Edgar Hoover had started working on the proposed deportation of Emma Goldman and Alexander Berkman. On August 23, 1919, when Emma was still in prison, Hoover prepared a memorandum on their case for John T. Creighton, Special Assistant to the Attorney-General. In view of his repeated claim that the Bureau of Investigation reported only the facts—"only what we find, without color or deductive evaluation"—Hoover's conclusion was interesting to say the least. "Emma Goldman and Alexander Berkman are, beyond doubt," finally evaluated Hoover, "two of the most dangerous anarchists in this country and if permitted to return to the community [sic] will result in undue harm." He worked tirelessly to prevent such undue harm.

For some obscure reason Hoover feared the outcome of deportation hearings for Emma in St. Louis; he advised that they be held in New York. Although such deportation cases fell under the jurisdiction of the Department of Labor, Hoover had a directing influence on the conduct of the government's actions against Emma, as the following passage in a letter from Immigrant Inspector W. J. Peters to Anthony Caminetti made clear: "Hoover thinks this whole arrangement is O.K., and that in view of the attitude of the court in the St. Louis jurisdiction [he] thinks it will be best if the case is heard at N.Y." The case was heard at New York.

Weinberger was officially informed that bail for Emma and Berkman (while they were being held for their hearings) would be $15,000 each. Weinberger again protested, but the Department of Labor refused to lower their bonds.

Since Secretary of Labor W. B. Wilson had set bail for such cases at $1,000, why was the bail of both Emma Goldman and Alexander Berkman fifteen times this amount? Hoover and Caminetti, the subservient Commissioner-General of Immigration, were apparently primarily responsible. Caminetti recommended no reduction in the bonds of Emma and Berkman, for, as he put it, the "Dept. of Justice authorities apparently entertain the view that, if anything, the bonds in behalf of both of these aliens should have been even in a larger sum, and $15,000 was fixed upon as somewhat in the nature of a compromise." In other words, Hoover, who was handling these cases for the Department of Justice, wanted to demand even more excessive bail![1]

Berkman had already undergone a hearing before he left Atlanta. An immigration inspector and J. Edgar Hoover heard Berkman state his position. Despite the severe ordeal he had just experienced—he was kept in solitary confinement for almost eight months—Berkman showed he still possessed his old spirit. When he remarked that he felt it was his duty to do his best for the community, he was asked: "Regardless of the laws thereof?" His reply went to the heart of his and Emma's conflict with the government: "Following the dictates of my conscience." Since Berkman openly declared his disbelief in both government and violence, holding them to be synonyms, and since he claimed to be merely a citizen of the world, his deportation was assured.

Spurred on by a Senate resolution, Secretary of Labor Wilson set the date for Emma's hearing on November 16. So much pressure came from Congress and the Department of Justice, however, that he moved up the date of the hearing to October 27. Immigrant Inspector A. P. Schell, Hoover, and other officials conducted the hearing. Weinberger appeared as Emma's counsel.

She was a most unco-operative witness against herself. Vehemently protesting the "Star Chamber Proceedings," she handed her inquisitors a statement of defiance:

If the present proceedings are for the purpose of proving some alleged offense committed by me, some evil or antisocial act, then I protest against the secrecy and third-degree methods of this so-called "trial." But if I am not charged with any specific offense or act, if—as I have reason to believe—this is purely an inquiry into my social and political opinions, then I protest still more vigorously against these proceedings, as utterly tyrannical and diametrically opposed to the fundamental guarantees of a true democracy. Every human being is entitled to hold any opinion that appeals to her or him without making herself or himself liable to persecution.

She flatly refused to answer whether she claimed citizenship through her father or through Kersner. Despite her "unfriendly" attitude, she remained free on bail until a decision was rendered by the responsible officials.

---

[1] Caminetti's response went a long way to document Post's contention that the Department of Justice had an "undue influence" on the Department of Labor.

2

A few days later Hoover informed Caminetti that information he had received from New York made it advisable to close the case against Emma Goldman "at the earliest possible moment." Very probably Hoover had merely learned that Emma and Berkman were embarking on a lecture tour.

With the heresy hunt gaining momentum, a lecture tour was about like a stroll during a hurricane. Weinberger and other friends strongly advised them not to make the tour. But disregarding such counsels of caution, Emma and Berkman audaciously went ahead with their plans, for they felt it was imperative that they present the argument for the Russian Revolution, speak out against the "Palmer Raids," and say goodbye to many old friends. Surprisingly, in view of the public temper of the day, the tour was a resounding success. All the sensational press reports of police interference and all the quasi-official admonitions to boycott their meetings did not prevent huge audiences from attending their lectures in Chicago and Detroit. The size of their audiences was both a registration of protest against the Red Scare and a testimonial to the two veteran fighters for unpopular causes.

Yet time had run out. On November 29, Louis F. Post, Emma's old friend who found himself in the predicament of administering "Know Nothing immigration laws," signed her deportation order. As a mild protest in Emma's case, Post ventured "to infer that she is one of those disbelievers in violence who anticipate forcible resistance to peaceable development of anarchistic policies, and therefore and in support of those policies justify the use of force as a defense against force." A genuine libertarian, Post was sorely troubled and tempted to resign. Nevertheless, he stayed at his desk, for "whether or not I liked the law did not enter in. I was not a maker of laws but an administrator of a law already constitutionally made."

Emma never forgave Post for his act. His plea of official necessity rang hollowly when she compared Post with another friend, Frederic Howe, who resigned as Commissioner of Immigration at Ellis Island rather than order deportations he believed unjust. Post merited her sympathy, however, for his anguished attempt at self-justification in his Deportations Delirium (1923) and his other remarks in his unpublished autobiography suggested strongly that he never completely forgave himself.

In any event, the order was signed. Weinberger was directed to produce his clients at Ellis Island before twelve o'clock noon, December 5.

In Chicago Emma and Berkman were at a farewell banquet in their honor when reporters rushed in with the information that Henry Clay Frick had just died. Did Berkman care to make any comment? "Deported by God," dryly observed Frick's old enemy—or rather was reported to have observed. Not at all apocryphal, however, was Caminetti's cryptic wire: the case of Emma Goldman "is closed and alien ordered deported."

3

Such a pronouncement was just a bit premature. Both sides recognized that the key to the whole proceedings was the disputed validity of Jacob A. Kersner's denaturalization.

Emma had commenced efforts to shore up her position while she was still in prison. While there she had received an offer of aid from Sam Sickles, a stranger of "some prominence" who lived in Carruthersville, Missouri. Sickles had read Kate O'Hare's prison letters in the New York *Call* and therewith offered to adopt Emma Goldman. Next Harry Kelly, an old friend, a native American anarchist and former associate of Kropotkin, offered to marry Emma and thus put her citizenship beyond question. Weinberger advised her to reject both of these generous proposals. After examining the records in the Kersner case, he decided "that there is a reasonable doubt in our favor"; they might as well rely on the Kersner thread, weak as it was, for "snapping the thread will appear like persecution and not like law."

The missing or dead Kersner thus became the key pawn. If he had died before April, 1909, or if he were alive and could prove that he had not obtained his citizenship illegally, the government possibly could be stalemated.

One of Emma's nephews conducted an investigation of his own. After some discreet inquiries in upstate New York, he discovered that Kersner was probably hiding "because of certain criminal proceedings against him." The fugitive had assumed the alias Jake Lewis. The nephew concluded with the fear that there was "no possibility of establishing his death because the records up to December 20, 1906, are complete and conclusive."[2]

With the help of this information, Weinberger traced Kersner to Chicago. Here the trail was lost as Leon Green, a member of the Retail Clerks International Protective Association, blundered badly. He reported that he was unable to find any trace of the missing man,

[2] The relative ease with which a layman traced Kersner this far suggests that the government might well have known of Kersner's whereabouts in 1909.

either in the office of his supposed employer or in the records of any of the likely organizations. Unfortunately, Green simply did not look far enough, carefully enough. Yet if Weinberger and others working for the defense had been granted more time, perhaps through a more systematic inquiry they might have picked up Kersner's trail again. Post, however, denied their request for additional time.

The government had a real advantage in this race to find the missing ex-husband. It had already spent a considerable sum—$25,000 or more was the estimate one source gave to Weinberger—in assembling information on Kersner in 1908–9. Now an enlarged and developed governmental agency could be set in motion to take up the hunt.

Hoover's General Intelligence Division succeeded where Green had failed. On November 21 an immigration official wired Washington that "Mr. Hoover advises he has proof of death of Emma Goldman's husband. Important that same be made part of her hearing. Recommend that case be reopened to insert new evidence." Hoover's agents had come up with a sheaf of records and other evidence. A death certificate showed that Jacob Lewis, a tailor, had died in Chicago on January 18, 1919. Numerous sworn statements indicated that Jacob Lewis was really Jacob Kersner. Barney H. Joseph, a friend and fellow worker of Kersner thirty years before in Rochester, supplied a motive for Kersner's use of an assumed name: he had not wanted anybody to connect him in any way with his former wife, for in "after years, after he saw her life, from what he gave me to understand, he hated her very name." Though this may very well have been true, the unfortunate Kersner was probably more strongly motivated by the criminal charges awaiting him in the East. In any event, the documents dispatched to Washington were just what the government needed. Hoover triumphantly observed that they were "sufficient to refute any allegation which may be made by Weinberger to the effect that Emma Goldman's husband died prior to 1909."

And they arrived just in time for Emma's hearing before Judge Mayer on December 8. Weinberger led off with the contention that the government had no proof Kersner was alive at the time of his denaturalization and that even if he were, Emma's citizenship had not been taken from her by the proceedings. Federal Attorney Caffey then merely stated as a "fact" (the evidence was not put in the record), that Kersner was alive to January 18, 1919. (He refused to tell the shocked Weinberger where Kersner had died.) Judge Mayer found that Emma Goldman was "not at any time a citizen of the United

States"; he repeated his opinion of 1917 that "the Court views both of these defendants as enemies of the United States of America and of its peace and comfort." Mayer did, however, grant them time for an appeal to the Supreme Court.

Weinberger immediately filed a brief with Justice Brandeis for a writ of error. After Brandeis presented the writ to the entire Court, the Justices refused a stay for Berkman, but granted Weinberger a week to submit the record and argument for Emma. Emma elected, however, to accompany Berkman to Russia; she withdrew her application for a writ on December 12. The time was short; the expense of printing the records was great; the outcome was uncertain. Had she chosen to make this last fight, probably the Supreme Court would have decided against her. Nevertheless, the Department of Justice was relieved, for it had been worried by the appeal. Solicitor-General Alex C. King warned Caffey not to proceed with undue haste, for the Court was scrutinizing rather closely all proceedings described as "summary"; it was Solicitor King's opinion that "if questions are substantially raised on the record," the Court would grant a writ of error, even though it might ultimately rule against her.

The thread had snapped and Emma's personal war with the government was over. The most amusing comment on the war's end was made by United States Attorney Francis Caffey. Beginning with the falsehood that Emma had been informed in 1909 of the suit to revoke Kersner's citizenship, Caffey continued with this reassuring pronouncement: "Throughout the Government's dealing with Emma Goldman clean-handed justice has prevailed."

4

Now all that remained was to ship Emma Goldman and "her consort Berkman," as Hoover described him, out of the country. But how? It was embarrassingly awkward to dump them in Russia, for at the moment the United States had no diplomatic relations with the new Russian Socialist Federated Soviet Republic. Just a few years later, in 1922, the courts were to balk at sending aliens to a country the United States had not recognized. Now, however, with the anti-radical feeling in full tide, this inconvenience was merely a minor challenge to official ingenuity. As Congressman Isaac Siegel of the House Immigration Committee put it, some "left-handed diplomatic arrangement" was to be tried. A ship containing the deportees was scheduled to "sail past the Statue of Liberty on the outward bound trip" before Christmas.

An old sea-rolling army transport, the "Buford," which had been acquired from Britain during the Spanish-American War, was chartered by the busy Hoover. By December 17 the authorities announced themselves prepared to "remove all alien radicals ready for deportation, among whom were the 'famous' Emma Goldman and Alexander Berkman." In all, 249 "anarchists" were to sail away from Paradise on the "Buford." To be more accurate, only 51 anarchists were to be deported. Among the others there were 184 who allegedly advocated violent overthrow of the government and 14 who were found guilty of moral turpitude or of being public charges. Although Secretary of Labor Wilson had insisted that no deportee having a wife or child should be placed aboard the "Buford," his order was disregarded at Ellis Island. Of the twelve families the government admitted to separating by these deportations, only five had been reunited over a year later. So great was the haste to save the United States from these pitiable individuals that some of them were not even allowed to pick up sufficient clothing for the cold winter voyage.

Though their ship sailed under sealed orders, it was an open secret that the deportees would be taken somehow to Russia. The day before their departure an open letter to Emma Goldman appeared in Soviet Russia, an official organ of the Bolshevik government. Ludwig Martens, the unrecognized "Ambassador" to the United States, extended a welcome to Emma and the other refugees. In his letter, however, there was a jarring note—a note which was in fact strikingly parallel to the position on dissent advanced by Judge Mayer at the end of Emma's trial in 1917: "Soviet Russia persecutes nobody for his beliefs or political or economic theories," Martens asserted, and everybody could express his beliefs, "as long as he does not engage himself in active cooperation with the enemies of the Russian workers—especially at this crucial time. . . ." The revolutionary ambassador and the conservative judge were agreed on this one point: Emma Goldman and every other person have, of course, free speech, but. . . . Just as this pregnant "but" effectively banished Emma Goldman from the United States, so Marten's use of it foreshadowed her experience during the next months in Russia.

But she could hardly have known this when, at 4:15 on the frosty Sunday morning of December 21, she and her fellow exiles set out on the long trip back to where they had come from. One journalist flew to calculated literary heights in describing the scene: "hugging their grips and old fashioned, foreign looking portmanteaus, their Old World tin trunks—small affairs in weird colors—extra overcoats and boxes of apples and oranges, the Reds trooped into the big, warm, brave, brilliantly lighted room." To his mind, they looked like a party of immigrants "waiting in Grand Central Station for a train to take them somewhere in the new land of opportunity." Instead, a launch took them to the "Buford."

Gleeful officials saw them off. Among those in the farewell party were Congressman Isaac Siegel of the House Immigration Committee, William J. Flynn, who was the new Chief of the Bureau of Investigation and reputedly a great "anarchist-chaser," and J. Edgar Hoover, who was in no small measure responsible for the spectacle—he had worked long and hard to get these particular passengers one-way passage and he had made most of the arrangements for the sailing. The birthday of the Poor Carpenter was at hand and perhaps the season had something to do with the holiday mood of the victorious authorities. Filled with the spirit of the occasion, one congressman shouted out, "Merry Christmas, Emma!" as she boarded the "Soviet Ark." Emma thumbed her nose at the festive legislator.

Or thus went the anecdote.[3] It should have happened just that way, in any event, for the image was perfect: the short little woman stood for an instant glowering down upon her official tormenters in their launch below and upon the forces of suppression in the sleeping country behind them; she then jerked a thumb to her nose in a gesture of defiance to all those who made life less livable in her beloved America. True, this image was harsher than the one of the young girl with the pathetically eager face who landed at Castle Garden thirty-four years earlier; but a lot had happened in the meantime. As if to offer mute testimony to this effect, the Statue of Liberty, also an arrival of some thirty years before, still looked out toward Europe with "its huddled masses yearning to breathe free," but her torch was unlighted. The inner meaning of this scene was best captured in a drawing, "The Sailing of the Buford," which Boardman Robinson did for the *Liberator*. In Robinson's sharp artistic indictment, as the old ship with her cargo of heretics wallowed past Bedloe's Island, smoke from her stacks

---

[3] It is probably based on Hoover's recollection of the event, for it appears in the quasi-official book by Don Whitehead on *The FBI Story* (New York: Random House, 1956), p. 48.

drifted back and obscured the face and upper torso of the Mother of Exiles.

The official reaction to the sailing was understandably quite different. J. Edgar Hoover, for instance, rather enthusiastically predicted that more Reds would be deported aboard other "Arks."

Possibly the conservative reaction was best expressed by an editorial in the New York *Times* (December 23): "The Buford gives us the sweet sorrow of parting at last with two of the most pernicious of anarchists, Emma Goldman and Alexander Berkman. . . . Well, Americans know the revolutionary aliens now. They are determined that these soldiers of disorder shall be driven out."

But the best reaction of all was that of a District of Columbia attorney who moodily observed: "With Prohibition coming in and Emma Goldman going out, 'twill be a dull country."

CHAPTER XXV

THE RATIONALIZED CONFORMITY

So ended the decades of struggle, the years of official vilification and misrepresentation. The outright chicanery of the Kersner denaturalization, the fabrication of spy charges, the arbitrariness and vindictiveness of excessive bail and unreasonable searches and seizures—these made up only part of the unlovely record. Not a generous emotion, capable of prompting a gallant deed, apparently ever moved Chambers, Zamosh, Bonaparte, Harr, Straus, Caffey, Content, McCarthy, O'Brian, Palmer, Hoover, or any other official enemy of Emma Goldman. Reflect on the absurdity of a government which at one time or another put its Departments of Justice, Labor, Post Office, and State, its apprehensive judges, and its agitated legislators to the task of silencing a little woman —surely the state showed itself to be, as Thoreau had characterized it, as "timid as a lone woman with her silver spoons." Emma should have been flattered: her great opponent betrayed unmanly fears.

Yet an analysis of the record may yield something more fruitful than bitter humor and righteous indignation. The social and political reaction to Emma Goldman revealed, I venture, a definite shift in the locus of the attack on her civil rights in particular and, since she was for many the outstanding symbol of radicalism, perhaps of the attack on the civil rights of other rebels as well. The shift was from what may be termed *vigilante authoritarianism* toward *bureaucratic authoritarianism*.

Vigilante authoritarianism operated primarily at the city or local level. It was often of an extralegal or illegal nature. Vigilantes in San Diego burned letters in Reitman's buttocks, twisted his testicles, and tried to ram a cane into his rectum. Often such a hated stranger was beaten, tarred and feathered, and threatened with much worse as he was thrown out of town. At their gentlest, vigilantes merely suppressed free speech and protest meetings. At their roughest, they castrated, or shot, or hanged the objects of their fury. Obviously, then, at no time in her thirty years of activity did Emma Goldman live in a "Golden Age of American Freedom." The vigilantes were rough opponents indeed. But Emma showed herself capable of standing up to this kind of terroristic opposition and eventually facing it down. Think of the towns, aside from San Diego, in which she was suppressed initially, but in which she had her say finally.

Bureaucratic authoritarianism, on the other hand, succeeded in making the entire United States forbidden territory for her. The distance between the two authoritarianisms was the distance between the raging mob in San Diego in 1912 and the quietly efficient hearing on Ellis Island in 1919. Bureaucratic authoritarianism operated primarily on the national level. Even during the Red Scare, it had the semblance of legality; as it developed, it was to become quite respectably legal. It was not, as a rule, physically violent in dealing with dissenters, for it worked through the trial or, preferably, the administrative hearing. Nevertheless, the consequences of bureaucratic authoritarianism—say, deportation—were often more painful than tar and feathers.

To be sure, the shift in the attack on Emma did not entail a smooth or complete change-over from vigilante to bureaucratic authoritarianism. From the first the vigilante stamp was on the Red Scare, with its illegal arrests, brutal tortures, calculated starvation, intimidation and beating of speakers, invasion of homes, burning of books. Yet the crucial point is that the scare was in fact administered from Washington. All the pent-up collective dread of difference was manipulated and channeled into the institutional framework provided by governmental agencies and bureaus—by, most notably, the Bureau of Investigation and the Bureau of Immigration. Put another way, Palmer, Hoover, Caminetti, and their subordinates became a kind of Swiss Guard for the religion of nationalism.

The course of the government's campaign showed these suppressive agencies grinding into the lead in action against radicals, or at least alien radicals, years before the outbreak of the Red Scare. Seen from this perspective, the scare was hardly a mere "wave of hysteria" or "spasm of terror" which came at the end of the Great Crusade. For twenty years officials had been working to suppress Emma Goldman. The anarchist exclusion act of 1903 and the denaturalization act of 1906, while evidence of the continuing campaign against alien radicals, did not quite enable the government to deport Emma and all the other irritating strangers in the land. But with the World War, officials had their golden chance: they could draw on popular anxieties to establish a program under which Emma Goldman and others could be imprisoned and deported. Given this institutional background of the scare, it was clearly more than one of America's sporadic waves of terror—waves which presumably crest and then flow back to their previous level.

In his classic essay on bureaucracy, Max Weber pointed out that the demand "for order and protection ('police') in all fields exerts an especially persevering influence in the direction of bureaucratization. A steady road leads from modification of the blood feud, sacerdotally, or by means of arbitration, to the present position of the policeman as the 'representative of God on earth.' "[1] In abbreviated form, the reaction to Emma Goldman suggested precisely such a long-range development. The change was from feud-like, hit-or-miss conflicts with city fathers and their local police to a serious, continuing struggle with professional "anarchist-chasers" who had a constantly enlarged bureaucratic apparatus at their disposal.

This shift was tied closely to the accelerated industrial growth of the times, the growth of economic concentration, the rise of urban giants, the extension of state controls to many areas of economic and social activity. All of these developments subjected the individual to a network of increasingly rationalized (in terms of precise relationships of means to ends) controls. On the national level the primary means of enforcing these controls was the Bureau of Investigation. During the war and after, this startlingly expanded branch of the Department of Justice openly, if not admittedly, assumed the functions of a political police service.

As the preceding chapter makes clear, the bureau's part in the rationalization of conformity was not a small one. The efficiency of J. Edgar Hoover's direction of the deportation proceedings against Emma, compared with P. S. Chambers' rather sloppy handling of Kersner's denaturalization, was perhaps one index of the more effective methods of dealing with nonconformity. Another, despite the multiple differences between the two situations, was that in 1898 Emma Goldman could safely be an anarchist and vehemently oppose the Spanish-American War, while for the same "crimes" two decades later she was locked up and the full weight of Hoover's General Intelligence Division was thrown behind the effort to deport her for once and all. Or the rationalization of conformity was marked by the growth of the bureau as a clearinghouse for information on radicals and alleged radicals. Possibly the library of Emma and Berkman, which was seized in 1917, formed the nucleus for the collection of radical material which the General Intelligence Division established through other seizures, contributions, and even purchases. It was especially ironic that the card index seized

---

[1] *From Max Weber*, eds. H. H. Gerth and C. Wright Mills (London: Kegan Paul, Trench, Trubner & Co., Ltd., 1947), p. 213.

in the *Mother Earth* office may well have had a similar fate (the New York *Times*, June 16, 1917, had observed that the anarchist index would simplify the work of the secret police). With or without Emma's index as a start, Hoover, a former employee of the Library of Congress, installed such an index of radicals when he was named to head the General Intelligence Division. By the time of Palmer's report to the Senate (November, 1919), Hoover had data on Emma Goldman and another 59,-999 radicals in his files; the following year he reported 200,000. Thus information, rumor, and fantasy about citizens and aliens could be collected and prepared for use by an officialdom of antiradicals. Against individual radicals such as Emma Goldman, Hoover could draw on these files, direct the activities of agents in the field, and co-ordinate the efforts of his division and other governmental agencies working on the case. Day in and day out, then, Hoover could throw against dissentients the crushing, metallic power of bureaucratically organized time, energy, and money.

These strides toward the rationalization of conformity, however, were purchased at a prohibitive cost. The policeman as the "representative of God on earth" simply had no place in an open society and a democratic political order. By going a long way toward the elevation of the policeman to this position, Americans turned away from their more open past. More to the point here, they sanctioned the establishment of a political police apparatus which succeeded in deporting Emma Goldman.

DEATH OF EMMA GOLDMAN

Triumphant at the final breath,
    Their senile God, their cops,
All the authorities and friends pro tem
Passing her pillow, keeping her concerned.
But the cowardly obit was already written;
Morning would know she was a common slut.

Russians who stood for tragedy
    Were sisters all around;
Dark conscience of the family, down she lay
To end the career of passion, brain a bruise;
And mother-wonder filled her like a tide,
Rabid and raging discipline to bear.

In came the monarchist, a nurse,
    And covered up her eyes;
Volkstaat of hate took over; suddenly
The Ego gagged, the Conscious overpowered,
The Memory beaten to a pulp, she fell.
It remained to hide the body, or make it laugh.

Yet not to sink her name in coin
    Like Caesar was her wish,
To come alive like Frick, conjecture maps,
Or speak with kings of low mentality,
But to be left alone, a law to scorn
Of all, and none more honored than the least.

This way she died, though premature
    Her clarity for others;
For it was taught that, listening, the soul
Lost track and merged with trespasses and spies
Whose black renown shook money like a rat
And showed up grass a mortmain property.

KARL JAY SHAPIRO, *Person Place and Thing*

CHAPTER XXVI

MATUSHKA ROSSIYA

"Hurrah, hurrah, hurrah! Kerensky deposed! Bolsheviki in control! Land to be returned to the people. Armistice & peace! I am wild with joy," Berkman had exultingly confided to his prison diary on November 8, 1917. "I never before have known such a happy moment. Indeed this is the happiest moment of my life. . . . Ah, for a few friends & champagne to celebrate this great, this wonderful, blessed news." A short while later Emma Goldman rushed into print with *The Truth about the Boylsheviki* (1918), a pamphlet which vigorously supported the "glorious work" of the Bolsheviki. In a fog of warm defensiveness, she defined the Bolsheviki as "the plural term for those revolutionists who represent the interests of the largest social groups. . . ." Somehow she had obtained the notion that the Bolsheviki "have no imperalistic designs. They have libertarian plans, and those that understand the principles of liberty do not want to annex other peoples and countries."

At the time of their deportation, then, Emma and Berkman both had committed themselves to support Lenin and his followers. True, Emma had reservations which Berkman did not fully share. From the "Buford" she wrote her niece of doubts about her ability to work with the Communists: "I could never in [my] life work within the limited confines of the state—Bolshevist or otherwise." Russia, she feared, compared with America, was "likely not so good. . . . I long for the land that has made me suffer so. Have I not also known love and joy there? And the work which I have built up so patiently and painfully and the friends I made. I have been very rich in spite of all. . . ." Despite these longings for America and her misgivings about work in the Communist state, however, she returned to mother Russia in January, 1920, with spring in her heart and a firm resolution to help the Bolsheviki:

At last I was bound for Russia and all else was almost blotted out. I would behold with mine own eyes *matushka Rossiya*, the land freed from political and economic masters; the Russian *dubinushka*, as the peasant was called, raised from the dust; the Russian worker, the modern Samson, who with a sweep of his mighty arm had pulled down the pillars of decaying society.

The twenty-eight days on our floating prison passed in a sort of trance. I was hardly conscious of my surroundings.[1]

2

The next two years gave Emma and Berkman an extraordinary opportunity to examine revolutionary Russia up close. Knowing the language, they needed no interpreter to talk to anyone, from Lenin to factory workers and peasants. From January to July, 1920, they discussed the course of the revolution with hundreds of Russians in Petrograd and Moscow. Then, at a time when travel in Russia was made almost impossible by the hopelessly overburdened and dislocated railroad system, they made a long, four-month trip to the Ukraine as members of a commission charged with collecting historical materials for the Petrograd Museum of the Revolution. In such cities as Kharkov, Kiev, and Odessa and in such small southern towns as Kremenchug and Znamenka, Emma and Berkman were able to gather not only documents on the revolution but also the views of many groups—local Communists, the persecuted Left Socialist Revolutionists, trade union leaders, harassed members of the intelligentsia, hunted partisans of the agrarian anarchist Nestor Makhno, victims of the Cheka in the forced-labor camps, Zionists and other Jews in pogrom-ridden villages. While General Wrangel's momentary victories over the Red Army kept them from going on to the Caucasus, in November and December they traveled as far north as Archangel on another expedition for the museum. The range and depth of these experiences soon enabled the two old comrades to penetrate to the inner life of the Russian people. What they saw was profoundly disquieting.

Within months of her arrival, Emma discovered that the enchanted Russian forest was really haunted by the absolute Bolshevik state. All local independence and mutual helpfulness were being choked by the miles of red tape which streamed out of Moscow. One needed a *propusk* or pass to go anywhere. There were thirty-four different kinds of rations—with the best naturally going to the "active" members of the Communist party. In Moscow and other cities people rushed frantically by one another, so absorbed in hunting food and so afraid of the secret police that they did not stop to aid the children and women who fell

---

[1] *My Disillusionment in Russia* (London: C. W. Daniel Co., 1925), p. 3. The American edition of the same title, published by Doubleday, Page & Co., in 1923, was marred by the omission of the final third of the text. The omitted chapters were later published under the title, *My Further Disillusionment in Russia* (Garden City, New York: Doubleday, Page & Co., 1924). The English edition, cited above, is complete.

from exhaustion. Arrogant commissars and their subordinates deliberately wasted time, while thousands of perplexed people spent days and weeks waiting in corridors and offices for attention. Almost everywhere she observed incredible mismanagement, favoritism, corruption, centralized authoritarianism. It was a nightmare realized. One of its harshest sides was the militarization of labor. The great flour mill of Petrograd, for instance,

looked as if it were in a state of siege, with armed soldiers everywhere, even inside the workrooms. The explanation given was that large quantities of precious flour had been vanishing. The soldiers watched the millmen as if they were galley slaves, and the workers naturally resented such humiliating treatment. They hardly dared to speak. One young chap, a fine-looking fellow, complained to me of the conditions. "We are here virtual prisoners," he said, "we cannot make a step without permission. We are kept hard at work eight hours with only ten minutes for our *kipyatok* [boiled water] and we are searched on leaving the mill." "Is not the theft of flour the cause of the strict surveillance?" I asked. "Not at all," replied the boy; "the Commissars of the mill and the soldiers know quite well where the flour goes to." I suggested that the workers might protest against such a state of affairs. "Protest, to whom?" the boy exclaimed; "we'd be called speculators and counter-revolutionists and we'd be arrested." "Has the Revolution given you nothing?" I asked. "Ah, the Revolution! But that is no more. Finished," he said bitterly.

At first Emma was willing to accept the Communist argument that all this could be explained in terms of external dangers. First and foremost, there was the allied blockade, Zinoviev or Gorky or Ravich would impatiently point out in reply to her questions, and then there were Kolchak, Denikin, Yudenich and other counterrevolutionists, the Menshevik "traitors," and the Social Revolutionists of the Right. The harsh centralization was "absolutely necessary," for the Bolsheviki obviously had to defend the revolution. Yet Emma continued to be disturbed by thoughts she could not down. Perhaps some of the evil was inside Russia, not outside. Why not send the freezing population of Petrograd out to the nearby forests for fuel? she asked Zinoviev. He admitted that such direct action might reduce suffering, but added that it would interfere with crucial political policies, notably that of concentrating all power in the hands of the Communist party. Upon reflection, Emma concluded that this was a dear price indeed to pay.

Of course the rationalized terror bothered Emma most. On her first night in Petrograd, Zorin, her Communist host, had assured her that capital punishment had been abolished and a general political amnesty declared. But lying awake other nights, she heard the oppressive silence of Petrograd broken by occasional shots. Did this mean that Zorin had lied? To her great distress, she discovered that it did. Anarchists and other dissenters were thrown into overcrowded prisons for their ideas, denied any defense, even condemned to death—all this in revolutionary Russia! As the Russian novelist Korolenko summarized the situation for her, "if the gendarmes of the Tsar should have had the power not only to arrest but also to shoot us, the situation would have been like the present one."

Sorely troubled, Emma asked Angelica Balabanoff, a dedicated Communist who was at that time still close to Lenin, for some kind of explanation. When Emma began her anguished questioning, she suddenly broke into a fit of weeping. As Miss Balabanoff wrote in her memoirs, Emma "poured forth all her shock and disillusionment, her bitterness at the injustices she had witnessed, the others of which she had heard. Five hundred executed at one time by a revolutionary government! A secret police that matched the old Okhrana! Suppression, persecution of honest revolutionists, all the unnecessary suffering and cruelty— was it for this the Revolution had been fought?"[2] Struggling with her own doubts, Miss Balabanoff tried to explain away Emma's by holding that life itself was at fault: it was the "rock on which the highest hopes are shattered. Life thwarts the best intentions and breaks the finest spirits." She promised to arrange a meeting for Emma and Berkman with Lenin, who knew all about life.

True to her word, Miss Balabanoff sent Vladimir Ilyitch a note and a copy of *The Trial and Speeches of Alexander Berkman and Emma Goldman* (1917). A few days later she received a reply from Lenin: " 'Dear Comrade,' he wrote, 'I read the pamphlet with immense interest' (he underlined the 'immense' three times). 'Will you make an appointment with E. G. and A. B. for next week and bring them to me? I shall send a car for you.' "[3]

So one day they went to see the great man in the Kremlin. Greeting them with apparent cordiality, Lenin fixed his sharp eyes on the pair and fired a volley of questions: When could the social revolution be expected in America? Was the American Federation of Labor completely bourgeois? What about the I. W. W.? Lenin praised Emma and Berk-

---

[2] *My Life as a Rebel* (New York: Harper & Bros., 1938), p. 254.

[3] *Ibid.*, p. 255.

man for their speeches in court and held out a bright future in Russia for *ideiny* anarchists—anarchists of ideas—who were co-operative. Berkman interrupted to ask why anarchists were in prison. Nonsense, Lenin insisted emphatically. No anarchists of ideas were in prison; some bandits and followers of Makhno had been imprisoned, but no *ideiny* anarchists. Emma expressed some skepticism about Lenin's distinction and asserted her reluctance to work with the soviet government so long as her companions were in prison for opinion's sake. Lenin broke in to assail her sentimental view of free speech: it was merely "a bourgeois notion. There can be no free speech in a revolutionary period." They should take up some useful work to regain their "revolutionary balance."

3

With each passing day, Emma found it more difficult, though her life depended on it, to achieve the kind of "balance" suggested by Lenin. Every position she was offered seemed to demand total surrender of her independence. When she proposed to Lenin that a Russian society for American freedom be established, he expressed interest, but ruled that it would have to be directed by the Third International. Luncharsky, the Commissar of Education, invited her to join him in his work, but only if she were ready to give up being a "free bird." By the time Petrovsky offered her a post as head instructress in the military Nurses' Training School, she was convinced that she should take no job which tied her to the government.

Berkman also found it almost impossible to adjust to the demands made by Lenin and his followers. On one occasion he was asked by Radek to do a quick translation of Lenin's manuscript on "The Infantile Sickness of Leftism." Once he had read it, Berkman realized that it was an attack, an unfair attack, he felt, on all his ideals. He astonished Radek by refusing to translate it unless he were allowed to add a preface. After this act of *lèse majesté*, leading Communists became perceptibly cooler in their attitude.

Nevertheless, Berkman continued to defend their hosts against Emma's criticism. He admitted that the bureaucracy had become suffocating and that there were many inequalities and injustices, but he argued that Russia would outgrow these evils once the blockade was lifted. The important thing was that the revolution had gone beyond mere political change to root out the larger part of the capitalist system. In return for this great achievement, he was willing to excuse much. In the fall of 1920 he was still asking critical anarchist comrades if they had anything to propose in place of the dictatorship: "Not the faults and shortcomings of the Bolsheviki are at issue," he argued, "but the dictatorship itself. Does not the success of the Revolution presuppose the forcible abolition of the bourgeoisie and the imposing of the proletarian will upon society? In short, a dictatorship?"[4] Well into 1921 Berkman continued to believe in the possibility of establishing better relations between the soviet government and dissident political groups.

Berkman's stubborn defense of the Bolsheviki and Emma's growing alienation from them produced a serious rift between the two old friends. When Emma cried out against all the brutal repression, Berkman pointed out to her that the revolution could not be judged "by a few specks of dust." As Emma later reminded Berkman of these days in one of her letters: "And what is more dear Sash[,] deep down in your soul you are still the old Adam. Didn't I see you in Russia where you fought me tooth and nail because I would not swallow everything as justification of the Revolution. How many times did you throw it into my teeth that I had only been a parlour revolutionist, that the end justifies the means, that the individual is of no account etc., etc.?" Berkman could only reply that "your opposition to the Bolsh seemed to me too sentimental and womanish. I needed more convincing proofs, and until I had them I could not honestly change my attitude."

Berkman was in truth more the revolutionist, while Emma was more the rebel. He could excuse much in terms "of historical necessity"; she never made her peace with "historical necessity." When the revolution became oppressive, Emma was more likely to oppose the oppression and become a heretic. Tom Bell, an old Scottish anarchist and a lifelong friend of Peter Kropotkin, Emma, and Berkman, cut through to the core of the matter in one of his letters to Berkman:

You know, Alec, that I have a strong affection for you and that I had a strong affection for our dear old Peter. Yet if I had to cleanse my soul I should have to tell you that in regard to you both in that dark period in Russia I should not have been surprised too much if I had heard that either or both of you were forgetting the Anarchist part of your Anarchist-Communism and being led astray by the Communist part. . . . But about Emma! Her ideas in that matter were never supposed to be different from yours or Peter's. Yet never for a moment, never for an instant did I doubt that in the long run Emma at least would come out alright with her sound instincts and fundamental good sense, and that at once she would take up the fight.

[4] Berkman, *The Bolshevik Myth* (New York: Boni & Liveright, 1925), pp. 256–57.

Yet Berkman, too, however less certainly than Emma, proved to be fundamentally a rebel: when he could no longer defer choosing, he showed that he preferred heresy to orthodoxy—even to "revolutionary" orthodoxy.

4

For Berkman and everyone else who had eyes to see, the moment of forced decision came in March, 1921. Once described by Trotsky as the "pride and glory of the Russian Revolution," the Kronstadt sailors had fought on the Bolshevik side in the October Revolution which deposed Kerensky. Three years later, however, their dissatisfaction with the oppressive rule of the Bolsheviki erupted when a series of strikes broke out in Petrograd. The sailors supported the demands of the strikers for better rations and greater self-determination for their unions; they also seized upon the occasion to protest the organized terror and to demand free speech, free press, and free assembly. Lenin, Trotsky, and Zinoviev typically interpreted these demands for greater freedom as a counterrevolutionary plot. All the soviet state's forces of suppression were swiftly mobilized.

Emma Goldman and Alexander Berkman viewed this turn of events with great apprehension. On March 5 they sent a letter to Zinoviev in which they declared that the time had come to speak out: "To remain silent now is impossible, even criminal." Asking the Communists to set up an impartial commission to arbitrate the dispute, they implored: "Comrades Bolsheviki, bethink yourselves before it is too late. Do not play with fire; you are about to take a most serious and decisive step." Their answer came in the evening of March 7, when they heard artillery attacking Kronstadt.

For ten terrible days and nights, until Kronstadt surrendered on the seventeenth, the remorseless slaughter continued. Emma and Berkman wandered helplessly in Petrograd's streets or sat in unbelieving agony in the Hotel International. Berkman's brief diary entry for the time had its own eloquence: "Days of anguish and cannonading. My heart is numb with despair; something has died within me. The people on the streets look bowed with grief, bewildered. No one trusts himself to speak. The thunder of heavy guns rends the air." The guns, sent by Trotsky to shoot the counterrevolutionists "like partridges," killed instead about 18,000 friends of the Russian Revolution.

A picture taken a little later in Moscow captured Emma's mental and physical condition. Without her glasses, which had been smashed, her eyes gazed directly at the camera from their sunken, underscored settings. Her entire face looked unusually lean, even haggard—in part explainable, no doubt, by the simple observation that she was hungry. (She and Berkman had enough food for themselves, but with starvation on all sides, she commenced cooking for two and finished by feeding a dozen. "I do not need to tell you," she wrote a friend, "that I was the one who remained hungry, this not once but every day.") But her face suggested most a horror, a bottomless horror, of which black despair and bitter anguish were merely the surface expressions. More than physical distress, her face suggested a conscience as raw as an open wound.

Inevitably the months after Kronstadt were merely an anticlimax. Both Emma and Berkman refused to accept food rations from the blood-stained government. Moving into small quarters in Moscow, they lived like thousands of other ordinary Russians, hauling their own wood, preparing their own food, caring for their own clothes. Their rooms were often filled with comrades and friends who arrived at all hours of the day and night. Their visitors' moods varied from deep dismay to heady exaltation. Anarchists came for support, bringing news of other arrests, comrades on hunger strike in one of Moscow's prison's, or additional acts of persecution by the Communists. Of quite another character and mood were their visitors from the United States. Big Bill Haywood, in full flight from his sentence to Leavenworth and from his followers in America, came to chat enthusiastically about the glorious Russian experiment, the possibility of revolutionizing the American masses from Russia, and the need to realize that the ends justified all means. Also in the first flush of their evangelical fervor were such old acquaintances as Bob Minor, Mary Heaton Vorse, William Z. Foster. For different reasons, both the hunted anarchists and the naïve American enthusiasts added to Emma's and Berkman's despair. For all their callers, however, Emma practiced her best culinary magic and gave generously of her physical and moral resources.

Aside from acting the good hosts, there was little the two comrades could do. They worked halfheartedly to establish a Peter Kropotkin Museum—their great teacher had died in February—only too aware that such a venture was both a grotesque anomaly and a virtual impossibility in a country dominated by Lenin's Leviathan. In the summer of 1921 most of their energies were directed to arousing the interest of some foreign syndicalists, delegates to the Red Trade Union Congress, in the fate of imprisoned anarchists. While they managed to help secure the release of a few anarchists, actually they were almost helpless before the advancing terror. The end came with the execution by the Cheka of Fanya Baron, their close friend, and of Lev Chorny, the beloved poet. Russia under Bolshevik rule had become unbearable.

Berkman commenced clandestine negotiations to leave the country. Reluctant to go this way, Emma applied for their passports. To her surprise, these were granted. In December, 1921, Emma Goldman and Alexander Berkman crossed the border into Latvia. All of Russia seemed a fresh grave.

CHAPTER XXVII

THE BOLSHEVIK MYTH

Along with Alexander Shapiro, a veteran syndicalist who was also fleeing Russia, the two comrades arrived in Riga, Latvia, in early December
of 1921. From there they hoped to travel to Germany, where an anarchist congress was scheduled for later in the month. After days of irritating
delay they learned that their application to enter Germany had been
refused. Almost as disturbing, the Latvian government refused any
further extension of their permits to remain in Riga. Faced with an
impossible quandary, unable to leave and unable to stay, Berkman again
began to explore the possibilities of a *sub rosa* route to Germany. Only
at the last minute came word that comrades in Stockholm had secured
Swedish *visé* for them.

Their relief was short-lived. They were taken from the train for
Reval, Estonia, by the Latvian secret police, searched thoroughly, locked
in solitary confinement over the Christmas holidays, and finally released
with lame, if profuse, apologies for the "unfortunate mistake." From
the Latvian police and from friends in Berlin they learned later that
their difficulties had been the work of the Cheka: the cynical Bolsheviks,
it seemed, had avoided international protests by granting the application of Emma and Berkman for their passports, but at the same time
the Russian secret police had made every effort to make sure that these
passports would do the pair no good. Prompted by the Cheka, other
countries would do the dirty work of the Bolshevik by branding their
two opponents as undesirables. Had this plan worked, Emma and Berkman, with no place else to go, would have had to return to Russia and
to silence about their recent experiences. This interpretation was plausi-
ble and had some evidence to back it up.

Unknown to Emma and her friends, however, was some other evidence which made it almost equally likely that the United States had a
hand in the affair. Commissioner Young in Riga transmitted to Washington excerpts from Berkman's diary, copies of his personal letters,
descriptions of their credentials to the anarchist congress, lists of names
and addresses from Berkman's notebooks. Now how did Young come

into possession of these stolen materials? Did he arrange to have the hated deportees arrested for this purpose? Less likely, though conceivable, he and the Russian agents co-operated in the venture, Most likely, he merely secured his information from the obliging Latvian authorities. In any event, whatever the reasons for their arrest, the two anarchists had good reason to be reminded of the long reach of governmental arms.

On January 3, still on the job, Young informed Secretary of State Hughes that Emma Goldman and Alexander Berkman had left the preceding day for Sweden.

2

In Stockholm their first thought was to tell the rest of the world of the Russian terror. The Swedish anarchist and anarcho-syndicalist papers, the *Arbetaren* and the *Brand*, published interviews with them and carried their appeals for all the imprisoned politicals in Russia. Berkman sent off some articles to the New York *Call*, the Socialist daily, and to other radical papers. Emma felt a crushing responsibility to reach a larger audience, however, both for the sake of the politicals and for her earlier presumption for having written in America her exceedingly naïve pamphlet on *The Truth about the Boylsheviki*. So just a few days after their arrival in Sweden, Emma mailed an article on the martyrdom of Maria Spiridonovna, the veteran Russian revolutionary, to her niece Stella Cominsky, with instructions that she try to have the article published in the *Nation* or the *New Republic*.

Emma's willingness to let the liberal press have her articles without pay was in character, but still remarkable. In Riga and later in Stockholm representatives of the New York *World* and the Chicago *Tribune* had offered her substantial sums for such a series. And at this time Emma and Berkman were virtually without funds and cut off from any real opportunity for an income (in Russia Berkman had been robbed of some sixteen hundred dollars of their money, so that when he and Emma arrived in Riga they had less than seven hundred dollars). Yet Emma's desire not to give aid to the enemies of the Russian Revolution—she sharply distinguished the revolution from the subsequent Bolshevik misrule—impelled her to inform her niece that she would not think of accepting the offers of the capitalist press: "But of course I do not propose that they should have anything from me."

Unfortunately liberals were quite unwilling to publish accounts of Communist brutality toward political prisoners. When Stella Cominsky carried Emma's article to one editorial office after another—to the

Nation, the *New Republic,* the *Freeman*—she received the same response in each, a polite, firm, "No thanks!" Emma found herself in a distressing dilemma: if she did not accept an offer from the *World* or *Tribune,* then she could make her views known to only a small circle of radicals. If she accepted such an offer, she would be charged with having sold herself to the enemy for a few pieces of silver. Berkman and Shapiro strongly advised her not to accept the offer, for, they assured her, workers everywhere would be suspicious of her accounts in any such capitalistic setting. She was pained by Berkman' hostility to the plan, though she recognized a large measure of truth in what he said—she had herself earlier criticized Catherine Breshkovskaya for accepting support from wealthy patrons for her lectures against the Communists. On the other hand, some comrades, notably Errico Malatesta, Max Nettlau, and Rudolf Rocker, argued that under the circumstances Emma's primary obligation was to make her experiences as widely known as possible. With or without this kind of support, Emma felt a compelling responsibility to speak out, even if it meant opprobrium. She wired Stella Cominsky to accept the *World* offer of three hundred dollars each for five or six articles. In the end she sent the *World* seven articles, all of which were published in late March and early April, 1922.

3

Meanwhile, Emma and Berkman were trying to find a relatively permanent refuge in some country. After their articles began to appear, Karl Branting, the Socialist prime minister, warned them that it was "inadvisable" for them to appear in print—Branting obviously feared that they might inadvertently interfere with his current delicate negotiations to recognize the new Russian regime. With considerable courage the prime minister defied the attacks of the opposition press and extended their permits to stay for a month, but he also let them know that this was the last extension they could expect.

Anarchist comrades in a number of other countries—Germany, France, Czechoslovakia, Austria—redoubled their efforts to get visé for the two Ishmaels. Finally Czechoslovakia granted Emma a permit. Sick of applying for official favors, Berkman wrathfully rejected Emma's pleas that he seek permission to accompany her; instead he stowed away on a tramp steamer bound for Germany. Just before his ship left, Austrian visé arrived, but Berkman would not be deterred from his plan —especially since the Austrian foreign minister insisted that they sign a pledge to refrain from political activity while in his country.

Emma also refused to sign the pledge and turned regretfully to underground schemes to enter Germany. These proceeded so far that a friend had made arrangements with some sailors he knew to have Emma smuggled into Denmark. Fortunately her conspiratorial efforts failed, for when she returned to Stockholm the German counsul handed her a *visé* for ten days.

4

Once in Berlin, Emma easily secured an extension of her permit to stay. She moved into a small apartment and set about picking up the pieces of her life. Her first major project was a book on her Russian experience. Before she started, however, she needed a few days of leisure to collect her thoughts; she hoped at the same time to resume an affair which had commenced in Stockholm.

There Emma and a young man named Arthur Swenson had established a sweet and, to Emma, a flattering companionship—while Emma was now fifty-two years old, Swenson was only thirty. Swenson's intelligence, his fluent English—he had spent some time in the United States and still proudly displayed his wobbly button—his devotion, and his youthful blond, blue-eyed good looks drew Emma with a force that suggested she hoped to regain her own past and thereby erase the unhappy present.

After Emma left for Berlin, Swenson wrote plaintively that his longing for her was so great he could not sleep. Emma had changed his life: "Before I met you I did not live. I doubted everybody and condemned almost everything. Now the sun shines with a radiant glow and I know all mankind is of good and not of evil." Their differences of age did not mean a thing, he protested, for his love belonged to her only. His deepest wish was to come to her in Berlin.

With some trepidation, Emma bade him to come. Her worst fears were realized upon his arrival, for she immediately sensed that his ardor had cooled. Eight harassing months followed. At first she sought to regain something that had disappeared forever and then she tried to content herself with Swenson's friendship—she was reluctant to send him away, for he was without means and in trouble with the Swedish authorities for evading conscription. Moreover, when Berkman observed that Swenson's affection for Emma had waned, he believed that she was just allowing herself to be used and he became antagonistic to the Swede. The situation became impossible for Emma. Finally, after Swenson could no longer hide his feelings for her young secretary, Emma decided to end the painful experience. In a moving letter she emphasized that she was not blaming him, "even if my heart refuses to submit to the verdict of my mind. You are thirty and I am fifty-two. From the ordinary point of view, it is natural that your love for me should have died. It is a wonder it should ever have been born. How then can it be your fault? Traditions of centuries have created the cruel injustice which grants to the man the right to ask and receive love from one much younger than himself and does not grant the same right to the woman." She implored him not to rush away in anger, but to leave her "in the same beautiful spirit as one separates from something dead, something one had loved and cherished." Swenson showed his good will and his understanding of her suffering by quietly going out of her life—she did not hear from him again for over a decade.

5

It was during this difficult period that Emma commenced her book. After a slow start, she was soon back in Russia, reliving the march of events which had come to a climax with Kronstadt. As usual, she turned to Berkman for editorial assistance. This time, however, her preoccupation with her own interests led her to take advantage of her friend.

While he had already written pamphlets on various aspects of the Russian problem, Berkman also planned to write a book on the "Bolshevik Myth." For such a study, his Russian diaries were indispensable. When Emma unthinkingly asked to use his diaries for her work, Berkman experienced considerable distress. After he had granted her request, he was informed that a prospective publisher was no longer as interested in his diary. As Berkman wrote a friend in October, 1922:

You see, dear Mac, the man who made me that offer is the local representative of the publishing house that is to publish E.'s book. You will understand my feeling of comradeship when I tell you that I have consented, willingly and cheerfully, that E. make use of all the data, material, documents etc. which I had accumulated (and translated) for her book. Moreover, E.'s forte is the platform, not the pen, as she herself knows very well. Therefore my days and weeks are now taken up, really entirely, as editor. It is not only that I get no time for my own work, but my Diary and my book (if I ever get to it) must of necessity contain the very same things, data and documents, in exactly the same wording even, as E.'s book, for the translations are all mine. As her book will be out first, what interest could my book (or even Diary) have on the very same subject. . . . It is a tragic situation. Of course, my writing is different in style, and to some extent in point of view, but the meat I have given away. And yet I could not do otherwise. . . .

To be sure, Berkman's Bolshevik Myth (1925) was published within a few months and discerning critics proclaimed it superior to Emma's book. But the fact remained that Berkman had to provide Emma with materials he had himself collected and translated; he had to drop his own work to help her edit her manuscript and even help with the writing of her theoretical Afterword; and he had to forego any advance such as she received—instead he had to give Boni and Liveright guarantees against any loss they might suffer in taking his book. On occasion in the past Emma had accepted proofs of Berkman's friendship in ways which brought her dangerously close to outright exploitation. In this incident she exhibited a certain moral insensitivity.[1]

When Doubleday and Page sent her copies of her book, it was Emma's turn to be distressed. For her title, "My Two Years in Russia," the publishers had substituted My Disillusionment in Russia—"a veritable misfit," she felt, for it implied her rejection of the revolution and not merely and specifically her repudiation of the Bolshevik tyranny. What was worse, the book appeared with the last twelve chapters missing! Her frantic cablegrams eventually elicited the information that Doubleday and Page had received what they believed to be the complete manuscript from the McClure Syndicate; perhaps someone in the literary agency had unintentionally failed to include the final installment of Emma's manuscript when it was sent to the publishers. After receiving guarantees for the cost of printing, the publishers agreed to issue the missing chapters in a separate volume under the title of My Further Disillusionment in Russia. Emma was scarcely comforted: by this point her work had all the appeal of a one-legged, stillborn infant.

The response of the book reviewers seemed a suitable denouement. The obvious incompleteness of the book was perceived by only two reviewers, one a critic for the Cleveland Plain Dealer and the other a Buffalo librarian. The "reviewers" either had not read the book carefully or had not read it at all. Liberal critics generally indulged themselves in ad hominem arguments and then felt free to dismiss the evidence Emma presented. Typical of this approach was the review by Jerome Davis in the New Republic. Davis thought it natural that she and Berkman should be antagonistic to the Communist regime, since as anarchists they were opposed to government anywhere—he did grant, however, that they presented a good deal of "spicy gossip" in their works.

[1] Years later, after Berkman's death, Emma read the letter quoted above. In an initialed marginal note, she penned: "Poor Old Sasha, your feeling was unnecessary. Bolshevik Myth great." Apparently she still did not fully comprehend why it had been "a tragic situation" for Berkman.

On quite another level was the review by Henry Alsberg, an old friend, in the New York *Post*. Alsberg admitted the general validity of her charges, but he took her to task for her romanticism, for her failure to recognize that "grim necessity, the driving need to preserve, not the revolution but the remnants of civilization, had forced the Bolsheviki to lay hands on every available weapon, the Terror, the Tcheka, suppression of free speech and press. . . ." The Communist press's predictable response was that the book was the product of an agent for the reactionaries, of a "lying American sensation monger," of a "hysterical, shameless liar." Conservative reviewers were inclined to give her a pat on the head for her opposition to the Communists. The editor of the New York *Herald Tribune* even departed from the paper's long-established policy of intense hostility by noting that the books of Emma and Berkman were rather disconcerting commentaries on "so-called civilization's ability to use its materials. . . . Are we partly wrong and they partly right?" H. L. Mencken put the matter more directly in a syndicated article entitled " The United States Sustains a Loss in Berkman and Emma Goldman." Their books, perhaps the best on the Russian debacle, showed that they had an ability to "write simple, glowing and excellent English." Mencken concluded that the United States was not so rich in literary talent and honest criticism that it could afford to kick them out of the country: "It was a great mistake, I am convinced, to let so shrewd, forthright and frank a fellow go and La Goldman with him. The defect in our system is that it uses men badly—that it throttles more talent than it makes any use of."[2]

The amputated form of her published work prevented any critic from commenting on her Afterword, an interesting analysis of the forces behind the Russian Revolution and an attempt to outline a general anarchist theory of revolutions. In lines remarkably parallel at points to the recent analysis of George Kennan, she and Berkman argued persuasively that the revolution at its outset was a spontaneous break toward freedom—it was the result of "the passionate yearning for liberty nurtured by a century of revolutionary agitation among all classes

---

[2] In a letter to Frank Harris, Emma revealed that she was not swept off her feet by Mencken's glowing tributes: "I am rather in doubt as to Mencken's sincerity when he waxes warm about my style. I am inclined to think that he uses both Berkman and myself as a medium to prick the American sensibilities regarding its literature and general culture." While this was a shrewd observation, Mencken later proved that his interest in her went further than merely her usefulness as a "medium" or instrument. In 1930 he petitioned the Department of Justice to allow her to return to the United States. He also tried to exert pressure of her re-entry by working with various friends in Congress. When he had to admit defeat, his regret was apparently quite genuine.

of society." One fine day the oppressive, anachronistic power of the Czar was no more. At this stage there was an imperative need for "the broadest exercise of the creative genius of the people." The Soviets, the co-operatives, the labor organizations, and the intelligentsia were instruments which had the potential for effective guidance. The tiny band of Bolsheviki, however, had other plans. Although at first Lenin and his followers swam with the tide of popular feeling by voicing ultra-revolutionary slogans and by suffering the popular forces to manifest themselves, they soon began to oppose this current. When they felt secure enough, they sheared away the power of the Soviets, made the trade unions over into creatures of the Communist state, and destroyed the autonomy of the co-operatives. Thus the revolution, which in essence was the negation of authority and centralization, was diverted by the Bolsheviki into authoritarian, centralized channels. All real power was appropriated by the omnicompetent state; the Communist party kept an iron grip on the state through systematic violence. Once again the people had been betrayed into exchanging one set of masters for another.

Yet the ultimate betrayer of the revolution was not the handful of Leninists, but "the authoritarian spirit and principles of the State," the "fanatical governmentalism" for which the people themselves were not without responsibility. Anarchists simply had been unsuccessful in alerting the masses to this catastrophic consequence. If there is ever to be a revolution which will not extend the area of coercion, she declared, then anarchists will have to forego their preoccupation with limited group activities and isolated individualistic endeavor in order to make men everywhere thoroughly familiar with true libertarian principles. Above all, anarchists must show more effectively that there is no greater fallacy than the notion the end justifies all means. Inevitably, the means used become "part and parcel of the final purpose." The final purpose or "ultimate end of all social change is to establish the sanctity of human life, the dignity of man, the right of every human being to liberty and well-being." This great end absolutely cannot be achieved in Russia or anywhere else through a contempt for human life, through the practice of deceit, hypocrisy, and murder. To believe that it can is to believe in the Bolshevik Myth.

6

Quite understandably her analysis of the unhappy aftermath of the Russian Revolution inflamed German Communists. Several hundred of them broke up the one large meeting in Berlin which she had called in behalf of the imprisoned Russian politicals. Since she had expected such bigotry from enthusiastic believers in the myth, she was not unduly disturbed. Much more discouraging was the official warning not to continue her public criticism of the Russian regime.

Denied any effective expression of her views in Germany, she turned, with no great enthusiasm, to the possibility of settling in England. It seemed a remote chance, for two years earlier Bertrand Russell and Colonel Josiah Wedgwood had tried unsuccessfully to get the Home Office to grant her asylum. Fortunately the political atmosphere had since changed, and Frank Harris, at the moment in Berlin, confidently assured her that the matter could easily be arranged. Harris pledged the Home Office that Emma "would never become a charge on English charitable institutions," for, besides himself, there were dozens who would keep as a sister one whose whole life was a "passionate crusade on behalf of the helpless and dispossessed." He also enlisted the support of George Slocombe, editor of the *Daily Herald*, George Lansbury, Hamilton Fife, and other Labourites. The upshot was a visé, granted by Home Secretary Arthur Henderson in the summer of 1924.[3]

On November 12, 1924, shortly after Emma's arrival, Rebecca West arranged a dinner for her in London. On this impressive occasion, the English left, some two hundred and fifty strong, formally welcomed the veteran rebel to England. Havelock Ellis, Edward Carpenter, H. G. Wells, Lady Warwick, Israel Zangwill, and Henry Salt sent messages of greeting. Colonel Wedgwood, Miss West, and Bertrand Russell paid handsome tributes to her idealistic career. When Emma rose, she was greeted with loud applause. Her vehement attack on the Soviet government and its merciless treatment of politicals, however, raised loud cries of protest. Was she going back on her past? Was she throwing in with the Tories? When she sat down, Bertrand Russell recalls, "there was dead silence except from me."

A comparable lack of enthusiasm met her efforts to form a committee to aid Russian political prisoners. Of the Labour leaders, most of whom were disturbed by the similarity between her depiction of events in Russia and the anti-Communist charges of the Tories, only Colonel Wedgwood and Miss West consented to join. After a meeting in his

[3] Berkman remained in Berlin to head the Joint Committee for the Defense of the Imprisoned Revolutionists in Russia. With the help of Isaac Don Levine, Emma, and others, he also collected materials for *Letters from Russian Prisons* (ed. Roger Baldwin; New York: Albert and Charles Boni, 1925), still an important source on early Bolshevik oppression.

home, Harold Laski wrote that Emma had better go her own way without hoping for help from the Labour party. Laski listed the reasons individual leaders gave for their decision: Some felt that an attack on the Communists was an "adventure" on which the Labour party "must not, at any cost, embark"—obviously it was impolitic to give any aid and comfort to the Conservative opposition. Others felt that any action would have to await corroborating evidence—specifically, the report of the Trade Union Delegation to Russia. Others felt that Emma was more anxious to attack the Bolsheviki than "to obtain privileges" (!!) for the politicals. But the most interesting argument was advanced by Bertrand Russell, who had met Emma in Russia and who had been guided around Moscow by Berkman.

Russell wrote Emma directly that he could not participate in her work:

... I am not prepared to advocate any alternative government in Russia: I am persuaded that the cruelties would be at least as great under any other party. And I do not regard the abolition of all government as a thing which has any chance of being brought about in our life times or during the twentieth century. I am therefore unwilling to be associated with any movement which might seem to imply that a change of government is desirable in Russia. I think ill of the Bolsheviks, in many ways, but quite as ill of their opponents. ... I am very sorry to have failed you, and I hesitated for a long time. But the above view is what, in the end, I felt to be the only possible one for me.

Emma was painfully disappointed by Russell's stand. She had already suggested that if he did not wish to associate himself with her, he should form his own committee; but in any event, she implored, do not "remain silent in the face of such wrongs."

Respect for Russell and diffidence about seeming importunate apparently prompted Emma to discontinue their correspondence. But in her reply to Laski she ripped into Russell's argument. She held, ironically, that it was illogical. His point that there was no other political group of an advanced nature to take the place of the Bolsheviki seemed to her completely "out of keeping with the scholarly mind of a man like Russell." Even if it were so, what bearing did that have on a stand for political justice for the victims of the government? Besides, with every other political organization broken up and the "adherents wasting their lives in Russian prisons and concentration camps, it is difficult to say what political group is likely to be superior to the present on the throne of Russia." On this shaky foundation of illogicality and lack of evidence, was Russell really suggesting that "all liberty-loving men and women must sit supinely by while the Bolsheviki are getting away with murder?" Would Russell have hesitated to use his pen and his voice in behalf of political victims of the Czar?

The question, as I understand it, is the Dictatorship and the Terror, such as a Dictatorship must make use of, not the name of the particular Group at the back of it. This seems to me to be the dominant issue confronting various men and women of Revolutionary leanings, and not, who is being persecuted, or by whom.

She wondered, finally, if Russell, "like Mr. Clifford Allen and many good people in the Labour and Socialist movements, believe[s] that the 'Bolsheviki' are engaged in an experiment which is going in the right direction."

Another man for whom Emma had great admiration failed to rise to her expectations. Havelock Ellis declined to speak out against the Russian persecution. In a letter he wrote sympathetically:

I certainly understand your attitude in regard to Russia today, though my own feeling is that Russia must work out things in her own way. Every social condition is, in some degree, affected by the social condition that preceded it, and if that was cruel, what follows cannot be entirely good. Apart from that, every social edifice can only be built up out of human nature and as human nature is a mass of contradictions[,] these contradictions must be mirrored in the practical operation of the social scheme. I am sure that under any social system you would feel bound to protest, and in so doing you would be performing a valuable service for humanity.

Probably reflecting that Ellis' laissez faire attitude toward the Russian terror was cold comfort indeed for the dead Kronstadt sailors and the imprisoned victims of the Communists, Emma merely questioned whether the past need be photographically reproduced, whether the Jacobin terror must attend every revolution. People should learn something from experience. She herself had learned from this latest revolution "the imperative necessity of intensive educational [work] which would help emancipate people from their deep-rooted fetiches and superstitions. With many revolutionists I foolishly believed that the principle [sic] thing is to get people to rise against the oppressive institutions and that everything else will take care of itself. I have learned since the fallacy of this on the part of Bakunin, much as I continue to revere him in other respects. . . ."

It is difficult not to believe, after careful consideration, that in these exchanges with some of the best minds in England the virtually self-educated Emma Goldman emerged triumphant. But it was only an intellectual and moral triumph, for—always with the bright exception of Rebecca West—one after another of the leading English liberals and radicals turned down her invitation to cry out against the Bolshevik Myth. Unlike Russell and Ellis, some obviously wished she had not brought the matter to their attention. Emmeline Pethick Lawrence, a Member of Parliament, refused abruptly to take any part in a "futile protest" since her country was not involved: "I do not want to hear or read in detail of atrocities which I know only too well are happening. . . ." Others sympathized with her work but were very busy with other tasks. Henry W. Nevinson, for instance, wished her "every possible success in your efforts to make life for those poor victims endurable"; but, he added, work on a book made it impossible for him to join her committee.

In a summary of the situation for Berkman, Emma wrote that things in England were almost hopeless among the intellectuals "steeped in the Russian spook": The tragedy was "that Bolshevism has gotten under the skin of advanced people and . . . they are loath to do anything against it, while those who have not been infected with the poison belong to the reactionary gang with whom one can not affiliate." It was discouraging.

7

American liberals and radicals were just as great a disappointment. Even among some of her former co-workers there was a conviction that she had betrayed the international proletariat. Rose Pastor Stokes demanded that Emma at least be burned in effigy. Another radical breathlessly charged that she had "sold out to the reactionary papers." Moissaye J. Olgin, editor of *Freiheit*, averred that she was hurt because she had not been given more attention in Russia; he declared that "the Communists are in the saddle because they have the confidence of all Russia, but Miss Goldman has not found that out."[4]

---

[4] The charge that Emma had "sold out" was nonsense. We have already seen that she first offered her *World* articles to the liberal journals for nothing. She was also unwilling to capitalize on the anti-Communism of *My Disillusionment*. For instance, she refused to let Frank Harris use it in his efforts to have English authorities grant her a *visé*. When in 1925 she was informed by her American publishers of the "belated academic recognition" bestowed upon her work through its adoption as reference reading by the University of North Carolina Extension Division, she wrote a friend that "I am not happy about the N.C. business. It is my stand on Russia." Moreover, through the years she turned down a number of offers from suspect sources or declined offers with un-

Scott Wood felt that she had failed to understand Russia. Agnes Inglis and Ben Reitman both expressed their sympathies for the Communists and let her know that they thought she had been unfair in her criticism of the New Order. Reb Raney, a woman who had once worked in the *Mother Earth* office in New York, shrilly proclaimed that Emma was not admired for taking money from the conservative press to attack "the Russian endeavorers . . . who but a cur would throw mud at a baby trying to walk?" Agnes Smedley wrote more rationally that her years in China had convinced her that the Communists were "the only ones who offer any hope for the peasants." She did not want to see Emma again, for "I do not want to think of you with bitterness."

Among the liberals the response was pretty much the same. B. W. Huebsch, the publisher, wrote to a friend that when Emma was in the United States she was a "positive and interesting figure," but now, in her disappointment that the Soviet government was not anarchistic, "she seems to be only a blurred carbon copy of herself." Returning

---

acceptable conditions attached. Two illustrations only: In 1924 *Colliers* magazine offered her four hundred dollars for an article on the conditions and institutions in the United States which compared *favorably* with those of the Old World. She replied that she was willing to point out the good points of America, if at the same time she could deal with the damnable things. *Colliers* wanted no such balanced approach. In 1925 she was asked by the British Women's Guild of Empire to speak to them about conditions in Russia. She sent Mrs. J. D. Campbell, the Honorable Secretary of the Guild, her regrets, adding that she had to be careful under whose auspices she spoke: "You are opposed to the Revolution as well as to the Bolsheviki."

More subtle was the Communist-inspired charge that Emma's and Berkman's bitterness was due to their disappointment in not being given "soft jobs," as Bill Haywood put it. Mr. Charles Madison, in his *Critics and Crusaders* (New York: Henry Holt & Co., Inc., 1948), recently pulled this old chestnut out of the fire: "Emma and Berkman had naïvely assumed that the Russian Revolution, even though directed by extreme Marxists, would create the libertarian utopia. Moreover, as leading American radicals they had expected positions of eminence. Finding themselves merely tolerated . . . they magnified the 'dull gray spots' until they could see nothing else." To counteract precisely this sort of vilification, Angelica Balabanoff, the first Secretary of the Third International, went out of her way in *My Life as a Rebel* to point out that, after watching Emma and Berkman closely during their stay in Russia, she was convinced "they were happy to make any contribution to the 'Workers' Fatherland.'" Even after their disillusion mounted, "they cheerfully went on working without complaints or recriminations." All Emma and Berkman needed to do in order to have power and comfort was to set aside their sense of justice and decency. More specifically, Emma could have had positions in education, nursing, or, probably, in international propaganda had she been willing to give unquestioning obedience to Lenin and his party.

But Emma kept faith with her principles. One of the first of the radicals who became anti-Communist, she was also one of the few who did not make a pendulum-like swing to the political right. Throughout this dark and bitter struggle with the myth she kept her balance.

from Russia, John Haynes Holmes informed a reporter that Emma was "heartily detested" there for the articles which she wrote for the New York World. Holmes later informed Emma directly that he was "terribly shocked" by her stand on Russia.

The formidable hold the myth had on many liberals came out clearly in her correspondence over the years with Roger Baldwin, her former protégé. In 1928 Baldwin admitted that while he deplored the evils in Russia, "I do not protest against them as much as I do against similar evils in other countries, for the simple reason that such protests might be used by the common enemies of us all—the capitalist and imperialist press." He preferred a working-class dictatorship to a capitalist dictatorship and "in this practical world you come pretty near having to choose." In 1931 he was even prepared to grant that "in ultimate terms you are right. As to arriving at ultimates in the mad process of struggle today I see a different road." In yet another letter he wrote "I am further so pragmatically minded that I can accept—with reluctance and doubt—the Soviet system because it works toward a far better goal than capitalism, while maintaining the principles of anarchist-communism as the only desirable solution of the world's struggle for liberation." After this, what could Emma say? She reminded herself of the extenuating circumstances, of the fact that it had taken months in Russia for her to free herself from the hold of the myth. But she was all too aware that Baldwin's letters revealed that virulent moral schizophrenia which caused its victims to cry out in righteous rage against oppression in the west and to remain respectfully silent before much worse in the east.

Emma expressed this troubled awareness during an exchange of letters with Freda Kirchwey of the Nation. Advancing all the old clichés about grim revolutionary necessity and the forced choice between communism and fascism, Miss Kirchwey stated the position in all its grotesqueness:

It may be, as you say, that liberals and radicals fail to point out the oppressive measures of the Soviet government. If this is not strictly true, it is true enough to justify your charge. . . . These groups welcome and admire so many of the fundamental economic, social, and political changes brought about by the Russian Revolution that an outright opposition like yours based on Russian policy toward political dissenters seemed one-sided and non-realistic—like pouring out the baby with the bath. . . . [Besides, the job of criticizing the Soviets was done so viciously by the capitalist press during the early years that journals like the Nation felt called upon to counteract this attack.] . . . all governments maintain themselves by force and the measure of repression varies almost directly with the degree of stability and security achieved by any given group in power. . . . at least [Russia] exercises its power in support of a system that has largely abolished the control of private capital and is working to achieve for the first time in the modern world a collective society. . . . I feel that at a time when fascist dictatorship is the dominant instrument of oppression in Europe, you have been at least guilty of a lack of proportion in the emphasis you place on Russia's sins.

Emma's reply slashed into the spongy center of Miss Kirchwey's argument:

The trouble with you, my dear, and all the others who are carried away by the Soviet experiment, is that you fail to realize that the methods employed by the Communist state are inherent in the dictatorship. . . . I cannot share enthusiasm . . . [for] the "collective society" the Soviet government is attempting to create. I hardly need to emphasize my stand on private capitalism. I have fought it all my life. But collective slavery is nothing to be excited about or any improvement on the slavery created by the capitalistic class. It is merely a change of masters. . . . The fact that the bourgeois press has and does misrepresent Russia should not have bearing on those who all their lives have fought for libertarian ideas. . . . It seems to me that liberals cannot consistently smooth over every outrage committed in the name of socialism, at the same time objecting to the suppression of liberal ideas at home.

Utterly opposed to abandoning the individual to the tender mercies of an abstract historical necessity, Emma pressed her opponent: "You see, my dear, my understanding of revolution is not a continued extermination of political dissenters. I was once told by Robert Minor that individual human life does not matter at all. I consider that an outrage of revolutionary ethics. Individual life is important and should not be cheapened and degraded into a mere automaton. That is my main quarrel with the Communist state."

CHAPTER XXVIII

"NOR FEEL AT HOME ANYWHERES"

Only at Oxford, curiously enough, was Emma Goldman really able to break through the wall of indifference which had closed in shortly after her arrival in England. When several members of the American Club at Oxford invited her to address their group, she of course accepted. Moved by the knowledge that American boys wanted to hear her, she was even more stirred by their response to her remarks. As the Rhodes scholar who introduced her recalls, "she talked for two hours, without notes, in copious detail, with magnificent management of her theme—and brought the house down with a Jeffersonian ending on freedom of the mind. She was weeping as a hundred American boys crowded around to meet her—another hundred of English boys just didn't count with her."[1]

Warm support for Emma's views also came from Rebecca West, a woman of very great brilliance and moral courage. Miss West took time out from her own full schedule to help Emma find a publisher and to write a long introduction for an English edition of *My Disillusionment in Russia.* "For our own sakes we must understand Bolshevist Russia," declared Miss West, "and we must not shrink if our understanding leads to the same conclusion as the Conservative Party regarding the lack of material for admiration and imitation in the Bolshevist Government." For such an understanding *My Dissillusionment* was important, because "Emma Goldman is one of the great people of the world. She is a mountain of integrity." Unfortunately Miss West's fellow Socialists—filled with the wonders of the Communist state reported by the British Trade Union Delegation—remained unconvinced.

After one successful meeting at South Place Institute, Emma experienced a deadening frustration in her attempts to reach the general public. There was nothing to do but carry on with Yiddish lectures in London's East End and English lectures wherever she could find a

[1] Wright Thomas to me, March 29, 1956. Samuel Eliot Morison, then a visiting Professor at Oxford, writes: "She was about the finest woman orator I have ever heard" (Letter, February 6, 1957).

place—but the halls seemed to grow smaller, colder, and more dismal from one meeting to the next.

Six months of heartbreaking effort only brought her to a standstill. Her conviction hardened that the damp, cold English weather, which she found more unbearable than the frozen Russian winters, was no more chilling than the English character. "Even the best English paralyze me," she wrote Berkman. "They are so indifferent, so God damned selfcentered, nothing touches them. It's like Prof. [Samuel Eliot] Morison wrote me, 'I have been trying to get English students to learn something of American history with the same result as you. If only one could make the English angry. The only man who could do it was Samuel Adams when he threw tea in Boston harbor. . . .' Certainly nothing makes the English snob angry, or ruffles him except the destruction of property."[2]

The enthusiastic reception of Emma by the Welsh coal miners and their families was a welcome contrast. The obvious hunger and poverty of the colliers, however, tugged at Emma's conscience for a denunciation of the system which produced their misery. In a sense, her attacks on the Russian dictatorship and her silence about English economic oppression, she reflected, made her just another missionary —she was appealing for "charity for China" when those at home were in need. Yet she could do little or nothing about domestic problems so long as she was in England merely as a visitor and was tolerated only because of her attitude toward Russia.

Luckily a friend whom Emma had first met in Scotland in the 1890's came forward at this point to do her a "good turn." James Colton, a widower in his mid-sixties, made her an offer of marriage. Known in the collieries of South Wales as "no respecter of persons"—one way of saying that his rebellion showed—Colton had educated himself with virtually no help and had thought his way through to a libertarian position. His proposal was a gesture both of friendship for Emma and of defiance to the Establishment. "One important bit of work I was in England in," he explained to Berkman in a letter, "it was what Brought me to London. it will rank with me as a Memory of how two fighters Thwarted the Powers that Be. i have no doubt you have heard about it by this time. i had a Comrades Duty to Perform, to hit back at our Enemie for the Cruel treatment Meted out to you

<hr>

[2] EG to AB, May 28, 1925, IISH, AB.

and Emma and for that i am Thankful."[3] Emma accepted Colton's act with deep gratitude, for it meant her one chance to secure a passport and other credentials. She paid Colton's fare to and from London and reimbursed him for the loss of two and one-half days of work in his colliery. A short while after their marriage, Emma wrote to her "husband" how grateful she was: she had her passport, "thanks to you[,] my faithful comrade. I can not find words to express my appreciation of your sweet solidarity."[4]

2

Now a British subject, legally at least, Emma could try to put roots down in England. Her most pressing problem, after so many months of activity for the Russian politicals, was how to make a living. Uncertainty of income was her one certainty. She even thought of opening a beauty parlor, for she knew of no place in London where one could get the kind of "shampoo, massage and scalp treatment as is given in A[merica]"—for capital, in lieu of more tangible assets, she had "a prescription for the cure of dandruff which works like magic"![5] While

[3] Colton to AB, July 22, 1925, IISH, AB. Colton had almost no formal education, for he had earned his own way from the time he was eight years old.

[4] EG to Colton, November 20, 1925—this letter is in the possession of Mr. J. C. Colton, Lougher, Glamorganshire, South Wales. In her Red Rose: A Novel Based on the Life of Emma Goldman (London: Jarrolds, Ltd., n.d.), Ethel Mannin indulges herself in full fictional license at this point. Once the ceremony is over, Miss Mannin has "Red Emma" nonchalantly dash away from "Jim Evans" after slipping him "a ten shilling note on the station platform, urging him to 'treat' himself and one or two of the boys to the pictures." The real Red Emma had no such flippant attitude toward Jim Colton, and she did more than slip him a few shillings for the cinema. Over the years she helped him whenever her own meager resources permitted. In 1929, for instance, she collected a bundle of clothing for Colton, who was in especially great need at the moment, and wrote a covering letter in which she pointed out that he fully deserved help and sympathy: "I know how fine in spirit you are yourself. People learn to appreciate kindness and to respond to it often in times of need" (EG to Colton, May 18, 1929, also in the possession of J. C. Colton). She also continued to express her gratitude for Colton's act, as in another observation to Berkman that she owed her passport to the generosity of the collier: "I can't thank dear, old, kindly Colton enough for it" (EG to AB, January 11, 1932, IISH, AB).

Needless to add, the press gleefully misinterpreted the marriage. The New York Times (November 21, 1926) rhapsodized that the Goldman-Colton romance had covered twenty years: Cupid was "armed with a coalpick when he dug his way to Emma Goldman's heart." The editor of the New York World (November 22, 1926) mused that Emma must have lost her seemingly "unquenchable flame of rebellion." Disillusioned and without her old ardor, she had turned her back on her past: "Is it not clear why she sought finally so obvious a solace as matrimony?" As clear as the East River, might have echoed the reply.

[5] EG to AB, July 11, 1925, IISH, AB.

she had made a success of a comparable venture in New York, by this time such entrepreneurial schemes were hardly more than a measure of her perplexity. Much more serious were her attempts to gain an income through writing. She wrote occasional articles for the *Westminster Gazette*, the *Weekly News*, and the London *Times*, and she made regular contributions to *Time and Tide*. Free-lance writing, however, provided no real solution. For each of her columns in *Time and Tide* she was paid only a guinea, from which she had to deduct ten shillings for her typist. Given these "starvation wages," as she called them, to rely on her pen for support was to rely on a frail reed indeed.

Striking out obstinately against a "life hedged in by pennies," Emma turned again to the platform and lectures on the drama. Obstacles loomed large on all sides. She was not well known in England. Her poor and scattered anarchist comrades could be of little help. Perhaps most important, one worked through organizations in England. Time after time she was politely informed that her kind of free-lance work just "isn't done in England." Never reluctant to lay the old aside, she pushed ahead. A timely appointment as overseas representative of the American Provincetown Playhouse introduced her to the avant-garde of the English theater. Walter Peacock and Bache Matthews, both of the Birmingham Repertory Theatre, and Barry V. Jackson, its founder, received her hospitably and helped interest the British Drama League in her work. With one foot in the door, she sent out hundreds of letters and circulars to the various societies of playgoers. In one circular she announced: "I can speak on any of the Russian dramatists, as per enclosed Syllabus, on the life and work of August Strindberg, the Swedish dramatist, the German Expressionists, on Eugene O'Neill and his works, or the plays of Miss Susan Glaspell." In London she organized a Drama Study Circle and also scheduled some Yiddish lectures on Russian plays. When O'Neill's new play, *Desire under the Elms*, was banned, she tried to have the Drama League sponsor a public protest meeting. Although she was bitterly disappointed in the results of all these efforts, they were still impressive: She had booked autumn and winter engagements for a single lecture or a series of lectures in London, Bristol, Bath, Birmingham, Manchester, and Liverpool.

To prepare for her lectures she dipped into the "bottomless tank" of the British Museum, that majestic haven where so many other bruised exiles had gone for intellectual sustenance and refuge. Most of the summer she spent full days in the museum, reading works in

Russian, German, Yiddish, and English. One of her discoveries was an unsuspected passion for research. She soon wrote Berkman: "The way I do is to fill myself on each author, all that has been written about him or most of it, and his plays. . . . it is really good for me, it makes me go ahead in a systematic and 'disciplined' manner. I never had time enough to do my work in that way. Perhaps now in my old age I will learn." She was determined to make her lectures more thoughtful than those in America. "I must work doubly hard," she wrote another friend, "not to disgrace my American friends and those here who vouched for me."[6]

Inevitably the response to her lectures fell short of her expectations. Her independent lectures in Bristol and London were especially disappointing, for she had hoped to show that "it was done in England." Despite the support of Rebecca West, Frank Harris, Barry Jackson, and others, her London series on the Russian drama was not well attended. In Manchester her lecture on O'Neill filled the hall, but she felt that few understood her points: "God what a bunch the English middle class is," she wrote Berkman. "The American is freedom and alertness personified in comparison."[7] Nevertheless, her appearances before the playgoers' societies and other groups led her to believe that in time, perhaps a few years, she could gain a regular income from her lectures. She was also encouraged by the interest of C. W. Daniel, her English publisher, in her work. Daniel presented her with stenographic notes of her lectures and urged her to work them over into a book.

A few months off from her grinding routine was more than welcome. Settling in Saint-Tropez, a small village in the south of France, she soon completed "Foremost Russian Dramatists: Their Life and Work." In her discussion of the early Russian playwrights and of Griboyedov, Gogol, Ostrovsky, Pisemsky, Turgenev, Tolstoy, Chekhov, Gorky, and Andreyev, she showed her customary grasp of the explicit meaning and spirit of her subject. The weeks she had spent in the British Museum and her sympathy for the playwrights who struggled with the problem of creativity in her native land gave the study an intensity and depth of insight lacking in most of her previous essays on the drama. That her study also had benefited from a rejection of her earlier mimetic theory of art was obvious: "The epoch commands man to lose himself in the collectivity and demands of him a sacrifice

[6] EG to AB, September 23, 1925, IISH, AB; EG to Harry Weinberger, May 15, 1925, WMC.

[7] EG to AB, November 9, 1925, IISH, AB.

of his individuality, of feelings, of personal happiness," she concluded. "It also exacts obedience and condemns meditation but man continues to defend his right to crazy thought, impetuous love, disarming tenderness, unaccountable passions, and the spiritual freedom he has won." No longer was art merely reality's looking glass.

Just as she was finishing her writing in September, 1926, disturbing news arrived from Daniel. His publishing business had suffered a series of losses after the general strike of the preceding spring; he could, therefore, no longer undertake to publish her manuscript.[8] At about the same time the New York friend who had promised her financial backing for a lecture tour of Canada wired that the tour would have to be canceled—it turned out that he was afraid that she might be injured physically by her Communist enemies. Utterly unwilling to lose the little momentum she had laboriously built up, Emma wired an appeal to some other friends for a loan to cover her passage to Canada. The money arrived almost immediately. With a wry glance backward at England, where so many things just were not done, she sailed for Canada in the fall of 1926.

3

At her first lecture in Montreal Communist threats of physical injury proved that the fears of her erstwhile backer were not baseless. Yet when alarmed friends urged her to seek police protection, she scornfully rejected their pleas with the dry reminder: "I have never called for the police, but the police have often called for me."[9] Ignoring her Communist opponents when she could and shouting them down when she had to, she delivered a series of Yiddish lectures, addressed a large meeting in English in behalf of the Russian political prisoners, and organized a permanent group of women to raise funds for these victims of Communist oppression. In Winnipeg she helped another group of women organize to raise funds and she successfully lectured on the drama to a number of audiences. In Edmonton she again faced down her Communist hecklers to deliver her lectures to almost every labor and liberal organization in the city.

But it was in Toronto that she made the greatest impact. At first

[8] Her "Foremost Russian Dramatists," IISH, EG, remained unpublished. It knocked around in the offices of a dozen publishers and was refused by all of them. It was, nevertheless, a much more profound study than her *Social Significance of the Modern Drama,* for which she had easily found a publisher in 1913.

[9] Montreal *Daily Star,* October 29, 1926.

the city was a disappointment. Known as the "city of intellectuality," it hardly lived up to its reputation. True, there were "five thousand students in the local university," she later wrote a friend, but "the university life is as far removed from the life of the people in this city, as if the seat of the university were in Moscow and not Toronto." And the churches hardly enlivened intellectual life: "Both Catholic and Anglican hold the city by the throat, and mould the habits and opinions of the people of Toronto. No book or lecture can have any success that does not have the stamp of approval of the churches. Perhaps you will understand the whole situation when I tell you that the librarian of the public library . . . declared: 'No, we do not censor books, we simply do not get them.' He certainly spoke the truth."[10]

Emma met Toronto's challenge with a series of meetings, lectures, and press releases. Although in one breath she pleased her audiences by telling them that Canada was freer than Russia, in the next she jabbed at their complacency by assuring them that this was no cause for celebration. The complete public apathy in the face of the arrest and imprisonment of Ernest V. Sterry was a case in point. Sterry, a free-thinker who had once sold pamphlets for Emma in New York, had been convicted of blasphemous libel for referring to God as "this irate old party." To Emma's mind Sterry was imprisoned simply for exercising his right to freedom of speech and thought. Gradually, after she had lashed her audiences for their indifference to the suppression of such fundamental civil rights, others joined their protests to hers. The Reverend W. A. Cameron, a prominent, orthodox Baptist, for instance, sharply denounced such religious persecution by civil authority—Sterry's conviction was, Cameron charged, "a return to the old days of religious slavery."[11] While Sterry still had to serve his sixty-day sentence, the reaction which Emma touched off promised to make such cases more difficult to prosecute in the future. She was tempted to go further in challenging the power of the churches, she wrote Berkman, "but with the idiotic blasphemy law which is very rigid one does not know just what may fall under it. I certainly have no desire to go to prison for the Lord."[12]

Rather she attacked obliquely by lecturing on birth control. She stated the argument for planned parenthood, but carefully refrained

10 EG to Ben Capes, January 27, 1928, IISH, EG.

11 New York *World*, April 10, 1927.

12 EG to AB, May 17, 1927, IISH, AB.

from discussing methods—she declared that while her earlier discussion of methods in the United States had been of value as social protest, the logical procedure was for each individual to seek advice in a clinic or from his private doctor. When the inevitable outcry went up, Inspector McKinney of the Toronto police pointed out that nothing could be done to prosecute her as long as she discussed no techniques of preventing conception. Dr. C. J. Hastings, Medical Officer of Health, went further by expressing the opinion that Emma's lecture on birth control was very sane; what he liked was its angle of attack "as women's rights."[13]

The Toronto Star, one of the city's major newspapers, gave Emma unexpected help in these efforts to whip up public interest in things that mattered. Used to reporters of little understanding and less sympathy, she was startled to find one from the Star, Mr. C. R. Reade, who was well read on the theory of anarchism and prepared to take her efforts seriously. It was a pleasant change to lecture on the drama and then to observe her lecture covered fairly and admiringly in the press. On November 30, 1926, for instance, the Star reported a "Brilliant Disquisition on Ibsen by Emma Goldman," in which her knowledge of the playwright's fundamental ideas as well as the minute details of his plays made for "lecturing in excelsis." That Emma Goldman had not been allowed to speak at the University of Toronto the Star found laughable—the authorities apparently feared that like the Pied Piper she would draw all the students after her. In an interview (December 18, 1926) the Star generously quoted her attack on academic formalism: "In all the sciences today, in art, literature and music you find the same desire to get away from the bonds of academic and confining formulas. The futurists, the cubists, what have they been but anarchists, rebels against the coercion of burdening tradition? In music— why music is filled with ultra-revolutionary movements. Jazz? Yes, jazz is anarchistic, the very spirit of youth, essentially a revolt against outworn traditions and restrictions." And in a feature article on "Toronto's Anarchist Guest," Frederic Griffin informed the readers of the Star Weekly, December 31, 1926, that they had in their midst probably the most interesting woman in the world, a woman who had lived more fully, rebelled more strenuously and unselfishly, suffered more vividly, and thought more vigorously than any other: "It is hard to reconcile the Canadian view of Emma Goldman, of this placid, ex-

---

[13] Toronto Daily Star, April 28, 1927.

perienced woman of the philosophic outlook and the scholarly mind who apparently finds nothing at the moment so interesting as to give such of the bourgeoisie as care to attend academic lectures on Ibsen, Tchekov, and other dramatic giants with the idea of the wild woman whom the United States jailed for her incendiary beliefs and finally threw her out for her inflammatory teachings."

With such a forum for her ideas and publicity for her work, Emma stimulated public interest in her ideas and discovered a cultural undercurrent of people who were, as she observed, "trying to reach out for the newer and better things in literature, art and social ideas." Never, her new friends insisted, had Toronto responded so well to libertarian ideas. Would she not stay and continue the good work? Her expenses would be taken care of. Emma decided to stay on in Toronto through 1927, though she would not think of letting the local anarchists pay her bills—mostly workingmen with families, they were in no position to make this sacrifice. She paid her own way, drawing on surplus receipts from her drama lectures and on cash presents from relatives and friends in the United States.

Yet, no matter how hospitably she was received in Toronto, she was tantalized by the nearness of the United States and distracted by its inaccessibility—as far as she was concerned, the country might as well have been on another planet. She had some small hope that she might be permitted to return temporarily. Isaac Don Levine, a journalist acquaintance, worked through Frank L. Polk, Undersecretary of State during the Wilson administration, to secure permission for her re-entry. Polk found that Secretary of State Kellogg had no objection in principle to a limited stay for Emma, but he took the position that this question was under the jurisdiction of the immigration authorities. Solicitor Davis finally informed Levine that the project was impossible, because of "the situation in China and developments in Haiti."[14] Well aware that there would always be some situation in China or Timbuctoo, Emma seriously considered the alternative of simply boarding a train for Detroit. Though she had no expectation that she would be allowed to stay, the move would force the authorities to deport her a second time—it would "help to make America ridiculous again," she predicted to Berkman.[15]

[14] Levine to EG, November 19, December 15, 1926, IISH, EG; W. S. Van Valkenburgh to EG, April 8, 1927, IISH, EG.

[15] EG to AB, December 22, 1926, IISH, AB.

Eventually she decided against such a sensational "border stunt." Yet even after she had given up the scheme, her desire to return to her friends and her work in the United States burned as brightly as ever. Indeed it was her main motive in going to Canada in the first place: "You might as well know once and for all my dear," she wrote Berkman, "that I will never be able to free myself from the hold A[merica] has on me, nor feel at home anywheres. . . . Because I knew this all the years since we were sent out[—]that is why I went to C[anada]."[16]

In August, 1927, her remoteness from the United States did "gird her to torture," as Evelyn Scott wrote in one of her letters, for it was then that the State of Massachusetts moved with finality to kill Nicola Sacco and Bartolomeo Vanzetti, the shoemaker and the fish peddler who had been convicted, on flimsy evidence and prejudice, of the murder of a paymaster and a guard during a robbery in South Braintree. The same tide of antiradical hysteria which had swept Emma from the country had surged over the two men in 1920 and condemned them to die for a crime they probably did not commit. Along with many others, Emma was convinced that they were convicted not of murder but of anarchism. In Toronto Emma could merely hold a protest meeting in the Labor Temple against the death-like determination of Massachusetts to execute its victims, send what money she had raised to the International Sacco-Vanzetti Defense Committee, and bitterly reflect that she could have done much more if she had been back in the United States: "I feel like a fool to be talking about theoretic stuff, lectures on nothing," she wrote Berkman, "instead of rushing out to add my voice to the cry against the impending butchery." She was little comforted by a letter from Rosa Sacco which informed her that her husband and Vanzetti had spoken of Emma with respect. To Berkman, Emma emotionally reported: "I am going through the agony of 40 years ago in a more conscious form. Then I had my life before me to take up the cause for those killed. Now I have nothing. Now I realize how little I have achieved in the forty years if a new crime is about to be committed and the world protests only in words."[17]

Still enveloped in her feeling of futility, Emma booked passage for France at the end of February, 1928. Over the years many friends,

[16] EG to AB, December 23, 1927, IISH, AB.

[17] EG to AB, August 8, 1927, IISH, AB; EG to Rosa Sacco, September 3, 1927, IISH, EG.

among them Howard Young and Theodore Dreiser, had urged her to write her autobiography. Before she left Toronto she received word from Peggy Guggenheim that Howard Young had started raising a fund to enable her to commence writing—Miss Guggenheim announced that she was starting the fund with a five-hundred-dollar contribution. With Edna St. Vincent Millay as chairman, a group of friends and sympathizers had raised some twenty-five hundred dollars by the time she sailed from Montreal. This was enough for Emma to commence the chronicle of her life.

CHAPTER XXIX

THE STILL INNER VOICE

Saint-Tropez, the little fishing village where Emma had already spent a summer working over her manuscript on the Russian drama, seemed to her an ideal place to settle. Some New York friends, among them Arthur Leonard Ross, who had become her attorney, and Mark Dix, one of her well-to-do admirers, raised a little over three thousand dollars to buy her a modest cottage in which she could live and work. "Bon Esprit," her new home, rested among the vineyards on the hills above the town. From her windows she could look out upon the blue Mediterranean—lonely, timeless, lost in the distance on its way to Africa; for a more active view she could look down upon the small fishing boats rocking quietly in the water along the shore below. With this serenity of setting she could hope to summon the inner strength she needed to relive her turbulent years.

The loss of her own archives (which had been confiscated by the Department of Justice in 1917) made her fear that she would not be able to write the detailed, precise work she had in mind. To be sure, her old friend Agnes Inglis, curator of the Labadie Collection at the University of Michigan, could send her fat scrapbooks of clippings, old programs, and forgotten pamphlets; other friends could do research on newspaper files in the United States and send her the results of their investigations; still others could be expected to write her their recollections of specific events in which they had taken part. But she still needed more data. Fortunately for Emma—and anyone else interested in her career—she had become an inveterate letter-writer during her years of wandering. Indeed, she had turned to this medium not only as a means of communicating with associates scattered all over the world but also as a major means of self-expression. As Max Nettlau, the shrewd anarchist historian, once observed, this habit marked her in part as a woman of an earlier century: "In letters happily, though tip top up to date otherwise," Nettlau wrote, "you are eighteenth century, doing honour to the good old art of letter writing, which the wire and telephone have strangled, and this is a good thing, as a thoughtful way of communication by letters is an intellectual act of value of its own, which rapid talk cannot replace. . . ."[1] Thanks to her practice of "the good old art," when she made an appeal to her correspondents, they returned hundreds of her letters. From these she was able not only to reconstruct the chronology of events, but also to recapture directly her past moods and thoughts. The huge pile of letters added up to a kind of diary.

Berkman's help was also indispensable. Now living in nearby Nice, Berkman encouraged her to get started, offered to edit sections of the work as she finished them, and in turn sought her advice for the book he was writing—indeed, he wrote, "I need your aid more in my work than you do my help."[2] (His book was published in 1929 under the title of *Now and After: The ABC of Communist Anarchism*.)

When Berkman inquired of her what steps should be taken against the "active enemies" of an anarchist revolution, Emma replied that he had to come out unreservedly for "the unlimited right of free speech, press and assembly. Anything else will create all the evils you want the revolution to fight."[3] If there were an armed attack, then certainly there would be a need to repel it by force of arms; but there really should be no need "even in the most critical period of the revolution as [long as] everyone is given a chance to participate in the rebuilding of society. . . ." In any event, prisons and capital punishment were not justifiable, no matter what the offense. A few days later, obviously not completely satisfied with her response to Berkman's question, she returned to the topic in another letter: "Unless we set our face against the old attitude to revolution as a violent eruption destroying everything of what had been built up over centuries of painful and painstaking effort not by the bourgeoisie but by the combined effort of humanity, we must become Bolsheviks, accept terror and all it implys [sic] or become Tolstoyans."[4] The problem was of sufficient urgency for her to conclude: "I insist if we can undergo changes in every other method of dealing with social issues we will also have to learn to change in the methods of revolution. I think it can be done. If not I shall relinquish my belief in revolution." Thus did Emma give Berkman the benefit of her advice and at the same time order her own thoughts on how to deal in her memoirs with the crucial problems

[1] Max Nettlau to EG, February 16, 1929, IISH, EG.

[2] AB to EG, n.d., IISH, EG.

[3] AB to EG, June 25, 1928, IISH, EG; EG to AB, June 29, 1928, IISH, EG.

[4] EG to AB, July 3, 1928, IISH, EG.

of freedom, violence, and power. One thematic red thread running throughout her chapters would be the key insight that the means used must be appropriate to the ends in mind.

While she would no more write a book without Berkman's assistance than she would join the Communist party, as she once remarked, she still was uncertain whether he would be "able to stand himself as I conceived and presented him."[5] Her apprehensions grew when Berkman went to work and expressed the opinion forcibly that she had depicted him as too harsh, too much the fanatic. The growing tension between the two was recorded from time to time by Berkman in his diary:

[January 30, 1930] The Mss., after I correct it, looks worse than an ordinary battlefield. Some pages: half of it crossed out by me, on the other half every word, literally, changed by me. I hope she'll never write another book. No such luck.

Emma's response to his attitude was also recorded by Berkman:

[April 25, 1930] "I don't mind the slicing—I mind your gruff comments. You say this has no bearing on my life. Don't you think you should let me decide that?" In a previous note she wrote me: "I realize how difficult it is to revise the book. Do you realize how difficult it is for me to accept your help in this case? You could not have chosen a better simile than 'the surgeon with the bloody knife.' "

Yet Berkman's merciless wielding of his blue pencil was necessary, for Emma was, like Thomas Wolfe, a great exponent of putting in even more than the full story. And her unwillingness to yield after every disagreement was necessary, for Berkman wanted to excise episodes which had to remain if her autobiography was to be a full and candid account of her years. Although the conflict was hard on them both at the time, the upshot was a meaningful collaboration. When it was all over, Berkman wrote a mutual friend: "The book is great, I think. It is well done in every respect. Some details could have well been left out, but you know E. G.—she fought me on every passage and page I cut out."[6] A little earlier Emma wrote her nephew that "Sasha had been brave in the revision." Berkman and she had been "riveted together by his act and my share in it and a thousand agonies following."[7] All the more remarkable then, she observed, was his detached view and his generous criticism.

[5] EG to Demi Coleman, January 8, 1930, IISH, EG.

[6] AB to M. Eleanor Fitzgerald, February 9, 1932, IISH, AB.

[7] EG to Saxe Commins, July 14, 1931, IISH, EG.

Bothered by fallen arches, swollen veins, bad eyesight, and emotional fatigue, Emma drew on her last reserves to bring her autobiography to a close in early 1931. With more than a sigh of relief, she wrote Arthur Leonard Ross: "I am sending you a cable today conveying the great news that I have at last operated on the appendix of Living My Life and Jesus Christ and God know that no operation would cause anyone more agony or such struggle as the last six months have been."[8]

2

Her struggle was by no means over, however, for Alfred A. Knopf, her publisher, refused to consider selling the two-volume work for less than seven dollars and fifty cents. One reason for Knopf's stand was their contract, in which he gave Emma a seven-thousand-dollar advance and guaranteed her 10 per cent royalties on the first five thousand copies and 15 per cent thereafter.[9] Another reason Knopf insisted on the higher price was that he thought five dollars too low: it was "virtually no money"—at this price the booksellers would think something was wrong with the work.[10]

From the outset Emma urged that her book not sell for more than five dollars. "I am anxious to reach the mass of the American reading public," she wrote Agnes Inglis, "not so much because of the royalties, but because I have always worked for the mass."[11] Knopf remained firm, however, and when the book finally appeared in the shops at the end of 1931, sales were predictably slow. In this year of deep depression, for a publisher to bring out a biography for seven dollars and fifty cents was to be absurdly optimistic—it was about like trying to sell diamond tiaras to needleworkers. And novelist Evelyn Scott's reaction was to the point: "What irony," she wrote Emma, "that your book of all in the world must be given this exclusiveness."[12]

The brisk circulation of Living My Life in libraries across the United States provided additional proof, if any were needed, that a reasonably priced edition need not have had this exclusiveness. For the week ending January 16, 1932, Living My Life was one of the six "general books" most in demand in the Detroit Public Library (although it was not one of the "Best Sellers" in Detroit bookstores or on Bren-

---

8 EG to Ross, February 1, 1931, LC.

9 Ross to EG, October 2, 1929, IISH, EG.

10 Knopf to EG, April 23, 1931, IISH, EG.

11 EG to Inglis, April 11, 1930, LC.

12 Scott to EG, August 9, 1931, IISH, EG.

tano's New York listing). In New York the Syracuse University librarian listed it as one of the "important books of the year." In Des Moines the city librarians recommended it as one of the best nonfiction works of the year.[13] This recommendation by librarians was seconded by a number of newspapers, among them the Washington *Post*, the Richmond *Times Dispatch*, the New York *Times*, the Boston *Transcript*, and the Buffalo *Times*, and by magazines such as the *New Yorker*, the *Saturday Review of Literature*, and the *Nation*. With this kind of support the book sold fairly well in some areas—the Milwaukee *Journal*, October 31, 1931, for instance, reported *Living My Life* sixth on a list of local bestsellers. But even such evidence hardly revealed the true number of her readers, as Arthur Leonard Ross pointed out, for there was good reason to believe "that because of the price . . . the book has traveled from home to home."[14] It was a mistake, then, for her to turn from statistics on sales to the assumption that her work was a "flop."

Reviewers who were favorably impressed outnumbered those who were not by about three to one. While the Hackensack *Record*, September 12, 1931, found only "trite writing and bald conceit" in *Living My Life*, there was general agreement that it was well written: the *New Yorker*, November 23, 1931, held that it was valuable as a document and "interesting too, as sheer reading"; the Baltimore *Evening Sun*, November 14, 1931, liked its style which, though often declamatory, was also "frank, direct, and brisk"; and the Boston *Herald*, January 9, 1932, complimented it for its excellent English, "even the high literary quality that marks it."

Conservative reviewers granted the substance of the autobiography a grudging respect. *Time*, November 9, 1931, under the characteristic heading "Old Red," maintained that everybody "admires a fighter who has a heart. Now that Emma Goldman's career is finished, you may even find it possible to add a kind of warmth to your disapproving admiration of her." Although the Des Moines *Register*, January 10, 1932, found the book simply "a thousand dull pages of fornication and fanaticism," other papers, such as the Tucson *Star*, November 8, 1931, and the Murfreesboro *News Journal*, November 7, 1931, revealed that they were changing their minds about "Red Emma." The Tennessee paper, for instance, admitted that "probably the name Emma

[13] Detroit *News*, January 17, 1932; Oswego *Palladium Times*, February 1, 1932; New York *Herald Tribune*, December 29, 1931.

[14] Ross to EG, January 22, 1932, IISH, EG.

Goldman would not inspire our contempt if we gave a calm, fair, objective reading to her new autobiography."

Liberals had a much more complex reaction. Their response ranged from R. L. Duffus' admiring front-page review in the New York *Times Book Section*, October 25, 1931, to a vicious attack by Laurence Stallings in the New York *Sun*, November 20, 1931. The nature of Stallings' review was foreshadowed by his title, "The Unmarried Life of Emma and Company or Goldman, Goldman, Goldman Uber Alles." Stallings evidently could not forgive Emma her response to Lenin, the man with the "greatest political wisdom of the century." Thus Stallings slashed at the "gamey, lecherous one" for her failure to realize that, "faced with every danger from without and infected with every trouble from within . . . Lenin needed a disciplined and ruthless disregard of individual sensibilities." By way of contrast Stallings presented Emma as a contemptible, reactionary old woman who was resting after her labors "in the bosom of her legal husband," tending fires, and from time to time putting away "a bit of silver" for her old age. In a thoughtful analysis in the *New Republic*, December 30, 1931, Waldo Frank avoided meretriciousness and venom, but also concluded that Emma's "failure to understand Russia is an anarchist failure to understand and hence to work upon the world. Her story of a great anarchist (there is something about this woman that is great) becomes the most eloquent defense of communism." Freda Kirchwey agreed in the *Nation*, December 2, 1931, that in terms of objective results, the book was a record of defeat: "But as a study in subjective achievement what a personal triumph these volumes reveal." Victims of the Bolshevik Myth, Frank and Kirchwey still could not quite suppress a gasp of admiration for Emma as an individual.

English reviews of her work, on the whole much less penetrating and understanding than the American, were a commentary on Emma's feeling that she and the English had a temperamental incompatibility which would never be resolved. For a review the London *Daily Express*, October 20, 1932, printed a piece entitled "Love Life of an Anarchist" which merely listed her lovers. Other papers emphasized her "amorous dalliances" (*Everyman*, October 29, 1932) or her "chronic egoistic excitation" (London *Morning Post*, October 25, 1932). In the best analysis to appear in an English publication, a reviewer in the *Times Literary Supplement*, October 27, 1932, put the book down with astonishment and profound sadness: "Over thirty years of violent, almost frantic activity—to what end?"

The *Times* reviewer and his fellows apparently were unable to see that the end was to live a meaningful life. Her autobiography was a work of art primarily because to a large extent her life was as well. No English reviewer came up with the insight advanced by Ordway Tead, an editor of Harper and Brothers: "Her life story is an antidote—a strong, heady, disconcerting antidote—to personal complacency, social hard heartedness, and spiritual introversion. Whatever the ultimate assessment of her influence and value, it is well to have driven home that the forces she attacked still give battle, still crush the human spirit, still have to be rebelled against."[15]

3

A lifelong responsibility for attacking the forces which crush the human spirit was no easy burden, especially when these forces became overwhelming. During the inevitable letdown which followed the writing of her memoirs, she actually yearned for the soothing silence of retirement. But, she complained to Berkman,

the still voice in me will not be silenced, the voice which wants to cry out against the wretchedness and injustice in the world. I can compare my state with that of a being suffering from an incurable disease. He knows there is no remedy. Yet he goes on trying every doctor, and every kind of quack. I know there is no place where I can or will gain a footing and once more throw in my lot with our people who continue the struggle of liberation.[16]

Yet with the still inner voice urging her on, she could only sail on, as before, into the wind.

In the spring of 1932 she unerringly headed for the storm center in a lecture tour which was to take her through all of the major German cities and as well to Copenhagen, Oslo, and Stockholm. She sounded the keynote of her tour before a thousand Danes at the University of Copenhagen. Speaking on "Dictatorship: A World Menace," she warned them against its "foul spirit . . . threatening the happiness and culture of this and future generations."[17] From Berlin she playfully wrote Berkman that "it would be great fun to interview Hitler. Of

---

[15] *Yale Review*, June, 1932. Somewhat less important but still deserving notice was the fact that *Living My Life* was a valuable historical source. As Upton Sinclair wrote, "the historian of our period will be grateful to you and Lincoln Steffens" (Sinclair to EG, November 10, 1931, IISH, EG).

[16] EG to AB, November 18, 1931, IISH, EG.

[17] New York *Times*, February 14, 1932; EG to AB, February 15, 1932, IISH, AB.

course I'd have to do it under my good old Scotch name, Colton."[18]
More soberly, she added she had in mind a first-rate article; however,
she feared that it and her tour would be off if "the Hitler gang gets
in." Her conviction that "Hitler and his bloodhounds are fast approaching" hardened when she was approached on the street one day
by two confident Nazis who grimly promised her an end like Rosa
Luxemburg's.[19] Although such promises did not strike her as empty
threats, she was not unduly alarmed. What bothered her most was the
misery in Berlin. "The sights make one lose all hope in humanity,"
she wrote Berkman. "The lack of courage and self respect of the
masses who can put up with the horrible bureaucracy, the endless
waiting in lines in the cold and wet for a few measely [sic] marks
they are doled out. It is a harrowing sight. I am all in from the picture.
I feel every effort to awaken the masses seems a waste, and one's own
life utterly useless."[20] Nevertheless, with that still voice crashing in her
ears, she accepted an invitation from the German League for Birth
Control and Sexual Hygiene (*Deutsche Verband für Geburtenrege-
lung and Sexualhygiene*) to return for a lecture tour in March, 1933.

Uncanny timing—in March Hitler swept into power. Sensing the
black reaction in the air, Berkman wrote to Emma of his anxiety
about her proposed tour: "it looks as if radical meetings are out of the
question from here out. . . . Hitler and his gang have at once raised
the iron hand and it seems . . . that always succeeds with the masses."
Emma agreed it was foolish to think of meetings in Germany, but "if
the Reichsverband will really go ahead I can not let them down whatever the consequences may be to me."[21] The time had definitely
passed, however, for Emma's kind of lectures in Germany; she was not
called on to make good her promise.

That March Emma stayed instead in England and labored to arouse
some kind of protest over the murderous course of the Nazis. For those
who had dismissed Emma as a professional anti-Communist, it was
something of a surprise to hear her denunciation of German as well
as Russian tyranny. And denounce she did: "tonight at my lecture,"
she wrote Berkman, " I am going to sail into the gathering and tell

[18] EG to AB, March 6, 1932, IISH, EG.

[19] EG to Beckl, May 25, 1932, LC. While on her way to prison in 1919, Rosa Luxemburg was beaten to death and her corpse was thrown in a river. Miss Luxemburg was
at the time a frail and elderly woman.

[20] EG to AB, April 9, 1932, IISH, AB.

[21] AB to EG, March 5, 1933, IISH, EG; EG to AB, March 8, 1933, IISH, AB.

them what I think of the callousness to the atrocities going on in Germany. Perhaps I can shame them into contributing enough to organize a big protest meeting."[22] Although she was unable to stir Socialists and trade-unionists to any protest, she again had the opportunity of telling them quite frankly what she thought of their frigid reserve.

A rather amusing incident occurred that same month which emphasized the gulf separating her from the general English outlook. To celebrate the appearance of an English edition of Living My Life, a "literary luncheon" was held for Emma at Grosvenor House on March 20. Tributes were paid her by Henry W. Nevinson and Rebecca West —the latter digressed to put Emma beside Willa Cather as one of the two best cooks among the living writers—and Paul Robeson paid his respects with two well-chosen songs, "Sometimes I Feel Like a Mornin Dove" and "Roll de Chariot Along." Some difficulty had developed, however, before all this could take place. As reported in newspapers in the United States: "The traditional toast to the king was omitted at a luncheon at fashionable Grosvenor House today, to spare the feelings of the anarchist Emma Goldman, who threatened to leave if the toast were given. The king's health is always drunk before smoking is permitted and the speakers are introduced at public functions in England."[23] Many Englishmen must have felt, along with the distant Windsor, Canada, Border Cities Star (March 6, 1933) that this was a "Deliberate snub to King George."

But as Robeson had implied in his rich bass, Emma had to "Roll de Chariot Along" in her own unique fashion. In November of 1933 she was back in Holland urging her audiences to combat dictatorship. (She did not propose, of course, that Holland or other countries go to war against Germany, for it was to her mind World War I which had made Hitler possible; she did want, however, world opinion aroused against the Nazis, she wanted workers to take economic action against them, and she wanted her listeners to extend every possible aid to those who opposed Hitler and to those who were his victims.) She did not get far with this message. In Hilversum, the Dutch police informed her that she would not be allowed to speak on the internal conditions of the Netherlands or criticize any other government. Emma's response was a smashing denunciation of Hitler's strangulation of freedom. Always at her best under this kind of opposition, she obviously was in possession of her old fighting spirit—

22 EG to AB, March 3, 1933, IISH, EG.
23 New York Times, March 2, 1933; Chicago Tribune, March 2, 1933.

as she jubilantly reported to Berkman, "I am no longer tired."[24] In Rotterdam, however, the police prevented her from delivering her lecture on dictatorship. In Amsterdam the police failed to keep their fast-moving visitor from addressing a successful meeting in the Trade Union House, but they caught up with her in Appledorn with orders from the ministry for her expulsion. After she had picked up her things in The Hague, detectives put her on a train and escorted her out of the country. Emma felt the reason for her expulsion was that Holland "manufactures ammunition for Germany. I was expelled, because of it, after my third lecture on the German situation." Berkman argued that it meant "you are still dangerous—there is no doubt of it. And especially the powers that be fear talks on dictatorship now, because they are all anxious to have dictatorship."[25] This was not entirely fair, for the Dutch expelled Emma and later other opponents of the Nazis in part because of their fearful and forlorn hope of placating the increasingly belligerent neighbors just over their eastern border. It was true, however, that they regarded Emma as a dangerous guest.

Now that Holland, the last country on the continent in which she hoped to be active for a few weeks each year, was closed to her, she again took up plans for a tour of Canada and the possibility of a visit to the United States. A return to the country she loved was a live possibility largely because Mabel Carver Crouch, a well-known liberal, dropped in on Emma unexpectedly at Saint-Tropez, promised to form a committee dedicated to bringing her back to America, and then worked seriously on the project when she got home. Emma's hopes were not high, for several other friends—Isaac Don Levine, Theodore Dreiser, H. L. Mencken—had already thrown themselves futilely against the thick wall of official American hostility to her re-entry. Mabel Carver Crouch, however, brought to the task an unprecedented drive and enthusiasm. With the support of a committee composed of

[24] EG to AB, November 20, 1933, IISH, AB.

[25] EG to Freda Kirchwey, July 14, 1934, IISH, EG; AB to EG, November 25, 1933, IISH, AB. The Dutch secret police, incidentally, had long been interested in her and Berkman. One of their reports indicated that their outlook (and awkwardness in handling evidence) was little different from that of their counterparts in the United States. The Chief of the Third Section of the General Staff of the Dutch Army transmitted to the American Legation on February 6, 1922, a report on the activities of the two anarchists—INS 52410/43C; DS 311.6124 K/47. In the United States, the Third Section Chief declared, "they had a very luxurious life and received much money from the anarchists." Emma, a very clever speaker, along with Berkman, appealed "to all classes of people" and adeptly launched ideas "at the proper moment." The Chief concluded they were dangerous undesirables who should be kept out of the Netherlands, England, and the United States.

liberals and radicals—among them John Dewey, John Haynes Holmes, Sherwood Anderson, Dorothy Canfield Fisher, Sinclair Lewis, Anna Sloan, Harry Elmer Barnes, A. J. Muste, Quincy Howe, Robert Morss Lovett, Dorothy Kenyon, and Amos Pinchot—Mrs. Crouch spurred Roger Baldwin and the American Civil Liberties Union into action. Baldwin was soon able to report that Secretary Perkins was willing to have Emma return for a visit, provided the Department of Labor and her sponsoring committee established a specific understanding on the length and purpose of her tour and a list of the subjects on which she proposed to speak.[26] Shortly after Emma arrived in Montreal on December 10, 1933, Baldwin wired that it was necessary for her to give the committee authority to determine the subjects and auspices of her lectures; he added that the reasons would be explained later—she could trust the judgment of the reception committee. Emma had hardly given her reluctant permission when she learned that the Department of Labor had stipulated that she lecture only on the drama and literature.

There followed an almost comic complication. Without funds to go anywhere else—indeed with hardly anywhere else to go—Emma objected strenuously to Miss Perkins' formalistic conception of literature and refused to abandon her own theory of literary criticism merely to gain admittance to the United States. Every art form, she pointed out to Baldwin, is an expression of life, of life which is barren without ideals and dreams:

Having adhered to this conception of literature and drama, in fact every form of art, I could not buy my rentry to A[merica] with a complete reversal of my conception of art. That does not mean I look upon literature or the drama as my "friends" the Communists do, as a means of propaganda. But I do insist that every creative expression must have its being in the social and political fabric of the time.

She would therefore not emasculate literary or dramatic works by discussing them out of their social context, nor would she mislead the committee by false promises to do so. In reply Baldwin urged her to give her consent as a "sporting proposition" that she would be allowed to lecture on the drama and literature as she wished once she was in the country.[27] On this basis she accepted the conditions; at long last, on February 1, 1934, she came home for ninety days.

[26] Baldwin to EG, December 4, 1933, NYPL, EGP.

[27] For this incident, see Baldwin to EG, December 22, 1933, January 2, 5, 1934, NYPL, EGP; EG to Baldwin, January 3, 1934, NYPL, EGP.

CHAPTER XXX

RETURN OF THE PRODIGAL DAUGHTER

Emma Goldman was formally welcomed home at the Town Hall Club. Only three hundred of the eight hundred applicants gained places—for this number to apply at one dollar and fifty cents a plate was in itself a handsome tribute in this depression year. Leonard Abbott, Roger Baldwin, John Dewey, Henry Alsberg, Harry Kelly, and John Haynes Holmes all joined in warmly greeting the exile and in paying their respects to her career—the *Nation* reported that their speeches and "the mood of the audience were marked by an almost religious ardor."[1] In a mellow mood, she spoke briefly of the trip of the "Buford" and of her comrades who were deported with her almost fifteen years earlier.

The whirl of activity had commenced. She had rather reluctantly turned down an offer of two thousand dollars a week to appear in a vaudeville circuit: "With our precarious chance of making a living," she admitted to Berkman, "the offer loomed high." Nevertheless, the *Daily Worker* sneeringly charged that, with the royalties from her antisoviet books gone, "Emma Goldman is here to make cash."[2]

James B. Pond, head of the lecture agency which was managing her tour, had secured a room for Emma at the Hotel Astor. When she left her train at Pennsylvania Station she had walked to her hotel in observance of a strike of the cab drivers; but at the Astor, in all the confusion of the newsreel cameramen, the reporters, and her friends, she failed to notice that it was picketed. Her enemies immediately raised the charge that she had deliberately walked through the hotel picket line. Reporters wanted to know why, and their criticism mounted when she did not immediately move out.[3] An apparently endless line of people began knocking on her door. Her telephone rang ceaselessly from morning to night. Soon she

---

[1] *Nation*, CXXXVIII (March 21, 1934), 320.

[2] EG to AB, January 6, 1934, IISH, AB; *Daily Worker*, February 2, 1934. The *Worker*, with its own inimitable humor, detected an affinity between Emma and the Trotskyites.

[3] New York *Times*, February 3, 1934.

complained to Evelyn Scott that at this rate, after the ninety days were over she would have seen "nothing of New York or the rest of the country or of the people and friends I love most."[4]

2

The pace was assuredly fast. On February 11 she spoke to a capacity audience from John Haynes Holmes's pulpit in Community Church. During the course of her remarks she referred to Germany as a "nation led by degenerates." This provoked the German ambassador to make a formal protest to the State Department. The Labor Department soon reacted by informing her that it had no objection to her discussion of political issues just so long as she did not arouse foreign legations or congressmen to protest.[5]

The German ambassador was not alone in his belief that Emma should be silenced. The redoubtable Daughters of the American Revolution refused to rent Constitution Hall in Washington to Ann Lord, Emma's personal representative and press agent on the tour. In the course of its report on the claims and counterclaims of Miss Lord and the manager of the hall, the Washington *Herald* (February 17, 1934) explained to its readers who Emma was: "Emma Goldman, after vast pacifist agitation during the World War, was deported from the United States largely through the efforts of Edgar Hoover, Chief of the Department of Justice, fifteen years ago." Mr. Hoover was still on the job, of course, and could hardly have been pleased by Emma's re-entry. He assigned some agents to keep her under surveillance. One of their reports provided a diverting footnote to the long struggle between the lawman and the rebel: As Mr. Hoover wrote, "a confidential report received by this Department relating to Communistic [sic] activities concerning a speech made by Emma Goldman in Pittsburgh, April 11, 1934," revealed that she had lectured on *Living My Life*—she had discussed her years in the United States, her experience with the Fascists, her belief that the people of the United States were very lucky still to have the freedom to speak out, and her conviction that Americans should never give up

[4] EG to Scott, February 24, 1934, IISH, EG.

[5] Baldwin to EG, February 15, 1934, IISH, EG; EG to AB, February 19, 1934, IISH, AB. Unrepentant, Emma continued to use a very broad definition of drama and literature for her "non-political" lectures. She lectured on "The Drama of Europe" and "you can rest assured," she wrote Berkman, "I led blows straight from the shoulder on the menace of Fascism and dictatorship" (March 23, 1934, IISH, AB). She also lectured on such subjects as "Germany's Tragedy" and the "Collapse of German Culture."

this freedom. The agent's account made clear that her lecture was a kind of Jeffersonian celebration of civil freedoms and thus, in a democracy, beyond reproach. Nevertheless, Mr. Hoover maintained in a confidential memorandum to Assistant Attorney-General Joseph B. Keenan that the report "may indicate that her activities in this country at the present time are in violation of the agreement upon which she was permitted to enter the country for a ninety-day stay."[6] Hoover's memorandum was dated May 4, 1934. But the wheels of justice had slipped, as Mr. Hoover might have discovered had he turned from his confidential reports to his calendar or even to his daily newspaper: Emma Goldman was no longer pursuing "her activities in this country at the present time." Her three months behind her, she had been in Canada for several days![7]

Given the Federal Bureau of Investigation's preoccupation with "Communistic activities," it was passingly ironic that the Communists also disapproved of Emma's lectures. At first, foregoing for the moment their sneers at her crass, counterrevolutionary money-hunger, the Communists had proposed a bit of blackmail: they would not interfere with her tour, they secretly assured her manager, if she would agree to give their International Defense League all the money she collected for political prisoners.[8] When she wrathfully rejected their proposal, the Communists retaliated with a refusal to run her paid advertisement in the *Daily Worker*,[9] boycotted her meetings, and attacked her in the general press. Thus the Madison *State Journal*, March 27, 1934, reported that local Communists had labeled her a "reactionary" who would save capitalism by fascism.

As if to complete the circle, the New York *American* (April 7,

---

6 Hoover, "Memorandum for Assistant Attorney General Keenan," May 4, 1934, and Keenan to Secretary of Labor Perkins, May 11, 1934, DJ 133149.

7 On the day Hoover sent off his apprehensive memorandum *La Presse* of Montreal reported without alarm that the city's grandmotherly visitor carried her age well: "Elle paraît porter tranquillement ses 64 ans." She had arrived in Montreal on May 2, 1934 (Montreal *Star*). The following day a local interview with her was reported in the Montreal *Gazette*.

On June 14, 1934 an even more belated and equally unenlightened warning to Washington officialdom came in the form of a telegram to the Immigration and Naturalization Service from its Los Angeles office: the West Coast agent reported that Emma was "engaged in agitating among longshoremen strikers," according to information supplied him by the local United States Attorney—INS 52410/43D. By then Emma had been out of the country for almost a month and a half; on her tour in the United States she had gone no farther west than St. Louis.

8 EG to AB, February 7, 1934, IISH, AB.

9 New York *Evening Post*, February 9, 1934.

1934), one of the Hearst papers, identified "Red Emma" for its read-ers as "for many years the leading Communist in the United States." But apart from the Hearst press—and it was not quite as unreliable as the *Daily Worker*—many newspapers treated Emma with surpris-ing honesty and fairness. Some followed the lead of the New York *Herald Tribune* (January 19, 1934), which braced itself for her arrival by editorializing that though "our old friend" Emma would soon be back, the nation "might still survive." The *Washington Herald* (February 24, 1934) granted that her nimble wit had become "more nimble with increasing age, her tongue as fiery, her answers as ready for a question barrage of 15 newspapermen." Doubtful that her ideas had improved much, the Baltimore *Evening Sun* (March 1, 1934) still pointed out that she was a notable person because she had been battered by the police and "exiled by a terrified Government." The Chicago *Daily News* (March 22, 1934) generously told its readers of her "fine sense of humor" and her "keen show of intel-ligence." The most complimentary statement, however, came from the editorial page of the Madison *Capital Times* (March 29, 1934). "The intelligence and vitality of Emma Goldman impressed deeply her four hundred hearers in Madison," declared Ernest L. Meyer. "Battered by life, life flows from her steadily, hotly; her blood and passion are the weapons she has dedicated to her revolutionary cause. Freedom for herself she has always had,—whether in jail or in exile her winged words hunted out her persecutors, stinging them where they wallowed in beefy complacency, and fettered to smug-ness which is more degrading than bars." Meyers characterized as gross libel the Communist charge that she had "sold out": "She is opposed to the annihilation of the individual spirit whether the massacre proceed from Mussolini or Marx. . . ."[10]

3

Despite these unexpected boosts from some papers, her tour was, on the whole, a financial failure. James Pond, her manager, argued that public hostility was to blame. "Last month we got 1,500 news-paper clippings about Emma Goldman," he explained to her niece. "A great mass of these clippings are decidedly opposed to her. In

---

[10] Meyer added in a letter to Emma (May 22, 1934, IISH, EG) that after her lecture "for days when I met some of the group, we talked about you, and agreed that as a clear, forceful presenter of facts on important world issues, you make all the professors look pallid."

other words, there is quite a national anti-Emma Goldman senti-
ment."[11] But the attitude of a number of influential papers was sympathetic; even unfavorable publicity need not have kept large numbers
of people from attending her lectures.

Emma believed that Pond's mismanagement of her lectures was
a more likely reason for their disappointing financial returns. He
handled her tour "in a big way," as though she were Admiral Byrd,
another of his agency's clients.[12] His expensive, sensational publicity
techniques repelled rather than attracted those most likely to be
interested in her lectures—he so misunderstood his lecturer and her
public that he directed part of his appeal to organizations like the
American Legion and then expressed surprise at their lack of response.
He rented expensive, overly large auditoriums, theaters, and even
arsenals and armories for her lectures. As she complained to Berkman, "Pond jumps into a city for a day or two, grabs hold of the
first theater manager he can lay hands on, gives him carte blanche
to pay high rentals and spend fortunes on advertising, and dashes
out again. Some types who booked me were as ignorant as new born
babes. They thought I was some circus performer, rope walker, or
trick musician. None of them attract the very people interested in
hearing me."[13] Finally, in his haste to handle her tour "in a big way"
and secure a hatful of profits, Pond charged from fifty cents to two
dollars for admission to her lectures, or what amounted to exorbitant
prices during a depression year. He overlooked the fact that low admission charges in the long run meant larger audiences and greater
returns, for Emma's primary appeal was to impecunious or unemployed radicals, liberals, and laborites who could not, or would not,
pay fifty cents to hear a lecture. For Emma the "proof of the pudding"
came in Chicago, where her comrades handled the arrangements and
set admission prices at thirty-five and forty-five cents. There she spoke
to two thousand people in the New Masonic Temple and to capacity
audiences at Mandel Hall, Lincoln Center, and the Labor Lyceum.[14]
Other successes at meetings organized by her friends in Detroit and

[11] Pond to Stella Cominsky, March 10, 1934, NYPL, EGP. Pond may have exaggerated
somewhat, for many of the clippings which I have seen were not "decidedly opposed to
her."

[12] James B. Pond to A. L. Ross, January 15, 1934, IISH, EG.

[13] EG to AB, March 23, 1934, IISH, AB.

[14] Chicago Daily News, March 21, 22, 1934; Anna Olay, "Emma Goldman in Chicago," Road to Freedom, June, 1934; EG to Henry Alsberg, April 9, 1934, IISH, AB.

Pittsburgh underscored her conviction that Pond's high admission prices and general mismanagement were basically responsible for her small audiences in other cities.

Yet, notwithstanding this evidence that her lectures could be popular if they were properly handled, Pond's "bungling of the grandest opportunity of a lifetime" was only part of the story. The other part was the changed nature of American radicalism. As one of Emma's nephews rather sadly remarked, "there are new definitions in the air and new concepts that shove all the old ones—ten years old—into the limbo of the forgotten. . . . The worker who doubts must be exterminated under the new dispensation. The skeptical mind is the counter-revolutionary mind; obedience and overalls are the passports to the cooperative commonwealth."[15] And pointing to her own bitter experience among radical and liberal writers who were mesmerized by their "Salvation Army revivalist feeling about the Communist movement," Evelyn Scott warned Emma that the Communist boycott of her lectures would be decisive in some quarters.[16]

And so it was. It was an unpleasant truth—one which she was understandably reluctant to recognize, despite her years of struggle against the Bolshevik Myth—that in the early 1930's American radicals and liberals looked on her ideas as, at best, hopelessly old-fashioned. In his important book, *Farewell to Reform*, published in 1932, John Chamberlain set forth this representative attitude:

A woman of an essentially "pure" nature, she defines anarchism in such a way as to make it seem the most intelligent of creeds—until one bethinks oneself to remember that problems of organization, of means, of institutions for human concourse, are left in a delightfully vague region of the non-necessary. It is here that one is thrown, inevitably, back into the arms of either capitalism or socialism. . . . Yet anarchism has gone its way into the past; the Emma Goldmans—atomic, incapable of organization towards definite ends—make no sense in a corporate world. If anarchism has any future, it is far beyond the horizon, and beyond the Communist horizon, once the state has "withered" away as a coercive instrumentality.[17]

In a world where "the problems of organization" would soon be solved by Communist managers, she was as out of place as an iron-tired

---

[15] Saxe Commins to EG, May 29, 1934, IISH, EG.

[16] Scott to EG, March 1, 1934, IISH, EG.

[17] *Farewell to Reform* (New York: Liveright, Inc., 1932), pp. 84–85. As his quotation marks suggest, Chamberlain was somewhat cynical about the "withering" away of the state; in his opinion anarchism really had about as much relevance for the future as astrology.

carriage on a paved highway. "Emma Goldman is a symbol of the world situation," declared the Nation, a symbol to radicals and liberals "that freedom cannot be rolled under by the tanks and tractors of centralized power; she offers them courage to go on believing in principles that have lost their meaning on both fronts."[18] Yet only a handful of the older rebels could be expected to rise to the curious courage of belief "in principles that have lost their meaning on both fronts." The choice had become fascism or communism; Emma rejected these alternatives; therefore, apart from some fugitive nostalgic and contradictory notes of praise, the young generation on the political left ignored her lectures or attacked them.

"There is no stemming the tide of the intellectual rush to Communism," Berkman morosely wrote from Nice. Perhaps after the Bolsheviki establish their control in other countries the "people will see that we were right, but I fear THEN there will be no chance to propagate our ideas, for the Communists will crush us as they did in Russia."[19] Emma's experience with American intellectuals and her uphill efforts in Canadian radical and liberal circles to lecture in a hostile, pro-Communist atmosphere offered persuasive evidence in support of Berkman's prophecy. On all sides she observed "young people who do not think for themselves," who "want canned or prepared stuff," who "worship at the shrine of the strong-armed man."[20]

But in December, 1934, began the Communist Great Purge (the Moscow Trials were to follow). Soon the political hallucination which had gripped so many was thrown off by a few. Sensing the beginning of the long overdue disenchantment, Emma hurried off to Berkman a clipping on the resignation of Horace Kallen, Clifton Fadiman, Carl Van Doren, and Suzanne La Follette from the Communist-controlled International Defense League: "It had to be wholesale murder," she added grimly, "before they would budge from their infatuation of the Communist gang."[21] Later, in January, 1935, she had John Haynes Holmes, one of the veteran adversaries of her anti-

[18] "Emma Goldman," Nation, CXXXVIII (March 21, 1934), 320. This view was not, of course, restricted to American intellectuals. Thus Victor Gollancz, the English publisher, wrote Emma (March 17, 1933, IISH, AB) that he was not interested in any anti-Communist works: "My own view . . . is that in the present state of the world the support of the present regime of Soviet Russia is one of the first essentials. I would not care, therefore, to publish a book which was in the nature of an attack."

[19] AB to EG, July 27, 1934, IISH, AB.

[20] EG to AB, September 15, 1934, IISH, AB.

[21] EG to AB, January 5, 1935, IISH, AB.

communism, to tea while he was in Montreal: "it is interesting to hear Holmes say," she reported, " 'well E.G., you and Berkman are coming into your own. You were the first to disclose the butcheries in Russia. Now we all know and have to admit it.' You see, it required the 'purge' to rouse the Holmes, [Oswald Garrison] Villards and a few others. The rest have remained indifferent or continue to justify the murder."[22] Although the Bolshevik god remained on his throne, heresy was slowly spreading. At last she had reason to hope that recognition of the validity of her anti-Stalinism would not be postponed indefinitely—or more positively, that recognition of the importance of her defense of individual freedom did not lie far beyond Chamberlain's Communist horizon.

[22] EG to AB, January 24, 1935, IISH, AB.

CHAPTER XXXI

NO PLACE TO LAY THEIR HEADS

Ninety days in the United States stirred up all the old, gnawing questions of the meaning of America. Granted that her adolescent dream of it as another Paradise had been visionary, was there nothing in its present condition which offered grounds for more modest hopes? Should she not be forever estranged from a land in which she had been harassed by the police, hounded by officials, and roughly locked away in prison? How then could she explain the unbroken grip of America on her deepest feelings? In a word or two, how could she explain her woefully one-sided love affair with a land which not only failed to return her affection but persisted in treating her as an eminently undesirable alien?

Earlier, from abroad, she had analyzed the American crisis as "the inevitable result of the collapse of material values. America built up her illusionary wealth, and proclaimed it the only deity worth worshiping[—]that having tumbled down like a house of cards, there is nothing to take its place[,] no inner strength to fall back on, no spiritual integrity to reach out for a new ideal."[1] Her return to the United States gave her no reason to change her mind about American materialism. Indeed, in an article she wrote for *Harper's*, she remarked on the extent to which it had been rationalized:

In fact, the pattern of life has become standardized, routinized, and mechanized like the canned food and Sunday sermons. The hundred-percenter easily swallows syndicated information and factory-made ideas and beliefs. He thrives on the wisdom given him over the radio and cheap magazines by corporations whose philanthropic aim is selling America out. He accepts the standards of conduct and art in the same breath with the advertising of chewing gum, toothpaste, and shoe polish.[2]

In one of her lectures in Canada shortly after leaving the United States she predicted the "inevitable failure" of the National Recovery

---

1 EG to Stewart Kerr, February 2, 1932, NYPL, EGP.

2 "Was My Life Worth Living?" *Harper's Magazine*, CLXX (December, 1934), 52–58.

Administration. The people had made a great mistake when they "saw in Roosevelt a New Messiah and sat back and waited for miracles."[3]

But there were some hopeful signs as well. In the same lecture she praised Roosevelt for having introduced "a more liberal tone" into American life and for helping—unwittingly—to awaken the country to a deeper social awareness. She took Berkman to task for his blanket condemnation of the New Deal: Although it was childish and a failure already, "it has the adventurous spirit of the people; elsewhere it would have meant Fascism." What she wanted to stress was that "America brings out adventure, innovations, experimental daring which except for Russia no European country does."[4] And in her *Harper's* article she refused to despair over the many things wrong with America: "On the contrary, I feel that the freshness of the American approach and the untapped stores of intellectual energy resident in the country offer much promise for the future." For her, America was still the land of promise.

2

On a more personal level she felt with augmented force the anguish of her expatriation. A few days at home caused her as never before to realize that uprooting meant more than a forced removal from familiar surroundings and the work of nearly a lifetime. It meant also to be cut off from any direct enjoyment of the love and understanding of family and friends.[5] For less outgoing emotional natures, deracination was hard to bear; for Emma, it was pure torment.

Her distress was briefly eased by the visit in late August of Dr. Frank G. Heiner. She had met Heiner, a graduate of the Chicago College of Osteopathy and now one of Professor Ernest W. Burgess' graduate students in sociology at the University of Chicago, when she lectured at Lincoln Center.

Although Heiner had never met her before, he had long been one of her admirers. At one of the banquets in Chicago given in her honor, his wit and speaking ability had caught her attention. She had been pleased to find him, for in all the United States, she had written Berkman, "we have no outstanding person who knows the

[3] Toronto *Star*, May 29, 1934.

[4] EG to AB, May 27, 1934, IISH, AB.

[5] Emma explored the more general meaning of expatriation in "The Tragedy of Political Exiles," *Nation*, CXXXIX (October 10, 1934), 401-2.

American psychology and knows how to gain their confidence. I have discovered one remarkable man in Chicago. Alas, he is blind, has been since he was two months old."[6] In spite of his handicap, Heiner and Emma had worked out a program intended to revive American anarchism—Heiner had responsibility for writing a series of leaflets for wide distribution and for seeking every available opportunity to lecture to organizations and groups. After she left Chicago, he had gone ahead with their plans, but he also had sought a more intimate relationship. Convinced that her "great spontaneous tenderness which absorbs one and tremendous vitality and sexual passion" were what he had always sought in a woman, Heiner adoringly had asked to become her lover. Rejecting his "offer of sweet love," she had reminded him that he was thirty-six and she sixty-five; even radical comrades who smiled at the relationship of a mature man and a much younger woman were sure to disapprove of the reverse; she knew, more importantly, that his proposal would not work, for she remembered all too clearly her painful experience twelve years earlier with the young Swede.[7] Heiner had brushed aside these objections and her further fears over coming between him and his wife. On the issue of their disparity in ages, he had written that "my aching need of you has no reference to time." Mary Heiner, a remarkable woman who fought to have her husband overcome his handicap and refused to interfere with his freedom, informed Emma that she had no objection to her husband going to Toronto. Only then had Emma given her consent to his visit.

There followed two glorious weeks, as Emma forgot about her exile and reveled in the "world of beauty" Heiner brought with him. Unwilling to leave him alone for long in his prison of darkness, she put aside the article she was writing for *Harper's* to spend every

[6] EG to AB, April 9, 1934, IISH, EG. Actually, Heiner had been blinded by an accident at the age of six months—Chicago *Sun-Times*, May 5, 1957.

[7] EG to Heiner, April 17, 1934, IISH, EG. Most of Heiner's letters in this correspondence were undated, but obviously were written at this time or in response to later letters from Emma.

It is worth noting that the young Swede of painful memory turned up during her tour of the United States. Now happily married to Emma's former secretary, Arthur Swenson reaffirmed his affectionate admiration and his desire to see her: "For after all, Emma dear," he wrote, "you have left a greater impression upon me than anybody else. And you changed my whole philosophy of life. You made me see and understand and appreciate everything that is beautiful in life, which I otherwise never may have been aware of. . . . All I want to do is to feel the presence [of your] magnetic personality and receive that magnificent inspiration which radiates from you" (Arthur Swenson to EG, February 28, 1934, IISH, EG).

available minute with him. Years later he recalled that their hours together "meant everything to me":

> She stimulated me as much mentally as physically. . . . In Toronto, in many hours of conversation, she confided in me, her hopes, her fears, her views, her tastes, her admirations and aversions, her likes and dislikes, her background, associations, and experiences. Conversation with her was like reading a dozen books at once. Beyond the Anarchist movement which she knew intimately, she had met most of the interesting people of her time.[8]

Equally elated by Heiner's presence, Emma wrote her niece that

> it has increased my faith in humanity to find in Frank such an indomitable will to overcome all the terrible difficulties his handicap had put in his way. And it has streng[thened] my belief in freedom as the highest expression of man. You see dearest I found in Frank complete harmony in ideas, in the world we aim to build, in our need for art and beauty and in complete fulfillment of my woman soul. Is this not a great wonder, at my age? And in this cold and ugly world?[9]

But the spell could not last. Heiner returned to Chicago and Emma again faced the harsh reality of her exile in "empty" Toronto.

On into the fall of 1934 she held on to a slim chance that she might be readmitted to the United States. Colonel D. W. MacCormack, Commissioner of Immigration, had earlier expressed a willingness to consider a six-month stay. When Baldwin submitted her application in September, however, MacCormack refused to give it his approval; Miss Perkins, his superior, ultimately supported his stand. Baldwin wrote that the Secretary of Labor had informed him in a telephone conversation that she personally was interested in seeing Emma back, but that she could not risk it because of the San Francisco general strike, the mounting antiradical, antialien attack of

[8] Letter to me, February 17, 1957.

[9] EG to Stella Cominsky, September 9, 1934, IISH, EG. Although Heiner continued to express a desire to come to her again, even after she returned to France, Emma gradually broke off their relationship. She did not want to come between Heiner and his wife; she continued to be disturbed by the difference in their ages. After two years of sporadic correspondence she finally decided to bring the affair to an end (EG to Frank Heiner, March 2, 1936, IISH, EG).

It was an ironic tribute to the strength of the Bolshevik Myth that Heiner lost his faith in anarchism and eventually joined the Communist party—"a distressing fact to remember," he later wrote. "I met some grand people among them but while I love my memories of the Anarchist movement, despite its absurdity, I can think of the whole Marxist ideology and its parties only with loathing" (letter to me, March 27, 1957). Heiner died suddenly of a heart attack in April, 1957, still prizing his recollection of Emma's "loveliness of spirit."

the Hearst newspapers and the Chicago *Tribune,* and the general worsening of the public attitude toward aliens.[10] Miss Perkins did observe, however, that if Emma remained in Canada until the congressional session was well advanced, then her application might be reconsidered. Emma decided to stay on, though she was under no illusion about her chances: "Such craven cowardice as these pseudo liberals display," she exclaimed. "It's too farcical to fear that my presence would have any effect on Congress. It is true however that the Hearst sheets and the Chicago Tribune have been spitting gall against all aliens. But I am not at all deceived about the excuse McCormack [sic] and Perkins are giving. I am sure they'll find another excuse in the spring."[11]

Still, when her application was indeed refused, it came as something of a shock. At the time she was distracted by reports that Dr. Morris Goldman, her favorite brother, was slowly dying; she was also at her wit's end about how to pay for her fare back to France— the months of tedious lecturing in Toronto and Montreal had left her with only about sixty dollars. At this point her hand shook a bit— she asked the wife of a radio executive of her acquaintance whether she knew anyone who could speak to Roosevelt in her behalf: "It is only that I am in a desperate state," she explained apologetically, "or I wouldn't go to the humiliating extent of asking anyone to see Roosevelt for me."[12] When nothing came of this gesture of desperation she soon recovered her poise and went ahead with her plans to leave North America for good. A prosperous friend paid the cost of her ticket. Booking passage on the "Ascania," which sailed on May 3, 1935, Emma wrote ahead to Berkman that she was coming. With her customary tenacity, she added that in spite of her setbacks, she had retained her vigor: "I am as strong as a bull and I have inexhaustable [sic] energy."[13] But the truth was that she was sick at heart to be leaving America. As she wrote Baldwin a little later, "for a revolutionist and internationalist it is indeed disgraceful to be rooted to the soil of one country. Perhaps one can not adjust oneself easily in later years as one does in one's youth. Whatever the reason I have to admit defeat. The ninety days of my return

10 "Memorandum RNB to Stella Commins [Cominsky] and A. L. Ross," October 26, 1934, IISH, AB.

11 EG to AB, October 29, 1934, IISH, AB.

12 EG to Mildred Mesirow, February 16, 1935, IISH, EG.

13 EG to AB, April 17, 1935, IISH, AB.

dispelled whatever doubts I had on that score. I know now I will remain an alien abroad for the rest of my life."[14]

3

One of history's caprices made Leon Trotsky a neighbor-in-exile of Emma Goldman and Alexander Berkman. In 1935 Trotsky was living incognito in the small Alpine village of Domène, a couple of hundred kilometers north of Saint-Tropez. Isolated from his friends and for the first time without secretaries, oppressed by the recent suicide of his daughter in Germany, and haunted by Stalin's persecution of his family in Russia, Trotsky set aside—for a rare moment—his polemics and ideological pronouncements to assess somberly the consequences of estrangement for the individual. "The depth and strength of a human character," he wrote, "are defined by its moral reserves. People reveal themselves completely only when they are thrown out of the customary conditions of their life, for only then do they have to fall back on their reserves."[15] Although they could agree with "the butcher of Kronstadt" on almost no other point, Emma and Berkman, who had preceded Trotsky into exile by a decade, could have immediately recognized the truth of his diary entry: Exile did indeed draw on all the individual's moral reserves.[16]

Of all the Communist lies, none was further from the truth than the fantasy that had the two anarchists living luxuriously on the French Riviera from the proceeds of their betrayal of the revolution. The actual condition of their lives was given its tone by petty and sometimes not so petty hardships. No matter how she scrambled, Emma never made enough from her lecturing and writing to make ends meet. She was helped very considerably by the gift of her cottage, "Bon Esprit." On birthdays and other infrequent occasions donations from friends and associates arrived to ease the press of day-to-day expenses. Still, she was able to skimp along only because,

[14] EG to Baldwin, June 19, 1935, IISH, AB.

[15] *Trotsky's Diary in Exile, 1935*, trans. Elena Zarudnaya (Cambridge: Harvard University Press, 1958), p. 70.

[16] When Trotsky was attacked by his former Communist comrades in Copenhagen in 1932, he had to accept police protection. Emma then had sardonically remarked to Berkman: "What do you say to our friend Trotsky? Some irony that he had to accept the ...protection of the capitalist police.... History does play tricks with the mighty.... But yesteryear the butcher of Kronstadt, today humble and subdued" (EG to AB, December 1, 1932, IISH, EG).

beginning in 1934, her brother Morris Goldman sent her a monthly check for thirty dollars.

Despite Emma's willingness to share what little she had, Berkman was in a more serious predicament. While editing the *Bulletin of the Relief Fund* for Russian political prisoners, he tried to maintain himself in Nice by translations and ghost writing. In 1928 he translated Emil Bernhard's *The Prisoner*, a five-act play which was performed by the Provincetown Players. With the playwright's recommendation he translated Eugene O'Neill's *Lazarus Laughed* into Russian for the Moscow Art Theater. In 1935 his translation of Yefim Sosulia's short story, "The Dictator" was accepted by *Esquire*. Yet translators are notoriously underpaid and Berkman was no exception. For the translation of plays by Gogol and Ostrovsky, published in America by Macaulay in 1927, for instance, he received only a hundred and fifty dollars. His earnings from ghost writing were no more substantial. Only a few dollars came in from editing and writing part of Talbot J. Taylor's "Between Panics," an inside story of international financial chicanery, for the publishers found this account of stock market rigging too hot to handle. Some preparatory work for Isadora Duncan's autobiography raised his earnings a little. In 1931 he made more by helping the journalist Frank Scully and one or two others rewrite and complete the biography of Shaw by the dying Frank Harris.[17]

All this hack work fell short of bringing in enough to live on. In the summer of 1933 Berkman got the idea of buying some tents and setting up a camp for vacationers near Emma's cottage in Saint-Tropez. Unhappily, after buying the tents and setting up the camp, Berkman and Emma had only two customers.[18] Berkman then proposed that they open a vegetarian restaurant, but Emma dispiritedly replied that his idea "would also be a failure as most things we have undertaken. . . . In business undertakings one must have a knack for such and we do not have it."[19] Berkman was so despondent he next took the fantastic and uncharacteristic step of spending a hundred

[17] *Bernard Shaw* was published in New York in 1931 by Simon and Schuster. Though Harris was presumably the author, Scully and Berkman and others had written most of the work and Shaw himself had then rewritten parts and edited the whole manuscript. Apparently no critic detected that Harris was only nominally the author.

[18] EG to Ben Capes, July 31, 1933, NYPL, EGP.

[19] EG to AB, September 23, 1933, IISH, EG.

francs for a lottery ticket—as "a trial" he apologetically noted to Emma.[20]

Ships never or rarely ever come in when they are needed most, however, and in March, 1934, Berkman's plight became even more serious: "Broke and in debt," he cabled an American friend from Nice. "Giving up apartment. Urgently need seventy five dollars."[21] The following month he thanked Emma, who was then lecturing in Canada, for sending sixty dollars. The draft was especially welcome since he "had been sitting here for almost two weeks without a cent. Some days not enough to buy food or carfare."[22]

Bad as it was to have "not enough to live and too much to die," as Emma once summed up their condition, it was worse to be subject to the whims of the authorities of a strange country. Her marriage to Colton gave Emma a British passport and a measure of protection. Nevertheless, in March, 1930, while staying at "Bon Esprit," she was confronted with an expulsion order, dated March 26, 1901, and signed by Waldeck-Rousseau, the former premier of France who had been dead for over a quarter of a century. The police gave her ten days to leave. After much bother and only after she had enlisted the help of the famous attorney Henri Torres did she secure the revocation of the antique order.[23]

Carrying only a Nansen passport, issued by the League of Nations for stateless persons, Berkman was more vulnerable than Emma to official arbitrariness. On May 1, 1930, he was arrested, taken to the Préfecture in Nice, photographed, fingerprinted, and then put on a train for Belgium. In Brussels he was arrested, told he had to return to France, but eventually was allowed to proceed to Antwerp. Torres helped Emma secure permission for Berkman to return for three months. Berkman then had permission to be in France, but the French consul in Brussels absolutely refused him a visé to get there. "What to do?" he recounted to a friend. "Well, I got acquainted with some diamond people in Anvers, got friendly etc., and finally managed to get over the border with their help."[24]

Orders of expulsion came almost as rapidly as the change of ministries. Bribes and the efforts of a few French friends stopped his

20 AB to EG, November 16, 1933, IISH, AB.

21 AB to Michael Cohn, March 15, 1935, IISH, AB.

22 AB to EG, April 7, 1934, IISH, EG.

23 EG to A. L. Ross, April 29, 1930, IISH, EG.

24 AB to Michael Cohn, June 6, 1930, IISH, AB.

expulsion in November, 1930, and secured him a three-month stay which was automatically renewable. But on June 28, 1931, he was again ordered out of the country. Berkman began to suspect that old Czarist enemies or Bolshevik agents in the Sûreté—though he had given up editing the *Bulletin of the Relief Fund* in 1930—were determined to destroy his refuge in France. This suspicion was given some support on July 6, 1931, when *Le Petit Marseillais* carried an item on "*Propagande antimilitariste à Toulon*" to which his name was linked—he had in fact been in Toulon only once for less than an hour a couple of years earlier. Later it was the United States, however, which appeared to be surreptitiously behind the efforts to have him expelled. "We have the information from officials very high in authority in the Ministry of Interior," Berkman wrote Roger Baldwin, "that it is the U.S. that is pushing the case against me."[25] One French official confidentially explained that all the persecution was because the Ministry had received the information or misinformation that Berkman had killed a man on the Canadian border; another noted that Berkman's role in the Frick case was the basis for the intercession. But, despite their disagreement over details, both officials agreed it was the United States that wanted Berkman out of France. He was puzzled over the absence of any discernible motive: "Yet, who can tell?" he remarked to the sculptor Jo Davidson. "Perhaps some personal enemy in the U.S. Secret Service at Washington is back of the whole matter."[26] Whoever was behind all the orders, his expulsion was stopped in 1931 by the renewed efforts of the lawyer Torres, a friendly deputy named Pierre Rénaudel, and a galaxy of writers and intellectuals, including Albert Einstein, Thomas Mann, John Dewey, Romain Rolland, Charles Vildrac, and Bertrand Russell, all of whom petitioned Premier Laval to let Berkman remain where he was.[27]

Thereafter Berkman could rest easier, for the move to deport him fizzled out. Yet he was still subject to the badgering of the local gendarmes and to regulations which discriminated against foreigners. For years he had to secure renewals of his stay every three months. Frequently he was visited by detectives for information and expensive "tips." He was refused a labor card which would have given him the right to seek some kind of manual work. Finally, in

25 AB to Baldwin, October 1, 1931, IISH, AB.

26 AB to Davidson, September 18, 1931, IISH, AB.

27 Copies of the various wires and letters are in IISH, AB.

1935, his application for permission to move to Saint-Tropez during Emma's absence was denied under a new law which required aliens to get permission from the police to move from district to district.[28] Berkman felt that it all came down to a kind of imprisonment.

4

Another drain on their moral reserves, apart from official persecution and economic privation, was the presence of Emmy Eckstein, a German Jewess who had become Berkman's companion. While Emma was in Canada in 1927, Berkman had invited Emmy Eckstein to join him in Nice. Unwilling to live alone and heartsick over the course of events in Europe, especially in Russia, he had an obvious need for the devotion and care he expected from the young woman whom he had met in Berlin five years earlier. Perhaps he was also still trying to make up for his lost prison years—she was thirty years younger than he.

Emmy Eckstein was a most unlikely companion. Her family was in itself cause for worry. As Berkman described her background, "her damned mother is a hysterical woman who writes to Emmy only to scare her and to tell her of her own imaginary illness, travels around all the time for pleasure and complains she is poor. . . . Sister also a neurasthenic, almost crazy. Am trying to get her to go home to Berlin. She is a nuisance. All of them have a bad inheritance from their profligate father, who was a Hungarian baron or something."[29] Emmy Eckstein herself was babyish, neurotic, and possessed of all the petty bourgeois prejudices which Berkman despised. In a good summary of their problems, Berkman wrote:

Emmy is a very sensitive and imaginative kind of girl, easily depressed. Moreover, she is a stranger in our ranks and is by no means of my way of thinking. Has very decided ideas of her own, bourgeois ideas, but deeply ingrained. Thinks it terrible to live with me free, for instance. Just overpowered by her affection, she says, but always feels she is doing wrong. So one must understand such a psychology. Being a stranger in our ranks she feels also that others consider her as such, even an interloper. Which they do of course. Besides, there is also the instinctive prejudice among most people against an elderly person living with a younger one. . . . On the whole she has a lot to contend against, and I am not always patient as you know.

[28] AB, "Form Application to Préfet of Police, Var," March 14, 1935, IISH, EG.

[29] AB to EG, Monday [January], 1928, IISH, EG.

As if this were not already enough to turn a marriage counselor's hair white, Berkman added that, although "her love is very exceptional . . . she is incredibly jealous. It is enough for me to get a letter in a woman's handwriting to make her miserable. But I have been trying to break her from this and she seems to be growing more reasonable. . . ."[30]

But Berkman was not confident of her growing reasonableness. The following day, January 31, 1928, he recorded another quarrel in his diary: "I feel I live in a glass case, every movement observed, always watched like a thief or a prisoner. . . . Even brings thoughts of suicide. I am tired of such a life and after her great love I don't want that of any other woman." He continued to suffer torments over their relationship, as the following diary entries show:

[May 2, 1928] Great trouble. Woman upstairs burned foot. Emmy asked me to go up. Then shouted "stay there" etc.

[November 15, 1928] Made bad atmosphere last eve[ning] by her eternal suspicion. Saw old letter from a man on my desk. Written in Russian. Looked to her like a woman's handwriting. . . . I feel I live in an atmosphere of suspicion.

[November 30, 1928] Big trouble. Repeated to me what counterrevolutionary officer above us once told her. "So, have it easy. Workers have to work." He is right, she said. Her social attitude is something shocking and terrible to me. . . . I feel in her—rather in her attitude—the enemy of our entire world and ideas.

[January 19, 1929] Jealous in a pathological way.

[February 4, 1929] Big trouble. Insanely jealous of Lillian in Washington.

[October 20, 1931] Have had lots of quarrels with Emmy. Every day almost.

[August 7, 1932] I went with Eve and Emmy to Café Paris. When Eve arrived she acted as if not to kiss me as is her wont. I got up from table, pulled her up and kissed her. I wanted her to feel that she can be with me in the presence of Emmy the same as always. There have been before remarks about Emmy's jealousy. Well, Emmy got wild and made scene—"don't talk to me." That night was terrible.

And so on and on. In spite of Berkman's insistence that his diary was private—on the front page of one of the small, memorandum books he used he wrote: "Don't Read This. Strictly Personal and Private"—Emmy Eckstein obviously disregarded his wishes, for on August 5, 1933, she penned in a note to the "sweet little book" in which she sought its forgiveness for being on the "wrong track." A

30 AB to EG, January 30, 1928, IISH, EG.

few days later, August 30, 1933, disgusted by this further invasion of his privacy, Berkman gave up trying to keep a diary: "Life has become too stupid a thing. There is no purpose in it anymore. Besides misunderstandings with E.G., misunderstandings with Emmy. Is there ever any real understanding anywhere?"[31]

Emmy Eckstein was, of course, a prime cause of many of Berkman's misunderstandings with Emma. It was enough for Berkman to get a letter from Emma to set Emmy Eckstein off into one of her quarrels with Berkman. She hated and feared Emma, most of the time, for the latter's forty years of shared life with Berkman. She quite understandably felt left out of the things that really counted for the two older people. What was a little less understandable was her violent response to this inevitable situation. Most of the time she simply expressed an active hatred for Emma. During an especially bitter quarrel in 1931, for instance, she lashed out: "Wollen Sie mich heute verstehen, Emma, dass ich die Frau Sasha's bin, wie Sie auch nennen moegen: Frau, Sweetheart, Geliebte" ("Now understand me, Emma, I am Sasha's wife, whatever else you want to call me: mistress, sweetheart, darling").[32] After Emma wrote a letter rejecting this injunction, Emmy Eckstein wrote a hysterical note to Berkman about Emma, "Eine Frau mit weissem Haar und weisen blauen Augen": "I don't want to see those bad eyes again." She believed Emma was so malicious that even when she brought her flowers, as she sometimes did, "each flower has a knife."[33]

Emma's response to Emmy Eckstein was spelled out in her letters to Berkman in which she observed that his lady friend was "obsessed by her sense of possessions," the victim of "her own unfortunate jealousy." She pointed out to Emmy Eckstein that she was not the "only one who has broken with home, parents, friends, tradition." When Emmy Eckstein stubbornly insisted that she be regarded as Berkman's wife, Emma charged that she was still caught up in her past, in "the narrow, stifling confines of a life barren of human interest, centered only on one's family, one's furniture and silverwear [sic], one's dog."[34] On the other hand, Emma defended Berkman's

[31] Berkman's Diary is in IISH, AB. Of course not all the entries recorded their quarrels. On a few occasions Berkman noted: "Good with Emmy" or "peace for a considerable time."

[32] Emmy Eckstein to EG, May 31, 1931, IISH, AB.

[33] Emmy Eckstein to AB, n.d. [October, 1931], NYPL, EGP.

[34] EG to Emmy Eckstein, June 10, 1931, IISH, AB.

relationship with Emmy Eckstein when outsiders wrote to ask if their impossible liaison had finally ended. Thus she wrote the Danish writer, Karen Michaelis: "No, Sasha did not break with his lady love. Why should he? She is terribly devoted to him, even if it is the devotion which often killeth rather than cures. But I am inclined to think that Sasha loves that devotion and I am glad for him to have it."[35] And Emma did desire to get on with Emmy Eckstein, at least for Berkman's sake. When the younger woman swung in her unstable way from her hostility to a rather extravagant affection—usually these swings occurred when Emma was away on one of her tours—Emma did not rebuff her. In 1934 Emmy Eckstein wrote Emma: "I am sure that you would be surprised how much I have changed re my attitude to Sash. I was of course too much rooted in that thought that a man belongs altogether to a wife. Mit Hart und Haar. But, if I well remember, I even was that way the last time you were with us. . . ."[36] Emma replied that she was glad that Emmy Eckstein no longer thought she was taking Berkman away from her. She later added: "My dearest, I am glad you want to be my friend. Not that I have ever considered you my enemy. But I did think you did not understand me and that you resented my friendship with Sasha."[37] Unhappily, shortly after Emma returned to France in 1935, she and Emmy Eckstein shattered their new understanding with another quarrel.

Ultimate responsibility for all the strife and disharmony of this complex triangular relationship was clearly not Emmy Eckstein's alone. In the last analysis Berkman was himself partially responsible: It was his infatuation for a person so foreign to his and Emma's experience, ideas, and values which brought them all together to play out these pathetic scenes. Moreover, he felt with some justice that Emma was partially responsible, that she unwittingly made life hard for any of his feminine companions: "You say I have always been between two fires in this regard," he wrote Emma. "Partly true, because you must know yourself that you have a squelching effect upon other women, and particularly upon younger and inexperienced

[35] EG to Michaelis, August 8, 1929, IISH, EG.

[36] Emmy Eckstein to EG, July 16, 1934, IISH, AB.

[37] EG to Emmy Eckstein, July 30, 1934, IISH, AB. Berkman wrote hopefully to Emma that she would "be surprised how she has really taken you to heart. Emmy seems to have transferred her love for her mother . . . to you" (AB to EG, November 4, 1934, IISH, AB).

women. Still more particularly upon those that have been in my life. You are too strong for them, and they feel it, consciously or unconsciously. . . ."[38] In truth caught between two fires, Berkman defended one woman to the other. He admitted to Emmy Eckstein that Emma was outspoken, "in fact too outspoken, especially about her feelings, for she hurts people often unnecessarily and often when she does not even intend it and does not know it." But this was not a case of persecution and he warned her that only a "sickly state of mind" would allow her to think that it was.[39] He admitted to Emma that Emmy Eckstein was hurt too easily but sadly added that "even if unconsciously you have embittered her life. And by reflex it has also brought a good deal of bitterness in my life."[40]

Never easy to live with, Emma became more irascible during the ordeal of exile. "E.G. is dictatorial and interfering," Berkman confidentially wrote a mutual friend, "and she has a way of making life miserable for you without saying anything to which you can give a rough and suitable answer. The more is the pity. And the worst of it is that E.G. herself has not the least idea of it. She is a great woman in some ways, no doubt of that; but living close with her is just impossible."[41] There was truth in what Berkman said, but he was wrong in thinking that Emma had no idea of her own irritability. In 1934 she wrote Emmy Eckstein that "if I have seemed impatient and unkind to you my dear it was only due to my own inner void, and unsatisfied longing for what I left behind."[42] And the following summer, after another eruption, Emma wrote Rudolf Rocker that she was terribly restless and that perhaps the friction was "entirely my fault."[43]

5

In the face of all these pressures and conflicts, the friendship of Emma Goldman and Alexander Berkman showed no signs of weakening. On his sixty-fifth birthday Emma observed that the one treasure she had rescued from her long struggle was her friendship with him: "it is not an exaggeration when I say that no one ever was so rooted in my being, so ingrained in every fiber as you have been and are to

[38] AB to EG, January 30, 1928, IISH, EG.

[39] AB to Emmy Eckstein, October 16, 1931, NYPL, EGP.

[40] AB to EG, October 29, 1932, IISH, EG.

[41] AB to M. Eleanor Fitzgerald, November 11, 1932, IISH, AB.

[42] EG to Emmy Eckstein, May 9, 1934, IISH, AB.

[43] EG to Rocker, August 22, 1935, IISH, EG.

this day. Men have come and gone in my long life. But you my dearest will remain forever."[44] Berkman had already written that their friendship could survive occasional mutual criticism and that, speaking for himself, nothing on earth could effectively come between them. Then in February and March of 1936 Berkman had to undergo two prostate gland operations. He kept knowledge of the second operation from Emma, not wishing to worry her while she was on a lecture tour in South Wales. But in a letter, annotated "to be mailed only in case of my death," he wrote: "I just want you to know that my thoughts are with you and I consider our life of work and comradeship and friendship, covering a period of about 45 years, one of the most beautiful and rarest things in the world. In this spirit I greet you now, dear immutable Sailor Girl, and may your work continue to bring light and understanding in this topsy-turvy world of ours." If he were to die, she should not grieve too much: "I have lived my life and I am really of the opinion that when one has neither health nor means and cannot work for his ideas, it is time to clear out."[45]

The time had apparently arrived. The financial failure of Emma's American tour meant that "Bon Esprit" would have to be put up for sale and that Berkman could count on little assistance from his hard-pressed comrade. Try as he would, he could see no way to keep alive other than by depending completely on the generosity of friends; proud as ever, he was utterly unwilling to accept this degrading way to maintain what he had come to regard as his "useless" life. Emmy Eckstein was seriously ill and required an operation—she suffered from a dislocation and extension of her stomach, which caused her pain and made normal digestion impossible. Berkman himself was in constant pain for months after his second operation.

For Emma's sixty-seventh birthday, on June 27, 1936, Berkman planned to take an excursion boat, the "Isle-de-beauté," to Saint-Tropez for a surprise visit. But on the twenty-fourth he suffered a relapse. With regret he had to write that he could not come: "I embrace you heartily and hope that this birthday may bring you some joy and brighten the days that will follow."[46] Without him, however, it was a sad birthday. "My dear," she wrote Berkman, "whom else should I write on this day but you. Only there is nothing to tell. I keep think-

44 EG to AB, November 19, 1935, IISH, AB.

45 AB to EG, March 23, 1936, IISH, AB.

46 AB to EG, June 24, 1936, IISH, AB.

ing what a long time to live. For whom? For what? But there is no answer. . . . [Your visit] would have been a grand surprise and your room so nice and clean and inviting."[47] He never read her letter. The following morning, at 2:00 A.M., she received a telephone call from Nice: during an especially severe attack, Berkman had fired a bullet into his side. So miscast for a role of violence was this essentially gentle intellectual that he bungled his suicide. The bullet he had fired perforated his stomach and lower lungs and lodged in his spinal column. It was sixteen hours before death finally came.

"I don't want to live a sick man," Berkman had written. "Dependent. Forgive me Emmie darling. And you too Emma. Love to all. Help Emmie. Sasha." Hit harder by Berkman's death than by any other catastrophe in her life, Emma set about clearing up his affairs and making arrangements to have the hysterical Emmy Eckstein cared for.[48] Aside from his manuscripts, diaries, and letters, Berkman had left little to be disposed of. His estate amounted to eighty dollars. But Emma and a few friends knew that his legacy was in another coin. "As for my fame, (God help us!) and your infame," Eugene O'Neill once declared to Berkman, "I would be willing to exchange a good deal of mine for a bit of yours. It is not hard to write what one feels as truth. It is damned hard to live it."[49]

[47] EG to AB, June 27, 1936, IISH, AB.

[48] Emma made plans to send Emmy Eckstein twenty-five dollars a month and got another friend to do likewise. She also tried to have her go with Dr. Michael Cohn to America as a governess, but there were difficulties over her passport—primarily because she had been Berkman's mistress—and Cohn finally reached the point that he could not stand the difficult young woman. "How could you do it after knowing me for so many years?" he angrily asked Emma. After she sold "Bon Esprit" in 1937, Emma sent Emmy Eckstein some more money. Following her sixth stomach operation the unfortunate young woman spent almost a year in a clinic before she died in 1939.

[49] O'Neill to AB, January 29, 1927, IISH, AB.

CHAPTER XXXII

SPAIN: THE VERY TOP OF THE MOUNTAIN

Word of Emma Goldman's retirement had been making the rounds for years. "Goldman is past now," Laurence Stallings had chortled in 1931—he could not even admit his obvious pleasure "in baiting a toothless tiger."[1] Several years later the editor of *Harper's* also had marked her case closed: "It is strange what time does to political causes. A generation ago it seemed to many American conservatives as if the opinions which Emma Goldman was expressing might sweep the world. Now she fights almost alone for what seems a lost cause; contemporary radicals are overwhelmingly opposed to her. . . ."[2] Utterly unwilling to be relegated to the past, she ignored these premature obituary notices: "I am very far from retirement," she grimly informed an interested young couple in 1936. "In fact I am more than ever [determined] that my life should end as it began, fighting." Yet she did not reckon with Berkman's suicide within a few months. After this blow, alone now in a way she had never been before, she felt herself slipping deeper and deeper into a mood of grief and despair.

At this moment, on the nineteenth of July, 1936, the Spanish workers offered the first real resistance to European fascism by beating off a military insurrection and by putting down the cornerstones for a far-reaching social revolution. Guided by their faith in anarchism, which had strong roots in Spain going back to the time of Bakunin, the revolutionists set up agrarian and industrial collectives and seriously sought to introduce a future of freedom and equality. Emma followed the news of their heroic efforts with an intensity of interest which soon made her own personal problems seem almost inconsequential. She was therefore overjoyed when Augustine Souchy, Secretary of the Comité Anarcho-Syndicaliste, called on her to serve in the great undertaking. His letter "contained an invitation to come to Barcelona," she jubilantly reported to her niece. "Believe me my

[1] *New York Sun*, November 20, 1931.

[2] *Harper's Magazine*, CLXX (December, 1934), 52.

heart jomped [*sic*] and the crushing weight that was pressing down on my heart since Sasha[']s death left me as by magic."[3]

2

Members of the powerful Confederación Nacional del Trabajo (CNT) and the Federación Anarquista Ibérica (FAI) welcomed her with open arms when she arrived in Barcelona in September, 1936. Ten thousand of her comrades turned out for a mass meeting to hear her place them under the responsibility of being a "shining example to the rest of the world." For the first time she was in a city where the anarchists were in control and the prospect was enormously pleasing: "I have come to you as to my own," she declared, "for your ideal has been my ideal for forty five years and it will remain to my last breath."[4] Brushing aside for the moment her misgivings over the idealistic innocence of the Spanish anarchists, she took up the struggle with all her old vigor and spirit. There was work to be done and she was needed.

The Catalonian workers wanted her to take charge of the CNT-FAI press service and propaganda bureau in England. So that she would be able to speak with firsthand knowledge, they made every effort to show her their major accomplishments and their major problems. She was even helped to travel to the Aragon front, where she could see for herself whether the anarchist troops had been "militarized." Now sixty-seven, the old lady sat in trenches within hearing distance of Franco's snipers and talked to Buenaventura Durruti, the already legendary leader of the anarchist troops, and to "simple, unsophisticated workers, who had flocked to the front to stake their all in freeing Spain."[5] She came away from the front reassured by the lack of barrack discipline and the belief of the soldiers, from officer to private, in equalitarianism. Despite her concern that this revolution, like all modern revolutions, had to spring from the loins of war, she was pleased that the anarchists had the reputation of being the best fighters on the line.

Aware that the underlying problem of Spain was its feudal agrarian

[3] Souchy to EG, August 18, 1936, IISH, EG; EG to Stella Cominsky, August 22, 1936, NYPL, EGP.

[4] *CNT-AIT-FAI Boletín de Información*, September 25, 1936. (The AIT was the Spanish section of the International Workingmen's Association [L'Association International des Travailleurs]; Emma was in charge of an English-language edition of this bulletin.)

[5] "Visiting the Fronts," unpublished manuscript, n.d., LC.

system, she visited as many agricultural collectives as she could. She was particularly impressed by Albate de Cinca, a collectivized village in the Province of Husea. The large estate, which had formerly belonged to an absentee owner, had been divided among the five thousand residents, each family receiving a share proportionate to its size. Although much of their land had lain fallow for years and they had little modern machinery, the new owners had made remarkable progress in their common venture. They were understandably proud of their acquisition of a threshing machine and of their ability to cultivate the land efficiently without the direction of any outside manager or state agent. "The Cinca comrades saw it to be their duty to demonstrate the superior quality of work in common," Emma observed, and was even more pleased by the fact there was no Cheka, no state machinery in sight.[6]

The collectivization of the factories had proceeded less dramatically, for the workers were handicapped by the opposition of the Madrid government, the flight of many technicians and managers, the increasing difficulty of obtaining raw materials from abroad, and the loss of major areas of both domestic and foreign markets. Nevertheless, she was "amazed at the capacity of the supposedly untaught workers." The Metal Syndicate was an outstanding example. Within two days it had converted an automobile assembling plant into a munitions factory "and when I arrived in September 1936 it was already working three shifts and producing the only arms loyalist Spain had at her disposal during that critical period."[7]

What she saw added to her conviction that the Spanish anarchists had proved that the Bolshevik pattern of revolution was not inevitable, that it was possible to have a constructive revolution worked out in freedom. After her visits to the collectives she informed a large meeting of the youth of the FAI that "your revolution will destroy forever [the notion] that anarchism stands for chaos."[8] No one could expect a revolution to run smoothly and this one was being carried out under the extraordinarily difficult conditions of an armed attack. (From her point of view there was only one answer to this: "I have and do maintain," she wrote, "that an armed counter-revolutionary and fascist attack can be met in no way except by an armed

---

[6] "Albate de Cinca," unpublished manuscript, n.d., LC.

[7] "The Lure of the Spanish People," unpublished manuscript, n.d., LC.

[8] CNT-AIT-FAI Boletín de Información, October 15, 1936.

defence."⁹) All things considered, she was not prepared to be sharply critical of such excesses as the destruction of churches. After all, how could one be too critical of a people who, in the face of the approaching danger on the Madrid and Sargossa fronts, sent a thousand delegates to Barcelona to discuss the modern school and the dangers of centralization?

Before she left for England, she was taken high in the Pyrenees to see a libertarian educational experiment.

By way of confession I have to own up that I was literally pulled up a mountain of 4,000 feet above the level of the sea, and this only with the help of Professor Mawa on the one side and the young children of Comrade Prig Elias on the other. A troupe of children singing lustily led the way. Another troupe with a cinema operator followed. I admit it was an exhausting feat but I would not have missed it for worlds. On the very top of the mountain we found a small white peasant house, and a patch of land. We were greeted by a large streamer which contained in bold letters the name of the colony—MON NOU (New World). Its credo read as follows: "Children are the new world. And all dreamers are children; those who are moved by kindness and beauty. . . .¹⁰

It was with a kind of anticipatory regret that she came down from this mountain of idealism to the "old murderous world" below, down to her hotel on the Plaza de Cataluña. Never again would she be so happy.

3

Although she almost preferred dying in Spain to living in England, she went to London in December to enlist the economic and moral support so desperately needed by her Spanish comrades.

The international response to the Spanish conflict made her task virtually hopeless from the beginning. The Tory government in Britain had persuaded France and other nations to adhere to a so-called doctrine of nonintervention out of fear both of provoking a showdown with the German and Italian backers of the insurgents and of antagonizing General Franco, who dominated territory in which many British nationals had sizable investments. (The United States obligingly followed suit in January, 1937, with a Roosevelt-sponsored neutrality act which denied supplies to the loyalists.) In October, 1936, Russia commenced an unofficial intervention on the loyalist

---

⁹ EG to Tom Bell, October 4, 1936, NYPL, EGP.

¹⁰ "Lure of the Spanish People," LC.

side, but did so, of course, to further its own interests. These interests included checking the expansion of Germany, maintaining its defensive alliance with France, and strengthening the previously insignificant Spanish Communist party. These interests did not include supporting the libertarian Spanish revolution at the double risk of weakening its own authoritarian influence in Spain and of alienating, during this united front period, its property-conscious allies in France and elsewhere. In a sentence, the one thing uniting all the major powers was their opposition to the Spanish Revolution.

Trade-unionists and Socialists abroad might still have been expected to demonstrate some solidarity with the Spanish workers, but, as Emma soon discovered, they had easily accepted the line that the war against Franco had to come first and the revolution afterward. In vain did the CNT-FAI protest that the revolution and the war were inseparable—to pursue the latter without the former was to rob the people of their will to resist fascism and to postpone the revolution indefinitely, perhaps forever. To the matter-of-fact Labourites, however, this was little more than infantile leftism, a leftism which blocked the necessary centralization of military and industrial effort. Eventually some even accepted the Stalinist-inspired view that the revolutionists were "stabbing the Republic in the back" as part of a perfidious Fascist plot. The upshot of all this "realism" and misrepresentation was that the European working class maintained a peculiarly detached attitude toward the decisive Spanish conflict. Its involvement hardly went beyond minor contributions to the various aid funds.

No individual could have turned the tide of opinion which was running against the Spanish anarchists, but Emma Goldman did what she could. She opened a propaganda office in London for the CNT-FAI and edited an English-language edition of its Spanish bulletin. To combat the systematic denigration of the anarchist position in the press she organized letter-writing campaigns and wrote letters of her own to the Manchester *Guardian*, the *Daily Telegraph*, the *Evening Standard*, and other papers. She contributed articles to *Spain and the World*, a fortnightly journal. She took the lead in arranging concerts, exhibitions of Catalan art, and film showings to raise money for her comrades. She organized the Committee To Aid Homeless Spanish Women and Children, with herself as the "Honorable Secretary," Stella Churchill as treasurer, and Sir Barry Jackson, Sybil Thorndike, Lady Playfair, and other prominent persons as sponsors. Later she persuaded Havelock Ellis, C. E. M. Joad, John Cowper Powys, Fenner Brockway, Rebecca West, George Orwell, and Herbert Read to lend their names and support to another of her committees, the International Anti-Fascist Solidarity, which was one more attempt at "resurrecting the dead in England."[11]

The dead stubbornly refused resurrection. Honest confidence men were scarcely more rare than left intellectuals who honestly and sympathetically portrayed the cause of the Spanish anarchists. She learned from bitter experience what George Orwell was to discover later, that it was almost impossible to get anything printed or said in their defense. And it was not until the publication of Orwell's *Homage to Catalonia* (1938), as she wrote a friend, that there was a break in the "conspiracy of silence against us. . . . For the first time since the struggle began in 1936 someone outside our ranks has come forward to paint the Spanish anarchists as they really are. . . ."[12] Exasperated beyond words with the English intelligentsia, she became more grim, more contemptuous of those who were unwilling even to hear the anarchist side of the story, and more determined than ever that they should hear it.

She needed all of her unbelievable tenacity to get through the countless lectures she delivered in behalf of the CNT-FAI. In *Lover under Another Name* (1953), Ethel Mannin has shown Emma, with whom she was closely associated in those days, in action at a more or less typical meeting. Although part of a work of fiction and written long after the event, Miss Mannin's account has the ring of substantial authenticity: A "short thickset scowling elderly woman with grey hair and thick glasses," Emma entered the crowded hall and sat "glowering ferociously at the audience." When she rose to speak, her supporters cheered, the Fascists booed, and the Communists cat-called and sang "L'Internationale." Cries rang out to call the police:

But Red Emma roared on, announcing that she had had fifty years of dealing with mobs and no one could shout her down. And by God she was right. No one could. I couldn't keep some lines from *The Marriage of Heaven and Hell* out of my mind:

"Rintah roars, and shakes his fires in the burden'd air;
Hungry clouds swag on the deep."

11 EG to Harry Kelly, January 1, 1938, NYPL, EGP.
12 EG to Rudolf Rocker, May 6, 1938, NYPL, EGP.

I always liked that word "swag." Red Emma's voice swag on the waves of opposition.

Her speech over and the collection made, she still did not let her hearers go, but "began pitching into the audience for its smallness—though the hall was packed—and the paltryness of its three-hundred-pound contribution to the cause for which the Spa-aa-nish people, she yelled at them, were giving their life's blood." The audience sat "enchanted under the attack, and when she had finished applauded wildly."[13]

Toothless Old Tiger indeed!

4

But by now she was playing mainly on her nerve, for, in addition to the insuperable or almost insuperable obstacles she faced in England, she was deeply disturbed by some of the compromises of her Spanish comrades. While still in Barcelona in 1936 she had written that "the end evidently does justify the most impossible means . . . and what is more tragic is that there is no return to first principles. On the contrary, one is pulled deeper and deeper into the mire of compromise."[14] The ends were the defeat of Franco and the survival of the revolution. But defeat of Franco apparently demanded participation in the moderate popular-front government in Madrid—in November, 1936, the world had been treated to the curious spectacle of anarchists becoming ministers of state. Much worse, from Emma's point of view, was the acceptance of arms (with the inevitable strings attached) from the Soviet Union in order to wage the fight against Franco and attempt to bypass the nonintervention policy of the capitalistic nations. Bogged down by these basic compromises, the anarchists found themselves part of the government, though they hated and feared any government; they found themselves shoulder to shoulder with the Communists, though they hated and feared their ingrained authoritarianism and felt that participation in the united front was in some measure a betrayal of the anarchists who languished in Russian prisons; they found themselves fighting in increasingly disciplined, centralized armies, though they hated and feared the consequences of war and militarism.

From the beginning Emma had privately argued against the course

[13] *Lover under Another Name* (London: Jarrolds, Ltd., 1953), pp. 136–39.
[14] EG to Mark Mratchny, November 3, 1936, LC.

chosen by the leaders of the CNT-FAI. Even before Berkman's death she had written her old friend opposing the participation of the Spanish anarchists in elections and utterly rejecting the idea of any common activity with the Communists. She felt that such a denial of anarchist philosophy was both futile and dangerous—it was, moreover, absurd, for the Communists were just as great enemies of the anarchists as the Fascists and would, if they were given a chance, turn on the anarchists and destroy them.[15] Now she argued with the leaders of the CNT-FAI for an acceleration of the revolution, the retention of people's militias, the use of strikes, and other straightforward revolutionary measures. She warned them that their acceptance of ministries would undermine their usefulness and cut them off from their rank and file, that militarization was antithetical to the spirit and principles of anarchism, and, above all, that their collaboration with the Communists was fatal.[16]

As in a game of chess, each move of the Spanish anarchists lead to another. Emma's personal horror was that she knew this but was unable to convince her comrades that each of their compromises made a final debacle more inevitable. Her letters were filled with the painful realization of impending disaster:

[November 14, 1936] All is not well. Our people are in a hornet's nest. . . . Apropos of Russia darling, I hate to disappoint you. Russia never does anything handsomely.

[January 5, 1937] The so-called United Front hangs on a straw. We would only make it harder for the CNT-FAI if we were to come out with plain talk.

[May 4, 1937] Well, I have taken my place with the Spanish comrades. I can not accept their every act, but their courage, fortitude and even more their passionate devotion to the Revolution make me decide I am with them to the bitter end.[17]

As she wrote this last letter, Communists were fighting anarchists in the Barcelona streets.

From early 1937 the Communist-controlled Valencia government had been slowly strangling the revolution through carefully devised taxes and decrees which placed the collectives and armed forces of

---

[15] EG to AB, March 24, 1936, IISH, AB.

[16] EG to Mark Mratchny, November 3, 1936, LC; EG to Alexander Shapiro, May 2, 1937, IISH, EG.

[17] EG to Stella Cominsky, November 14, 1936, NYPL, EGP; to Mark Mratchny, January 5, 1937, LC; to Rudolf Rocker, May 4, 1937, IISH, EG.

the workers under centralized control. On May 3, 1937, the government attempted to seize the Barcelona telephone exchange held by the anarchists. Members of the CNT-FAI resisted this final provocation. Fighting broke out with the government forces taking the initiative against the anarchists, the barricades were quickly put up, and the infamous "May Days" had commenced. But the anarchist spokesmen, unwilling to weaken the anti-Franco forces by waging an all-out fight, soon called the workers off the barricades. Restrained by no comparable scruples, the Communists and their allies then commenced a long line of reprisals against the "Trotskyites" and the "uncontrollable" anarchists. Political prisoners filled the jails in the old, familiar pattern. The bitter end of the revolution had come, as Emma had predicted, with the Communists leading the counter-revolution.

Still Emma publicly defended the leaders of the CNT-FAI and appealed for understanding of their predicament. She continued to keep her major criticisms of their compromises to her private correspondence and discussions. For the first time in her life, she had one set of opinions for the outside world and another set for her intimate friends. Galling from the first, her position became more intolerable as the tragedy progressed.

At the end of 1937 Marino Vasquez, National Secretary of the CNT, requested Emma to be a delegate at an extraordinary session of the International Workingmen's Association. At the meeting in Paris Emma was attacked on the right by those who thought, like Max Nettlau, that she had already been too critical of the actions of the CNT-FAI and on the left by those who thought, like Alexander Shapiro, that she had become an apologist for their egregious compromises and mistakes. A left oppositionist all her life, Emma had to hold her own inner doubts in check to make the best of her new experience of defending a centrist position: "Did I not know that the Spanish people see in government a mere makeshift, to be kicked overboard at will—and that they had never been deluded and corrupted by the parliamentary myth, I should perhaps be more alarmed for the future of the C.N.T.-F.A.I. But with Franco at the gate of Madrid, I could hardly blame them for choosing a lesser evil—participation in the Government rather than Dictatorship, the most deadly evil."[18] Although her statement was filled with compassion

---

[18] "Address to the Delegates at the Extraordinary Congress in Paris of the I.W.M.A.," n.d., NYPL, EGP.

for the dilemma of the Spanish anarchists, it lacked any real conviction that their decisions could be justified. Probably no one at the session was less convinced than Emma herself by her argument based on historical necessity and the lesser evil.

In publicly defending the course pursued by the Spanish anarchists, Emma was indeed swept away by her sympathies. As she put it in one of her letters, she felt about the CNT-FAI inconsistencies "as a mother feels toward her condemned son." To another comrade she declared that "it is as appropriate to sit in judgement over our comrades now as it were to sit in judgement on a man condemned to death. All theories must be set aside at present and our efforts increased to our utmost to help our comrades. . . ."[19] Although her sympathy for her Spanish comrades did her credit and undoubtedly her perspective on Spanish problems was changed by hearing the roar of bombs in Barcelona, she could not set theories aside without reaping the consequences. She knew at the time, what others have only since learned, that even a victory over Franco with USSR help meant ultimate defeat. Her failure to point this out, publicly and plainly, represented a retreat from her most effective political role, that of uncompromisingly honest criticism. The defense of basic compromises of principle might better have been left to the professional politicians.

In the last analysis, however, Emma remained essentially a rebel rather than a revolutionist. To a novelist friend who questioned the worth of revolutions if they "stifle the creative spirit," she promised: "One thing you can rest assured—that if the C.N.T.-F.A.I. were really to conquer—were really to become the sole economic and spiritual force and were then to attempt repression, I would be the first to sever my connection with them."[20] Then she would rebel against the revolution itself. Her motherly forgiveness, which had caused her to stray from her real political vocation, did not extend to any tampering with basic freedoms.

Even though she had long lived with a presentiment of their defeat, she was overwhelmed by grief when her Spanish comrades finally went under. In spite of all the compromises and frustrations, she had had a real glimpse in Spain of the New World which she had worked for decades to bring into being. On that first trip of hers

[19] EG to W. S. Van Valkenberg, April 4, 1938, IISH, EG.
[20] EG to Evelyn Scott, July 19, 1938, IISH, EG.

in 1936 she had seen a community in which ideals were actually working. It was a community which was not dedicated either to money-grubbing or to the rationalized terror: bootlicking subservience of the many to the few had been replaced by genuine I-and-thou fraternal relationships; men and women were encouraged to be free; and children were encouraged to dream. Picasso's very great painting of a woman with a dead child in "Guernica" (1937) expresses the kind of screaming mental anguish Emma felt when this community was crushed. "It's as though you had wanted a child all your life," she told a friend, "and at last, when you had almost given up hoping, it had been given to you—only to die soon after it was born!"[21]

As a last gesture of support, she went to Canada to raise money and sympathy for the lost cause. In Toronto on her seventieth birthday, June 27, 1939, she received a message that meant a great deal to her. Marino Vasquez, the CNT leader who had taken refuge in Paris, greeted the tired old lady in the name of the Spanish Libertarian Movement. His tribute, complete with Latin flourishes, was only a trifle overdrawn: "You are the incarnation of the eternal flame of the ideal which you have demonstrated in your life. The Spanish militants admire and revere you, as Anarchists should admire and value those of a great heart and abiding humanism for all mankind. . . . We declare you our spiritual mother."[22]

[21] Ethel Mannin, *Women and the Revolution* (New York: E. P. Dutton & Co., Inc., 1939), p. 137.

[22] Vasquez to EG, June 12, 1939, LC.

CHAPTER XXXIII

TO THE FINAL BREATH

By all odds Emma Goldman should have at last been ready for a rocking chair on a front porch somewhere. But in the autumn of 1939, shortly after the outbreak of the "imperialist" war she had vowed to oppose, four of her Italian friends in Toronto were arrested and charged, under a new War Measures Act, with having subversive literature in their possession. With no hesitation she took up the fight, organized a committee, secured a "cracker-jack" fighter for an attorney, and helped secure dismissals of the indictments against three of the boys. How could she rest easy in the face of the "frame-up of the Red Squad" and the generally "vicious police force here"?[1] It was just like old times in the United States!

The fourth Italian, Arthur Bartoletti, was held to answer a charge of being an alien and having an offensive weapon. Bartoletti, a militant anti-Fascist, had earlier disclosed the existence of a Fascist school in Windsor. Emma was convinced that this was what was behind his detention and feared that he might be deported to Italy—a deportation which meant almost certain death. She organized a Save Arthur Bartoletti Committee and appealed to friends in the United States for help. Nearly exhausted by this last campaign, she rather incoherently wrote a friend that she had "kept at [my typewriter] machine day[s] and half the nights bombarding our New York Italiens and Spaniards, and in a number of other cities for money." A few days later she admitted to another friend that she was "almost worn out from the struggle which I have been carrying on almost single handed."[2] Though her efforts were perhaps crucial in helping her Italian friends, she had pushed herself too hard—her magnificent, apparently inexhaustible energy had all but disappeared. In January, 1940, she wrote that one of the Italians was ill and that she had been going "every day to the place where he lives to take his

---

[1] EG to M. Eleanor Fitzgerald, November 13, 1939, NYPL, EGP.

[2] EG to M. Eleanor Fitzgerald, November 13, 1939, NYPL, EGP; to Harry Kelly, November 17, 1939, NYPL, EGP.

temperature and look after him in other ways."[3] Her heart, which had already given unmistakable signs that it was weakened, now began to cause her acute distress. Still she climbed the stairs up to her Italian comrade's room and still she walked to catch streetcars to her meetings.

As she wished, she went out fighting. On February 17, 1940, she suffered a stroke. On the fourteenth of May she died. On the eighteenth of May she achieved another wish by returning to the country she had loved: The Immigration and Naturalization Service granted the dead exile re-entry to the United States. She was buried in Chicago's Waldheim Cemetery, near the graves of her Haymarket comrades.

2

The living, flesh and blood Emma Goldman had her share of faults. She was something of a prima donna—she could exercise an imperiousness which was woefully inharmonious with her anarchistic principles and could be crudely insensitive to the feelings of others. As Berkman observed, she was not an easy person to live with. Tom Bell got at the heart of the matter when he once wrote that an old friend could have drawn up an appalling list of things Emma should not have done:

He could have told of times without number in which she had been impatient, irritable, unreasonable, unjust, altogether wrong—times when she showed that she had digestive and sexual organs, when her liver was out of order or her ears hot, when she thrashed a man of straw, said just the wrong thing, and would not listen to argument. Times innumerable.

Like most human beings, she fell a little short of being an angel. But Bell was also right when he continued by saying that the old friend

might however not yet have forgotten times when she was patient and sweet with that fellow whom she knew to be a sincere comrade even though he was indeed a dreadful bore, times when she was generous and big-minded, times when amid all the uproar she kept her head. Times too when in spite of it all she could be jolly and comrade-like, when she could join in the laugh even when the joke was on her. . . . She never, never once failed us in a crisis. Emma then always rose to her full height, always.[4]

Very likely this was why, since her career was marked by an extraordinary series of crises, studies of Emma Goldman, including her

[3] EG to Liza Kadolsky, January 26, 1940, NYPL, EGP.
[4] Bell to AB, February 23, 1933, IISH, AB.

own autobiography, seem drawn to a scale larger than life: During all the critical periods she stood on her tiptoes.

And perhaps the realization that Emma never failed to rise to her full height in a crisis helps to explain her unusual capacity for friendship. Her correspondence reveals a remarkable range of friends, from distinguished writers to social outcasts and prisoners. All of them must have seen in her, in addition to her courage and energy, an almost unlimited fund of compassion. As Henry Alsberg once observed in astonishment, "you have protected so many of the naked and helpless (physical and spiritual)[,] been a mother to so many a staunch friend, without asking questions or demanding account. . . ."[5]

Though she was by no means a seminal social or political thinker, she made her ideas an integral part of her life and used them to achieve her full height. Her one serious lapse was on the issue of violence. Even after she had rejected the ethicality of individual acts of violence, she still had not, at the end of her life, discarded the illusion that large-scale violence—in this case the defensive violence of her Spanish comrades—could bring about her ultimate ends of peace, freedom, and justice. Yet she went further than all but a very few of her contemporaries in honestly confronting the complicated problem of the relationship of means to ends, and her constant stress on neglected and unpopular truths enriched American and European life.

No matter where she found them, she fought against the administrators who regarded people not as ends in themselves but as means to institutional ends. She opposed rationalized conformity in the United States and rationalized terror in Russia. She correctly diagnosed as a moral malady the special pleading, discouraged determinism, and historicism which led liberals to apologize for Communist oppression and bloodshed. She effectively criticized the naïve faith of liberals and Socialists in the omnicompetent state and in the sufficiency of economic reform. Indeed, her attempted spiritualization of politics, her contempt for those who were absorbed in governmental mechanics, her emphatic assertion of the need for small, countervailing groups—all of these views provided a needed counterstatement to prevailing orthodoxies on the political left.

To the final breath she waged an unrelenting fight for the free individual. The opening lines of Karl Shapiro's otherwise perceptive poem, "Death of Emma Goldman," are wrong: Emma died triumphant. She had lived to the end a life of unique integrity.

[5] Alsberg to EG, June 18, 1929, IISH, EG.

BIBLIOGRAPHICAL ESSAY

PERSONAL PAPERS AND PUBLIC RECORDS

The turbulence of Emma Goldman's affairs and her almost constant movement from place to place swirled some of her papers, such as those seized by the Department of Justice in 1917, behind the walls of official secrecy; other of her papers were scattered across most of the countries of the Western world. Fortunately for the biographer, she had the entirely commendable habit of keeping the letters of her wide range of correspondents and of making copies of the stream of letters, usually filled with the details of her activities and with candid accounts of her intellectual and emotional life, which she sent off in return. But these letters and her manuscripts might well have disappeared forever, had it not been for the alertness and historical awareness of her family, her friends, and the librarians who commenced early to gather files of her materials. Thus, although there is still a paucity of evidence for her childhood and adolescence, there are surprisingly rich primary sources for most of her life. This biography would have been impossible without the following collections:

Joseph A. Labadie Collection (LC) at the University of Michigan. Use of these materials presents some problems, for the late Agnes Inglis, to whom the collection owes so much, followed an anarchistically individualistic filing system, based in part on associations which are not readily apparent to the outsider. To find Emma Goldman's correspondence, for example, the student must first know that she was considered a "Libertarian" and then look for her name in this category. Other papers are in the "Anarchism" section under her name. The files are not in any strict chronological or topical order, nor are the packages numbered. But these are minor problems. The student will find here some of her early letters and an especially good collection of scrapbooks and pamphlets and of manuscripts on the Spanish Civil War.

Emma Goldman Papers at the New York Public Library (NYPL, EGP). These papers are chronologically arranged, with the exception of one box labeled, "Typescripts, Misc." This collection is best for her family correspondence and very good for her correspondence with American radicals and liberals. When Roger Baldwin turned over some of the files of the American Civil Liberties Union to the NYPL, part of his correspondence with Emma was placed in these papers. Here one also finds many of her old lectures and lecture notes.

Harry Weinberger Memorial Collection (WMC) at Yale University. These papers are also well arranged, primarily by legal cases, and are indispensable for letters and documents on her legal struggles.

Goldman Files in the Department of Justice, Department of State, and Post Office Department holdings in the National Archives. These files are numerically arranged. DJ 186233–13, for instance, refers to the principal Department of Justice file on Emma Goldman, composed of four large folders. The Immigration and Naturalization Service, which until June, 1940, was part of the Labor Department, now has separate files in the Department of Justice holdings—INS 52410/43 is the most important file in this collection. There are some relevant papers in the numerical files of the Department of State—most useful are DS, Vol. DCCXXI, Cases 10093 to 10133, and DS, Vol. DCCCXXI, Cases 12612 to 12655, and DS 311.6124 K 47. The relevant Post Office Department file is PO 46647. These files are, of course, of fundamental importance for the government's campaign against Emma.

Goldman-Berkman Archives at the International Institute for Social History (IISH) in Amsterdam. These archives are roughly arranged according to subjects or correspondents, but the divisions are incomplete and much of the material is where one would least expect to find it. Yet here one finds Emma Goldman's correspondence with Berkman and most of her important manuscripts. Almost every current of radical activity and thought left some deposit in these papers. Here is her correspondence with Eugene Debs, Victor Berger, Morris Hillquit, Upton Sinclair, Lincoln Steffens, Fremont Older, Theodore Dreiser, Eugene O'Neill, John Dewey, Bertrand Russell, Harold Laski, Aldous Huxley, and many others. Unquestionably, these archives are best for the last twenty years of her life.

Other collections or files of papers which I have found helpful are the following: Louis F. Post Papers, Library of Congress; Theodore Herfurth Papers, State Historical Society of Wisconsin; Czolgosz Papers, Buffalo Historical Society; People v. Czolgosz, Erie County Court House, Buffalo; People v. Emma Goldman, Court of General Sessions, New York City. I have also made use of the hearings and reports of legislative investigations, the report of proceedings and debates in the *Congressional Record*, and Supreme Court decisions. Finally, I have benefited from interviews or telephone conversations with Stella Cominsky Ballantine, John Beffel, Irving Abrams, Lillian Kisliuk, Adelaide Schulkind, Curtis Reese, and others.

BOOKS

The published books of Emma Goldman were the following: *Anarchism and Other Essays* (New York: Mother Earth Publishing Assoc., 1911); *The*

Social Significance of the Modern Drama (Boston: Richard G. Badger, 1914); *My Disillusionment in Russia* (Garden City, N.Y.: Doubleday, Page & Co., 1923); and *My Further Disillusionment in Russia* (Garden City, N.Y.: Doubleday, Page & Co., 1924)—the entire, unmutilated text was published in *My Disillusionment in Russia* (London: C. W. Daniel Co., 1925); *Living My Life* (New York: Alfred A. Knopf, Inc., 1931); and *Voltairine De Cleyre* (Berkeley Heights, N.J.: Oriole Press, 1933).

One of her book-length studies was never published: "Foremost Russian Dramatists," 1926, copies of which are to be found in the IISH, EG.

Berkman's published works included *Prison Memoirs of an Anarchist* (New York: Mother Earth Publishing Assoc., 1912); *Bolshevik Myth* (New York: Boni & Liveright, 1925); and *Now and After: The ABC of Communist Anarchism* (New York: Vanguard Press, 1929).

PAMPHLETS

By their nature, pamphlets are ephemeral. Copies that are not destroyed are hard to find. The following chronological list, however, contains the titles of nearly all her pamphlets; at the very least it contains the titles of her most important writings in this form.

Patriotism: A Menace to Liberty. New York: Mother Earth Publishing Assoc., 1908(?).

What I Believe. New York: Mother Earth Publishing Assoc., 1908.

A Beautiful Ideal. Chicago: J. C. Hart & Co., 1908.

The White Slave Traffic. New York: Mother Earth Publishing Assoc., 1909(?).

Anarchism: What It Really Stands For. New York: Mother Earth Publishing Assoc., 1911.

The Psychology of Political Violence. New York: Mother Earth Publishing Assoc., 1911.

Syndicalism: The Modern Menace to Capitalism. New York: Mother Earth Publishing Assoc., 1913.

Marriage and Love. 2d ed. New York: Mother Earth Publishing Assoc., 1914.

La Tragédie de l'émancipation féminine. Saint Joseph, Orleans, France: La Laborlease, 1914(?).

Philosophy of Atheism and the Failure of Christianity. New York: Mother Earth Publishing Assoc., 1916.

Preparedness: The Road to Universal Slaughter. New York: Mother Earth Publishing Assoc., 1916(?).

Trial and Speeches of Alexander Berkman and Emma Goldman in the United States District Court, in the City of New York, July, 1917. New York: Mother Earth Publishing Assoc., 1917.

The Truth about the Bolysheviki. New York: Mother Earth Publishing Assoc., 1918.

A Fragment of the Prison Experiences of Emma Goldman and Alexander Berkman. New York: Stella Comyn, 1919.

The Crushing of the Russian Revolution. London: Freedom Press, 1922.

Dos Años in Russia. New York: Aurora, 1923.

War against War. The Hague: International Anti-Militarist Bureau, 1925(?).

Russia and the British Labour Delegation's Report. London: British Committee for the Defense of Political Prisoners in Russia, 1925.

Trotsky Protests Too Much. London: Anarchist Communist Federation, 1939(?).

The Place of the Individual in Society. Chicago: Free Society Forum, 1940(?).

ARTICLES

Since they were often published in short-lived anarchist publications, her articles are sometimes even more fugitive than her pamphlets. But one has her many contributions to *Mother Earth*, which began publication in March, 1906, and stopped in August, 1917, and also to the *Mother Earth Bulletin*, which was published from October, 1917, through April, 1918. In the 1930's she contributed regularly to the *CNT-AIT-FAI Boletín de Información*, *Spain and the World*, and the *Spanish Revolution.* The following list, arranged chronologically, includes her most important contributions to newspapers, periodicals, and books:

"Anarchy," *Labor Leader*, XXI (June 5, 1897), 19.

"What I Believe," *New York World*, July 19, 1908.

"Die Masse," *Der Sozialist* (Berlin), August 1, 1911.

"Russia," *New York World*, March 26 through April 4, 1922.

"Bolsheviks Shooting Anarchists," *Freedom* (London), January, 1922.

"Persecution of Russian Anarchists," *Freedom*, August, 1922.

"The Bolshevik Government and the Anarchists," *Freedom*, October, 1922.

"Russian Trade Unionism," *Westminister* (England) *Gazette*, April 7, 1925.

"Women of the Russian Revolution," *Time and Tide* (England), I (May 8, 1925), 452.

"Appeal by Alexander Berkman, Emma Goldman, and Others," in *Letters from Russian Prisons*, ed. Roger Baldwin. New York: Albert and Charles Boni, 1925.

"Johann Most," *American Mercury*, VIII (June, 1926), 158–66.

"Reflections on the General Strike," *Freedom*, August–September, 1926.

"The Voyage of the Buford," *American Mercury*, XXIII (July, 1931), 276–86.

"The Assassination of McKinley," *American Mercury*, XXIV (September, 1931), 53–67.

"Emma Goldman Defends Her Attack on Henry George," *The Road to Freedom*, November, 1931.

"America by Comparison," in *Americans Abroad, 1918–1931*, ed. Peter Neagoe. The Hague: Servire Press, 1932.

"Most Dangerous Woman in the World Views U.S.A. from Europe," British Guiana *New Day Chronicle*, February 21, 1932.

"The Tragedy of the Political Exiles," *The Nation*, CXXXIX (October 10, 1934), 401–2.

"Was My Life Worth Living?" *Harper's Magazine*, CLXX (December, 1934), 52–58.

"There Is No Communism in Russia," *American Mercury*, XXXIV (April, 1935), 393–401.

"Anarchists and Elections," *Vanguard*, III (June–July, 1936), 19–20.

"Berkman's Last Days," *Vanguard*, III (August–September, 1936), 12–13.

"The Soviet Executions," *Vanguard*, III (October–November, 1936), 10.

"Emma Goldman's First Address to the Spanish Comrades at a Mass-Meeting Attended by Ten-Thousand People," *CNT-AIT-FAI Boletín de Información*, September 25, 1936.

"Enlarged Text of Emma Goldman's Radio Talk in Barcelona, 23 September 1936," *CNT-AIT-FAI Boletín de Información*, September 25, 1936.

"Whom the Gods Wish To Destroy They First Strike Mad," *CNT-AIT-FAI Boletín de Información*, October 6, 1936.

"The Soviet Political Machine," *Spain and the World*, I (June 4, 1937), 3.

"Naive Anarchists" (Letter), *New York Times*, July 4, 1937.

"Madrid Is the Wonder of the World," *Spain and the World*, October 13, 1937.

"Reports on Spain," *Spanish Revolution*, December 6, 1937.

"On Spain," *Spanish Revolution*, March 21, 1938.

Preface, in Camillo Berneri, *Pensieri e battaglie*. Paris: Edito a cura dei Comitato Camillo Berneri, 1938.

"Letters from Prison," in *The Little Review Anthology*, ed. Margaret Anderson. New York: Hermitage Press, 1953.

Since the footnotes for chapters i through xxvii are largely explanatory, chapter bibliographies serve here to indicate in a general way some of the manuscript sources and secondary books and articles which have been helpful. Readers interested in more specific citations may, let me suggest again, turn to my dissertation, "Emma Goldman: A Study in American Radicalism" (University of Minnesota, 1957).

Chapter I GHETTO GIRLHOOD

Given the absence of manuscript sources for these early years, the best accounts are in *Living My Life;* the long introduction by Hippolyte Havel to her *Anarchism and Other Essays;* the somewhat unreliable sketch by Frank Harris in *Contemporary Portraits,* 4th ser. (New York: Brentano's, 1923); and the synopsis and notes for her autobiography in the IISH. Charles Madison relies on her autobiography for his account of her life in *Critics and Crusaders* (New York: Holt, 1947–48). Also to be used with care are Margaret Goldsmith, *Seven Women against the World* (London: Methuen, 1935); Ethel Mannin, *Women and the Revolution* (New York: Dutton, 1939); and Lloyd Morris, *Postscript to Yesterday* (New York: Random House, 1947).

For the plight of Jews in Czarist Russia, see the especially suggestive essay by Paul N. Milyukov, "The Jewish Question in Russia," in *The Shield* (New York: Knopf, 1917). The introductory section of Solomon M. Schwartz's *Jews in the Soviet Union* (Syracuse: Syracuse University Press, 1951) is good. Louis Wirth, *The Ghetto* (Chicago: University of Chicago Press, 1928), is indispensable. Also useful are works such as Milton Steinberg, *The Making of the Modern Jew* (Indianapolis: Bobbs-Merrill, 1934), and Ismar Elbogen, *A Century of Jewish Life* (Philadelphia: Jewish Publication Society, 1944).

Chapter II ST. PETERSBURG

For radical currents within the ghetto, see A. L. Patkin, *The Origins of the Russian Jewish Labour Movement* (Melbourne: Cheshire, 1947). Some works which I have found helpful in cutting through the confusion of nihilism and populism and of both with terrorism are Peter Kropotkin, *Memoirs of a Revolutionist* (New York: Houghton Mifflin, 1899); Avrahim Yarmolinsky, *Turgenev* (New York: Century, 1926); Michael Karpovich, *Imperial Russia* (New York: Holt, 1932); Stepniak, *Underground Russia* (London: Smith, Elder, 1890); Koni Zilliacus, *The Russian Revolutionary Movement* (New York: Dutton, 1905); and Richard Hare, *Pioneers of Russian Social Thought* (New York: Oxford University Press, 1951). Nicholas Berdyaev's *The Origin of Russian Communism* (London: Bles, 1937) is filled with insights.

Chapter III ROCHESTER: FLOWER CITY IN THE GARDEN

Emma missed landing on Ellis Island by five years, for it was not until 1890 that it was designated an immigrant station. Nevertheless, see Edward Corsi, *In the Shadow of Liberty: The Chronicle of Ellis Island* (New York: Macmillan, 1935). A popular but informative account of the poetess of the Statue of Liberty is to be found in H. E. Jacob, *The World of Emma Lazarus* (New York: Schocken, 1949). Paul Masserman and Max Baker, *The Jews Come to America* (New York: Bloch, 1932) is spotty but useful for background. Very good for tensions among the immigrants is Stuart E. Rosenberg, *The Jewish Community in Rochester, 1843–1925* (New York: Columbia University Press, 1954). The charge that Garson demanded sexual favors from his female employees was made in one of her letters to her attorney, Arthur Ross (June 25, 1928—IISH, EG). Industrialists have sometimes looked on their mills as harems. For the British precedents, see G. M. Young, *Portrait of an Age* (London: Oxford University Press, 1936).

Chapter IV THE MAKING OF A RADICAL

Many useful suggestions on the proper use of autobiographies and biographies are contained in Gordon W. Allport, *The Use of Personal Documents in Psychological Science* (New York: Social Science Research Council, 1942); unfortunately much less helpful is Louis Gottschalk *et al.*, *The Use of Personal Documents in History, Anthropology, and Sociology* (New York: Social Science Research Council, 1945). For an interesting effort to lay out the proper questions for analyzing personal documents, see John Dollard, *Criteria for the Life History* (New Haven: Yale University Press, 1935).

For contemporary accounts describing the anarchists as lunatics, see Karl Blind, "The Rise and Development of Anarchism," *Contemporary Review*, LXV (January, 1894), 140–52; James M. Beck, "The Suppression of Anarchy," *American Law Review*, XXXVI (March–April, 1902), 190–203— Beck characterized "the Goldman woman" and other anarchists "as mental as well as moral perverts"; and "Anarchists Again," *Independent*, LXIV (March 12, 1908), 554–55. For Roosevelt's interpretation of the psychology of anarchists, see his *Presidential Addresses and State Papers* (New York: Review of Reviews, 1910). An early and influential use of physiognomy to account for the actions of anarchists was Cesare Lombroso's paper, "Illustrative Studies in Criminal Anthropology: The Physiognomy of the Anarchists," *Monist*, I (April, 1891), 336–43. Closely allied with Lombroso's positivistic point of view, except that fixed mental rather than physical features were given primary weight, was Augustin Hamon's *Psychologie de l'anarchiste-socialiste* (Paris: Stock, 1895). Later efforts to relate personality and political beliefs to constitutional determinants were Ernest Kretschmer's *Physique and Character* (New York: Harcourt, Brace, 1925) —according to Kretschmer's typology of physical types, Emma should have been a cheerful organizer, a conciliatory diplomat, and a hard-headed calculator!—William Sheldon's *Varieties of Human Physique* (New York: Harper, 1940), and Harold Lasswell's *Psychopathology and Politics* (Chicago: University of Chicago Press, 1930). Lasswell believed the "leanness of the 'fanatical agitator' " a "scientific conception." On the relationship between radicalism and intelligence, see a recent article by M. Sanai and P. M. Pickard, "The Relation between Politico-Economic Radicalism and Certain Traits of Personality," *Journal of Social Psychology*, XXX (November, 1949), 217–27. On the general origins of radicalism, see the perceptive essays of Walter Weyl in *Tired Radicals* (New York: Huebsch, 1921) and George W. Hartmann, "The Psychology of American Socialism," in Donald Drew Egbert and Stow Persons (eds.), *Socialism in American Life* (Princeton: Princeton University Press, 1952), Vol. I. For a helpful Freudian interpretation of radicalism, see J. C. Flugel, *Man, Morals, and Society* (New York: International Universities Press, 1945). In attempting to deal with the psychological origins of Emma Goldman's radicalism, I have found very suggestive Erich Fromm's *Escape from Freedom* (New York: Farrar, Rinehart, 1941) and his *Man for Himself* (New York: Rinehart, 1947); also useful were Hadley Cantril, *The Psychology of Social Movements* (New York: Wiley, 1941); Jean Piaget, *The Moral Judgment of the Child* (New York: Harcourt, Brace, 1932); and Henry A. Murray *et al.*, *Explorations in Personality* (New York: Oxford University Press, 1938). Two books have been especially important in my assessment of the shaping social forces: Robert K. Merton, *Social Theory and Social Structure* (Glencoe, Ill.: Free Press, 1949), and Everett V. Stonequist, *The Marginal Man* (New York: Scribner's, 1937). Fortunately, as I make clear in this chapter, Emma puzzled often over the origins of her radicalism and wrote on the subject frequently.

Chapter V THE DREAM

On Most, see Emma's article in the *American Mercury*, VIII (June, 1926), 158–66; Max Nomad, *Apostles of Revolution* (London: Secker, Warburg, 1939); and Most, *Memoiren* (New York: Selbstverlag des Verfassers, 1903). For general accounts of radical activity during this period, see Lillian Symes and Travers Clement, *Rebel America* (New York: Harper, 1934); C. M. Destler, *American Radicalism, 1865–1901* (New London: Connecticut College Press, 1946); Daniel Bell, "Marxian Socialism in the United States," in Donald Drew Egbert and Stow Persons (eds.), *Socialism in American Life* (Princeton: Princeton University Press, 1952), Vol. I; and Ira Kipnis, *The American Socialist Movement* (New York: Columbia University Press, 1952). For native American individualistic anarchism, see James J. Martin, *Men against the State* (Dekalb, Ill.: Allen, 1953), and Eunice M. Schuster, "Native American Anarchism," *Smith College Studies in History*, XVII (October, 1931–July, 1932), 118–87.

For the origins of communist anarchism, see Bert F. Hoselitz, Preface, in Michael Bakunin, *The Political Philosophy of Bakunin*, ed. G. P. Maximoff (Glencoe, Ill.: Free Press, 1953); R. M. Wenley, *The Anarchist Ideal* (Boston: Badger, 1913); E. V. Zenker, *Anarchism: A Criticism and History of Anarchist Theory* (New York: Putnam's, 1897); Bertrand Russell, *Proposed Roads to Freedom* (New York: Holt, 1919); Herbert L. Osgood, "Scientific Anarchism," *Political Science Quarterly*, Vol. IV (March, 1889); and, still the standard work on its subject, George Adler, *Geschichte des Sozialismus und Kommunismus von Plato bis zur Gegenwart* (Leipzig: 1899). For Kropotkin, see the books I have cited in the text and the biography by George Woodcock and Ivan Avakumovic, *The Anarchist Prince* (London: Boardman, 1950).

Chapter VI   HOMESTEAD: IN THE BEGINNING WAS THE DEED

Berkman's correspondence and diaries are to be found in the IISH. See also, of course, his very important *Prison Memoirs of an Anarchist*. "Fedya" re-entered the lives of Emma and Berkman when they were both in exile in the 1920's and 1930's; a number of his letters and of their letters to him are in the IISH.

For general accounts of the Homestead lockout, see Henry David, "Upheaval at Homestead," in *America in Crisis*, ed. Daniel Aaron (New York: Knopf, 1952); Samuel Yellen, *American Labor Struggles* (New York: Harcourt, Brace, 1936). The best account of the "Gospel of Wealth," of which Henry Clay Frick was such a practical, devoted follower, is in Ralph Gabriel's *Course of American Democratic Thought* (New York: Ronald Press, 1940). Matthew Josephson's *Robber Barons* (New York: Harcourt, Brace, 1934) is still useful, as is Veblen's *Theory of the Leisure Class* (New York: Modern Library, 1934). For Frick see the informative but shoddy biography by George Harvey, *Henry Clay Frick* (New York: Scribner's, 1928); much more sensitive and intelligent is Edmund Wilson's short essay, "Fremont and Frick," in *Shores of Light* (New York: Farrar, Straus & Young, 1952).

Chapter VII   BEING AN EVIL DISPOSED AND PERNICIOUS PERSON

For a colorful journalistic account of Nellie Bly, see Ishbell Ross, *Ladies of the Press* (New York: Harper, 1936). Nellie Bly's description of Emma appeared in the New York *World*, September 22, 1893.

I am indebted to Mr. Howard Barret, Clerk of Court of General Sessions, for helping me find the People *v.* Emma Goldman, Court of General Sessions of the City and County of New York, Minutes (filed September 6, 1893). Unfortunately this transcript is so full of discrepancies and gaps that it must be used with extreme caution.

Lincoln Steffens' *Autobiography* (New York: Harcourt, Brace, 1931) contains an excellent discussion of New York police methods and corruption during the 1890's; Steffens' points were fully documented by the Lexow Committee's *Report and Proceedings of the Senate Committee Appointed To Investigate the Police Department of the City of New York* (Albany: 1895).

Chapter VIII   AFTER BLACKWELL'S ISLAND

For a critical contemporary account, see J. G. Speed, "Anarchists in New York," *Harper's Weekly*, XXXVI (August 20, 1892), 798–99. Nellie Bly's description of Schwab's saloon appeared in the New York *World*, September 17, 1893. R. L. Duffus' *Lillian Wald* (New York: Macmillan, 1938) is the best biography of this leading social worker and also a good introduction to the work of other settlement workers.

Chapter IX   THE ASSASSINATION OF McKINLEY

For the best survey of the background and personality of Czolgosz, see L. Vernon Briggs, *The Manner of Man That Kills* (Boston: Badger, 1921). For a recent, more journalistic account, see Robert J. Donovan, *The Assassins* (New York: Harper, 1955). Margaret Leech's *In the Days of McKinley* (New York: Harper, 1959) is not very helpful on the assassination. A report of the one lecture of Emma which Czolgosz heard appeared in the Cleveland *Plain Dealer*, May 6, 1901. For Czolgosz's statements and related material, see *People v. Leon F. Czolgosz*, Courthouse Archives, Erie County, Buffalo, New York. Also useful are Louis F. Babcock's "The Assassination of President William McKinley," *Niagara Frontier Miscellany*, XXXIV (1947), 31–32; Emma's "The Tragedy at Buffalo," *Mother Earth*, I (October, 1906), 11–16; and Murat Halstead, *The Illustrious Life of William McKinley* (n.p.: Halstead, 1901).

Chapter X   MEANS AND THE DREAM

One of the chapters of *Anarchism and Other Essays* is devoted to a consideration of "The Psychology of Political Violence." Berkman's *Prison Memoirs of an Anarchist* is a remarkably perceptive, introspective analysis of the motives which induced him to attempt to assassinate Frick. Shortly after his release from prison, Berkman addressed himself to "Violence and Anarchism," an essay published in *Mother Earth*, III (March, 1908), 67–70. For the critical reaction of a Socialist, see Robert Hunter, *Violence and the Labor Movement* (New York: Macmillan, 1914). John Dewey made a number of interesting points on "Force, Violence, and Law," in *Intelligence in the Modern World* (New York: Modern Library, 1939). For a discussion of some of the anarchist terrorists, see Charles Malato, "Some Anarchist Portraits," *Fortnightly Review*, LXII (September 1, 1894), 315–33. Albert

Camus's chapter, "Individual Terrorism," in *The Rebel* (London: Hamilton, 1953) is the most brilliant and understanding discussion of the subject I have seen anywhere.

Chapter XI NATIONAL BUGABOO

For histories of the *Times*, see Elmer Davis, *History of the New York Times* (New York: Times, 1921); Meyer Berger, *The Story of the New York Times* (New York: Simon, Schuster, 1951). Kenneth Stewart, *News Is What We Make It* (Boston: Houghton Mifflin, 1943), deals with the *Times's* "fetish of objectivity." S. N. Behrman's amusing discussion of what Emma Goldman meant to him when he was a boy appeared as "Double Chocolate with Emma and Sasha," *New Yorker*, January 16, 1954. See William Marion Reedy's "The Daughter of the Dream," St. Louis *Mirror*, November 5, 1908, for his sagacious comments on Emma and the press; see also the derivative piece by George Creel, "Free Love," *The Independent* (Kansas City), Vol. XX (November 14, 1908). For appeals urging legislative action against Emma and other anarchists, see Senator J. C. Burrows, "The Need of National Legislation against Anarchism," *North American Review*, Vol. CLXXIII (December, 1901); James Beck, "The Suppression of Anarchy," *American Law Review*, Vol. XXXVI (March–April, 1902); *Congressional Record*, Vol. XXXV, Part, 1, pp. 113, 148; Robert Pinkerton, "Detective Surveillance of Anarchists," *North American Review*, Vol. CLXXIII (November, 1901) and a number of other articles in this same volume. Cleveland's remarks are quoted in Murat Halstead, *The Illustrious Life of William McKinley* (n.p.: Halstead, 1901). For a discussion of New York's "Criminal Anarchy Act" see Zechariah Chafee, Jr., *Free Speech in the United States* (Cambridge: Harvard University Press, 1942); Thomas I. Emerson and David Haber, *Political and Civil Rights in the United States* (Buffalo: Dennis, 1952); Milton Konvitz, *Civil Rights in Immigration* (Ithaca: Cornell University Press, 1953). Konvitz ably discusses the Turner case (Turner v. Williams, 194 U.S. 279).

Chapter XII MOTHER EARTH

To fit *Mother Earth* in its proper context, see Frederick Hoffman et al., *The Little Magazine* (Princeton: Princeton University Press, 1946). The memoirs of other editors are useful—see Margaret Anderson's *My Thirty Years War* (New York: Covici, Friede, 1930) and Max Eastman's *Enjoyment of Living* (New York: Harper, 1948).

Chapter XIII AMSTERDAM ANARCHIST CONGRESS

The proceedings of the Congress were printed in *Congrès Anarchiste tenu à Amsterdam, Août 1907* (Paris: La Publication Sociale, 1908). The paper of Emma Goldman and Max Baginsky, which they delivered at the Congress, was published as "The Relation of Anarchism to Organization," *Mother Earth*, II (October, 1907), 310–12. See also, of course, her *Anarchism and Other Essays*, wherein she defined anarchism as the "philosophy of a new social order based on liberty unrestricted by man-made law; the theory that all forms of government rest on violence and are therefore wrong and harmful, as well as unnecessary." Shaw's assertion that anarchism was simply an extreme form of democracy appeared in his essay, "The Impossibilities of Anarchism," later published in *Socialism and Individualism* (New York: Lane, 1911). For contemporary assessments of her views, see "Emma Goldman," *American Magazine*, LXIX (March, 1910), 605, 608; Hutchins Hapgood, "Emma Goldman's Anarchism," *Bookman*, XXXII (February, 1911), 639–40; "Emma Goldman's Faith," *Current Literature*, L (February, 1911), 176–78.

Chapter XIV THE KERSNER CASE

This chapter rests on evidence to be found in the National Archives. The most important file is DJ 133149. Secretary of Commerce and Labor Straus' letter to the Attorney-General, for instance, was dated February 11, 1909, and became part of DJ 133149. For the relevant Department of State letters and communications, see DS, Vol. DCCCXXI, 12623. A transcription of the court stenographer's minutes is in the WMC. In 1934 Emma wrote "A Woman without a Country," for the *Ladies Home Journal*, but the article was never published; a copy of the typescript is in the IISH, EG.

Chapter XV LIBERTY WITHOUT STRINGS

Hutchins Hapgood's *A Victorian in the Modern World* (New York: Harcourt, Brace, 1939) is an especially important autobiography for the present study. Hapgood was perceptive in his appraisals of Emma and the New York radical world generally. There is an unpublished autobiography of Reitman, "Following the Monkey," which was written in the mid-1920's. I am indebted to Mr. Jack Sheridan of Chicago for permission to see this typescript. Reitman was also author of *The Second Oldest Profession* (New York: Vanguard Press, 1931), which is a hodge-podge of religious sentimentalism, bohemian radicalism, and sensational self-advertising, all mixed with a genuine feeling for outcasts and with occasional insights into the life of the pimp. Newspaper reports and statements by Freeman and others on the suppression of Emma's talk on Ibsen were reprinted in a pamphlet published by the National Free Speech Committee, *Law Breaking by the Police Department of New York City at Lexington Hall.* . . . (1909). Maurice Browne's *Too Late To Lament* (London: Gollancz, 1955) and Frederic C. Howe's *Confessions of a Reformer* (New York: Scribner's, 1925) contain amusing anecdotes about Emma's free-speech activities. See *Current Liter-*

ature, XLIV (May, 1908), 461–66, for a survey of contemporary press attitudes on freedom for heretical speakers.

The Theodore Herfurth Papers in the Wisconsin Historical Society are best for the Ross affair at the University of Wisconsin. See also E. A. Ross, *Seventy Years of It* (New York: Appleton-Century, 1936); Merle Curti and Vernon Carstensen, *The University of Wisconsin* (Madison: University of Wisconsin Press, 1949), Vol. II; Theodore Herfurth, *Sifting and Winnowing: A Chapter in the History of Academic Freedom at Wisconsin* (Madison: University of Wisconsin, 1949); and *Mother Earth*, IV (February, 1910), 387.

Comstock's life is journalistically portrayed by Heywood Broun and Margaret Leech, *Anthony Comstock: Roundsman of the Lord* (New York: Boni, 1927). See also Ernest Sutherland Bates, *This Land of Liberty* (New York: Harper, 1930); Floyd Dell, *Homecoming* (New York: Farrar, Rinehart, 1933); and George Hellman, *Lanes of Memory* (New York: Knopf, 1927).

George Edwards' "Free Speech in San Diego," *Mother Earth*, X (July, 1915), 182–85, is a good survey of this struggle. For the free-speech fight of the wobblies, see Paul F. Brissenden, *The I.W.W.* (New York: Columbia University Press, 1919), and Ralph Chaplin, *Wobbly* (Chicago: University of Chicago Press, 1948). A partial copy of Lewis J. Duncan's letter is in the IISH, EG. For General Funston's condemnation of Buwalda, see the New York *Evening Post*, June 30, 1908. The Buwalda affair was fully covered in *Mother Earth*—see especially Volumes III and IV. James J. Martin's "Agnes Inglis," *Resistance*, XI (August, 1953), 11–13, is a good portrait. Dwight MacDonald has written an entertaining and informative profile of Baldwin entitled, "The Defense of Everybody," *New Yorker*, July 18, 1953; see also Lucille B. Milner, *Education of an American Liberal* (New York: Horizon Press, 1954).

Chapter XVI DEVIL'S GATEWAY

Alfred Kazin's *On Native Grounds* (New York: Harcourt, Brace, 1942) has a good description of the contagious enthusiasm of the times. See also Meyer Schapiro, "Rebellion in Art," in *America in Crisis* (New York: Knopf, 1952); Henry F. May, *The End of American Innocence* (New York: Knopf, 1959). For the "new woman," see Isadora Duncan, *My Life* (New York: Boni, Liveright, 1927); Mabel Dodge Luhan, *Intimate Memories* (New York: Harcourt, Brace, 1936), Vol. VIII; Lloyd Morris, *Postscript to Yesterday* (New York: Random House, 1947); Jane Addams, *Twenty Years at Hull-House* (New York: Macmillan, 1910); James W. Linn, *Jane Addams* (New York: Appleton-Century, 1935); Arthur W. Calhoun, *A Social History of the American Family* (Cleveland: Clark, 1919); Sidney Ditzion, *Marriage, Morals and Sex in America* (New York: Bookman, 1953); Samuel Schmalhausen and V. F. Calverton (eds.), *Woman's Coming of*

Age (New York: Liveright, 1931); Carl N. Degler, "Charlotte Perkins Gilman on the Theory and Practice of Feminism," *American Quarterly*, VIII (Spring, 1956), 21–39; her autobiography, *The Living of Charlotte Perkins Gilman* (New York: Appleton-Century, 1935); and Ida M. Tarbell, *All in the Day's Work* (New York: Macmillan, 1939). Floyd Dell's *Women as World Builders: Studies in Modern Feminism* (Chicago: Forbes, 1913) is an especially important contemporary interpretation. Simone de Beauvoir's *Second Sex* (New York: Knopf, 1957) is a brilliant modern statement of the kind of position Emma held.

Chapter XVII POPULARIZER OF THE ARTS

Emma enthusiastically discussed the beginnings of the little theatre in "History of the Drama in America," IISH, EG. Rebecca West's claims for Emma appear in her introduction to the latter's *My Disillusionment in Russia* (London: Daniel, 1925). On the introduction of the plays of Shaw in the United States, see Arthur Hobson Quinn, *A History of the American Drama* (New York: Harper, 1928); also Archibald Henderson, *Bernard Shaw* (London: Appleton, 1932). Margaret Anderson's acute comments appeared in *Mother Earth*, IX (December, 1914), 320–24. For a successful performance of what Emma was attempting in her *Social Significance of the Modern Drama*, see Eric Bentley, *The Playwright as Thinker* (New York: Harcourt, Brace, n.d.). One of Emma's manuscripts on Whitman is in the NYPL, EGP; the others are in the IISH, EG. Bernard Smith wrote a rather appreciative Marxist interpretation of her drama criticism in *Forces in American Criticism* (New York: Harcourt, Brace, 1939). For Van Wyck Brooks's generous assessment, see *The Confident Years* (New York: Dutton, 1952).

Chapter XVIII BIRTH CONTROL PIONEER

The best study of the background of birth control is Norman Himes, *Medical History of Contraception* (Baltimore: Williams & Wilkins, 1936); see also Himes, "Note on the Origin of the Terms Contraception, Birth Control, Neo-Malthusianism, etc.," *Medical Journal and Record*, CXXXV (1932), 495–96. For a very careful, thorough study of the individuals and organizations urging birth control, see Francis M. Vreeland, "The Process of Reform with Especial Reference to Reform Groups in the Field of Population" (unpublished Ph.D. diss., University of Michigan, 1929). Mary Ware Dennett's *Birth Control Laws* (New York: Hitchcock, 1926) is well done. See also Victor Robinson, *Pioneers of Birth Control* (New York: Voluntary Parenthood League, 1919). The real pioneer of American birth control was Charles Knowlton—see the reprint of his *Fruits of Philosophy* (Mount Vernon: Pauper Press, 1937) and R. E. Riegel, "American Father of Birth Control," *New England Quarterly*, VI (Spring, 1933), 470–90. For Margaret Sanger's side of the story, see her *My Fight for Birth Control* (New York: Farrar, Rinehart, 1931); *An Autobiography* (New York: Norton, 1938); and Lawrence Lader, *The Margaret Sanger Story* (New York: Doubleday, 1955). The conservative opposition was expressed with characteristic forcefulness by Theodore Roosevelt in "Premium on Race Suicide," *Outlook*, CV (September 27, 1913), 163–64.

Chapter XIX "MUNI! MUNI!": THE MOONEY CASE, 1916

Berkman's correspondence with Tom and Rena Mooney and with others about this case is in the IISH, AB. James B. Christoph, "Alexander Berkman and American Anarchism" (unpublished M.A. thesis, University of Minnesota, 1952) is substantially accurate on Berkman's role. Of fundamental importance is the United States National Commission on Law Observance and Enforcement, Section on Lawless Enforcement of the Law, *The Mooney-Billings Report* (New York: Gotham House, 1932). For the reaction of one of the most dedicated liberals in San Francisco, see Evelyn Wells, *Fremont Older* (New York: Appleton-Century, 1936). For the reports of the Mediation Commission and for other relevant documents, see DJ 185354 and DJ 186233–13. See also *Foreign Relations, Russia*, I (1918), 353–54; George Frost Kennan, *Soviet-American Relations, 1917–1920* (Princeton: Princeton University Press, 1956–58), Vol. I. Upton Sinclair's *Brass Check* (Pasadena: Sinclair, n.d.) is good for the press reaction.

Chapter XX 1917

There is, of course, a vast body of works on America's entry into the First World War. I have found nothing more helpful, for a brilliant statement of the issues, than George F. Kennan's *American Diplomacy* (New York: Mentor Books, 1952). Most of the evidence for the government's actions against Emma and Berkman is in DJ 186233–13. They were charged with violating Sections 37 and 332 of the U.S.C.C. and Section 5 of the Conscription Act of May 18, 1917.

Chapter XXI THE UNITED STATES V. GOLDMAN-BERKMAN

I am indebted to Mr. John Beffel for the loan of his copy of U.S. Courts: Supreme Court: *Transcript of Record*, October Term, 1917, no. 702. Emma Goldman and Alexander Berkman, Plaintiffs in Error, v. U.S. (District Court of the U.S. for the Southern District of N.Y.). For the documents on Emma's brushes with the law over bail, her funds in the New York Produce Bank, and so on, consult the WMC. Emma's and Berkman's speeches were printed in *Mother Earth*, XII (July, 1917), 138–61, and also in the pamphlet, *Trial and Speeches of Alexander Berkman and Emma Goldman* (New

York: Mother Earth Publishing Assoc., 1917); see also Leonard Abbott, "The Trial and Conviction of Emma Goldman and Alexander Berkman," *Mother Earth*, XII (July, 1917), 132. Also useful are the autobiographies of Margaret Anderson, Floyd Dell, Max Eastman, which I have already listed, and Art Young, *His Life and Times*, ed. John Beffel (New York: Sheridan, 1939). For a sketch of the life of their attorney, see Barbara V. Simison, "The Harry Weinberger Memorial Collection," *Yale University Library Gazette*, XIX (January, 1945), 50–52. Tattler, "Notes from the Capital: Emma Goldman," *Nation*, CIV (June 28, 1917), 766–67, and "Uncle Sam's Obstreperous Niece," *Literary Digest*, LV (August 18, 1917), 54–57, afford some index to the depth and extent of the hostility of her contemporaries.

Chapter XXII   HEAVY GATES: THE PRISONER

This chapter leans heavily on *Letters from Kate Richards O'Hare to Her Family: From April 20, 1919 to May 27, 1920* (St. Louis: O'Hare, 1920)—I am indebted to Mrs. Marjorie Sibley for letting me use her copy of these letters. Extracts from Emma's "Letters from Prison," were published in the *Little Review Anthology*, ed. Margaret Anderson (New York: Hermitage Press, 1953); see also their pamphlet, *A Fragment of the Prison Experiences of Emma Goldman and Alexander Berkman* (New York: Stella Comyn, 1919). Emma had an interesting lecture, "Crime and Punishment," IISH, EG, in which she drew on her prison experiences. It is ironic that prison reform was given a boost by the imprisonment of radicals during the war—for a somewhat parallel English example, see Fenner Brockway, *Inside the Left* (London: Allen & Unwin, 1942). Ray Ginger's *The Bending Cross* (New Brunswick: Rutgers University Press, 1949) has an excellent discussion of the prison experience of Debs. The Bureau of Prisons file in the National Archives is labeled "Missouri-Goldman."

Chapter XXIII   EMMA GOLDMAN AND 59,999 OTHER REDS

The correspondence of John Lord O'Brian on the Har Dayal spy charges is in DJ 186233–13; in fairly sharp contrast is O'Brian's *John Randolph Tucker Lectures* (Charlottesville: University of Virginia Press, 1952). For Congressional activity, see *Bolshevik Propaganda: Hearings before a Subcommittee of the Committee on the Judiciary of the U.S. Senate*, 65th Cong., 3d sess. (Washington, D.C.: U.S. Government Printing Office, 1919). For a similar state investigation—one in which Emma figured—see New York Legislature, *Joint Committee Investigating Seditious Activities*, Clayton R. Lusk, Chairman (Albany, 1920). A. Mitchell Palmer's summary of the government's case against Emma Goldman and all the other Reds is in his *Letter from the Attorney General: Investigation Activities of the De-*

partment of Justice, 66th Cong., 1st sess., Sen. Doc. No. 153 (Washington, D.C.: U.S. Government Printing Office, 1919); see also the *Congressional Record*, LVIII, 6870, 7822. Very useful are Louis F. Post's *Deportations Delirium of Nineteen-Twenty* (Chicago: Kerr, 1923) and the National Popular Government League, *Report upon the Illegal Practices of the United States Department of Justice by Twelve Lawyers* (Washington: National Popular Government League, 1920). See also Constantine Panunzio, *The Deportation Cases of 1919–1920* (New York: Federal Council of Churches of Christ, 1921). A careful recent study is Robert K. Murray's *Red Scare: A Study in National Hysteria, 1919–1920* (Minneapolis: University of Minnesota Press, 1955). For Hoover's account, see his "Introduction" to Editors of *Look*, *The Story of the FBI* (New York: Dutton, 1947); see also Donald F. Whitehead's eulogistic *The FBI Story* (New York: Random House, 1956). Far and away the best study of the activities of Hoover and the General Intelligence Division is by Max Lowenthal, *The Federal Bureau of Investigation* (London: Turnstile Press, 1951). In addition to many of the autobiographies and biographies already listed, I found George Creel's *Rebel at Large* (New York: Putnam's, 1947) useful, though certainly mistitled.

Chapter XXIV BACK PAST THE STATUE OF LIBERTY

Many of the works listed for the previous chapter are, of course, relevant for this. The WMC is good for documents and correspondence on the legal aspects. The relevant files in the National Archives are DJ 186233–13, INS 52410/43B, and INS 54235/36.

Chapter XXV THE RATIONALIZED CONFORMITY

On a conceptual level, this chapter owes most to Max Weber—see H. H. Gerth and C. Wright Mills (eds.), *From Max Weber* (London: Kegan Paul, Trench, Trubner, 1947). Also suggestive is Robert Hutchins' Preface to Thomas I. Emerson and David Haber, *Political and Civil Rights in the United States* (Buffalo: Dennis, 1952). In a series of articles in the *New Republic*, which appeared in January and February, 1956, John P. Roche argued that "We've Never Had More Freedom," a thesis which is in sharp contrast to the one presented here. For a more qualified optimism, see Zechariah Chafee, Jr., *Thirty-five Years with Freedom of Speech* (New York: Roger Baldwin Civil Liberties Foundation, 1952); Bruce Catton, "Freedom, Faith and Courage," *The Fund for the Republic Bulletin*, April, 1957; and Walter Millis, "Outlook for Our Civil Liberties," *New York Times Magazine*, April 28, 1957. To put the deportations in a context with some historical depth, see John C. Stoessinger, *The Refugee and the World Community* (Minneapolis: University of Minnesota Press, 1956).

Chapter XXVI MATUSHKA ROSSIYA

Emma's correspondence with Berkman on their Russian experience is in the IISH; her correspondence with her family is primarily in the NYPL, EGP. A good overview of the American response to the new Bolshevik state is George Frost Kennan's *Soviet-American Relations, 1917–1920*, 2 vols. (Princeton: Princeton University Press, 1956, 1958). Angelica Balabanoff's *My Life as a Rebel* (New York: Harper, 1938) is very helpful for evaluating the role of Emma and Berkman in Bolshevik Russia.

Chapter XXVII THE BOLSHEVIK MYTH

Berkman's *Bolshevik Myth*, from which the chapter title is taken, and Emma's *My Disillusionment in Russia*, both of which are listed earlier are main supports here. Well worth reading are H. L. Mencken's articles, "Two Views of Russia," *American Mercury*, II (May, 1924), 122–23, and "The United States Sustains a Loss in Berkman and Emma Goldman," the Baltimore *Sun*, April 26, 1925 (syndicated column). One of the best sources is the work for which Berkman was mainly responsible, published under the name of the International Committee for Political Prisoners, *Letters from Russian Prisons*, ed. Roger Baldwin (New York: Boni, 1925). For a succinct statement of George Frost Kennan's analysis of the March revolution and after, see his "When the Russians Rose against the Czar," New York *Times Magazine*, March 10, 1957. The letters or copies of the letters Emma exchanged with Bertrand Russell, Harold Laski, Havelock Ellis, Roger Baldwin, and Freda Kirchwey are in the IISH, EG; some duplicates are in the NYPL, EGP.

Chapter XXVIII "NOR FEEL AT HOME ANYWHERES"

This chapter rests completely on manuscript and press sources. The footnotes finally make clear their nature and locations. Frederic Griffin's "Toronto's Anarchist Guest," Toronto *Star Weekly*, December 31, 1926, was especially useful.

Chapter XXIX THE STILL INNER VOICE

Some of the reviewers of *Living My Life* made a serious attempt to interpret the author's life. Particularly interesting, both for the light their reviews shed on the life of their subject and for the light they shed on the lives of the reviewers, were the following: Waldo Frank, "Elegy for Anarchism," *New Republic*, LXIX (December 30, 1931), 193–94; Roger Baldwin, "A Challenging Rebel Spirit," New York *Herald Tribune Books*, October 25, 1931; Freda Kirchwey, "Emma Goldman," *Nation*, CXXXIII (December 2, 1931), 612–14; Clara Gruening Stillman "Two Worlds," *Hound and Horn*,

VI (October–December, 1932), 143–57; Harry Hansen, "Once a Dangerous Woman," Brooklyn *Eagle*, October 30, 1931; Leonard D. Abbott, "Emma Goldman, 'Daughter of the Dream,'" *Road to Freedom*, April, 1932; Ordway Tead, "Emma Goldman Speaks," *Yale Review*, XXI (June, 1932), 851–52.

Chapter XXX RETURN OF THE PRODIGAL DAUGHTER

The extent of Communist influence on left politics in the 1930's is a matter of debate—for an evaluation supported by my research, see Irving Howe and Lewis Coser, *The American Communist Party* (Boston: Beacon Press, 1957), especially chapter vii, "The Intellectuals Turn Left." See also Daniel Bell, "Marxian Socialism in the United States," in Donald Drew Egbert and Stow Persons (eds.), *Socialism in American Life* (Princeton: Princeton University Press, 1952), Vol. I.

Chapter XXXI NO PLACE TO LAY THEIR HEADS

Emma attempted to sum up her feelings about America in her essay, "America by Comparison," in Peter Neagoe (ed.), *Americans Abroad, 1918–1931* (The Hague: Servire Press, 1932), and in an article, "Most dangerous Woman in the World Views U.S.A. from Europe," British Guiana *New Day Chronicle*, February 21, 1932. For the meaning of deportation, see her "The Tragedy of the Political Exiles," *Nation*, CXXXIX (October 10, 1934), 401–2, and "Was My Life Worth Living?" *Harper's Magazine*, CLXX (December, 1934), 52–58.

Chapter XXXII SPAIN: THE VERY TOP OF THE MOUNTAIN

In addition to the manuscript sources cited in this chapter, I have found George Orwell's *Homage to Catalonia* (New York: Harcourt, Brace, 1952) very helpful. See also V. Richards, *Lessons of the Spanish Revolution* (London: Freedom Press, 1953); David T. Cattell, *Communism and the Spanish Civil War* (Berkeley: University of California Press, 1956); Franz Borkenau, *The Spanish Cockpit* (London: Faber & Faber, 1937); Gerald Brenan, *The Spanish Labyrinth* (New York: Macmillan, 1943).

Chapter XXXIII TO THE FINAL BREATH

Next to Karl Shapiro's poem, perhaps the best assessment of the meaning of Emma's life was in a letter of Evelyn Scott, dated February 14, 1936, IISH—Miss Scott wrote to Emma that she regarded her as the only one who had been active in the United States without being conservative or won over to the defeat of personal liberty: "You were the only one there, I often feel, who had a third attitude and the power of personality to carry it into activities not representable in art. But you to me are the future they will, paradoxically, hark back to in time."

INDEX